The Functional Approach to Programming

A programming course should concentrate as much as possible on a program's logical structure and design rather than simply show how to write code. The functional approach to programming achieves this aim because logical concepts are evident and programs are transparent so can be written quickly and cleanly. In this book the authors emphasise the notions of function and function application which relate programming to familiar concepts from mathematics and logic. They introduce functional programming via examples but also explain what programs compute and how to reason about them. They show how the ideas can implemented in the Caml language, a dialect of the ML family, and give examples of how complex programs from a variety of areas (such as arithmetic, tree algorithms, graph algorithms, text parsing and geometry) can be developed in close agreement with their specifications.

Many exercises and examples are included throughout the book; solutions are also available.

Guy Cousineau is professor at École Normale Supérieure in Paris and head of the computer science laboratory.

Michel Mauny is Directeur de Recherche at INRIA-Rocquencourt, and head of the Cristal research team, where the Caml language is being developed.

The Functional Approach to Programming

Guy Cousineau
École Normale Supèrieure, Paris

and

Michel Mauny
INRIA-Rocquencourt

CAMBRIDGE
UNIVERSITY PRESS

PUBLISHED BY THE PRESS SYNDICATE OF THE UNIVERSITY OF CAMBRIDGE
The Pitt Building, Trumpington Street, Cambridge CB2 1RP, United Kingdom

CAMBRIDGE UNIVERSITY PRESS
The Edinburgh Building, Cambridge CB2 2RU, UK   http://www.cup.cam.ac.uk
40 West 20th Street, New York, NY 10011-4211, USA   http://www.cup.org
10 Stamford Road, Oakleigh, Melbourne 3166, Australia

First published in French by Edisciences 1995 © Edisciences 1995

English edition © Cambridge University Press 1998

First published in English 1998

Typeset by the author [CRC]

A catalogue record of this book is available from the British Library

ISBN 0 521 57183 9 hardback
ISBN 0 521 57681 4 paperback

Transferred to digital printing 2003

To the best of our knowledge, none of the code included in this book in itself
contains any date sensitive elements that will cause Year 2000-related problems.
However, this statement implies no warranty in this matter, on the part
of the authors or the publisher.

Contents

Preface

This book has a number of objectives. First, it provides the concepts and a language to produce sophisticated software. Second, the book tries to make you step back a bit from programming as an activity by highlighting basic problems linked to programming as a discipline. In the end, we hope to share our own pleasure in programming.

The language we use—CAML—makes it possible to achieve all these goals. CAML belongs to the family of "functional" languages, all of which have the following qualities:

- They are particularly well adapted to writing applications for "symbolic computation"—the kind of computing that concerns computer scientists as well as mathematicians—in software engineering, artificial intelligence, formal computation, computer-aided proof, and so forth.

- Functional languages are built on a fundamental theory that derives from mathematical logic. This basis provides these languages with their semantics as well as their systems of types and proof.

- By the very way in which they are designed, these languages support a certain aesthetic in programming, an aesthetic which, like the aesthetic of a mathematical proof, is often an indication of their quality.

This book grew primarily out of a programming course given by Guy Cousineau at the Ecole Normale Supérieure between 1990 and 1995. The book also benefited from the teaching experience of Michel Mauny, who wrote Chapters 8 and 13 and contributed to the overall consistency of the book. The web site for the book (http://pauillac.inria.fr/cousineau-mauny/) includes supplementary materials including solutions to the exercises.

The approach to functional programming in this book owes a great deal to the experience gained during the development of CAML, first by the Formel Project and then by the Cristal Project at INRIA (the French National Institute for Research in Computer Science and Automation) in collaboration with Université Denis Diderot and the Ecole Normale Supérieure. Both authors thank all the members of the research teams involved as well as other people who helped us in writing this book, whether through their ideas or their comments about the preliminary drafts of the manuscript. We owe particular thanks to Gilles Bernot, Jean Berstel, Bruno Blanchet, Emmanuel Chailloux, Antoine Chambert-Loir, Lucky Chillan, Pierre Crégut, Pierre-Louis Curien, Vincent Danos, Roberto DiCosmo, Damien Doligez, Maribel Fernandez, Thérèse Hardin, Robert Harley, Gérard Huet, Xavier Leroy, Rodrigo Lopez, Valérie Ménissier, Giancarlo Nota, Jean-François Perrot, Laurence Puel, Daniel de Rauglaudre, Didier Rémy, Christian Rinderknecht, Emilie Sayag, Michèle Soria, Ascánder Suárez, Pierre Weis.

We also thank Kathleen Callaway who translated the book to English with great care and the anonymous referees who provided very useful suggestions.

Introduction

Programming

The spectacular development of the computing industry depends largely on progress in two very different areas: hardware and software. Progress in hardware has been fairly quantitative: miniaturized parts, increased performance, cost cutting; whereas the progress in software has been more qualitative: ease of use, friendliness, etc.

In fact, most users see their computer only through interfaces that let them exploit the machine while ignoring practically all its structure and internal details, just as if we drove our cars without ever opening the hood, just like we enjoy the comfort of central heating without necessarily grasping thermodynamics.

This qualitative improvement was brought to us by progress in software as an independent discipline. It is based on a major research effort, in the course of which computer science has been structured little by little around its own concepts and methods. Those concepts and methods, of course, should be the basis for teaching computer science.

The most fundamental concept in computer science is computing, of course. A computation is a set of transformations carried out "mechanically" by means of a finite number of predefined rules. A computation impinges on formalized symbolic data (information) representing, for example, numbers (as in numeric computations) or mathematical expressions (as in formal computation) or data or even knowledge of all kinds. The only characteristics common to all computations is the discreteness of their data (that is, the information is finite) and the mechanical way in which the rules are applied.

The role of computer science is first of all to provide the means to specify and execute computations and, at a more theoretical level, to study the properties of those computations, such as, for example, their cost. Concretely, we specify computations with the help of programs written in a programming language. Computations can also be studied more abstractly through algorithms. These two approaches give rise to two disciplines in computer science—programming and algorithms—disciplines strikingly different in their aims and methods.

As a discipline, the study of algorithms lists the classes of specific problems for which we compare the performance of different algorithms. To make such comparisons, we exploit a model of a machine that we assume to be reasonably universal; we then consider a calculation as an ordered set of elementary operations carried out by the machine. Results obtained in that way should be independent of the programming language used.

As for programming as a discipline, it is concerned foremost with the logical aspects of program organization. It draws on the study of algorithms to choose efficient data structures and high-performance algorithms, but its main principle is to provide programmers with concepts and methods for writing programs correctly, legibly, and in a way that is easy to modify and to re-use. Indeed, progress in programming is reflected largely by the evolution of languages and environments available to programmers.

Programming problems

Here are a few problems that arise naturally in programming as a disciplined activity:

- How do we specify what we expect from a program?

- How do we associate a program with a precise description of what that program computes?

- How do we ensure that a program is correct with respect to a given specification?

These problems are not purely intellectual curiosities. When a program, for example, manages security at a nuclear power station or the landing procedure of aircraft, we really have to know how to answer such questions. Quite independently of such obvious high risk applications, the industrial costs linked to putting a program into production and the financial consequences of certain kinds of errors in programming are considerable.

The most satisfactory way to answer those kinds of questions would be to specify what we expect of a program and to do so formally in a mathematical language so that we could effectively prove the equivalence of the two and verify their equivalence by computer. Unfortunately, we still do not know how to do that nowadays, particularly when we are faced with really huge programs. Research has provided methods and formal systems, but for the moment they are not applicable on a grand scale. Nevertheless, even though a formal proof of correctness verified by computer is not practical for most software, it is important that the correctness of programs should at least be an object of rational argument. For that reason, the teaching and learning of the concepts making it possible to reason about programs must be a component of any training in programming as a discipline, and this demand greatly influences our choice of a language.

In practice, for all questions linked to specifying and verifying programs, such concrete formal systems as specification languages and programming languages have a very important role; indeed, we cannot afford to ignore the exact nature of such formal systems. In order for a verification method to be useful, it must be largely automatic. For that reason, such formal systems must be completely explicit. We thus naturally arrive at preoccupations very similar to those in mathematical logic, most particularly those in proof theory.

Even if we forget about the formal proof of correctness of programs, however, it is clear that the programming language we use influences our capacity as programmers to produce correct programs within a reasonable period of time. In short, language choice affects productivity. Indeed, the driving force behind the evolution of languages since the beginning of computer science has been this quest for improved productivity.

Programming languages

One way of summarizing the history of programming languages is to consider it as a continuous effort to abstract high-level concepts in order to escape from the idiosyncrasies of particular machines. These high-level concepts come very close to mathematics or logic.

The earliest users of machines were totally dependent on machine structure, and they had to program by means of a set of very elementary instructions. The first major effort to get out of that situation was the design of FORTRAN. In 1958, it introduced symbolic notation for variables and used arithmetic expressions in programs. With the wisdom of hindsight, the effect of FORTRAN may seem a limited step, but in fact it changed fundamentally the very nature of programming by separating the structure of the programming language from the structure of the machine. This separation is based on the idea of a **compiler**—that is, a program that translates programs written by a user into programs executable by a machine.

After FORTRAN, research into programming languages developed rapidly in tandem with work on compilation. In particular, the language ALGOL (1960), of which PASCAL and ADA are remote descendants, was the basis for significant progress, such as refined studies about different modes for passing parameters as well as the introduction of richer data structures.

Independently, the language LISP, born in the same era as FORTRAN, has been the basis of some essential innovations. Created for the purpose of non-numeric applications in "artificial intelligence," LISP was extremely innovative. For example, it fostered the adoption of data structures that were simultaneously rich and simple, making it possible to represent all sorts of symbolic objects, including LISP programs themselves. It promoted the systematic use of recursion. It supported allocation and automatic recovery of memory. It fostered interaction. These innovations were somewhat obscured, however, by the fact that early implementations of LISP were not highly efficient in performance. Not until the early eighties did increasing memory capacity and efficient compilers make it feasible to develop large scale applications in LISP or to distribute LISP applications like Macsyma, a system for computer algebra and symbolic computation, more widely.

These languages developed pragmatically outside a theoretical basis or using an *ad hoc* theory. At the end of the sixties and the beginning of the seventies, a great effort was made to give programming a healthy theoretical basis in the use of logical tools such as λ-calculus and first order logic. λ-calculus was used by Landin and then by Scott and Strachey to define the semantics of programming languages. First order logic was used to develop systems of proof to establish the correctness of programs formally with respect to their specifications. The success of these approaches was somewhat limited due to the fact that the systems used were quite heterogeneous compared to the existing programming languages. The next step was thus to design programming languages actually based on these logical systems. Functional languages, based on λ-calculus, came about in this way, as did logical languages, such as PROLOG, based on first order logic.

The history of programming languages as we have explained it here is from the point of view of computing as a science. Computing as an industrial technique, however, has obeyed very different laws, and the popular success of programming languages has depended on very diverse conditions. Some languages, like ADA, for example, have been imposed by administrative fiat. Others, like FORTRAN, survive in spite of their weaknesses because vast libraries of programs have already been produced that way and can hardly be replaced without enormous financial investment. Other languages exist not so much because they themselves represent obvious progress but rather because they support an innovative application, as in the case of the C programming language with respect to UNIX. And in this context, finally, it is important to note that pure theory is not the only seed-bed of programming languages: object-oriented programming, for example, grew out of concrete experience in the production of human-machine interfaces.

The very diversity of programming languages along with their often unsatisfactory character is a manifestation of the current state of computer science. This fact does not prevent us from appreciating the considerable progress of the last fifty years; nor does it keep us from establishing criteria to compare and judge existing languages.

Programming languages are generally strange hybrids combining aspects inherited from the structure of computers with more abstract aspects attached to their mathematical tradition. Among the former, we number assignment and sequenced instructions. Those kinds of constructions are known as "imperative" because they correspond to the idea of a program as an ordered sequence of commands given to the machine. Among the latter, abstract aspects, we find, for example, the ideas of expressions and functions—features known as "declarative" because they have a meaning independent of any execution on a machine.

A programming course, if it has any ambition to broach the fundamental problems linked to this discipline, must be based on some language that has a semantics that can be formally defined and that lends itself to prove the correctness of programs. For those reasons, we chose a "functional" language, that is, one built on the basis of expressions and applications of functions. However, at the same time, the language we choose has to be reasonably universal; in particular, it must facilitate the production of applications for which it is quite hard to keep up a purely functional point of view—applications such as "systems programming" or "human-machine communication."

The language used

The language used in this book—CAML—seems to us a reasonable compromise between rigor and realism. With an essentially functional spirit, it still lets us make use of conceptual tools close to the mathematical tradition to specify and verify programs. It also lets us give a vision of programming less tangled up in technical details than if we had chosen a language in more current use.

In addition, CAML is also a realistic language that supports imperative programming when that is needed. It is well adapted to a programming course where one wants to distinguish the fundamental aspects of programming from those contingencies linked to machine properties and existing systems, still without ignoring them entirely.

The language CAML is a dialect of ML, a language designed by R. Milner at the University of Edinburgh at the end of the seventies. CAML grew out of work among researchers at LIENS and INRIA; it was developed at INRIA. A version known as CAML LIGHT, available for micro-processors, is used in this course.

The plan of this book

This book is made up of three parts. The first part presents the language CAML, not in an exhaustive way, by any means, but rather highlights its internal consistency and its underlying ideas. Chapter 3 shows you why this language lends itself so well to defining semantics and proving correctness of programs. You do not absolutely have to read that chapter before you get into the rest of the book. In fact, on a first reading, you might skip it.

The second part of the book is about writing relatively complicated programs so you can see the expressive power of the language. Each chapter corresponds to a different domain and can thus be read more or less independently. Each chapter can even serve as the basis for fairly large programming projects.

The third part presents problems about the implementation of CAML on a machine. There we define the principles for representing values on a machine as well as an evaluator, a compiler, and a type synthesizer.

Part I

Basic Principles

Functional programming is a style that uses the definition and application of functions as essential concepts. In this approach, variables play the same role as in mathematics: they are the symbolic representation of values and, in particular, serve as the parameters of functions. The fundamental syntactic idea is that of an expression, and we define functions, starting from expressions, by using variables as parameters.

For example, in the language CAML, the expression

fun x → 2∗x+1

designates the function that associates x with 2∗x+1.

If we wanted to define the same function in PASCAL or in C, we would write:

```
function F(x : integer) : integer;
begin
  F := 2*x+1
end
```

or

```
int F(int x) {
    return (2*x+1);
}
```

In PASCAL, as in C, our definition of the function includes a kind of parasite: the introduction of an arbitrary name F. In those languages, we cannot define a function without naming it. Even more parasitic, there is also an assignment operation, or a **return**, relevant in computer science jargon but *a priori* having nothing to do with the definition of a function. We also notice that in PASCAL and C, there are types present in the declarations, though this fact does not distinguish these languages from CAML in any major way. Types exist in CAML, too, though they are computed by the system, so there is no need to declare them.

What we need to remember from this example is that a functional style tends to preserve the simplicity and spirit of mathematical notation. For example, the fact that functions can be denoted by expressions means that functional values must be considered as values just like others. Consequently, they can be passed as arguments or returned as results from other functions. That is certainly the case in CAML, though not so in conventional programming languages.

The following text can be read in two different ways. You can see it as a presentation that uses the language CAML as its example, but you can also think of the text as a rational construction of a programming language from a very simple presupposition. Starting from the basic idea that the language must be founded on the concepts of expression and function, we will introduce other necessary concepts little by little so that we can program effectively within this framework.

As we go about this construction, we will deliberately use ideas and notation very close to mathematics. In fact, there is no practical reason for programming languages to eschew the mathematical tradition; indeed, there is every reason for us to take advantage of many centuries of effort that mathematicians have put into achieving concise, clear ideas that reflect the concepts in use. When we have to depart from those ideas, we will explain why and try to show whether this departure is more apparent than real; that is, whether it is due to profound or circumstantial reasons, such as, for example, reasons based on current compiler technology.

The few pages that follow analyze the differences between the idea of expression as it appears in mathematics, and as it is used in functional programming.

Among our merely apparent (but not real) departures from the mathematical tradition, we could list the problems of written form or syntax. In general, programmers write their programs as strings of characters belonging to the conventional ASCII alphabet. Accordingly, the mathematical written form

$$\sqrt{x^2 + y^2}$$

has to be replaced by sqrt(x*x + y*y) or sqrt(x**2 + y**2).

Our choice of a syntax in the form of character strings (or in computer science parlance, **concrete syntax**) is a non-trivial problem. In fact, it gives rise to an important discipline: syntactic analysis. However, it involves a problem that we can consider a minor one. The development of techniques for syntactic analysis allows us, in large part, to concentrate on the deep structure of expressions, or, as we say in computer science, on **abstract syntax**.

Even so, sometimes difficult problems are attached to the issues of syntax— such problems as the interpretation of the symbols used. In general, mathematical expressions entail a number of implicit conventions which in turn introduce many ambiguities that cannot be resolved except by context and intelligence on the part of the reader, or by the use of complicated typographic conventions. For example, in any linear algebra textbook, the expression $M_1 \times M_2$ quite probably designates the product of two matrices, whereas in other contexts, the operation $\times$ could have many different meanings. In a programming language, the means for linking the definition of a symbol to its uses must be defined in a precise, unambiguous way. Doing so poses problems of scope and environment, problems inherent in the use of any completely formalized language.

Moreover, a mathematical expression generally has more than one level of meaning. For example, an expression such as

$$x^2 + 2x + 1$$

designates a polynomial over the variable x as well as the function from $\mathcal{R}$ to $\mathcal{R}$ associated with it.

In computer science, the level of meaning on which we work must be completely explicit. Any expression written by a programmer will be evaluated as a **value** defined in a unique way. The correspondence between expressions and values is called the **semantics** of that programming language and must itself be defined unambiguously.

Thus we introduce a dichotomy between expressions (in the programming language) and values (as results of computations). This dichotomy has consequences: for example, when we want to write programs for formal computations, the formal expressions being treated are values themselves and thus must be distinguished from the expressions of the programming language being used. The expressions of the programming language being used play the role of a **metalanguage** with respect to the formal expressions being treated. This distinction between language and metalanguage is foreign to current mathematical practice. In contrast, it is an important distinction in logic for the same reasons that it is in computer science.

Finally, we have to mention the idea of type again. It is used implicitly in mathematics, but it is used in computer science in a way that is more precise and more constraining. For an expression to be capable of being evaluated, it is not sufficient for that expression to be merely syntactically correct. There is more to the problem than that. For example, in an expression like $f(x)$, where f is a function and x is an argument, it is necessary for x to belong to the domain of f in order for the expression to be evaluated and to have meaning. If that were not the case, then the mechanical application of evaluation rules would in general lead to an operation that would be impossible to carry out—to such anomalies as an attempt to compute the square root of a character string. That sort of behavior would either produce an execution error or a result completely lacking in meaning. For such reasons, we are led to classify the values of a language according to their **type**. Once values have a type, correct expressions are typed as well: their type is the type of their value. If this type can be computed before evaluation, then possible inconsistencies in the expression can be detected, and we can then guarantee that evaluation will not lead to the application of an operator to inappropriate arguments, an application that would produce an execution error.

The programming approach that we will use will be based on the idea of an expression that can be evaluated. In its "purest" version, in Chapters 1 and 2, this approach will facilitate equational reasoning about programs (presented in Chapter 3). Chapter 3 will first make more precise what we mean by "an expression that can be evaluated". The formal definition of the correspondence between an expression and its value constitutes what we call the **semantics** of the language we are using. This semantics provides the necessary basis for reasoning about programs and serves as the specification of an implementation. Section 3.1 defines the semantics of CAML, used later in Section 3.4 to verify the correctness of programs. The semantics also serves as the reference for the implementation defined in Part III.

To define the type of an expression formally, we define a typing rule for every construction in the language. The definition of typing rules like this is sometimes known as **static semantics**, in contrast to **dynamic semantics**, which defines evaluation rules. The adequacy of static and dynamic semantics can be demonstrated by proving that evaluation preserves the type of expressions. In that way, we get a guarantee that an expression for which the type has been statically computed (that is, computed before execution) can be evaluated without provoking a type error. The rules for determining types in our language are defined in Section 3.5.

Notice that in what we have just been saying, we have not mentioned the idea of **assignment**. That operation makes it possible to modify the value of a variable over time. It is essential in most conventional programming languages, and at the level of the programming language, it reflects a low-level machine operation: the actual modification of the contents of a memory cell. In a rational approach to programming, this operation entails a serious defect: it prevents us from reasoning about the equivalence of programs. For example, if f is a function and x a variable, an expression such as $f(x) + f(x)$ is not necessarily equivalent to $2f(x)$ if the function f makes assignments. Using this operation thus makes it very difficult to verify the correctness of programs formally.

Unfortunately, considerations about the efficiency of certain algorithms make it hard to exclude the use of assignment totally, so eventually we will introduce it in Chapter 4.

The definition of our programming language takes up four chapters. The first, titled "Expressions," defines the constructions in the language and explains how to use them. In that chapter, we limit ourselves to programs that work on very simple types, mainly numeric types. The second chapter, titled "Data Structures," describes how users can define their own types to manage complicated data. The third chapter, titled "Semantics," defines precisely the static and dynamic semantics of the language and indicates how to demonstrate that a program is correct. These first three chapters occur in a purely functional context. The fourth chapter, titled "Imperative Aspects," introduces the non-functional constructions of CAML and explains for which kinds of programming it may be necessary to use them. It also covers what their use implies about the semantics of the language.

Chapter 1

Expressions

This book includes a great many examples. These examples are presented as if they were typed on the keyboard of a computer during an interactive session in CAML. In consequence, they include lines written by the user along with responses from the system. The character **#** that appears at the beginning of examples is the system prompt. Text written by the user begins after that character and ends with a double semi-colon (;;). Everything between the **#** and the double semi-colon is thus due to the user. The rest is the system response. This system response includes information about type and value.

In the CAML system, the type of expressions entered by the user is computed **statically**, that is, computed before evaluation. Any possible inconsistencies in type are detected automatically and reported by an error message. This kind of type-checking is carried out without the user ever having to give any indication to the system about types—no type declarations as in other languages, like PASCAL or C.

Once the types have been synthesized satisfactorily, evaluation takes place, and then a result is computed and displayed. This display takes one of two different forms, depending on whether the text entered by the user is a simple expression or a definition.

The examples given here differ a bit in typography from those that actually appear on screen during a real working session; we modified them for legibility and aesthetic reasons. For example, the keywords of the language are printed in bold characters, and the arrows that appear on a terminal as two ASCII characters, ->, are presented here as only one character, →. Even so, we think the correspondence between the typography we use in the examples and the ASCII form you see on screen will still be obvious to you.

1.1 Expressions and Definitions

As we just indicated, expressions and definitions are displayed differently during an interactive CAML session. This section elaborates the difference between the two.

1.1.1 Expressions

The most conventional expressions are arithmetic. In our first example, we enter the expression $2 + 3$ and we get the system response.

```
#2+3;;
- : int = 5
```

In that response, the symbol "$-$" indicates the expression entered by the user; the int indicates the type of that expression (that is, it's an expression with an integer value); and 5 is, of course, its value.

In plain English, the system response can be read as:

The expression you just entered is of type int and its value is 5.

In a completely conventional and familiar way, arithmetic expressions in CAML can use parentheses to eliminate certain ambiguities. In the absence of parentheses, the symbols $*$ (for multiplication) and $/$ (for division) have priority over the symbols $+$ (for addition) and $-$ (for substraction). In case of ambiguity among symbols of the same priority, by default, CAML is left-associative; that is, $a + b + c$ is treated as $(a + b) + c$. Of course, if you use parentheses, you can explicitly organize expressions into groups as you want.

```
#1+2*3;;
- : int = 7

#(1+2)*3;;
- : int = 9

#1-2+3;;
- : int = 2

#1-(2+3);;
- : int = -4

#4/2*2;;
- : int = 4

#4/(2*2);;
- : int = 1
```

As you will see later, this way of parenthesizing is generalized for all CAML expressions, not just simple arithmetic.

1.1.2   Definitions

Definitions let you introduce new variables into your user environment and to associate values with those new variables. As in mathematics, here the idea of a variable lets you designate values symbolically. It also lets you factor certain computations by naming a computed value so that it can be re-used later any number of times. In CAML, variables can be introduced by means of the construction **let**. As you no doubt know, the name of a variable in a programming language is called its **identifier**. In CAML, identifiers necessarily begin with a letter and consist of letters, digits, and the symbols "_" (underscore) or ' (prime).

```
#let x = 2+3;;
x : int = 5

#let pi = 3.14;;
pi : float = 3.14
```

Such definitions in CAML have exactly the same status as such phrases as

$$\text{Let's assume } x = 2+3$$

or

$$\text{Let's assume } pi = 3.14$$

in mathematics. The variables x and pi when defined in that way can be used throughout the rest of a working session.

```
#x*x;;
− : int = 25
```

1.1.3   Local Definitions

In CAML, you can also define things locally; that is, you can limit the scope to an expression.

```
#let x = 2 in x+1;;
− : int = 3

#let a = 3 and b = 4 in a*a+b*b;;
− : int = 25
```

These definitions do not have global scope. The definition of x, for example, is valid only in the expression x+1. After evaluation, the variable x is the one defined earlier.

```
#x;;
- : int = 5
```

Input such as **let** x=2 **in** x+1 taken as a whole is handled by CAML as an expression, not as a definition.

There is also a syntactic variation on the construction **let** x=e_1 **in** e_2. That variation involves the construction e_2 **where** x=e_1.

```
#x+1 where x=2;;
- : int = 3

#a*a+b*b where a=3 and b=4;;
- : int = 25
```

These two forms of local declaration are strictly equivalent.

1.2   Elementary Types

The main basic types provided by CAML are integers (**int**), floating-point numbers (**float**), Booleans (**bool**), strings (**string**), and characters (**char**).

1.2.1   Integers

In CAML, the integers lie between -2^{30} and $2^{30} - 1$. The operators that you can use on the type int are these:

+	addition
−	subtraction
*	multiplication
/	integer division
mod	modulo

Integer operations in CAML carry out exact arithmetic calculations as long as there is no overflow. However, there is a CAML library that lets you compute with integers of arbitrary size. In Chapter 10, we outline the main principles of its implementation.

1.2.2 Floating-Point Numbers

Floating-point numbers are used for approximate calculations. They are represented internally as a mantissa m and an exponent n for the number $m \times 10^n$. Such a number is displayed by the system as a decimal part possibly followed by the letter e and a relative integer, indicating the power of 10 by which you must multiply the first number. Any time a floating-point number is equal to an integer that can be represented by the type int, that number will be displayed by CAML without its decimal point. In such a case, only its type lets you know that it is a floating-point number.

```
#1.0;;
 - : float = 1
```

A number entered by a user is considered a floating-point number if it contains a decimal point or the letter e (or E) indicating the presence of an exponent.

According to the CAML type system, the types int and float are disjoint. There is no automatic conversion between them. That choice may be debatable, but it clearly separates exact computations from approximate ones. There does exist, nevertheless, a conversion function float_of_int to convert integers into floating-point numbers explicitly.

Floating-point operations are distinguished by a decimal point.

+.	floating-point addition
−.	floating-point subtraction
*.	floating-point multiplication
/.	floating-point division

This convention—of the decimal point in operators—is somewhat unusual and you might find it distasteful[1]. When you are working exclusively with floating-point numbers, you can use the operators +, −, *, and /. (For more details, see Section 1.2.3.)

The usual trigonometric functions operate on floating-point numbers.

---

[1]Overloading operators, that is, making the same symbol represent more than one operation on different types, is quite difficult to introduce into a language without explicit type declarations.

sqrt	square root
log	logarithm
exp	e^x
sin	sine
cos	cosine
tan	tangent
asin	arcsine
acos	arccosine
atan	arctangent

Here are a few examples:

```
#sqrt(2);;
> Toplevel input:
>sqrt(2);;
>        ^
> Expression of type int
> cannot be used with type float
```

A type-error will be detected there because the function sqrt expects a floating-point number, not an integer.

```
#sqrt(2.);;
```
$- : float = 1.41421356237$

```
#sqrt(float_of_int(2));;
```
$- : float = 1.41421356237$

```
#acos(-1.);;
```
$- : float = 3.14159265359$

```
#x*.x+.y*.y where x=sin(1.0) and y=cos(1.0);;
```
$- : float = 1$

1.2.3   Floating Mode

When you write a program using floating-point numbers exclusively, you can get into a mode where the operators $+$, $-$, $*$, and $/$ are interpreted as floating-point. All you have to do is use the command #open "float".

Commands that modify the system normally begin by the symbol # to distinguish them from expressions.

You get back into normal mode (that is, integer mode) by the command #close "float".

```
##open "float";;
```

```
#2.1+3.2;;
```
− : *float* = 5.3

```
#x*x+y*y where x=sin(1.0) and y=cos(1.0);;
```
− : *float* = 1

```
##close "float";;
```

1.2.4 Booleans

The Booleans, also known as truth values, consist of two constants, **true** and **false**. Functions that make comparisons ($=, <, >, \leq, \geq$) have a Boolean result.

```
#1<2 ;;
```
− : *bool* = **true**

Boolean values can be combined by means of logical operators such as **not** (negation), **&** (conjunction), and **or** (disjunction).

```
#1≤2 & (0<1 or 1<0) & not(2<2);;
```
− : *bool* = **true**

Boolean values are particularly useful in the construction **if−then−else**.

```
#let x=3 in
 if x<0 then x else x*x;;
```
− : *int* = 9

This construction is different from the one in more conventional languages: it impinges on expressions, and it is an expression itself.

1.2.5 Character Strings

In CAML, character strings are objects of type **string**. They are enclosed by the double-quote symbol ("). Concatenation of strings is indicated by the circumflex symbol (^).

```
#"a string" ^ " of characters";;
```
− : *string* = "a string of characters"

1.2.6 Characters

The character type (**char**) is used mainly for input and output. Characters appear between backquotes.

```
#'a';;
```
$-: char = $ 'a'

The internal ASCII code for characters is given by the function int_of_char.

```
#int_of_char 'a';;
```
$-: int = 97$

1.3   Cartesian Product

Chapter 2 explains how data is organized into complex structures corresponding to types defined by the user. For the moment, we will form complex values simply by using the mathematical idea of a Cartesian product.

The values themselves can be grouped in pairs or even in tuples. For that purpose, a comma serves as the separator between elements, just as in traditional notation. However, external parentheses are not obligatory. (For more detail about that idea, see Section 1.6.) The type "Cartesian product" is denoted by the symbol $*$.

```
#(1, 1.2);;
```
$-: int * float = 1, 1.2$

```
#(1+2, true or false, "hello");;
```
$-: int * bool * string = 3, true,$ "hello"

```
#((1,2), (3,4));;
```
$-: (int * int) * (int * int) = (1, 2), (3, 4)$

Types such as these

$$t_1 * t_2 * t_3, \qquad (t_1 * t_2) * t_3 \qquad \text{and} \qquad t_1 * (t_2 * t_3)$$

are considered different from one another. The first of those forms indicates a set of triples, the second a set of pairs where the first component is also a pair, and the third is a set of pairs where the second component is also a pair.

The functions fst and snd let you access the first and second component of a pair.

```
#snd(1+2, 3+4);;
```
$-: int = 7$

```
#fst((1,2),3);;
```
$-: int * int = 1, 2$

```
#let p=(1,2) in
 (snd(p), fst(p));;
```
$-: int * int = 2, 1$

Later we will show you how to define functions to access components of arbitrary tuples.

Notice that the Cartesian product lets you handle only collections of objects of fixed size. To deal with objects of variable size, you have to use the type list. (For more about lists, see Section 2.2.6.)

1.4 Functions

In CAML, functions are defined by notation that closely resembles mathematics.

1.4.1 Defining Simple Functions

To define sq as a function that associates a floating-point number x with its square x^2, we write this:

```
#let sq(x) = x*.x;;
sq : float → float = ⟨fun⟩
```

The type of a function is denoted by an arrow, just as it is conventionally. This information about type is all that the system offers after a function definition. The system prints only ⟨fun⟩ as the "value" part.

It is theoretically possible to give a representation of functions, but this representation can only be the expanded text defining the function (which could be very large), and furthermore, this text is difficult to reconstitute from the internal representation of function values. In Chapter 12, you will actually see a description of the internal representation of functions.

Functions defined by the user can be used later just like predefined functions.

```
#sq(2.0);;
− : float = 4
```

Functions of more than one argument are defined in the same way, though of course they use a tuple of arguments in place of a single argument.

```
#let module(x,y) = sqrt(sq(x)+. sq(y));;
module : float * float → float = ⟨fun⟩

#module(3.0,4.0);;
− : float = 5
```

In CAML, evaluation depends on the fact that the definitions of functions that we have just introduced are in fact effective. To compute the value of f(v) where f is a function defined by **let** f(x) = e, all you have to do is to evaluate the expression e in which you have replaced x by v.

The basis of CAML programs is the function. A program is made up of a number of function definitions followed by an expression to evaluate. The value of that expression is the result of the program.

Exercise

1.1 Write a function that takes three floating-point numbers a, b, c as its arguments and tests whether the equation $ax^2 + bx + c = 0$ has any solutions.

1.4.2   Function Expressions

In CAML, it is also possible to denote functions without giving them names. For example, earlier we gave the name module to the function that associates the two variables, x and y, with the value $\sqrt{x^2 + y^2}$. It could be denoted this way:

```
#fun(x,y) → sqrt(sq(x) +. sq(y));;
− : float * float → float = ⟨fun⟩
```

The operation that builds the function (**fun** $(x_1, \ldots, x_n)$ → **e**) from an expression e containing the variables $x_1, \ldots, x_n$ is called **abstraction**.

The expression (**fun** $(x_1, \ldots, x_n)$ → **e**) is called a **function expression**.

Such an expression can be used in place of the name of a function and in particular can be applied to its arguments.

```
#(fun(x,y) → sqrt(sq(x) +. sq(y))) (3.0,4.0);;
− : float = 5
```

This way of denoting functions gives them the status of a value in their own right. Certain expressions in CAML denote functions the way other expressions denote numbers or pairs. It is thus *a priori* superfluous to have a special construction in the language in order to declare a function. In fact, it is quite possible to write:

```
#let sq = (fun x → x *. x);;
sq : float → float = ⟨fun⟩
```

This definition is equivalent to the one we gave earlier for the function sq, which can in fact be considered as a more traditional equivalent form.

1.4.3 Higher Order Function Expressions

Since functions are considered as values in their own right, it is natural for them to appear as arguments or results of other functions. Functions that take other functions as arguments or that return functions as results are said to be **higher order**, and we refer to them as "functionals" to distinguish them from ordinary functions.

Let's consider for example the functional h that associates the function $\frac{f(x)}{x}$ with every function $f(x)$. We could define it like this:

#let h = (**fun** f → (**fun** x → f(x)/.x));;
h : (*float* → *float*) → *float* → *float* = ⟨**fun**⟩

You might think that parentheses are lacking in the way the type of h is written. Actually, the form given by CAML results from a convention that we will explain later, in Section 1.6, when we discuss syntax. For now, you should read this type as (float → float) → (float → float).

Near 0 (zero), h(sin) is close to 1.

#(h(sin))(0.1);;
− : *float* = 0.998334166468

h(sin) is an expression with its own meaning; it denotes a function of type float → float. It can be applied to an argument (as we just did), but it can also be used in various ways; for example, it can be linked to an identifier.

#let k = h(sin);;
k : *float* → *float* = ⟨**fun**⟩

#k(0.1);;
− : *float* = 0.998334166468

#k(0.00001);;
− : *float* = 0.999999999983

Notice that instead of defining k by **let** k = h(sin), we have also been able to write **let** k(x)=(h(sin))(x). We can easily show in fact that for every expression e not depending on x, the expression (**fun** x → e(x)) designates the same function as the expression e. As you saw, the definition **let** k(x) = (h(sin))(x) is equivalent to **let** k = **fun** x → (h(sin))(x) which has the value of **let** k = h(sin).

If we use the construction **fun** in cascades, we get something a little dense to read, so by convention, instead of writing this:

$$\textbf{fun } x_1 \rightarrow (\ldots \rightarrow (\textbf{fun } x_n \rightarrow e) \ldots)$$

we can write this more simply:

$$\textbf{fun } x_1 \ldots x_n \rightarrow e.$$

For example, for h, we can write this:

#let h = **fun** f x → f(x) /. x;;
h : (*float* → *float*) → *float* → *float* = ⟨**fun**⟩

Other conventions for writing CAML legibly are presented in Section 1.6 about syntax.

Exercises
1.2 Given a function f:float → float and a small interval dx, the value of the derivative of f in x can be approximated by (f(x+dx)−f(x))/dx. Write a derivative function to associate the derived function f' defined by f'(x)=(f(x+dx)−f(x))/dx with any function f and an interval dx.
1.3 Write a smoothing function that takes a function f and an interval dx as its arguments and returns as its result the function for which the value in x is the average of f(x), f(x−dx), and f(x+dx).

1.4.4   Recursive Functions

In a definition of the form **let** x = e, the variables that appear in the expression e must have been defined already. It is possible for a variable x to appear in e but if so, then it involves an x which has already been defined before, not the one we are defining now. The following example illustrates that point.

#let x = 1;;
x : *int* = 1

#let x = x+2;;
x : *int* = 3

In contrast, when we define functions, it is often useful to call the function itself in its own definition. In such a case, we speak of a **recursive definition**. For example, when we want to program a function defined by recurrence, that is, by its own repetition, then the definition of f(n) actually calls f(n−1). In such definitions, we replace the construction **let** by a construction **let rec** that uses recursion explicitly.

For example, the recursive definition of the factorial function:

$$
\begin{aligned}
0! &= 1 \\
(n+1)! &= (n+1) \times n!
\end{aligned}
$$

becomes:

```
#let rec fact(n) =
    if n=0 then 1 else n*fact(n−1);;
fact : int → int = ⟨fun⟩
```

```
#fact(5);;
− : int = 120
```

Our earlier concern—to keep the definition of a value completely independent of the name of that value by means of the definition of the variable linked to it— might normally lead to our introducing notation like **fun rec** to denote recursive functions. However, that notation does not exist in CAML, though we will come back to this point later in Section 3.1 about evaluation.

Exercises

1.4 Write a function that computes a^n for a floating-point number a and an integer n. First, use the fact that $a^0 = 1$, $a^{(n+1)} = aa^n$. Then write a second function by using the property that $a^{2n} = (a^n)^2$ and $a^{2n+1} = a(a^n)^2$. Compare the complexity of those two functions.

1.5 Write a function computing the greatest common divisor for two positive integers.

1.6 Write a function to test whether an integer is prime.

1.4.5   Mutually Recursive Functions

We also need to define mutually recursive functions, such as those corresponding to crossed recurrences. For example, it is possible to write this in CAML:

```
#let rec even (n) = if n=0 then true else odd(n−1)
  and odd (n) = if n=0 then false else even(n−1);;
even : int → bool = ⟨fun⟩
odd : int → bool = ⟨fun⟩
```

1.4.6   Functions Defined by Case

In fact, the construction **fun** is more general than we have shown up to now. It actually allows you to define functions by case. For example, the Boolean negation that associates true with false and associates false with true can be written like this:

```
#let neg = fun true → false
         | false → true;;
neg : bool → bool = ⟨fun⟩
```

In a similar way, the exclusive Boolean **or** can be written like this:

```
#let xor = fun (false,false) → false
           | (false,true) → true
           | (true,false) → true
           | (true,true) → false;;
xor : bool * bool → bool = ⟨fun⟩
```

In those two examples, a function with a finite domain is defined by an exhaustive list of cases.

The idea of defining a function by cases is much more important, however, than these two examples demonstrate. In fact, it is possible to mix definitions by case along with variables.

For example, to define the exclusive Boolean **or**, we could also write this:

```
#let xor = fun (false,x) → x
           | (true,x) → neg x;;
xor : bool * bool → bool = ⟨fun⟩
```

Here the case includes a variable x which can be used on the right side of the arrow. We are midway between a definition by case like the one for **neg** and an ordinary definition using a variable as a parameter. Each case corresponds to a class of possible values. For example, the first case handles the class of values that are pairs where the first element is **false**. The variable x names the second component of the pair. By doing so, it lets us use it in the corresponding definition. A structure such as (false,x) is called a **pattern**[2], and the process of associating a pattern with an argument passed to the function is known as **pattern matching**.

In the preceding examples, the cases partition the domain of the function. That is, they are simultaneously disjoint and exhaustive. CAML also allows non-disjoint cases. For example, we could write the factorial function a bit more elegantly than before, like this:

```
#let rec fact = fun 0→1
                | n→n*fact(n−1);;
fact : int → int = ⟨fun⟩
```

The first case is included in the second because the second pattern consists of a simple variable that introduces no constraints on the value being matched. In the case of non-disjoint patterns, the order in which the cases are written by the programmer is used in the function call to choose the first pattern to match against the argument.

---

[2] Patterns that appear in a construction **fun** but that are not reduced to a constant or a variable must be enclosed by parentheses.

Notice that ordinary definitions of functions are simply a very special form of definition by case: there is only one case and the pattern is a variable or a tuple of variables.

In the same style as the definition of the factorial function, here is a definition of Fibonacci numbers:

```
#let rec fib = fun 0 → 1
              | 1 → 1
              | n → fib(n−1)+fib(n−2);;
fib : int → int = ⟨fun⟩
```

In a definition of a function by case, it may occur that certain cases are not foreseen. It may also occur, given the order among the cases, that certain ones may never be used. CAML indicates these kinds of situations by warnings.

```
#(fun 0 → 1);;
> Toplevel input:
>(fun 0 -> 1);;
> ^^^^^^^^^^
> Warning: pattern matching is not exhaustive
− : int → int = ⟨fun⟩

#(fun x → true | 0 → false);;
> Toplevel input:
>(fun x -> true | 0 -> false);;
> ^^^^^^^^^^^^^^^^^^^^^^^^^
> Warning: some cases are unused in this matching.
− : int → bool = ⟨fun⟩
```

Variables that appear in the same pattern must be distinct from one another. Even so, it is possible to replace parts of a pattern by the special symbol _ to match any value. That symbol can be used more than once in the same pattern, possibly even with different types. For example, the Boolean conjunction can be written like this:

```
#let conj = fun (true,true) → true
              | (_,_) → false ;;
conj : bool * bool → bool = ⟨fun⟩
```

or even like this:

```
#let conj = fun (true,true) → true
              | _ → false ;;
conj : bool * bool → bool = ⟨fun⟩
```

1.4.7   The **function** Construction

CAML allows two different forms of pattern abstraction: the form **fun** that we have already seen, and the form **function**. The form **fun** is the one that we will generally use in this book. It abstracts more than one pattern at a time. For example,

```
#fun true true → true
    | _ _ → false;;
 − : bool → bool → bool = ⟨fun⟩
```

When this function receives its arguments, their matching will proceed simultaneously on the two patterns in the first case (true and true). If pattern matching fails on either of the two patterns, then pattern matching goes on to the next case.

Since **fun** accepts cases that include more than one pattern, such cases sometimes need to be parenthesized so that the successive patterns can be correctly recognized by the compiler.

In contrast, the **function** construction (just like the construction **match−with** presented later) abstracts only one pattern per case, and its syntax can be more flexible. For example, the function conj, that you saw earlier, could just as easily be written like this:

```
#let conj = function (true,true) → true
                    | _ → false ;;
 conj : bool * bool → bool = ⟨fun⟩
```

1.4.8   The **match with** Construction

We should also note that cases are not limited to function definitions. The construction **match−with** also lets you make the value of an expression depend on a pattern matching operation. Here's its syntax:

```
match e with
  p₁ → e₁
| ...
| pₙ → eₙ
```

For example,

```
#match (3,5) with
   (0,_) → 0
 | (x,y) → x*y;;
 − : int = 15
```

Exercise
1.7 Write the Boolean function $(a \lor b \lor c)$ with the three parameters a, b, c by using a definition with three cases.

1.5 Polymorphism

Polymorphism is an important idea that you can most easily understand if we first explain the idea of type variables.

1.5.1 Type Variables

Think for a moment about the function fst (which accesses the first component of a pair), and consider its type. To determine the type of the expression fst(1,true), we first have to assume that the function fst is of type $((\text{int} * \text{bool}) \rightarrow \text{int})$, whereas to determine the type of fst(true,1), we have to assume that the type of fst is $((\text{bool} * \text{int}) \rightarrow \text{bool})$.

So for CAML, just what is the type of the function fst?

To know the answer to that question, you simply have to ask:

```
#fst;;
- : α * β → α = ⟨fun⟩
```

In the way it writes the type of fst, CAML uses two variables of the type α and β[3]. The function fst has every type that you can get by replacing α and β by any types. This way of determining the type of a function like fst is quite natural. As long as it is legal to build pairs by means of values of any type, it is natural that the functions to access those components of the pair should take into account that possibility. A type discipline (in the sense that this is a discipline—a set of rules—applied before we arrive at a type system) is said to be **polymorphic** if it allows the use of variable types. A function is said to be polymorphic if its type is polymorphic[4].

It is easy and natural to write polymorphic functions. Here are a few examples.

Projection

```
#let fst(x,y) = x;;
fst : α * β → α = ⟨fun⟩
```

---

[3]In CAML syntax, these type variables are denoted 'a, 'b, 'c instead of α, β, γ. It seemed more aesthetically pleasing to us to present them to you as Greek letters.

[4]Notice that most current programming languages lack polymorphism, except of course those that are not statically typed, for example, LISP.

```
#let snd(x,y) = y;;
snd : α * β → β = ⟨fun⟩

#let proj_23 (x,y,z) = y;;
proj_23 : α * β * γ → β = ⟨fun⟩
```

Identity

```
#let id = fun x → x;;
id : α → α = ⟨fun⟩

#id(3);;
− : int = 3

#(id(id)) (id(3), id(4));;
− : int * int = 3, 4
```

Composition

```
#let compose(f,g) = fun x → f(g(x));;
compose : (α → β) * (γ → α) → γ → β = ⟨fun⟩

#let square(x) = x*x
 in (compose(square,square))(3);;
− : int = 81
```

You can ask CAML to choose a less general type than the one normally produced by the system. To do so, in an expression like e, where you want the type to be t you replace the expression by a **constraint expression** of the form (e:t). This technique also applies to arguments of functions. For example, you can also write this:

```
#fun ((x:int),(y:bool)) → (y,x);;
− : int * bool → bool * int = ⟨fun⟩
```

or this:

```
#fun (x,y) → ((y:bool),(x:int));;
− : int * bool → bool * int = ⟨fun⟩
```

or even this:

```
#fun ((x,y):int*bool) → (y,x);;
− : int * bool → bool * int = ⟨fun⟩
```

or likewise this:

#((**fun** (x,y) → (y,x)):int∗bool → bool∗int);;
− : *int* ∗ *bool* → *bool* ∗ *int* = ⟨**fun**⟩

The language CAML, of course, verifies that the constraint the user provides is compatible with the rules for determining type. It offers the most general type that is simultaneously compatible with the structure of the expression and the user's constraints.

#**fun** ((x:int),y) → (y,x);;
− : *int* ∗ α → α ∗ *int* = ⟨**fun**⟩

1.5.2 Type Synthesis

The type that CAML finds for the function **compose** highlights a certain system "intelligence" when it analyzes expressions entered by the user. CAML discovers that to compose f and g, it is necessary and sufficient for the domain of g and the domain of f to coincide.

If we stick to simple expressions, the mechanism for synthesizing types is quite simple, too. In the expression (**fun** (f,g) → **fun** x → f(g(x))), representing their composition, the variables f, g, and x appear. For the moment, let's call their types φ, ψ, and χ.

Since g is applied to x, we deduce that ψ is of the form $(\chi \rightarrow \alpha)$ and that the expression (g x) is thus of the type α.

Since f is applied to (g x), we deduce that φ must necessarily be of the form $(\alpha \rightarrow \beta)$ and that the expression f (g x) is thus of the type β.

Consequently, the expression (**fun** x → f (g x)) is of type $(\chi \rightarrow \beta)$ and the expression (**fun** (f,g) → **fun** x → f(g(x))) is thus of type $((\alpha \rightarrow \beta) * (\chi \rightarrow \alpha)) \rightarrow (\chi \rightarrow \beta)$.

Since no other constraint impinges on the types of f, g, and x, there is no need to specify the types α, β, and χ any further.

The type we find in this way is the most general one possible in the sense that all other types that we could have given it could be obtained by substitution, starting from the synthesized type, that is, by replacing (in this type) certain variables by expressions of types (or type expressions).

This means of synthesizing types that we have just detailed is essentially a mechanism for resolving constraints based on an algorithm known as the **unification algorithm**. We will say more about that algorithm in Section 5.2.4.

Notice that this description of type synthesis depends on the fact that we associate a unique type variable with each variable that appears in the expression for which we are determining the type. Every occurrence of the same variable must therefore be of the same type. For example, given the expression (**fun** f →

f 1, f true), we cannot determine its type in this way because the two occurrences of f cannot be of two different types.

However, CAML allows situations where the same variable can be of multiple types, as for example, id in the expression **let** id = **fun** x → x **in** (id 1, id true). Those kinds of variables are introduced by the construction **let**. To take this construction into account, type synthesis must be carried out in a stratified way. To determine the type of an expression **let** x = e_1 **in** e_2, we first compute the type t_1 for e_1; then we compute the type of e_2 under the hypothesis that x is of type t_1. If t_1 is polymorphic, that is, if it includes variables, then we rename these variables for each occurrence of x in e_2.

For example, to determine the type of **let** id = **fun** x → x **in** (id 1,id true), we first compute the type of id, that is, the type of (**fun** x → x). That computation gives us $\alpha \rightarrow \alpha$, and we attribute different types $\alpha_1 \rightarrow \alpha_1$ and $\alpha_2 \rightarrow \alpha_2$ to the occurrences of id in (id 1,id true). Then we see that α_1=int and α_2=bool, and that observation gives us the type int $*$ bool for the expression we are considering.

This way of working is equivalent to replacing the entire expression **let** id = **fun** x → x **in** (id 1,id true) by ((**fun** x → x) 1,(**fun** x → x) true).

Exercise
1.8 Determine the type of the expressions (**fun** f → **fun** (x,y) → (f x, f y)) and **let** id = **fun** x → x **in fun** (x,y) → (id x, id y). Verify your answer.

1.6   About Syntax

Now we are going to review a few syntactic difficulties and clarify some ideas that we introduced in earlier sections.

1.6.1   Application Notation

Concerning the application of functions, CAML takes the point of view that every function can be seen as a function with one argument. As long as this one argument may be a pair or a tuple, this point of view neither removes anything from nor adds anything to the language. So what is the point here?

In fact, it is easy to convince ourselves that this point of view is the only one possible about a polymorphic language. If we consider, for example, the identity function id (defined in Section 1.5) it is clear that it should be applied to values of any type, in particular, to values of a Cartesian product type, so we could as readily write id(1) as id(2,3). Thus the only reasonable point of view is to consider id as a function with one argument, and that one argument may be a simple value, a pair, or a more complicated object.

The syntactic corollary of this point is that the application can be denoted by simple juxtaposition. When we write id(2,3), the only purpose of the parentheses is to delimit the argument of id. Parentheses are not really necessary when we write id(1) or id(id), which could just as readily be written as id 1 or id id[5].

This notation of application as a simple juxtaposition is particularly well adapted to our use of higher order functions, as you will see now[6].

Our use of higher order functions gives a richer structure to expressions than the usual and customary one. When we write an application in the form (f e), not only e may be an expression, but also f. In the expression (h sin) 0.1, for example, the function (h sin) itself is applied to the value 0.1. With the purpose of simplifying the way we write such expressions and in particular with the goal of limiting the level of nested parentheses, we are led to the following conventions:

- A group of applications is parenthesized by default to the left. In other words, application is left-associative, so the expression h sin 0.1 is equivalent to (h sin) 0.1.

- The types of functionals are parenthesized by default to the right, so the type of the function h can be denoted (float $\rightarrow$ float) $\rightarrow$ (float $\rightarrow$ float) or as (float $\rightarrow$ float) $\rightarrow$ float $\rightarrow$ float.

  However, it cannot be written as float $\rightarrow$ float $\rightarrow$ float $\rightarrow$ float because that type is interpreted as float $\rightarrow$ (float $\rightarrow$ (float $\rightarrow$ float)).

1.6.2 Syntactic Analysis of Caml Expressions

Denoting application by simple juxtaposition does create unusual syntactic ambiguities. For example, when we write f 2,3, does it designate f(2,3) or (f 2),3?

To eliminate such ambiguity, we extend the idea of priority among arithmetic operators to other operators as well, like application and construction of pairs. Application is considered the operator of the highest priority. Consequently, it has priority over any other construction and in particular over arithmetic operators. At the other extreme, the comma has lower priority than arithmetic operators. The following examples highlight how these rules work in the system.

```
#let d x = (x,x);;
d : α → α * α = ⟨fun⟩

#let s x = x+1;;
s : int → int = ⟨fun⟩

#d 2,3;;
− : (int * int) * int = (2, 2), 3
```

---

[5]Notice, however, that the space between id and its argument is therefore obligatory because id1 and idid are acceptable identifiers. (For more about that idea, see Section 1.1.2 about identifiers.)

[6]This notation, by the way, comes from λ-calculus.

#d (2,3);;
− : (int ∗ int) ∗ (int ∗ int) = (2, 3), (2, 3)

#s 2∗3;;
− : int = 9

#s (2∗3);;
− : int = 7

In CAML, parentheses are used the same way as in arithmetic expressions in mathematics. They make structure explicit in expressions, and they force associations other than the default. By the way, we are always allowed to write more parentheses than strictly necessary. We do so, for example, when we are not sure about the priority observed by the system—frequently the case even among experienced CAML programmers!

1.6.3   Infix Operators Defined by the User

The binary operators written between their two arguments—most arithmetic operators—are known as **infix** operators. These operators represent functions like other operators, but from the point of view of a syntactic analysis of the language, they are interpreted differently. In particular, they cannot be used directly without arguments; that is, they cannot be used as functional values. If we were to write id(+), it would be syntactically incorrect.

In order to use these operators as functional values, we have to put a keyword in front of them: **prefix**.

#(**prefix** +);;
− : int → int → int = ⟨**fun**⟩

At times, the user may want to ask the system to treat certain identifiers as infix. It is possible to do so by means of the directive #infix. It takes a string of characters as its argument to represent the identifier. For example, if we want to use classic notation for function composition, we can declare the infix identifier o. Infixes must have a type of the form $t_1 \rightarrow t_2 \rightarrow t_3$.

#**let** o f g = **fun** x → f(g(x));;
o : $(\alpha \rightarrow \beta) \rightarrow (\gamma \rightarrow \alpha) \rightarrow \gamma \rightarrow \beta$ = ⟨**fun**⟩

##infix "o";;

#(sq o sq) 2.0;;
− : float = 16

1.7   Scope of Identifiers

The variables used in an expression cannot be free variables. In order to be exploited in an expression, a variable must appear in a definition (by the constructions **let** or **where**) or in a pattern to match (by the constructions **fun** or **match**). Each of these constructions defines a region of text where the variables that they have introduced can be used. For example, in an expression such as **let** $x = e_1$ **in** e_2, the scope of the definition of x is the expression e_2.

In the text of a program, the same identifier can be used more than once as the name of a variable. Consequently, we have to be able to connect the use of a variable unambiguously with its definition. In CAML, the principle we follow in doing so—like in mathematics—is that the occurrence of a symbol refers to its closest definition in the text. For example, in the case of definitions nested in the same expression like **let** $x = e_1$ **in** (**fun** $x \rightarrow e$), the binding by the construction **fun** prevails in the expression e.

This simple convention has consequences that we should underline in the case of function expressions with free variables (that is, variables that are not parameters of the function in which they appear). Consider this expression, for example:

```
#let x = 7 in
 let f z = z*x in
 let x = true in
 f 3;;
 − : int = 21
```

If we take account of the place in the text where the function f is defined, then the variable x that the function uses is the one defined by **let** $x = 7$. The fact that we redefine another x later by the same name as the preceding one does not modify the definition of the function f.

This convention that CAML follows about the scope of definitions is known as **textual scope** or **lexical scope** or **static scope**.

This idea of scope means that the value of a variable cannot be called into question by external definitions, and this property totally conditions the possibility of formally defining the type and the semantics of an expression. In the preceding example, the way we determine the type of f would not be possible if the variable x used by f could be redefined with a Boolean type.

1.8 More about Function Types: Equivalent Function Spaces

Defining functions in a language such as CAML is effective; that is, function definitions make it possible to evaluate mechanically expressions that include function calls. The price we pay for this efficacy is a certain rigidity.

For example, if e is an expression in two free variables x and y (let's say, 2*x+3*y), then there are four CAML functions abstracted from e. They are:

#let f_1=**fun**(x,y) $\rightarrow$ 2*x+3*y;;
f_1 : *int* * *int* $\rightarrow$ *int* = $\langle$**fun**$\rangle$

#let f_2=**fun**(y,x) $\rightarrow$ 2*x+3*y;;
f_2 : *int* * *int* $\rightarrow$ *int* = $\langle$**fun**$\rangle$

#let f_3=**fun** x y $\rightarrow$ 2*x+3*y;;
f_3 : *int* $\rightarrow$ *int* $\rightarrow$ *int* = $\langle$**fun**$\rangle$

#let f_4=**fun** y x $\rightarrow$ 2*x+3*y;;
f_4 : *int* $\rightarrow$ *int* $\rightarrow$ *int* = $\langle$**fun**$\rangle$

From a mathematical point of view, the differences among these functions are minor and correspond to trivial isomorhisms between function spaces. Nevertheless, these functions are different, and if we take the perspective of mechanical computation, getting from one to another is something we have to do explicitly.

Getting from f_1 to f_3 (and from f_2 to f_4) is known as **currying**[7]. Going the other direction is known as **uncurrying**.

It is easy to program these transformations in CAML:

#let curry f x y = f(x,y);;
curry : $(\alpha * \beta \rightarrow \gamma) \rightarrow \alpha \rightarrow \beta \rightarrow \gamma$ = $\langle$**fun**$\rangle$

#let uncurry f (x,y) = f x y;;
uncurry : $(\alpha \rightarrow \beta \rightarrow \gamma) \rightarrow \alpha * \beta \rightarrow \gamma$ = $\langle$**fun**$\rangle$

The transformations to interchange f_1 and f_2 on the one hand, f_3 and f_4 on the other, are written like this:

#let perm f (x,y) = f(y,x);;
perm : $(\alpha * \beta \rightarrow \gamma) \rightarrow \beta * \alpha \rightarrow \gamma$ = $\langle$**fun**$\rangle$

#let perm' f x y = f y x;;
perm' : $(\alpha \rightarrow \beta \rightarrow \gamma) \rightarrow \beta \rightarrow \alpha \rightarrow \gamma$ = $\langle$**fun**$\rangle$

---

[7]From the name of the logician Haskell Curry, who introduced combinatory logic, a formal system close to λ-calculus.

1.8.1 The Types of Predefined Operators

The predefined binary operators in CAML have Curryfied types.

#prefix +;;
$- : int \rightarrow int \rightarrow int = \langle \textbf{fun} \rangle$

#prefix *.;;
$- : float \rightarrow float \rightarrow float = \langle \textbf{fun} \rangle$

In addition to their infix form, these operators also have a prefix form.

#add_int;;
$- : int \rightarrow int \rightarrow int = \langle \textbf{fun} \rangle$

#mult_float;;
$- : float \rightarrow float \rightarrow float = \langle \textbf{fun} \rangle$

Check the reference manual for an exhaustive list.

1.9 Examples: Expressive Power

In this section, we will show you how to write a few functions to give you an idea of how expressively powerful functional programming is. In particular, these examples are meant to highlight the possibilities of functional parameters.

The applications we will deal with are oriented toward numeric calculations because non-numeric examples would necessitate declarations of types that will not be introduced until later chapters. However, the functionals used are essentially polymorphic and can be re-used in other contexts.

Many numeric calculations depend on the iteration of a function. Such is the case, for example, for all the approximate resolutions that solve equations by successive iterations. In those cases, we do not know the number of steps in the iteration *a priori*, but we depend on a test to learn whether we have achieved sufficiently precise results. In other cases, for example, in computing the ninth element of a sequence, we also iterate but this time, the number of iterations can be known from the beginning.

These two kinds of iteration along with the corresponding idea of summation correspond to the computation of series that will serve as our examples for functional programming.

1.9.1 Bounded Iterations

The CAML function iter (defined soon) corresponds to the idea of bounded iteration. It is defined with two parameters.

- n is the number of steps in the iteration.

- f is the function to iterate.

iter n f is thus the function f^n. Here is its definition.

#let rec iter n f = **if** n=0 **then** id **else** f o (iter (n−1) f);;
iter : *int* → (α → α) → α → α = ⟨**fun**⟩

#iter 4 (fun x → x∗x) 2;;
− : *int* = 65536

Notice that we could also have just as well defined this function by explicitly introducing a parameter x corresponding to the beginning value of the iteration.

#let rec iter n f x = **if** n=0 **then** x **else** f(iter (n−1) f x);;
iter : *int* → (α → α) → α → α = ⟨**fun**⟩

In this way, we define exactly the same function as the preceding one.

When we read its type, we notice that the parameter f is polymorphic, so it is not necessarily a purely numeric function. For example, we could apply iter to a function f that takes an argument and returns a result as pairs of numbers. In that way, we would get an efficient way to compute Fibonacci numbers.

Practically, the Fibonacci recursion is

$$u_{n+2} = u_{n+1} + u_n$$

By using a pair that contains two successive Fibonacci numbers, we thus have

$$(u_{n+2}, u_{n+1}) = f(u_{n+1}, u_n)$$

where f is the function which associates the pair $(x + y, x)$ with the pair (x, y).

#let fib n = fst(iter n (**fun**(x,y)→(x+y,x)) (1,0));;
fib : *int* → *int* = ⟨**fun**⟩

#fib 50;;
− : *int* = 1037658242

This function is much better than the one we showed you on page 27 because it computes each Fibonacci number only once. In consequence, the computation time is a linear function of n.

1.9.2   Unbounded Iterations

This second kind of iteration does not use an integer n to indicate the number of iterations to do; rather, it introduces a test of whether the value obtained so far is satisfactory or whether the iterations should continue.

> **#let rec** loop p f x = **if** (p x) **then** x **else** loop p f (f x);;
> *loop* : $(\alpha \rightarrow bool) \rightarrow (\alpha \rightarrow \alpha) \rightarrow \alpha \rightarrow \alpha$ = ⟨**fun**⟩

This function—loop—is more general than the function iter. In fact, we can construct iter from loop in the following way.

> **#let** iter n f x = snd(loop (**fun**(p,x)→ n=p)
> (**fun** (p,x)→ (p+1, f x))
> (0,x));;
> *iter* : *int* $\rightarrow (\alpha \rightarrow \alpha) \rightarrow \alpha \rightarrow \alpha$ = ⟨**fun**⟩

In Section 1.9.5, we will discuss the comparative powers of loop and iter further.

The function loop lets us program many computational methods by successive approximation, for example, such methods as looking for the roots of a function. Here we will study the binary method and Newton's method.

1.9.3   Binary Method

Given a continuous, monotonic function f and an interval $[a, b]$ over which $f(a)$ and $f(b)$ are of opposite signs, we know that we can find a root of f by dividing the interval $[a, b]$ in two parts and iterating this process on the half-interval that contains a root. This kind of binary search is also known as dichotomizing the interval.

If ϵ is the approximation we want, then the number of iterations needed to find the solution will be on the order of $\log(\frac{|b-a|}{\epsilon})$.

The function dicho takes a function f as its argument along with a pair of numbers (a,b) and a quantity epsilon to define the neighborhood of the root that we want to achieve.

dicho(f,a,b,epsilon) is loop is_ok do_better (a,b) where the function is_ok is the test whether to stop and do_better is the iterative step, both defined separately.

> **#let** dicho (f,a,b,epsilon) =
> loop is_ok do_better (a,b)
> **where** is_ok(a,b) = abs_float(b−.a) <. epsilon
> **and** do_better(a,b) =

```
    let c = (a +. b) /. 2.0 in
    if f(a) *. f(c) >. 0.0 then (c,b)
    else (a,c);;
dicho : (float → float) * float * float * float → float * float
    = ⟨fun⟩
```

Here is an approximation of π computed by searching for a root of the function $cos(\frac{x}{2})$.

```
#dicho((fun x → cos(x /. 2.0)), 3.1, 3.2, 1e−10);;
− : float * float = 3.14159265356, 3.14159265365
```

1.9.4 Newton's Method

First, let's review Newton's method. Let f be a function with a derivative. Let $(x, f(x))$ be a point on the graph of f. If $f'(x) \neq 0$, then the tangent to the graph at the point $(x, f(x))$ cuts the x axis at the point of the abscissa $x - \frac{f(x)}{f'(x)}$. In Newton's method, we iterate the transformation that associates x with $x - \frac{f(x)}{f'(x)}$. It is possible to show that if (in a given interval $[a, b]$ such that $f(a)$ and $f(b)$ are of opposite signs) f' and f'' are non-null with constant signs, then starting from any point in that interval, the iteration will converge.

We begin by defining a numeric derivative function. It will compute the approximate derivative by using a small interval dx.

```
#let deriv (f,dx) x = (f(x+.dx)−.f(x))/.dx;;
deriv : (float → float) * float → float → float = ⟨fun⟩
```

The function that implements Newton's method takes a function f as one of its arguments. It searches for a root of that function. It also takes an initial value, start, a value for the interval, dx, which we use to compute the derivative f', and another value epsilon, which determines the neighborhood we want to reach around the root.

```
#let newton(f,start,dx,epsilon) =
  loop is_ok do_better start
  where is_ok x = abs_float (f x) <. epsilon
  and do_better x =
  let f' = deriv (f,dx) in
  (x −. f x /. f' x);;
newton : (float → float) * float * float * float → float = ⟨fun⟩
```

This expression of the function newton, like the one for the function dicho, uses the construction where. This construction, first of all, expresses the essential ideas; we are leaving the details for later. However, experience in using it has shown us that it often leads to difficulties in limiting the scope of identifiers to what we want, so in general, we prefer to use the construction **let–in**. It is a little clumsier, but less ambiguous.

```
#let newton(f,start,dx,epsilon) =
    let f' = deriv (f,dx) in
    let is_ok x = abs_float (f x) <. epsilon
    and do_better x = x −. f x /. f' x in
    loop is_ok do_better start;;
newton : (float → float) * float * float * float → float = ⟨fun⟩
```

For example, we get an approximation of $\pi/2$ by searching for a root of the cosine function in the neighborhood of 1.5. If we then multiply the number we get by 2, we have an approximation of π.

```
#newton(cos, 1.5, 1e−10, 1e−10) *. 2.0;;
− : float = 3.14159265361
```

Likewise, we get an approximation of e by searching for a root of the function $\log(x) - 1$ in the neighborhood of 2.7.

```
#newton((fun x → log x −. 1.0), 2.7, 1e−10, 1e−10);;
− : float = 2.71828182846
```

1.9.5 About Iteration

In conventional programming languages, the ideas about iteration that correspond to the functions iter and loop are generally programmed by calls to loops. In practice, iter is usually written with a **for** loop, and loop itself is usually written with a **while** loop.

The forms that we have shown here make it possible for you to use parameters in the constructions for the body of the loop (that is, the function being iterated) and for the halting test. Rather than rewrite a loop for every application, all you have to do is to apply these functions to appropriate arguments.

From a theoretical point of view, these two kinds of iteration have different powers and characteristics. If we consider only positive integers and limit ourselves to functions f of type int → int, then the only functions that we can define by means of iter are called primitive recursive functions, while the functions we can define by means of loop constitute the class of (truly) recursive functions. Both classes have been defined and studied in the context of recursion theory in mathematical logic. The principal difference between them is that the class to which iter belongs produces total functions[8] by construction; that is, the computations are always guaranteed to terminate. In contrast, the class to which loop belongs allows us to write functions in which certain computations do not terminate.

Since in most applications it is a good idea to write only functions that are defined everywhere, one might think that programmers should limit themselves to iter. Unfortunately, that won't do because there are total recursive functions which are not primitive recursive. That means that those functions can be written in terms of loop but not by means of iter. We will come back to this problem of terminating computations in Section 3.4.

1.9.6   Summations

Once we can use functional arguments (that is, functions as arguments), mathematic notation, such as $\sum u_n$ or $\prod u_n$ where u_n is a sequence defined by a recursion of the form $u_{n+1} = f(u_n)$, can be translated immediately into programs.

For example, the function sigma computes $\sum_{n=a}^{n=b} f(n)$ for the function f over the integers in an interval $[a, b]$.

```
#let rec sigma f (a,b) =
   if a > b then 0
   else (f a) + sigma f (a+1,b);;
sigma : (int → int) → int * int → int = ⟨fun⟩
```

More generally, we can combine any set of values from one function by using any binary operation.

By the way, the idea of an interval can be replaced by the initial value, an incremental function for that value, and a halting rule.

The function summation generalizes all the calculations of summation. Its first pair of arguments (incr,test) gives the functions used to increment the parameter and to test when to halt. The second pair of arguments (op,e) gives the summation function and its initial value. (Usually, that initial value is its neutral element.)

```
#let rec summation (incr,test) (op,e) f a =
   if test a then e
   else op (f a) (summation (incr,test) (op,e) f (incr a)) ;;
summation : (α → α) * (α → bool)
           → (β → γ → γ) * γ → (α → β) → α → γ = ⟨fun⟩
```

---

[8]A total function is defined for every element in its domain; a partial function, in contrast, is defined only for part of its domain.

Summation over an interval of floating-point numbers [a,b] with an incremental step of dx can be written like this:

```
#let sum (op,e) f a b dx =
    summation ((fun x → x +. dx), (fun x → x >. b)) (op,e) f a;;
sum : (α → β → β) * β → (float → α) → float → float → float → β
    = ⟨fun⟩
```

With that function, we get a numeric integration function by using the fact that

$$\int_a^b f(x)dx \sim \sum_{n=0}^{n=\lfloor \frac{b-a}{dx} \rfloor} f(a+ndx)$$

```
#let integrate f a b dx =
    sum (prefix +., 0.) (fun x → f(x) *. dx) a b dx;;
integrate : (float → float) → float → float → float → float = ⟨fun⟩
```

```
#integrate (fun x → 1.0/.x) 1.0 2.0 0.001;;
− : float = 0.69389724306
```

Summation over an interval of integers [a,b] with an incremental step of 1 can be written like this:

```
#let summation_int (op,e) f a b =
    summation ((fun x → x+1), (fun x → x>b)) (op,e) f a;;
summation_int : (α → β → β) * β → (int → α) → int → int → β
    = ⟨fun⟩
```

With that function, we get functions corresponding to $\sum_{n=a}^{n=b} f(n)$ and $\prod_{n=a}^{n=b} f(n)$ with f of type (int → float).

```
#let sigma = summation_int (prefix +.,0.) ;;
sigma : (int → float) → int → int → float = ⟨fun⟩
```

```
#let pi = summation_int (prefix *.,1.) ;;
pi : (int → float) → int → int → float = ⟨fun⟩
```

We can use pi to define $n!$.

```
#let fact = pi float_of_int 1;;
fact : int → float = ⟨fun⟩
```

```
#fact 10;;
− : float = 3628800
```

And finally here is the partial sum of the series $\sum \frac{1}{n!}$.

```
#sigma (fun n → 1.0/.fact n) 0 20;;
− : float = 2.71828182846
```

1.10   Summary

We have presented the kernel of CAML. It is built on the idea that a program is an expression that can be evaluated, that computing a program corresponds to evaluating the expression.

Starting from an expression containing the variables $x_1, \ldots, x_n$, we can build the function (**fun** $(x_1, \ldots, x_n) \rightarrow e$). This construction is the operation known as **functional abstraction**. Its existence characterizes **functional languages**.

When we use functional abstraction, we are then able to define **higher order** functions; that is, functions that take other functions as their arguments or return other functions as their result. This facility gives a language great expressive powers, in particular, at the level of parameterizing programs.

CAML programs are automatically typed by the system. Many functions are of **polymorphic** type; that is, they involve type variables. Such functions can be applied to arguments of various types.

1.11   To Learn More

The idea of a functional language originated in mathematical logic. Around 1930, Alonzo Church invented λ-calculus [5], a formal system to define functions of only two constructions: functional abstraction[9] and functional application. This formal system proved equivalent to many other formal systems proposed to define the idea of a computable function (such systems, for example, as Turing machines or Curry's combinatory logic). The equivalence between these many formal systems lead to the formulation that we now call **Church's thesis**; that is, the hypothesis that these various formal systems do, in fact, accurately capture the intuitive idea of a computable function.

With the advent of computers, the idea of a computable function took on a very concrete aspect and was assimilated with the idea of a function that could be computed by a program. The Turing machine became the theoretical model from which we could formalize the way that a computer actually worked and thus study afterwards the fundamental problems of complexity. λ-calculus was then rediscovered in the sixties by computer scientists who wanted to define the semantics of programming languages in a rigorous way and to construct new languages on a solid theoretical basis.

The idea of a type also originates in mathematical logic. The theory of types developed mainly within the context of λ-calculus. The idea of types used in

---

[9]In λ-calculus, the abstraction of an expression e with respect to a variable x is denoted $\lambda x.e$. That notation loaned its name to the system.

CAML is essentially due to Curry. Nevertheless, you should realize that the idea of type as used in logic is much stronger than that used in computer science. In the spirit of Church, λ-calculus was meant to be a fundamental formal system of mathematics. The fact that the idea of a recursive function could be defined in that context produced a formal system that was indeed too powerful: it lead to logical paradoxes and thus to inconsistencies within the system. By adding types to λ-calculus, we could avoid those paradoxes, but in doing so, we greatly diminished its expressive power by forbidding recursion. In the branch of logic known as proof theory, the implementation of type systems and the study of their expressive power has been and remains a central activity.

In computer science, λ-calculus has dual interest, both immediate and long term. First of all, it can be considered as a point of reference for programming languages since it enables us to define the semantics of other languages. From this point of view, the fact that it allows us to define all computable functions is one of its indispensable qualities. Now, one of the effects of introducing a system of types is to limit expressive power to a subclass of total functions. In a language like CAML, we adopt a very elementary type system from a logical point of view, but we add the possibility of defining recursive functions by means of a special construction, **let rec**. In that way, we save consistency of function use, but we sacrifice the property of termination in favor of expressive power.

In the long term, more powerful type systems, as studied in proof theory could produce completely novel methods of program development. Types as used there are much richer and can be assimilated into logical formulas expressing the properties of programs. The fact that a program is correctly typed thus expresses the correctness of the program with respect to a specification expressed by its type system.

The language CAML used here belongs to a family of languages known as ML. The first definition of ML goes all the way back to 1978 [16]. R. Milner is credited with its design, based on earlier work by J. Landin. ML was originally a command language for LCF, a system to prove the correctness of programs. As compared to the logical language in which the properties of programs were expressed, ML could be called a **metalanguage**. In fact, that is the source of its name. Since those early days, ML has improved greatly and has been implemented in various ways, once as SML at Bell Labs in the United States, and as CAML in France [25, 42].

Chapter 2

Data Structures

Programs have to handle highly varied objects organized into categories, such as numbers, text, images, formulas, as well as other programs. These objects are for the most part foreign to the world of programming and involve quite diverse formal systems.

For each such category of objects, the programmer must define a representation in the objects of the programming language that he or she is using. This representation must satisfy criteria such as efficiency (by exploiting what the programmer has learned about algorithms) and clarity; that is, the way the data is structured should reflect the structure of the objects being represented. Representation of objects from the exterior world should not be some obscure encoding; rather, the conceptual, external structure should remain apparent.

In a typed language like CAML, the nature of an object lies in its type. It is thus natural to ask that the external structure of the objects being handled should be reflected in the types of their internal representation. For that purpose, the programmer must have the means to define a great variety of types.

In this chapter, we present the two principal type constructions that CAML offers: records and sums with constructors. You might think of a record as the product of named components, and a sum as the union of named components.

2.1 Record or Named Cartesian Products

Let's assume that we want to write programs working on complex numbers. We can imagine representing complex numbers by pairs (r,i) of type (float * float) giving the real and imaginary parts of such numbers.

That observation leads us to define addition, for example, like this:

```
#let add_complex (r₁,i₁) (r₂,i₂) = (r₁+.r₂, i₁+.i₂);;
add_complex : float * float → float * float → float * float = ⟨fun⟩
```

We see very quickly, however, that such a representation is inconvenient. For one thing, complex numbers are not the only objects that can be represented as pairs of digits. We can easily imagine representing intervals that way, too, for example, or even complex numbers themselves, but in polar form. If we represent complex numbers by simple pairs of floating-point numbers, we will not be able to rely on the type synthesis system to refuse to compose a function that produces complex numbers in polar form with another that takes, say, an interval as its argument, and a composition like that, of course, normally makes no sense.

Incidentally, using a Cartesian product is inconvenient in yet another way. If we are interested in structures that contain a great deal of information (such as a file containing a person's records, including last name, first name, address, all followed by various other types of detail) but we organize that information as a Cartesian product, then it will be painful—to say the least—for us to program because it will be very easy to make mistakes about the order in which details are arranged. For example, last name and first name are probably both data of type **string** so no type-checker will detect the error if a program mistakes a last name for a first name.

To manage this kind of object, in computer science we use a **record**. A record is a form of Cartesian product in which the various components (or fields) are identified so that we can access them by name.

In CAML, each type of record has a name given by the user at the time the record is declared.

For example, to define complex numbers, we could write:

#type complex = {re_part:float; im_part:float};;

We have thus defined the type complex as a type of record with one field, re_part, corresponding to its real part, and a second field, im_part, corresponding to its imaginary part. The list of fields in a record is written between curly brackets, and the definitions of the various fields are separated by semi-colons.

Objects of type record are written in notation close to that of the type itself: the symbol ":" is replaced by "=" and followed by a value (rather than a type). To access a field of an object, you use the expression representing that object, followed by a period and the name of the field you want to access.

#let cx_1 = {re_part=1.; im_part=0.};;
$cx_1 : complex$ = {re_part=1; im_part=0}

#let cx_i = {re_part=0.; im_part=1.};;
$cx_i : complex$ = {re_part=0; im_part=1}

#cx_1.re_part;;
$- : float = 1$

Functions that take records as arguments can be written in two different styles, depending on whether the structure of the record plays a part in the parameter of the function or whether the notation of dotted pairs is being used to access fields. For example, complex addition can be written like this:

#fun {re_part=r_1; im_part=i_1} {re_part=r_2; im_part=i_2}
    $\rightarrow$ {re_part=r_1 +. r_2; im_part=i_1 +. i_2};;
$-$: *complex* $\rightarrow$ *complex* $\rightarrow$ *complex* = ⟨**fun**⟩

or like this:

#fun c_1 c_2 $\rightarrow$
      {re_part=c_1.re_part+.c_2.re_part;
        im_part=c_1.im_part+.c_2.im_part};;
$-$: *complex* $\rightarrow$ *complex* $\rightarrow$ *complex* = ⟨**fun**⟩

Of course, the types of fields in records can also be user-defined types themselves.

#type planar_point = {xcoord:float; ycoord:float};;

#type circle = {center:planar_point ; radius:float};;

#type triangle = {ptA:planar_point;
             ptB:planar_point;
             ptC:planar_point};;

Exercises
2.1 Write functions using the type planar_point so that you can translate, rotate, and rescale.
2.2 Write the primary functions for complex arithmetic using the type complex defined on page 48.

2.2 Sums with Constructors

Fairly often we want to organize heterogeneous values belonging to various types into the same type. This problem is solved in CAML by a **type with constructors**. This idea is a kind of union, each component of the union corresponding to a constructor.

2.2.1 Constant Constructors

Some types can be defined by a finite list of values.

#type suit = Club | Diamond | Heart |Spade;;

The names "Club," "Diamond," "Heart," "Spade" are arbitrary names chosen by the user. The fact that they appear in a type definition confers special status on them. We call them **data constructors**, and they can then no longer be used as variables. Conventionally in CAML, we use names beginning with a capital letter for constructors. That convention makes it easier to recognize them visually.

Once it has been introduced in the definition of a type, a constructor can be used afterwards exactly like a numeric constant or a Boolean value.

```
#Club;;
```
− : *suit* = *Club*

```
#fun Club → 1 | Diamond → 2 | Heart → 3 | Spade → 4;;
```
− : *suit* → *int* = ⟨**fun**⟩

As a consequence, in CAML the type bool might not be a predefined type. The user can define it as

```
#type bool = true | false;;
```

2.2.2 Constructors with Arguments

Constructors may also have arguments. In the next example, we will introduce the type num defined as the union of the types int and float.

```
#type num = Int of int | Float of float;;
```

In this definition, **of** is a keyword which follows the name of a constructor and which is followed by the type of the argument of the constructor. The constructors Int and Float can be applied to arguments of type int or float to build a value of type num. Here's how we read that definition:

> "We get an object of type num either by applying the constructor Int to an object of type int or by applying the constructor Float to an object of type float."

```
#Int(3);;
```
− : *num* = *Int* 3

```
#Float(4.0);;
```
− : *num* = *Float* 4

Formally, Int and Float are canonic injections of the types int and float in the type num, which is their disjoint union. You can see that idea in Figure 2.1.

Moreover, constructors can be used in patterns in definitions by case. To show how, we will define an addition operation for the type num.

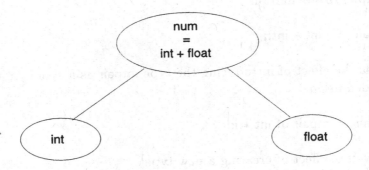

Figure 2.1. Disjoint sum of the types int and float

```
#let add_num = fun
    (Int m, Int n) → Int(m + n)
  | (Int m, Float n) → Float((float_of_int m) +. n)
  | (Float m, Int n) → Float(m +. (float_of_int n))
  | (Float m, Float n) → Float(m +. n);;
add_num : num * num → num = ⟨fun⟩
```

We can thus define a generic arithmetic that mixes integers and floating-point numbers.

When we write patterns with constructors, we are actually extending pattern matching naturally from the way we used it in the preceding chapter. Indeed, the real interest and utility of functions defined by pattern matching comes from constructors introduced by the user, as you will see later.

2.2.3 Types with Only One Constructor and Abbreviations

So far, we have been looking at types with several constructors. Sometimes it is useful to define them even when they include only one constructor. For example, to write geometric programs that handle angles, we might define this:

```
#type angle = Angle of float;;
```

If we treat angles as objects of type angle, we make the writing of programs slightly denser, but in compensation, doing so lets us use type synthesis to verify consistency: we will not run the risk, for example, of adding angles and lengths inadvertently.

This kind of definition should not be confused with type abbreviation, which also exists in CAML. The goal of type abbreviation is to make it simpler to write certain types, but it does not introduce any new types.

For example, this definition

#type intpair == int ∗ int;;

simply has the effect of introducing the type intpair as a synonym of int ∗ int whereas the definition

#type intpair = Intpair **of** int ∗ int;;

would have the effect of creating a new type[1].

2.2.4   Recursive Types

In contrast to the way values are defined, the definition of a type is considered recursive by default if the name of the type being defined appears in the definition. Recursive definitions of types with constructors have two major application domains. In CAML, they define conventional data structures for algorithms. They also define "abstract syntax."

Here, for example, is how to define the type binary tree with numeric information in the leaves.

#type inttree = Leaf **of** int | Node **of** inttree ∗ inttree;;

We read this definition like this:

> "An object of type inttree is either a leaf with an integer attached to it, or a binary node with two children of type inttree."

Here is an example of such a binary tree:

#Node(Leaf 3,Node(Leaf 4,Leaf 5));;
− : *inttree* = *Node* (*Leaf* 3, *Node* (*Leaf* 4, *Leaf* 5))

This tree is represented graphically in Figure 2.2.

Here's the function to compute the sum of values in a tree:

#**let rec** total = **fun** (Leaf n) → n
                | (Node(t_1,t_2)) → total(t_1)+total(t_2);;
total : *inttree* → *int* = ⟨**fun**⟩

---

[1]Type abbreviations are certainly useful in the interfaces of modules. They also simplify the way we write constraints.

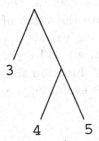

Figure 2.2. A binary tree

The definition of the type inttree is a structural definition of binary trees. It is useful for programming algorithms on trees but, on the other hand, it is quite unwieldy for building particular binary trees. Rather than having to write this:

#Node(Leaf 3,Node(Leaf 4,Leaf 5));;

we would rather have notation like this:

#(3,(4,5));;

In computer science, we distinguish the idea of **abstract syntax** from **concrete syntax**. Abstract syntax corresponds to the structural description and internal representation of objects. Concrete syntax is used for input and output in the form of character strings. Types with constructors make it possible for us to define abstract syntax in an elegant way. (The issue of concrete syntax is covered in Section 2.2.9.)

When we handle objects that are formal expressions, "abstract syntax" takes on its full meaning. The following example shows how to represent arithmetic expressions with integer value in CAML.

```
#type exp = Constant of int
          | Variable of string
          | Addition of exp * exp
          | Multiplication of exp * exp;;
```

According to this type-definition, an expression is either an integer constant or a variable or the addition of two expressions or the multiplication of two expressions. With that in mind, we are going to write a function, eval, to compute the value of an expression. In a certain way, this function is the prototype for evaluation functions in Chapter 11, those that take into account the evaluation of the language CAML itself.

Since expressions can contain variables, the evaluator has to recognize the value of these variables to compute the value of the entire expression. In computer science, a means of associating variables with their values is known as an **environment**. For the moment, we will represent environments by functions of type string →int. The evaluation function thus depends simultaneously on the environment and the expression to evaluate.

```
#let rec eval env expression =
   match expression with
     (Constant n) → n
   | (Variable x) → env x
   | (Addition(e₁,e₂)) → eval env e₁ + eval env e₂
   | (Multiplication(e₁,e₂)) → eval env e₁ * eval env e₂;;
eval : (string → int) → exp → int = ⟨fun⟩
```

In the same way that the function eval is a prototype of the evaluator, the following function, deriv, is a prototype of the program that formally computes expressions. The function deriv formally computes a derivative. To do so, it uses its first argument, a character string indicating the variable with respect to which we want to take the derivative of the expression.

```
#let rec deriv var expression =
   match expression with
     (Constant n) → Constant 0
   | (Variable x) → if x=var then Constant 1
                            else Constant 0
   | (Addition(e₁,e₂)) → Addition(deriv var e₁, deriv var e₂)
   | (Multiplication(e₁,e₂)) → Addition(Multiplication(e₁, deriv var e₂),
                                        Multiplication(deriv var e₁, e₂));;
deriv : string → exp → exp = ⟨fun⟩
```

That function is obviously rather crude and rudimentary since it does not simplify the expression it produces.

2.2.5   Polymorphic Types

Types defined by the user can be polymorphic. That is, you can use type-variables as parameters. This facility lets you actually code conventional data structures as CAML types, and thus define a binary tree, for example, without making the kind of information found in the leaves explicit.

```
#type α tree = Leaf of α | Node of α tree * α tree;;
```

The type inttree, defined in the preceding section, is a particular case of the type α **tree** that we have just defined. It is simply denoted int tree.

```
#Node(Leaf 3,Node(Leaf 4,Leaf 5));;
```
$- : int\ tree = Node\ (Leaf\ 3,\ Node\ (Leaf\ 4,\ Leaf\ 5))$

The function to compute the sum of numeric values contained in a binary tree with integer leaves is written now just as it was before:

```
#let rec total = fun (Leaf n) → n
              |  (Node(t₁,t₂)) → total(t₁)+total(t₂);;
```
$total : int\ tree \rightarrow int = \langle\mathbf{fun}\rangle$

This kind of polymorphism among types also exists for records as types. For example, a type defining a dictionary (that is, a data structure that stores information that can be retrieved by **key**) can be written like this:

```
#type (α,β) dict_entry = {content:α; key:β};;
```

Likewise, polymorphism occurs in abbreviations as well.

```
#type (α,β) dictionary == (α,β) dict_entry list;;
```

2.2.6 Lists

Among the many polymorphic types that we can define to represent data structures, the most frequently used is the type list. It can be defined like this:

```
#type α list = Nil | Cons of α * α list;;
```

A list is thus either the constructor Nil (that is, the empty list) or a nonempty list containing a first element (of type α) and the remainder (of type α list) containing the succeeding elements.

In fact, the type list is predefined in CAML and its elements are denoted by special syntax. The constructor Cons is denoted ::, that is, infix like the symbols + and *. In other words, it is written between its two arguments. The empty list is written as [ ].

```
#3::[ ];;
```
$- : int\ list = [3]$

Incidentally, the notation $[e_1;\ldots;e_n]$ can be used in place of $e_1::\ldots::e_n::[\,]$ to denote the list made up of values $e_1, \ldots, e_n$.

The function hd (for head) returns the first element of a list, and tl (for tail) returns the list without its first element. Concatenation, that is, the operation of sticking two lists together, is denoted by the infix symbol @.

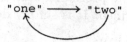

Figure 2.3. A value with a loop

#[[1;2];[3;4]];;
− : *int list list* = [[1; 2]; [3; 4]]

#[1;1+1]@[2+1;2+2];;
− : *int list* = [1; 2; 3; 4]

Section 2.3 tells more about how to use lists as structures.

2.2.7   Recursive Definitions of Values

In CAML, it is possible to define values recursively—values that are not functions but rather data structures. Such definitions suffer fairly strong restrictions.

For example, we can write this:

#let rec x= "one" :: y
 and y= "two" :: x;;
x : *string list* = ["one"; "two"; …; …]
y : *string list* = ["two"; "one"; …; …]

or even this:

#let rec t = Node(Leaf "one",Node(Leaf "two", t));;
t : *string tree*
 = *Node* (*Leaf* "one", *Node* (*Leaf* "two", *Node* (…, …)))

Structures created this way have loops. When we print them as character strings, they lead to infinitely long printouts if we do not limit them by convention. The graphic representation of the value x appears in Figure 2.3.

Such definitions are essentially limited to creating periodic data structures. We will have occasion to use them in the context of writing a CAML evaluator in Chapter 11. More interesting recursive definitions of values come from applying delayed evaluation (or evaluation by necessity) to data structures. This idea will be discussed in Sections 3.2 and 11.3.

2.2.8 Abstract Types

In contrast to the type constructions that we just presented, the idea of an **abstract type** does not exist in CAML, strictly speaking, and such a thing can be used only through a module. Nevertheless, it is an important concept that can be exploited in programming, independently of the language.

Here's the idea: certain objects with which we want to compute naturally have one or more possible representations. Complex numbers, for example, are like that: we could represent them by their real and imaginary parts or by their modulus and their argument. Both representations have advantages and drawbacks in terms of the efficiency of any application based on them. In such a situation, the wisest course of action is to postpone the choice about representation and to write programs that make no assumptions about it.

To do so, it suffices for us to assume that we have available a type complex, of variables containing complex constants such as 0, 1, and i, and operations for that type.

The type complex will be treated abstractly; that is, we do not know its representation, but we can nevertheless use it through the constants and functions defined for it.

In CAML, a **module** facilitates the writing of large-scale software by letting us assemble the components contained in files; such modules can then be compiled and thus implemented and debugged separately. Files with the suffix .ml contain modules and are associated with files with the suffix .mli defining their **interface**. By interface, we mean the set of types, exceptions, and values that the module "exports" to the exterior. Such files can be written before the module itself and thus used by other modules as well.

The interface of a module gives the type of each exported value. As for exported types, the interface may give either their complete definition or simply their name. In the case where only the name of the type is given, the programs refering to the module can use the type only through the values that depend on it. For example, you can imagine that an interface to a module of complex arithmetic might contain the following information.

```
type complex;;

value cx_0 : complex                                    (* the number 0 *)
and cx_1 : complex                                      (* the number 1 *)
and cx_i : complex                                      (* the number i *)
and add_complex : complex -> complex -> complex           (* addition *)
and mult_complex : complex -> complex -> complex        (* multiplication *)
;;
```

Programs refering to this module for complex arithmetic would have access to those constants and functions but not to the representation of the type.

2.2.9   Concrete Syntax of Data Structures

Types with constructors are well adapted to programming, but in contrast they are poorly adapted to data entry and the display of values. For example, it is quite inconvenient to be obliged to write this:

Addition(Multiplication(Variable "x",Constant 2), Constant 3)

simply in order to designate the expression x*2+3. Consequently, we need a way to associate appropriate syntax with values of types with constructors.

The language CAML provides various tools to define syntactic analyzers simply and thus associate concrete syntax with a given type of data easily. These tools are of two kinds. First, there are generators of syntax analyzers, known as CAMLLEX and CAMLYACC. They are based on the well known UNIX system software, LEX and YACC. Second, there is a tool to program lexical and syntactic analyzers directly, based on pattern matching of objects of type stream. (See Chapter 8 for more about that.)

In the rest of this book, when necessary, we will use conversion functions between concrete and abstract syntax. Such functions are programmed by means of pattern matching for the type stream, but we will not give their definitions.

For a CAML type ty, these functions are called ty_of_string and string_of_ty. In the case of a monomorphic[2] type ty, these functions have these types:

ty_of_string : string → ty
string_of_ty : ty → string

For example, for the type inttree, we will have the functions inttree_of_string and string_of_inttree.

```
#inttree_of_string "(2,(3,4))";;
```
− : inttree = *Node* (*Leaf* 2, *Node* (*Leaf* 3, *Leaf* 4))

For the type exp, we will have the functions exp_of_string and string_of_exp.

```
#exp_of_string "x*(y+1)";;
```
− : exp = *Multiplication*
                    (*Variable* "x", *Addition* (*Variable* "y", *Constant* 1))

In the case of a polymorphic type ty, for example, one of the form α ty, these functions will have for their types:

ty_of_string : (string → α) → string → α ty
string_of_ty : (α → string) → α ty → string

---

[2]A monomorphic type is a type with no variables.

That is, the functions for analyzing syntax and for printing with respect to the type with the parameters α ty will take similar functions for the type α as their argument.

Here is an example for the type tree:

```
#tree_of_string int_of_string "(2,(3,4))";;
− : int tree = Node (Leaf 2, Node (Leaf 3, Leaf 4))
```

2.3   Lists

Functions for lists most often take the form of definitions for two cases: the case of the empty list, and the case of the non-empty list.

Here are a few examples.

The length of a list

```
#let rec length = fun
    [ ] → 0
  | (a::l) → 1 + length l;;
length : α list → int = ⟨fun⟩
```

The concatenation of two lists

```
#let rec append l₁ l₂ =
    match l₁ with
      [ ] → l₂
    | (a::l) → a::append l l₂;;
append : α list → α list → α list = ⟨fun⟩
```

The mirror image of a list

```
#let rec rev = fun
    [ ] → [ ]
  | (a::l) → append (rev l) [a];;
rev : α list → α list = ⟨fun⟩
```

The sum and product of elements of a list of integers

```
#let rec sigma = fun
   [ ] → 0
 | (a::l) → a + sigma l;;
sigma : int list → int = ⟨fun⟩
```

```
#let rec pi = fun
   [ ] → 1
 | (a::l) → a * pi l;;
pi : int list → int = ⟨fun⟩
```

The application of a function f to all the elements of a list

```
#let rec map f l =
   match l with
     [ ] → [ ]
   | (a::l) → f(a)::map f l;;
map : (α → β) → α list → β list = ⟨fun⟩
```

```
#map (fun x → x*x) [1;2;3;4;5];;
− : int list = [1; 4; 9; 16; 25]
```

Flattening a list of lists

```
#let rec flat = fun
   [ ] → [ ]
 | (l::ll) → append l (flat ll);;
flat : α list list → α list = ⟨fun⟩
```

2.3.1   General Functionals for Lists

In the preceding functions, we made apparent a common structure:

- In the case where the list is empty, the value of the recursive function f is defined by a value that does not depend on f;

- In the case where the list is of the form (a::l), the value of f depends on a and f(l).

Consequently, it is possible to generalize this set of definitions with a single function parameterized by a constant and a function of two arguments.

```
#let rec list_hom e f l =
    match l with
      [ ] → e
    | (a::l) → f a (list_hom e f l);;
list_hom : α → (β → α → α) → β list → α = ⟨fun⟩
```

Here is how we express the functions defined in the preceding section, but this time we do so with the help of list_hom.

```
#let length = list_hom 0 (fun _ n → n+1);;
length : α list → int = ⟨fun⟩
```

```
#let append l₁ l₂ = list_hom l₂ cons l₁;;
append : α list → α list → α list = ⟨fun⟩
```

```
#let rev = list_hom [ ] (fun a l → append l [a]) ;;
rev : α list → α list = ⟨fun⟩
```

```
#let sigma = list_hom 0 add_int;;
sigma : int list → int = ⟨fun⟩
```

```
#let pi = list_hom 1 mult_int;;
pi : int list → int = ⟨fun⟩
```

```
#let map f l = list_hom [ ] (fun x l → f(x)::l) l;;
map : (α → β) → α list → β list = ⟨fun⟩
```

```
#let flat = list_hom [ ] append;;
flat : α list list → α list = ⟨fun⟩
```

(The function cons is defined as (fun a l → a::l).)

The function list_hom is a particular case of the functions that can be associated naturally with types with constructors. We call them **homomorphisms**. You will see other examples of such homomorphisms in Chapter 5 about trees and formal terms.

Among the predefined CAML functions, there are functions similar to list_hom; they are called list_it and it_list.

The function list_it differs from list_hom only in the order of its arguments. Here's its definition.

```
#let rec list_it f l e =
    match l with [ ] → e
        | (a::l) → f a (list_it f l e);;
list_it : (α → β → β) → α list → β → β = ⟨fun⟩
```

The order of the parameters for list_it was chosen so that the types of f and list_it f would be similar.

Here's the effect of that function:

$$\text{list\_it f } [a_1;\ldots;a_n] \text{ e} = \text{f } a_1 \text{ (f } a_2 \text{ (}\ldots\text{(f } a_n \text{ e)}\ldots\text{))} = \text{list\_hom e f } [a_1;\ldots;a_n]$$

The function it_list is a variation meant to highlight the possibility of combining the elements of a list in reverse order, like this:

```
#let rec it_list f e l =
    match l with [ ] → e
              | (a::l) → it_list f (f e a) l;;
it_list : (α → β → α) → α → β list → α = ⟨fun⟩
```

Here's the effect of that function:

$$\text{it\_list f e } [a_1;\ldots;a_n] = \text{f } (\ldots\text{(f (f e } a_1) \, a_2)\ldots) \, a_n$$

The two functions are related by these equations:

$$\text{it\_list f x l} = \text{list\_it } (\textbf{fun } x \, y \to \text{f } y \, x) \text{ l x}$$

and

$$\text{list\_it f l x} = \text{it\_list } (\textbf{fun } x \, y \to \text{f } y \, x) \text{ x l}$$

for every binary operation f, every list l, and every value x. Depending on the binary operation that we want to use, one of those forms will be more convenient than the other.

Notice the particular case where the function f is an associative operation + in which e is the neutral element:

$$\begin{aligned}
\text{it\_list} &+ \text{e } [a_1;\ldots;a_n] \\
&= \text{list\_it} + [a_1;\ldots;a_n] \text{ e} \\
&= \text{list\_hom e} + [a_1;\ldots;a_n] \\
&= a_1 + \ldots + a_n.
\end{aligned}$$

Exercises

2.3 Use the function it_list to write a function that takes a comparison predicate (of the type $(\alpha \to \alpha \to \text{bool})$) and a list of values of the type α as its arguments and provides a maximal element of the list for the comparison operation.

2.4 Write a similar function that simultaneously provides both a minimal and maximal element.

2.3.2 Partitioning and Sorting

It is often useful to be able to extract a sublist from a list where the elements of
the sublist satisfy a certain property. The function partition lets us separate a list
into two sublists according to a property. The result is a pair of lists, where the
second contains the elements satisfying the property and the first sublist contains
all the other elements of the original list.

```
#let partition test l =
   let switch elem (l₁,l₂) =
      if test elem then (l₁,elem::l₂) else (elem::l₁,l₂)
   in list_it switch l ([ ],[ ]);;
partition : (α → bool) → α list → α list * α list = ⟨fun⟩
```

The local function switch is of type $\alpha \rightarrow (\alpha\ list * \alpha\ list) \rightarrow (\alpha\ list * \alpha\ list)$.
Given an element x and a pair of lists (l_1,l_2), it adds the element to l_2 or to l_1,
depending on whether or not x satisfies the property test.

The function filter uniquely saves the elements satisfying the test.

```
#let filter test = snd o (partition test);;
filter : (α → bool) → α list → α list = ⟨fun⟩
```

```
#filter (fun x → (x mod 2) = 0) [2;3;5;8;9;12;15];;
− : int list = [2; 8; 12]
```

The function partition can be used, for example, to program the algorithm
known as quicksort. That algorithm chooses an element of the list, for example,
the first one, as a pivot and then partitions the list by comparing elements with
the pivot to sort the two sublists by recursive calls to quicksort. It then puts the
pivot between the two sorted sublists to get the final sorted result. The ordering
relation used is passed as a parameter in the form of a function comp of type α
$\rightarrow \alpha \rightarrow$ bool.

```
#let rec quicksort order list =
   match list with
      [ ] → [ ]
   | [a] → [a]
   | (a::l) → let l₁,l₂ = partition (order a) l
               in (quicksort order l₁)@(a::(quicksort order l₂));;
quicksort : (α → α → bool) → α list → α list = ⟨fun⟩
```

The second case of quicksort corresponds to the situation where the list to
sort contains only one element. There, the pattern [a] is equivalent to (a::[ ]).

The algorithm quicksort sorts a list in a number of operations proportional to $n \log(n)$ on average. In the worst case, it takes n^2. Applied to lists, it is, however, much less efficient in practice than when it is applied to arrays, to the degree that it entails building intermediate lists. The cost accrued by the construction of data structures will be made explicit in Chapter 12 when we describe allocation. A version of quicksort working on arrays is given in Section 4.4.1.

As a function, quicksort lets you see why polymorphism is interesting as well as why functional parameters are useful. Thanks to the fact that the order used for sorting is passed as a parameter, this function can be applied to all kinds of ordered sets.

```
#quicksort (prefix <) [6;3;9;1;2;7];;
- : int list = [1; 2; 3; 6; 7; 9]

#quicksort (prefix >) [6;3;9;1;2;7];;
- : int list = [9; 7; 6; 3; 2; 1]

#quicksort (prefix <.) [0.25;0.125;0.1095;0.3];;
- : float list = [0.1095; 0.125; 0.25; 0.3]
```

The function list_it also makes it easy to program a sort by insertion. It iterates an insertion function to put an element in an already sorted list. Here is the insertion function:

```
#let rec insert order elem list =
    match list with
        [] → [elem]
    | (a::l) → if order elem a then elem::a::l
                else a :: insert order elem l;;
insert : (α → α → bool) → α → α list → α list = ⟨fun⟩
```

It then suffices to apply the function repeatedly to the list to get the sort function.

```
#let sort order = list_it (insert order) [];;
sort : (α → α → bool) → α list → α list = ⟨fun⟩
```

Exercises

2.5 Write a function to sort a list of pairs according to an order defined by the first component of these pairs.

2.6 Given two orders, $<_1$ and $<_2$, on two sets, E_1 and E_2, the **lexicographic order** $<$ over $E_1 \times E_2$ defined by the orders $<_1$ and $<_2$ is defined as: $(x, y) < (x', y')$ if and only if $x <_1 x'$ or $(x = x'$ and $y <_2 y')$. Write a function that takes two comparison functions as its arguments and sorts lists of pairs according to the lexicographic order determined by those two orders.

2.3.3 Representing Sets by Lists

In computer science and data processing applications, we frequently encounter the problem of how to represent sets of objects. Our choice of a representation depends on the kinds of operations that we want to carry out on these sets. For example, the choice varies according to whether we will merely be adding, accessing, and removing elements of a set, or whether we also want to produce unions and intersections.

As a structure, a list may represent sets but in a fairly costly way, as searching for an element, on average, takes time proportional to the length of the list. We should choose this representation then only for relatively small sets or when we have no means of ordering the elements of the list; in that case, access time will be linear, regardless of the representation.

In our discussion, we will distinguish between ordered and unordered lists as the representation of sets.

Representing Sets by Unordered Lists

All the functions that we will define to handle sets take a relation as an argument. By relation, we mean an object of type $(\alpha * \alpha \rightarrow bool)$; it will serve as our equality predicate.

The function member tests whether an element belongs to a set.

```
#let rec member equiv e list =
   match list with
     [ ] → false
   | (a::l) → equiv(a,e) or member equiv e l;;
 member : (α * β → bool) → β → α list → bool = ⟨fun⟩
```

The function rem_from_list removes an element from a list. If the element in question does not belong to the list in the first place, then the list is not modified. If the element appears more than once in the list, all its occurrences will be eliminated. This function is used to define the function make_set, which builds a set from a list by eliminating redundant elements.

```
#let rec rem_from_list equiv e list =
   match list with
     [ ] → [ ]
   | (a::l) → let l' = rem_from_list equiv e l in
               if equiv(a,e) then l'
               else a::l';;
 rem_from_list : (α * β → bool) → β → α list → α list = ⟨fun⟩
```

```
#let rec make_set equiv list =
  match list with
    [ ] → [ ]
  | (a::l) → a:: make_set equiv (rem_from_list equiv a l);;
```
$make\_set : (\alpha * \alpha \rightarrow bool) \rightarrow \alpha\ list \rightarrow \alpha\ list = \langle\textbf{fun}\rangle$

The function rem_from_set removes an element from a set. In contrast to the function rem_from_list, it assumes that the element occurs at most once.

```
#let rec rem_from_set equiv e list =
  match list with
    [ ] → [ ]
  | (a::l) → if equiv(a,e) then l
               else a::rem_from_set equiv e l;;
```
$rem\_from\_set : (\alpha * \beta \rightarrow bool) \rightarrow \beta \rightarrow \alpha\ list \rightarrow \alpha\ list = \langle\textbf{fun}\rangle$

The function add_to_set adds an element to a set.

```
#let add_to_set equiv e l =
  if member equiv e l then l else e::l;;
```
$add\_to\_set : (\alpha * \alpha \rightarrow bool) \rightarrow \alpha \rightarrow \alpha\ list \rightarrow \alpha\ list = \langle\textbf{fun}\rangle$

The function union, of course, produces the union of its arguments, and likewise, inter takes the intersection of sets.

```
#let rec union equiv (l₁,l₂) = list_it (add_to_set equiv) l₁ l₂;;
```
$union : (\alpha * \alpha \rightarrow bool) \rightarrow \alpha\ list * \alpha\ list \rightarrow \alpha\ list = \langle\textbf{fun}\rangle$

```
#let inter equiv (l₁,l₂)= filter (fun x → member equiv x l₂) l₁;;
```
$inter : (\alpha * \beta \rightarrow bool) \rightarrow \beta\ list * \alpha\ list \rightarrow \beta\ list = \langle\textbf{fun}\rangle$

Notice that each of these operations takes quadratic time with respect to the size of the sets.

Representing Sets by Ordered Lists

As you might expect, the representation of sets by ordered lists involves ordered sets. This representation saves a factor of two in the cost of add, access, or remove operations, but it is really in union and intersection that the gain is significant: then we go from quadratic to linear costs. Furthermore, we get logarithmic time to search for an element when we use an array if we use a binary search method. (See Chapter 4 about that.) However, adding an element then becomes costly since arrays are not readily extendable. In Chapter 6, you will see how to represent ordered sets efficiently by means of balanced trees.

Functions that operate on sets represented by sorted lists take a pair of relations as an argument, (order,equiv). The first of those is the ordering relation used, and the other is the equality used. We could also combine order and equality in a function of three values, as we will do later in Chapter 6 about balanced trees.

The function member is modified so that it stops at the first element of the list greater than the element it is searching for.

```
#let rec member (order,equiv) e list =
    match list with
      [ ] → false
    | (a::l) → if order(a,e) then member (order,equiv) e l
                else equiv(a,e);;
member : (α * β → bool) * (α * β → bool) → β → α list → bool
        = ⟨fun⟩
```

The function add_to_set is a variation of the function insert, defined on page 64, but modified to handle the case where the element to add is already in the list.

```
#let rec add_to_set (order,equiv) elem list =
    match list with
      [ ] → [elem]
    | (a::l) → if order(elem,a) then elem::a::l else
                if equiv(elem,a) then a::l
                else a::add_to_set (order,equiv) elem l;;
add_to_set : (α * α → bool) * (α * α → bool) → α → α list → α list
        = ⟨fun⟩
```

The functions union and inter take advantage of the ordered structure to go through each list only once.

```
#let rec inter (order,equiv) = fun
      ([ ],_) → [ ]
    | (_,[ ]) → [ ]
    | ((a₁::l₁ as ll₁),(a₂::l₂ as ll₂))
        → if equiv(a₁,a₂) then a₁::inter (order,equiv) (l₁,l₂) else
          if order(a₁,a₂) then inter (order,equiv) (l₁,ll₂)
          else inter (order,equiv) (ll₁,l₂);;
inter : (α * β → bool) * (α * β → bool) → α list * β list → α list
        = ⟨fun⟩

#let rec union (order,equiv) = fun
      ([ ],l₂) → l₂
```

```
  | (l₁,[ ]) → l₁
  | ((a₁::l₁ as ll₁),(a₂::l₂ as ll₂))
    → if equiv(a₁,a₂) then a₁::union (order,equiv) (l₁,l₂) else
      if order(a₁,a₂) then a₁::union(order,equiv) (l₁,ll₂)
      else a₂::union(order,equiv) (ll₁,l₂);;
union : (α * α → bool) * (α * α → bool) → α list * α list → α list
      = ⟨fun⟩
```

2.3.4   Searching in a List

It is highly useful to be able to search a list for an element with a certain property. On page 63, we have already defined a function, filter, that extracts a sublist of elements having a given property. However, in many circumstances, we would be happy enough with the first such element satisfying a property, for example, if we already know that there is at most one. Our problem then is to decide what the search function should return when there is no element satisfying the property we are considering.

More generally, the problem is to know how to define partial functions. One way of introducing such functions is to use this type:

```
#type α option = None | Some of α;;
Type option defined.
```

and to give a partial function of type $\alpha \rightarrow \beta$ option. Here is an example of a function that searches a list by means of this device.

```
#let rec find prop list =
  match list with
    [ ] → None
  | (a::l) → if prop a then Some a else find prop l;;
find : (α → bool) → α list → α option = ⟨fun⟩
```

```
#find (fun x → (x mod 2) = 0) [3; 1; 7; 8; 13; 4];;
− : int option = Some 8
```

```
#find (fun x → (x mod 2) = 0) [3; 1; 7; 13];;
− : int option = None
```

A common example of using such a function occurs when we search an **association list**. A function of type $\alpha \rightarrow \beta$ with a finite domain can be represented by a list of type $(\alpha * \beta)$ list. We then get the value associated with a variable v of type α when we search the list for a pair where the left element is equal to v.

```
#let associate v l =
    match find (fun (x,y) → x=v) l with
      None → None
    | Some (x,y) → Some y;;
  associate : α → (α * β) list → β option = ⟨fun⟩
```

Another way of using partial functions is to add the idea of error or **exception** to the language to take into account the cases where a function does not return a result. This method has the merit of handling a group of exceptional situations that might arise in the course of a computation, including interruptions, and letting us abandon the normal course for certain calculations. We cover that idea in Chapter 4.

Exercises

2.7 A polynomial can be represented as a list of its coefficients, like this: $[a_0;a_1;\ldots;a_n]$. Write the functions for adding and multiplying polynomials represented in this way. Also write the evaluation function for a polynomial, given a value for the variable. Write the functions for taking the derivative and integral of the polynomial as well.

2.8 The representation of polynomials in the previous exercise is inconvenient in that its size is proportional to the degree of the polynomial, rather than the number of non-null terms. Define a CAML type for a representation that suppresses non-null terms. Write the functions needed for this new representation (addition, multiplication, evaluation, derivation, integration).

2.9 Remember the type α tree from page 54. Write a function to associate a set of values with a tree of this type.

2.10 We can associate a node or a leaf in a tree of type α tree with the list of binary choices to make in order to traverse the tree from the root to that node or leaf. For example, if we denote left by the letter l and right by the letter r, then in the tree Node(Leaf 3, Node(Leaf 4, Leaf 5)) in Figure 2.2 on page 53, rl represents the path designating the subtree Leaf 4. Given a tree t and a path of directions u, we will denote the subtree of t corresponding to u (if it exists) by $t_{/u}$. If it does not exist, then u can be decomposed into $u = u_1 u_2$ where $t_{/u_1}$ is a leaf of the tree. Define a type direction with two values, L and R, plus a function of type (direction list → α tree → α tree option) and starting from a list of directions dl and a tree t, provide $t_{/dl}$.

2.11 If all the values in a tree of type α tree are distinct, then the tree provides a binary encoding of the values it contains. For example, if we let 0 indicate left and 1 indicate right, then the tree in Figure 2.4 corresponds to the binary code (a $\mapsto$ 000), (b $\mapsto$ 001), (c $\mapsto$ 010), (d $\mapsto$ 011), (e $\mapsto$ 1). To decode such a group of binary values by a binary tree of type α tree and to produce the group of values of type α to which they correspond, all we have to do is traverse the tree, interpreting the binary symbols as indications of direction and returning to the root of the tree after getting to a leaf. In our example, the group "0011010" decodes as "bec." Write a function of type direction list → α tree → α list option to decode the binary groups of type direction list by means of a tree.

2.12 For a set of values that we want to code as binary, there are *a priori* a great many possible trees corresponding to various encodings. We can compare different encodings by comparing the average length of encoded messages. The following technique, due to Huffman, finds the code that is optimal from this point of view. We start from a set of

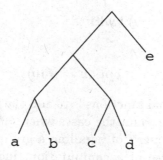

Figure 2.4. Tree for coding (a $\mapsto$ 000, b $\mapsto$ 001, c $\mapsto$ 010, d $\mapsto$ 011, e $\mapsto$ 1)

symbols $(x_1,\ldots,x_n)$ to code, and we associate with them probabilities $(p_1,\ldots,p_n)$ that they will appear. Then we build the list $[(\text{Leaf } x_1, p_1); \ldots; (\text{Leaf } x_n, p_n)]$. Then from this list, we iterate the construction that consists of choosing (from the list) the two pairs (a, p_a) and (b, p_b) where p_a and p_b are the two smallest probabilities and replacing them by the pair $(\text{Node}(a,b), p_a+p_b)$. When the list contains only a single pair, its first component is an optimal code for the original set. Write a function of type $(\alpha * \text{float})$ list $\rightarrow \alpha$ tree that implements this algorithm.

2.4 Summary

We have presented the main data types for CAML—the ones built from the Cartesian product of named fields (that is, records) and the sum of named cases (that is, types with constructors).

User-defined types are named, and after their definition, they acquire the same status as predefined types.

The Cartesian product and sum types can have parameters. In the type-environment available to a user, types without parameters can be seen as constant (type) constructors and types with parameters as type constructors with arguments. Every type definition enriches the type-environment.

Indeed, every type definition also enriches the syntax of patterns that can be used to define functions by case. This flexibility in use of pattern matching makes it natural to program highly varied functions for data structures. It also makes the language better adapted to symbolic computing.

2.5 To Learn More

You may be familiar with the idea of records as the Cartesian product of named fields from PASCAL (1971), but it had appeared in earlier languages such as PL/1

(1965), SIMULA (1967), or even COBOL (1960), and it has been propagated by many other languages since. The possibility of using parameters with these types is, nevertheless, a specialization due to polymorphism in languages in the ML family.

The idea of type with constructors was introduced in the language HOPE in the early eighties. It was then taken up again in ML and other functional languages.

ML made a fundamental choice to render type definitions **generative**; that is, each definition introduces a new type, different from all the pre-existing types, even if there was already a type with exactly the same structure as the type being defined. This choice is contrary to a **structural** view of types, where types are not named but defined solely by their structure, and where in consequence two structurally identical types are regarded as the same.

The choice ML makes is based on the idea that defining a type goes along with a certain *a priori* intention about how to use objects of this type. Each type corresponds to a concept and its objects have particular properties (their invariants) distinguishing them from other objects. By naming the type, we informally summarize this collection of unformulated properties.

The structural choice, in contrast, is based on the idea that the intention of a type is contained entirely in its structure; that is, in the type of its constructors or its fields. Nevertheless, we should note that the name of fields or constructors brings in an arbitrariness somewhat similar to that introduced by names of types.

To reconcile these two positions, we have to adopt an essentially logical point of view, where a type is defined by a set of formally expressed properties. An object would thus belong to a given type if and only if it had these properties. However, this approach collides against the fact that type synthesis assumes some way to carry out automatic proof—something well beyond what we know how to do today.

A great deal of research about **constructive types** is actually going on now. Perhaps in the future, it will give more logical content to the types used in programming.

Chapter 3

Semantics

This chapter is devoted to the semantics of the functional language that we described in the previous chapters. The point of its semantics is to define the meaning of expressions in this language; that is, to define precisely the value of each expression. The association between an expression and its value is created by rewrite rules; that is, rules that transform expressions textually. Those rules are presented and discussed in Section 3.1.

These rewrite rules are non-deterministic. That is, in general, for any expression under consideration, there is more than one rule that may be applied to it. The consistency of these rules rests on the fact that they form a convergent system. In other words, whatever the non-deterministic choices made, at every step it is always possible to make any two different computations converge toward the same expression. This property does not exclude the existence of infinite computations, but it does exclude the possibility of an expression having two distinct values. The value of an expression (when it exists), is therefore unique. We assert this convergence property here, but we will not try to prove it. References about the proof of convergence are found at the end of this chapter.

In practice, in order to implement an evaluator for a language, we have to define a strategy that lets us choose a rewrite at every step—we choose one such rewrite among the set of all possible rewrites. In Section 3.2, we present various strategies and compare them. To the degree that the same expression can produce either finite or infinite computations, we are obliged to distinguish between complete strategies that always lead to the value of the expression (when it exists) and incomplete strategies which may, in certain cases, lead to an infinite computation even though a finite one exists. The strategy in CAML—call by value—is an incomplete strategy, and we have to explain why this choice was made.

Section 3.3 uses what precedes it to define formally just what is the value of an expression.

Once we have formally defined semantics, we can reason about programs in order to prove properties about them. In Section 3.4, we develop a method of proof for properties of programs. The method is based on equational reasoning and the principle of recursion.

Finally, in Section 3.5, we take up the problem of type synthesis. Type synthesis rules formally define a set of types that can be associated with an expression. We also outline the fundamental properties of types and type synthesis (that is, the existence of a principal type and the compatibility between types and semantics).

3.1   Evaluation

Evaluation can be defined as a sequence of transformations leading from an expression to its value. These transformations are called **rewrites** and a sequence of rewrites is called a **reduction**.

3.1.1   Evaluation as Rewriting Expressions

For example, if we are interested in pure arithmetic expressions, the rewrites consist of replacing each subexpression made up of an operator applied to two numeric constants by the result of that application.

$$(2+3)*(4+5) \quad \rightarrow \quad (2+3)*(9) \quad \rightarrow \quad 5*9 \quad \rightarrow \quad 45$$

There is a certain freedom of choice among the subexpressions we choose to reduce. Here, too, we have been able to proceed from left to right:

$$(2+3)*(4+5) \quad \rightarrow \quad (5)*(4+5) \quad \rightarrow \quad 5*9 \quad \rightarrow \quad 45$$

It is clear that such reductions have the following properties:

- **Finiteness**: all the reductions terminate.

- **Consistency**: all the reductions lead to the same result.

The property of consistency results from a more general one known as **convergence**. A set of rewrite rules is said to **converge** if, in every situation where the same expression e can be rewritten in two expressions e_1 and e_2, there exists an expression e_3 such that e_1 and e_2 can be rewritten as e_3. This property is illustrated graphically in Figure 3.1. If we graphically represent the set of possible rewrites of the expression $(2+3)*(4+5)$, as we do in Figure 3.2, this property is immediately apparent in the drawing.

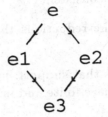

Figure 3.1. The property of convergence

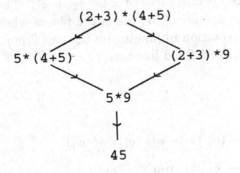

Figure 3.2. A graph of rewrites (or reductions)

When we move from arithmetic expressions to a programming language that supports the rewrite of recursive functions, the finite property of all reductions cannot be preserved. Nevertheless, convergence is preserved. However, in the face of infinite reductions, convergence does not imply consistency, at least not in the sense that we meant earlier that all reductions lead to the same result. Instead, we get a weaker form of consistency:

> **Weak consistency**: all the reductions that terminate lead to the same result.

Effectively, in rewrite systems that support infinite reductions, there may be expressions that simultaneously have finite and infinite reductions. Such systems can only be weakly consistent.

This property of weak consistency is valid only for purely functional languages. It is essential for program verification.

To get from simple arithmetic expressions to a language like CAML, we must define rewrite rules that take into account all the constructions in the language. For the moment, we will concentrate on functional abstraction and application. They will suffice for you to grasp the problem of evaluation.

Initially, we will limit ourselves to simple functional abstractions, that is, abstractions impinging on a single variable in the form (**fun** $x \to e$). The rewrite rule associated with the application of such a function exploits **substitution**, where a variable is replaced by an expression in some other expression.

The substitution of an expression e_2 for a variable x in an expression e_1 consists of replacing all the free occurrences of x by e_2 in e_1. The result is denoted by $e_1[x \leftarrow e_2]$. By "free occurrences," we mean the places where the variable x is not inside a functional abstraction impinging on the variable x. More precisely, as an operation, substitution is defined like this:

- $x[x \leftarrow e] = e$

- $y[x \leftarrow e] = y$

- $(e_1\ e_2)[x \leftarrow e] = (e_1\ [x \leftarrow e])\ (e_2[x \leftarrow e])$

- $(\textbf{fun}\ x \to e_1)[x \leftarrow e_2] = (\textbf{fun}\ x \to e_1)$

- $(\textbf{fun}\ y \to e_1)\ [x \leftarrow e_2] = (\textbf{fun}\ y \to e_1[x \leftarrow e_2])$

And here are two examples of substitution:

$(y + x\ y)\ [x \leftarrow (\textbf{fun}\ x \to x)] = (y + (\textbf{fun}\ x \to x)\ y)$

$(x + (\textbf{fun}\ x \to x)\ y)\ [x \leftarrow 2*y] = (2*y + (\textbf{fun}\ x \to x)\ y)$

In that latter example, the second occurrence of x (that is, the one inside the subexpression (**fun** x → x)) is not affected by substitution because it is not free. We could replace the expression (**fun** x → x) by the equivalent expression (**fun** z → z), highlighting the fact that the subexpression should not be touched by substitution.

Our definition of substitution so far is not quite complete because it does not take into account certain naming conflicts that may occur when an expression containing a free variable y is substituted in a function where y is a parameter (that is, a captured variable). For example, the result of the substitution ((**fun** y → x*y) x) [x ← 2*y] must not be ((**fun** y → (2*y)*y)(2*y)).

To avoid that problem, we could use the fact that it is always possible to rename linked variables as we did earlier by replacing (**fun** x → x) with (**fun** z → z). Thus, to reduce

$$((\textbf{fun } y \rightarrow x*y) \ x) \ [x \leftarrow 2*y]$$

we could replace this expression by

$$((\textbf{fun } z \rightarrow x*z) \ x) \ [x \leftarrow 2*y]$$

before making the substitution. Doing so finally gives the result

$$((\textbf{fun } z \rightarrow (2*y)*z)(2*y))$$

The reduction rule associated with the application of a functional abstraction is:

$$(\textbf{fun } x \rightarrow e_1) \ e_2 \quad \Rightarrow \quad e_1[x \leftarrow e_2]$$

For example, we could reduce the expression (**fun** x → x*x) (2+3) in this way:

$$\begin{aligned} &(\textbf{fun } x \rightarrow x*x) \ (2+3) \\ \Rightarrow \quad &(\textbf{fun } x \rightarrow x*x) \ (5) \\ \Rightarrow \quad &5*5 \\ \Rightarrow \quad &25 \end{aligned}$$

This rule makes it easy to evaluate higher order expressions. Here is an example that brings in the functions sq (defined as (**fun** x → x*x)) and **double** (defined as (**fun** f → **fun** x → f (f x))).

The evaluation of the expression double sq 5 could be done like this:

$$
\begin{aligned}
& \text{double sq 5} \\
=\ & (\textbf{fun } f \rightarrow \textbf{fun } x \rightarrow f\ (f\ x))\ \text{sq } 5 \\
\Rightarrow\ & (\textbf{fun } x \rightarrow \text{sq } (\text{sq } x))\ 5 \\
\Rightarrow\ & \text{sq } (\text{sq } 5) \\
=\ & (\textbf{fun } x \rightarrow x{*}x)((\textbf{fun } x \rightarrow x{*}x)\ 5) \\
\Rightarrow\ & (\textbf{fun } x \rightarrow x{*}x)(5{*}5) \\
\Rightarrow\ & (\textbf{fun } x \rightarrow x{*}x)\ 25 \\
\Rightarrow\ & 25{*}25 \\
\Rightarrow\ & 625
\end{aligned}
$$

3.1.2   Evaluation Strategies

To the degree that the process of reduction is not uniquely defined, an expression evaluator has to make choices. At every step in reduction, we have to choose which, among all the reducible subexpressions, to reduce. We will call any uniform procedure for making such choices an **evaluation strategy**. In contrast to the evaluation of simple arithmetic expressions, where the strategy did not influence the length of the reduction, we will see now that it is not at all the same case for the evaluation of programs.

An essential element for defining a strategy is how to handle applications. In the preceding examples, when we had to reduce an expression of the form $(\textbf{fun } x \rightarrow e_1)\ e_2$, we chose first to reduce e_2 before we applied the function. A different choice could have been possible. For example, we could also reduce this expression $(\textbf{fun } x \rightarrow x{*}x)\ (2{+}3)$ in this way:

$$
\begin{aligned}
& (\textbf{fun } x \rightarrow x{*}x)\ (2{+}3) \\
\Rightarrow\ & (2{+}3){*}(2{+}3) \\
\Rightarrow\ & (2{+}3){*}5 \\
\Rightarrow\ & 5{*}5 \\
\Rightarrow\ & 25
\end{aligned}
$$

Figure 3.3 shows the entire graph of rewrites that we could carry out for the expression $(\textbf{fun } x \rightarrow x{*}x)(2{+}3)$.

In the same spirit, another possible reduction of the expression double sq 5 is:

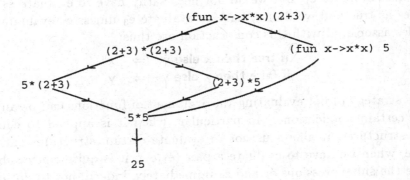

Figure 3.3. A graph of rewrites (or reductions)

$$
\begin{aligned}
&\quad \textbf{double sq } 5 \\
&=\;\; (\textbf{fun } f \rightarrow \textbf{fun } x \rightarrow f \ (f \ x)) \ \text{sq } 5 \\
&\Rightarrow\;\; (\textbf{fun } x \rightarrow \text{sq} \ (\text{sq } x)) \ 5 \\
&\Rightarrow\;\; \text{sq} \ (\text{sq } 5) \\
&=\;\; (\textbf{fun } x \rightarrow x*x)(\text{sq } 5) \\
&\Rightarrow\;\; (\text{sq } 5)*(\text{sq } 5) \\
&=\;\; (\text{sq } 5)*((\textbf{fun } x \rightarrow x*x) \ 5) \\
&\Rightarrow\;\; (\text{sq } 5)*(5*5) \\
&\Rightarrow\;\; (\text{sq } 5)*25 \\
&=\;\; ((\textbf{fun } x \rightarrow x*x) \ 5)*25 \\
&\Rightarrow\;\; (5*5)*25 \\
&\Rightarrow\;\; 25*25 \\
&\Rightarrow\;\; 625
\end{aligned}
$$

Notice that since we did not completely evaluate the argument before we applied a function, we had to duplicate certain reductions. Nevertheless, we should not hastily conclude from that example that it is always best to evaluate the argument because in certain cases, the argument of a function does not participate in the result and its reduction is useless.

$$
\begin{aligned}
&\quad (\textbf{fun } x \rightarrow 1) \ (\text{fact } 1000) \\
&\Rightarrow\;\; 1
\end{aligned}
$$

Notice that in place of (fact 1000), we could even have put an expression for which the reduction does not terminate.

Along the same lines, to evaluate a conditional statement

$$\textbf{if } e_1 \textbf{ then } e_2 \textbf{ else } e_3$$

we must evaluate e_1, but we do not necessarily have to evaluate e_2 unless e_1 evaluates as **true** and we do not have to evaluate e_3 unless e_1 evaluates as **false**. The rules associated with this construction are thus:

$$\textbf{if true then } x \textbf{ else } y \quad \Rightarrow \quad x$$
$$\textbf{if false then } x \textbf{ else } y \quad \Rightarrow \quad y$$

This strategy of not evaluating the argument of functions can be an excellent one for certain applications. In particular, when it is applied to constructors of data structures, it allows us not to evaluate certain structures entirely. For example, when we have to evaluate a pair (e_1, e_2), it is quite conceivable not to evaluate the subexpressions e_1 and e_2 immediately, indeed, not to do so until we access e_1 or e_2 by the functions **fst** or **snd** or even by a pattern match. (We will come back to this idea later.)

The fundamental property of evaluation by rewrites is that all reductions that terminate will lead to the same result[1]. This property of consistency in reductions belongs to functional programs: the result of a reduction is independent of the order of evaluation. That property is no longer true, however, when we introduce non-functional constructions into the language—such constructions as assignment, for example. (See Chapter 4 for more about that issue.)

Thus we can define the value of an expression as the terminal expression where all the reductions of that expression eventually arrive and terminate. An evaluation strategy is **complete** if it always leads to the same result (if that result exists). It is **incomplete** if there exist cases where the evaluation leads to an error or to an infinite reduction although some other reduction would lead to the result.

3.1.3   How to Deal with Recursion

The way we introduced recursion into CAML by means of the construction **let rec** is not entirely satisfactory. In effect, although ordinary functions can be denoted by expressions, recursive functions cannot be introduced unless we give them names.

In the evaluations that you will see, functions such as **double** or **sq** are replaced once and for all by their "text"—a replacement that is not possible for recursive functions since the text itself contains the name of the function. Thus it is necessary to introduce new notation for recursive functions if we want to take them into account in our evaluation mechanism.

One possible solution is to introduce a new constant Rec of type $((\alpha \to \alpha) \to \alpha)$ and to denote the function defined by **let rec** $f \, x = e$ simply as Rec (**fun** $f \, x \to e$).

---

[1] If we use functions defined by case, the result is true only if the pattern match is deterministic.

The evaluation rule associated with such functions is:

$$\text{Rec f} \;\Rightarrow\; \text{f (Rec f)}$$

Intuitively, Rec is a fixed point operator that associates a functional F having the type $(t \to t)$ with a fixed point denoted Rec F of type t; that is, a value having the property Rec F = F (Rec F).

If we add this new constant Rec to CAML, the definition

#let rec fact n = **if** n=0 **then** 1 **else** n*fact(n−1);;

can be written

#let ffact = **fun** f n → **if** n=0 **then** 1 **else** n*f(n−1);;

#let fact = Rec ffact;;

We can thus reduce fact(3) in the following way:

```
        fact 3
   =    Rec ffact 3
   ⇒    ffact (Rec ffact) 3
   =    (fun f n → if n=0 then 1 else n*f(n−1)) (Rec ffact) 3
   ⇒    (fun n → if n=0 then 1 else n*Rec ffact (n−1)) 3
   ⇒    if 3=0 then 1 else 3*Rec ffact (3−1)
   ⇒    if false then 1 else 3*Rec ffact (3−1)
   ⇒    3*Rec ffact (3−1)
   ⇒    3*Rec ffact 2
   ...
   ⇒    3*(2*Rec ffact 1)
   ...
   ⇒    3*(2*(1*Rec ffact 0))
   ...
   ⇒    3*(2*(1*1))
   ⇒    3*(2*1)
   ⇒    3*2
   ⇒    6
```

This way of handling recursion is the one adopted in λ-calculus where the combinator for fixed points is traditionally denoted Y. In untyped λ-calculus, Y can be defined, and that fact lets us get all the functions that can be computed without having to add a special construction to get recursive functions. In typed λ-calculus and in CAML, Y cannot be defined, a fact that explains our introduction of a special construction: **let rec**.

3.1.4   Another Way of Handling Recursion

We could also take a diametrically opposed perspective about how to handle recursion. Rather than systematically eliminate the names of functions, we could, in contrast, systematically name all of the functional expressions and introduce specific rules for each function name.

In this way, there are no more distinctions to make between ordinary functions and recursive functions. The rules for double, sq, and fact, respectively, are written like this:

$$
\begin{aligned}
\text{double } f\ x &\Rightarrow\ f\ (f\ x)\\
\text{sq } x &\Rightarrow\ x*x\\
\text{fact } n &\Rightarrow\ \textbf{if } n{=}0 \textbf{ then } 1 \textbf{ else } n*\text{fact}(n-1)
\end{aligned}
$$

This way of working has the advantage of being highly intuitive. It also extends naturally to definitions by case, with each case corresponding to a different rule[2]. Thus here is a definition by case of the factorial function:

#let rec fact = **fun** 0 → 1 | n → n*fact(n−1);;

which gives rise to two rules:

$$
\begin{aligned}
\text{fact } 0 &\Rightarrow\ 1\\
\text{fact } n &\Rightarrow\ n*\text{fact}(n-1)
\end{aligned}
$$

where of course the second is applied only when the first one cannot be applied. The application of the second rule is governed by the condition that $(n \neq 0)$.

Even so, this intuitive approach has drawbacks since some functions do not readily lend themselves to this treatment because of their free variables.

For example, if we consider the function defined by
let f x = (**fun** y → x*y) o (**fun** y → x*(y+1)),
it is not possible to replace that definition simply by this:

#let f_1 y = x*y;;

#let f_2 y = x*(y+1);;

#let f x = f_1 o f_2;;

because the definition of x in the definitions of f_1 and f_2 has been taken out of context and thus makes no sense.

Consequently, we have to make x a new parameter of f_1 and f_2. Thus we get this:

---

[2]as long as the cases are disjoint!

#let f_1 x y = x*y;;

#let f_2 x y = x*(y+1);;

#let f x = (f_1 x) o (f_2 x);;

We can prove that such a modification is always possible. This kind of transformation is used in certain implementations of functional languages where it is known as λ-**lifting**.

3.1.5 Behavior of Evaluation Processes

If we look again at a computation by substitution for the factorial function, and we prune off a few trivial steps, we will see a "geometric" property appear very clearly. The size of the expressions grows during the successive calls of the function and then decreases during the evaluation of the simple arithmetic expression built by these calls.

$$\begin{aligned}
&\text{fact}(3) \\
\Rightarrow\quad &3*\text{fact}(2) \\
\Rightarrow\quad &3*2*\text{fact}(1) \\
\Rightarrow\quad &3*2*1*\text{fact}(0) \\
\Rightarrow\quad &3*2*1*1 \\
\Rightarrow\quad &3*2*1 \\
\Rightarrow\quad &3*2 \\
\Rightarrow\quad &6
\end{aligned}$$

Every call of the function fact puts aside (so to speak) a multiplication that cannot be carried out until its second argument is known. That reserve operation is what makes the size of the expression grow.

It is possible to define the factorial function differently so that the computation is essentially different. This new definition uses an auxiliary function facti with two arguments.

#let rec facti n r= **if** n=0 **then** r **else** facti (n−1) (r*n);;
$\quad facti : int \rightarrow int \rightarrow int = \langle$**fun**$\rangle$

#let fact n = facti n 1;;
$\quad fact : int \rightarrow int = \langle$**fun**$\rangle$

The computation of fact 3 thus looks like this:

```
        fact 3
    ⇒   facti 3 1
    ⇒   facti 2 3
    ⇒   facti 1 6
    ⇒   facti 0 6
    ⇒   6
```

Here, the expressions that appear at each step remain constant in size, and the computation terminates when the last call of the function facti has been carried out. You can see a similar difference between the functions it_list and list_it in Section 2.3.

Of course this only remotely resembles what is actually going on in the machine, but the differences between these two computations reflect certain actual distinctions between the two real computations. In general, the way that expressions grow when they are rewritten as they are here corresponds to memory consumption in real computations. This memory actually takes the form of a stack used to store the calculations that are waiting their turn. (For more about that idea, see Chapter 12 about compilation.) This way of using memory is also the cause of an increase in computation time.

Functions like facti behave **iteratively**. In the jargon, we say they are **tail recursive**. They can be translated into a more efficient form. In contrast, functions like the first version of fact, which are truly recursive, express very directly and naturally the mathematical function that they compute.

In practice, how efficient these two forms of recursion are depends greatly on the compilation techniques in use.

3.2 Defining Strategies

There are complete evaluation strategies (complete in the sense we defined on page 80). Evaluation strategies that produce applications without evaluating the arguments are essentially complete. And it is quite possible to build implementations of functional languages based on such complete strategies.

In practice, however, it is more reasonable to opt for an incomplete strategy. Why? The crux of the problem is that it is difficult to adopt a purely functional programming style in all circumstances. If programs include an interactive aspect, they have to take into account certain constraints of the external world with which they interact—such constraints as sequentiality (that is, constraints on the order in which events occur). For example, when we program a dialogue with a user, questions must occur before the corresponding answers. It thus becomes necessary for the programmer to master the evaluation order of various parts of the program. In a complete evaluation strategy, the order of evaluation is necessarily decided by the evaluator—not the programmer—as a function of the needs of the computation, and thus evaluation escapes from the programmer's control.

The evaluation strategy known as **evaluation by value**, that is, where the arguments of an application are evaluated before their application, makes it possible for the programmer to master evaluation order. For that reason, this strategy is the one chosen for CAML so that the language can be extended to non-functional constructions needed to implement certain applications.

From a theoretical point of view, the choice of an incomplete strategy does not imply that we have to give up any proofs of correctness of programs. In effect, if we consider programs for which any evaluation terminates, (which is often the case), then every strategy is complete; in particular, the strategy "by value" is complete. The consequence of choosing the strategy "by value" is that to prove the correctness of a program, we must first prove that it terminates[3].

We are going to define various possible strategies, beginning with the one that is used in CAML. These strategies are precisely defined by a system of deduction rules.

We should note that these descriptions only remotely correspond to the way the language is implemented at the machine level. The real problems of implementation will be discussed in Chapter 11 about interpretation and Chapter 12 about compilation.

3.2.1 The Caml Strategy, or Evaluation by Value

We will begin our discussion of evaluation by value with an intuitive description of certain rules.

Evaluation Rules

- To evaluate a pair or a tuple, we evaluate their various members successively from right to left.

- To evaluate an expression **if** t **then** e_1 **else** e_2, we begin by evaluating t. If its value is **true**, we replace the entire expression by e_1. If its value is **false**, we replace the expression by e_2.

- A functional expression (**fun** x $\rightarrow$ e) or (**fun** $(x_1,\ldots,x_n)$ $\rightarrow$ e) evaluates as itself. It remains the same until it is applied to an argument.

- To evaluate an application, we evaluate the argument and then the operator; then we apply the operator to the argument. The operator can be a basic

---

[3]We could just as well show that, by construction, certain programs have this property of terminating.

operation, such as addition, in which case we immediately get the result. Otherwise, if the application is of the form (**fun** x → e)(v), we continue the computation by evaluating the expression e[x←v], and if the application is of the form (**fun** $(x_1, \ldots, x_n)$ → e) $(v_1, \ldots v_n)$, we continue the computation by evaluating the expression e[$(x_1, \ldots, x_n)$ ← $(v_1, \ldots, v_n)$].

- To evaluate **let** x=e_1 **in** e_2, we first evaluate e_1, which gives a value v_1; then we evaluate $e_2[x←v_1]$[4].

- To evaluate **let rec** f x = e_1 **in** e_2, we evaluate $e_2[f←\text{Rec}(\textbf{fun}\ f\ x → e_1)]$.

For completeness, we also have to indicate how to evaluate an application of the form Rec f. If we simply apply the substitution rule replacing "Rec f" by "f (Rec f)", we will immediately set off an infinite computation, because (to evaluate "f (Rec f)" later) we will have once more to evaluate "Rec f." The rule we have chosen for Rec is thus not well suited to CAML.

Nevertheless, it is possible to adapt it, so we will take this as our new rule:

$$\text{Rec f x} \Rightarrow   \text{f (Rec f) x}$$

An application of the form Rec e will be its own value and will lead to an evaluation only once it is applied to a supplementary argument. In this way, we can avoid the infinite calculation we mentioned earlier.

Evaluation Rules as Deduction Rules

Evaluation rules can also be regarded as deduction rules that let us define a relation denoted like this:

$$\vdash e \Rightarrow v$$

and signifying

The expression e has the value v.

Here, what we call a value is simply an expression we got by rewriting the original expression. In the case where the expression under consideration is a basic type or a user-defined type that employs only basic types and Cartesian product, then its value is a value in the conventional sense. In contrast, if the expression under consideration is a type where the functional arrow comes into play, then its value will simply be an expression containing function expressions. Notice that these expressions considered as values may contain reducible subexpressions. For

---

[4]The expression **let** x=e_1 **in** e_2 is thus considered strictly equivalent to (**fun** x → e_2) e_1.

example, the expression $(\textbf{fun } x \rightarrow x*(2+3))$ will be considered as a value even though it contains a reducible expression, namely, $(2+3)$.

For every construction in the language, we will give a rule represented in this form:

$$\frac{\text{List of Hypotheses}}{\text{Conclusion}} \text{ (Name)}$$

Here are the rules:

$$\frac{\vdash e_1 \Rightarrow v_1 \quad \dots \quad \vdash e_n \Rightarrow v_n}{\vdash (e_1, \dots e_n) \Rightarrow (v_1, \dots v_n)} \text{ (Tuple)}$$

$$\frac{\vdash e_1 \Rightarrow \textbf{true} \qquad \vdash e_2 \Rightarrow v}{\vdash \textbf{if } e_1 \textbf{ then } e_2 \textbf{ else } e_3 \Rightarrow v} \text{ (Cond1)}$$

$$\frac{\vdash e_1 \Rightarrow \textbf{false} \qquad \vdash e_3 \Rightarrow v}{\vdash \textbf{if } e_1 \textbf{ then } e_2 \textbf{ else } e_3 \Rightarrow v} \text{ (Cond2)}$$

$$\frac{}{\vdash (\textbf{fun } x \rightarrow e) \Rightarrow (\textbf{fun } x \rightarrow e)} \text{ (Fun1)}$$

$$\frac{}{\vdash (\textbf{fun } (x_1, \dots, x_n) \rightarrow e) \Rightarrow (\textbf{fun } (x_1, \dots, x_n) \rightarrow e)} \text{ (Fun2)}$$

$$\frac{\vdash e \Rightarrow op \qquad \vdash e_i \Rightarrow v_i \qquad \vdash op \; v_1 \dots v_n \Rightarrow v}{\vdash e \; e_1 \dots e_n \Rightarrow v} \text{ (AppPrim)}$$

$$\frac{\vdash e_1 \Rightarrow (\textbf{fun } x \rightarrow e) \qquad \vdash e_2 \Rightarrow v_2 \qquad \vdash e[x \leftarrow v_2] \Rightarrow v}{\vdash e_1 \; e_2 \Rightarrow v} \text{ (App1)}$$

$$\frac{\vdash e_1 \Rightarrow (\textbf{fun}(x_1,\ldots,x_n){\rightarrow}e) \quad \vdash e_2 \Rightarrow (v_1,\ldots,v_n) \quad \vdash e[x_i \leftarrow v_i] \Rightarrow v}{\vdash e_1 \ e_2 \Rightarrow v} \quad \text{(App2)}$$

$$\frac{\vdash e_1 \Rightarrow v_1 \quad \vdash e_2[x \leftarrow v_1] \Rightarrow v}{\vdash \textbf{let } x{=}e_1 \textbf{ in } e_2 \Rightarrow v} \quad \text{(Let)}$$

$$\frac{\vdash f \ (\text{Rec } f) \ x \Rightarrow v}{\vdash \text{Rec } f \ x \Rightarrow v} \quad \text{(Rec)}$$

$$\frac{\vdash e_2[f \leftarrow \text{Rec}(\textbf{fun } f \ x \rightarrow e_1)] \Rightarrow v}{\vdash \textbf{let rec } f \ x{=}e_1 \textbf{ in } e_2 \Rightarrow v} \quad \text{(Letrec)}$$

3.2.2 Another Strategy: Delayed Evaluation

If we start from the CAML strategy, and we want to get a complete strategy, then there are few things to modify: only the rules about tuples and about application.

The modified rule about tuples becomes this:

$$\frac{}{\vdash (e_1,\ldots,e_n) \Rightarrow (e_1,\ldots,e_n)} \quad \text{(Tuple)}$$

The rules about application are modified so that they do not require the computation of their arguments. Nevertheless, in the case of a function in more than one variable, that is, a function of the form ($\textbf{fun } (x_1,\ldots,x_n) \rightarrow e$), the arguments must be tupled in order to produce the application, so we will have two rules:

$$\frac{\vdash e_1 \Rightarrow (\textbf{fun } x \rightarrow e) \quad \vdash e[x \leftarrow e_2] \Rightarrow v}{\vdash e_1 \ e_2 \Rightarrow v} \quad \text{(App1)}$$

$$\frac{\vdash e_1 \Rightarrow (\textbf{fun}(x_1,\ldots,x_n){\rightarrow}e) \quad \vdash e_2 \Rightarrow (v_1,\ldots,v_n) \quad \vdash e[x_i \leftarrow v_i] \Rightarrow v}{\vdash e_1 \ e_2 \Rightarrow v} \quad \text{(App2)}$$

Finally, the rule about the construction Rec can assume this primitive form:

$$\frac{}{\vdash \text{Rec } f \Rightarrow f \ (\text{Rec } f)} \ (\text{Rec})$$

We call this process delayed evaluation.

The values we get as a result of delayed computation are not necessarily the same ones we would get in a computation by value. For example, since the arguments of pairs are not evaluated in this strategy, the expression (2+3,7) is a value, whereas in an evaluation by value, we pursue the computation to get (5,7). However, it is possible to show that for expressions belonging to simple types, the value we get is the same as the one in an evaluation by value, that is, a constant of the type under consideration.

To understand the strategy we define this way, consider the expression

$$(\textbf{fun}(x,y) \rightarrow x) \ ((\textbf{fun } x \rightarrow (x, \text{fact } 1000)) \ 3)$$

To find the value of that expression using the rules we just presented, we must necessarily use rule (App2) since that expression is a function where the parameter is a pair. To be able to apply that rule, the pair structure of the argument has to appear, so we must evaluate the argument, that is, the expression $((\textbf{fun } x \rightarrow (x, \text{fact } 1000)) \ 3)$.

To find the value of that expression, which is the application of a simple function, we must use rule (App1) which provides as its result the pair (3, fact 1000).

When we apply the function $(\textbf{fun}(x,y) \rightarrow x)$ to that pair, we get the result 3 without having to evaluate (fact 1000).

Thus to compute the expression according to a delayed evaluation strategy, we do this:

$$
\begin{aligned}
& (\textbf{fun}(x,y) \rightarrow x) \ ((\textbf{fun } x \rightarrow (x, \text{fact } 1000)) \ 3) \\
\Rightarrow \ & (\textbf{fun}(x,y) \rightarrow x) \ (3, \text{fact } 1000) \\
\Rightarrow \ & 3
\end{aligned}
$$

3.2.3 Extending Delayed Evaluation to Data Structures

The way we just handled tuples can be extended to any data structures with constructors. For example, when we use the list constructor Cons (::), it is not necessary to evaluate its arguments.

So that we do not complicate the way we write our application rule too much, we will limit ourselves to a restricted form of pattern matching. For a type that includes constructors $C_1, \ldots, C_n$, a function defined by cases on this type will always be of the form $\textbf{fun } p_1 \rightarrow e_1 \mid \cdots \mid p_n \rightarrow e_n$ where the p_i are of the form $C_i(x_1, \ldots, x_{n_i})$, with n_i being the arity of the constructor C_i.

For example, in a definition of lists like this:

#type α list = Nil | Cons **of** $\alpha * \alpha$ list;;

only patterns of the form Nil and Cons(x_1,x_2) will be allowed.

The new rules associated with constructors will be the following:

$$\frac{}{\vdash C(e_1,\ldots e_n) \Rightarrow C(e_1,\ldots e_n)} \text{ (Constr)}$$

$$\frac{\vdash e \Rightarrow (\textbf{fun} \ldots \mid C_i(x_1,\ldots,x_{n_i}) \rightarrow e_i \mid \ldots) \quad}{\vdash e\ e' \Rightarrow v} \text{ (Appcase)}$$

In a very significant way, these rules can change the complexity of certain programs. At the same time, they offer a programmer novel possibilities.

For example, the mathematical idea of sequence can be directly represented by infinite lists where the type is simply this:

#type α seq = Cons **of** $\alpha * \alpha$ seq;;

We will denote Cons as the infix constructor :: of lists, so the sum of two sequences is written simply:

```
#let rec sum = fun
    (a₁::l₁, a₂::l₂) → (a₁+a₂)::sum(l₁,l₂);;
```

The sequence of Fibonacci numbers can thus be defined simply like this:

```
#let rec fibs = 1::fibs₁
 and fibs₁ = 1::sum(fibs, fibs₁);;
```

In themselves, these definitions do not give rise to any computations. In contrast, accessing an element of the sequence will set off a computation of that element, and to compute it, we have to compute all the preceding elements. To access an element, we will use the function nth.

```
#let rec nth n (a::l) =
   if n=0 then a else nth (n−1) l;;
```

Here is the computation of the fourth Fibonacci number:

$$
\begin{aligned}
& \text{nth 3 fibs} \\
\Rightarrow\ & \text{nth 3 } (1\text{::}fibs_1) \\
\Rightarrow\ & \text{nth 2 } fibs_1 \\
\Rightarrow\ & \text{nth 2 } (1\text{::}sum(fibs, fibs_1)) \\
\Rightarrow\ & \text{nth 1 } (sum(fibs, fibs_1)) \\
\Rightarrow\ & \text{nth 1 } (sum(1\text{::}fibs_1, 1\text{::}(sum(fibs, fibs_1)))) \\
\Rightarrow\ & \text{nth 1 } (2\text{::}sum(fibs_1, sum(fibs, fibs_1))) \\
\Rightarrow\ & \text{nth 0 } (sum(fibs_1, sum(fibs, fibs_1))) \\
\Rightarrow\ & \text{nth 0 } (sum(1\text{::}sum(fibs, fibs_1), sum(1\text{::}fibs_1, 1\text{::}sum(fibs, fibs_1)))) \\
\Rightarrow\ & \text{nth 0 } (sum(1\text{::}sum(fibs, fibs_1), 2\text{::}sum(fibs_1, sum(fibs, fibs_1)))) \\
\Rightarrow\ & \text{nth 0 } (3\text{::}sum(sum(fibs, fibs_1), sum(fibs_1, sum(fibs, fibs_1)))) \\
\Rightarrow\ & 3
\end{aligned}
$$

In this example, it is clear that delayed evaluation can lead to great duplication in some computations if it is produced by rewriting expressions. Implementation techniques that use graph structures let us avoid those kinds of duplications.

3.3 Program Semantics

For you to understand program semantics, we need to examine rewrite semantics and to glance briefly at denotational semantics as well. As we do so, you will see why we pursued rewrite semantics rather than denotational semantics.

3.3.1 Rewrite Semantics

We have defined a set of textual rewrites that transform an expression into a value by successive steps. A value is then simply an expression that cannot be rewritten further. We say that such an expression is in **normal form** with respect to the rewrite rules under consideration. In the case where an expression is a simple type (such as integer, floating-point, or Boolean) the normal form corresponds to the value of the expression in the usual sense.

Since all computations that terminate lead to the same value, rewrites make it possible to define the value of an expression unambiguously. The value of an expression E, denoted $Val(E)$, will be the common value at which all terminating computations arrive, known as the **normal form** of E, when there exists at least one computation that terminates. Otherwise, the normal form of E will be undefined. The function Val thus defines the semantics of the language; that is, it is a way to associate a value (possibly undefined) with every expression in the language.

We have seen by the way how we could define an evaluation strategy by imposing constraints on the order in which these textual rewrites are carried out.

For a given strategy S, the value obtained as the result of a computation conforming to strategy S beginning from expression E is an expression E' satisfying the property $Val(E') = Val(E)$ if the computation terminates. Moreover, if the expression E is a simple type, then $E' = Val(E)$.

We will denote the evaluation function associated with a strategy S by Val_S. When E is a simple type, and $Val_S(E)$ is defined, we are sure that $Val(E)$ is also defined and that $Val_S(E) = Val(E)$. When E is not a simple type, we can only affirm that $Val(Val_S(E)) = Val(E)$.

3.3.2   Denotational Semantics

The fact that this language is functional makes its denotational semantics non-trivial. In effect, if we want to define the set of values D (its denotations) which this language manipulates, we must bear in mind the fact that functions are considered values, so we are obliged to assume that D contains the function-space D → D—which of course is impractical because in normal mathematics, D → D always contains strictly more elements than D. Thus we have to find an interpretation of D → D other than the entire function-space. We do so by defining a topology for D and then interpreting D → D as the space of continuous functions over D. As you can see, denotational semantics is a very interesting subject, but too complicated to be described in a course about programming like this one. For a good introduction to the topic, see [15].

The semantics we defined based on rewrites, in contrast, has the virtue of being intuitively easy to understand. It also incidentally justifies the technique for proving the correctness of programs that we will introduce in the next section.

3.4   Proving the Correctness of Programs

Proof about the properties of functional programs is based on equational reasoning (that is, we replace expressions by other expressions of the same value) and on inductive reasoning about data structures.

3.4.1   Equational Reasoning

The rewrite rules to evaluate programs can also be interpreted as equations or equalities. Let's assume in effect that an expression E' is obtained from an expression E by applying a rewrite rule (denoted $E \Rightarrow E'$). If E' is a well defined value, then E has the same value since we can associate a computation of E with every computation of E' simply by using the fact that $E \Rightarrow E'$. Reciprocally, if E has a well defined value, then by the convergence property, we know that we can reach the same value by starting from E'.

To sum up, the fact $E \Rightarrow E'$ entails $Val(E) = Val(E')$. We can thus use rewrite rules as equations or equalities about expressions.

Incidentally, it is possible to show that

$$Val(E) = Val(E') \text{ implies } Val(E \ [x \leftarrow E'']) = Val(E' \ [x \leftarrow E''])$$

As a consequence, equational reasoning establishes equalities that remain true for substitution.

For example, if we consider the functions

#let double f x = f (f x);;

#let compose f g x = f (g x);;

then equational reasoning lets us assert that for every function h and all values x,

double h x = h (h x) = compose h h x

We have thus demonstrated that the expressions double h x and compose h h x have the same value for all h and for all x.

Yet if we put ourselves in the context of a particular strategy S, the same equational reasoning no longer lets us assert that two expressions that we have shown to be equal by equational reasoning will lead to the same result when we apply strategy S. For example, if we define the recursive function

#let rec f x = f (f x);;

for which no computation terminates, the two expressions (**fun** x → 0) (f 1) and 0 are equal but the first one has no value in the strategy of CAML.

The only way we can interpret $E = E'$ within an incomplete strategy S is that if $Val_S(E)$ and $Val_S(E')$ are both defined, then $Val(Val_S(E)) = Val(Val_S(E'))$. If, moreover, the expressions belong to a basic type, then $Val_S(E)$ and $Val_S(E')$ are identical.

In fact, most programs for which we want to prove correctness do not involve infinite computations. In that case, for any strategy S, Val_S is defined everywhere, and equational reasoning is clearly valid. Nevertheless, we still have to demonstrate formally that our programs do not involve infinite computations; that is, we have to **prove termination**.

3.4.2   Taking Functions as Values into Account

It is rarely possible to demonstrate the equality of two functional expressions directly. For example, the two expressions (**fun** x → x) and (**fun** y → y) are not directly equal because they are syntactically different so no particular rule applies to them.

To solve such a problem, we simply have to consider the two functions equal if they always provide the same result when they are applied to the same argument. That is,

$$(\forall x, \; f(x) = g(x)) \quad \Longrightarrow \quad f = g$$

If f and g are functional expressions, to show f = g, it suffices to show that f z = g z for a variable z that does not appear in f nor in g.

For example, to show that (**fun** x → x) = (**fun** y → y), it thus suffices to observe that for all z, we have (**fun** x → x) z = z = (**fun** y → y) z.

Likewise, from our earlier proof, we get the result that for every function h,

$$\text{double } h = \text{compose } h \; h$$

However, we have to pay attention to the fact that in order to deduce f = g from f z = g z, it is necessary that the variable z appears neither in f nor in g. There is no way to deduce double = compose h from double h = compose h h.

3.4.3   Reasoning by Case

When the type of a variable is such that the variable can take only a finite number of values, we can reason by case about the value of the variable.

For example, let's assume that we want to prove this equality:

$$(\textbf{if } c \textbf{ then } f \textbf{ else } g) \; x = \textbf{if } c \textbf{ then } f \; x \textbf{ else } g \; x$$

Since c can take only the values true and false, all we have to verify is this:

$$(\textbf{if true then } f \textbf{ else } g) \; x = f \; x = \textbf{if true then } f \; x \textbf{ else } g \; x$$
$$(\textbf{if false then } f \textbf{ else } g) \; x = g \; x = \textbf{if true then } f \; x \textbf{ else } g \; x$$

3.4.4   Reasoning by Induction

Inductive reasoning as we will use it is an extension of reasoning by recurrence about integers; we will apply it to data structures as a set.

For integers, to demonstrate a property of the form $\forall n \; P(n)$, we show

- $P(0)$

- $\forall n \; (P(n) \implies P(n+1))$

if we write integers uniquely by using Z (for zero) and S (as the successor function), the principle of recursion is written like this:

- $P(Z)$

- $\forall n \ (P(n) \implies P(S(n)))$

In that notation, Z and S may be seen as constructors of an integer type which will be defined as:

#type nat = Z | S **of** nat;;

By analogy, if we now consider a data type as

#type btree = Empty | Bin **of** btree * btree;;

To prove a property of the form $\forall t \ P(t)$, we prove

- $P(\text{Empty})$

- $\forall t_1, t_2 \ P(t_1)$ and $P(t_2) \implies P(\text{Bin}(t_1, t_2))$

That proof may be seen as an induction on the size of the objects of type btree. It is, nevertheless, more elegant since it makes no direct reference to the size of objects and involves exactly one case for each constructor. It generalizes to the set of data structures defined by means of constructors.

3.4.5 Proof of Termination

The fact of whether a function is defined everywhere is an **undecidable** property. That is, there is no algorithm that can take the definition of a function as a given and then indicate whether it is defined for all data. Moreover, there is no algorithm that takes as a given the definition of a function and a particular value and then indicates whether the function is defined for that value.

The property of undecidability crops up in every formal system that defines the set of computable functions, such formal systems as Turing machines, λ-calculus, and programming languages. Proof that a function terminates can, consequently, be arbitrarily complex.

However, there are many situations where such a proof can be fairly simple. Let there be a recursive definition of the function f in which we use only elementary constructions and auxiliary functions that we know to be defined everywhere. To show that f is defined everywhere, it suffices to verify that the recursive calls of f found in the body of f have "simpler" arguments than the arguments of the function and that the basic cases are well defined.

For example, if we consider the factorial function

fact(0) = 1
fact(n) = n*fact(n−1)

we can show immediately by induction that the function fact is defined for all positive integers.

- fact(0) is defined and its value is 1.

- For every integer n, if fact(n) is defined then fact(n+1) is also defined and its value is (n+1)*fact(n).

Likewise for functions operating on a data type with constructors and for which recursive calls occur on a substructure of the initial value. For example, if we consider the function

#let rec mir = **fun**
   Empty → Empty
| (Bin(a_1,a_2)) → Bin(mir a_2, mir a_1);;

we can show immediately by induction on the type btree that the function mir is defined everywhere.

- mir(Empty) is well defined and its value is Empty.

- For every pair of trees (t_1, t_2), if mir(t_1) and mir(t_2) are defined then the value of mir(Bin(t_1, t_2)) is also defined.

This kind of definition is attached to the class of recursive primitive definitions. Their termination is practically evident from their construction.

In other situations, we can prove termination by highlighting the decrease in an argument of the function, where the decrease is characterized by an order relation that does not tolerate infinitely decreasing sequences. Such an order relation is known as well founded.

For example, in this exponent program, the exponent strictly decreases in order over the integers at every call because it is divided by two.

#let rec exp (m,n) = **match** n **with**
   0 → 1
| n → exp(m*m,n/2) * (**if** (n mod 2) = 1 **then** m **else** 1);;

That fact joined with the case $n = 0$ ensures termination for all positive n.

Among the well founded orders useful for proving certain properties about termination, we should also mention lexicographically defined orders on a Cartesian product. Given two orders $<_1$ and $<_2$ on two sets E_1 and E_2, the **lexicographic order** $<$ on $E_1 \times E_2$ defined by the two orders $<_1$ and $<_2$ is defined as:

$$(x, y) < (x', y') \text{ if and only if } x <_1 x' \text{ or } (x = x' \text{ and } y <_2 y')$$

It is easy to verify that if the orders $<_1$ and $<_2$ are well founded, then the order $<$ is well founded, too.

We can use lexicographic order, for example, on pairs of natural numbers to prove the termination of the following function, known as Ackerman's function:

```
#let rec ack = fun
   (0,n) → n+1
 | (m,0) → ack(m−1, 1)
 | (m,n) → ack(m−1, ack(m, n−1));;
```

Here is the main idea behind the proof: given a well founded order relation $<$ on a set E, to show a property $\forall x \, P(x)$, it suffices to show

$$(\forall y < x \; P(y)) \implies P(x)$$

Consequently, to show that the computation of $\mathsf{ack}(m, n)$ terminates for a pair (m, n) of natural numbers, it suffices to show that fact under the hypothesis that $\mathsf{ack}(m', n')$ terminates for all pairs (m', n') less than (m, n). In the case where m and n are different from 0, we can use the fact that $(m, n − 1)$ is less than (m, n) to conclude that the computation of $\mathsf{ack}(m, n − 1)$ terminates. If we then call p the value of that expression, we can once again use the fact that the pair $(m − 1, p)$ is less than (m, n) to conclude that the computation of $\mathsf{ack}(m − 1, p)$ also terminates and as a consequence the computation of $\mathsf{ack}(m, n)$ terminates as well. We have thus established that the function ack is total on natural numbers.

Now we will go on to prove properties of programs.

3.4.6   First Example: Mirror Image of Trees

Let's assume we are given these CAML declarations:

```
#type btree = Empty | Bin of btree * btree;;
```

```
#let rec mir = fun
   Empty → Empty
 | (Bin(a₁,a₂)) → Bin(mir a₂, mir a₁);;
```

Two equalities correspond to that program:

- mir(Empty) = Empty

- mir(Bin(a_1, a_2)) = Bin(mir(a_2), mir(a_1))

They will be used in the proofs.

Let's consider the property $\forall a \; P(a)$ where $P(a) \equiv (\text{mir}(\text{mir}(a)) = a)$.

To show that, it suffices to verify that:

1. $P(\text{Empty})$

2. $\forall a_1, a_2 \quad P(a_1) \& P(a_2) \implies P(\text{Bin}(a_1, a_2))$

Proof of $P(\text{Empty})$:

$$\text{mir}(\text{mir}(\text{Empty})) = \text{mir}(\text{Empty}) = \text{Empty}$$

Proof of $\forall a_1, a_2 \; (P(a_1) \& P(a_2) \implies P(\text{Bin}(a_1, a_2)))$

$$
\begin{aligned}
\text{mir}(\text{mir}(\text{Bin}(a_1, a_2))) & \\
= \text{mir}(\text{Bin}(\text{mir}(a_2), \text{mir}(a_1))) & \qquad \text{(definition of mir)} \\
= \text{Bin}(\text{mir}(\text{mir}(a_1)), \text{mir}(\text{mir}(a_2))) & \qquad \text{(definition of mir)} \\
= \text{Bin}(a_1, a_2) & \qquad \text{(hypothesis about recursion)}
\end{aligned}
$$

Notice that even if the initial type is modified to introduce parameters, the proof remains essentially the same.

```
#type (α,β) btree = Leaf of α | Node of β * btree * btree;;
#let rec mir = fun
   Leaf a → Leaf a
 | (Node(b,a₁,a₂)) → Node(b,mir a₂, mir a₁);;
```

The formula to prove simply becomes:

$$\forall x \; P(\text{Leaf}(x)) \; \& \; \forall a_1, a_2 \; (P(a_1) \& P(a_2) \implies \forall y \; P(\text{Node}(y, a_1, a_2)))$$

3.4.7   Second Example: Associativity of **append**

```
#let rec append = fun
   ([ ],l) → l
 | (a::l,l') → a::append(l,l');;
```

Here we want to establish the associativity of the function append; that is, we want to prove the property

$$\forall l_1 \ l_2 \ l_3 \ \ P(l_1, l_2, l_3)$$

where $P(l_1, l_2, l_3) \equiv \text{append}(l_1, \text{append}(l_2, l_3)) = \text{append}(\text{append}(l_1, l_2), l_3)$.

To do so, we will show

$$\forall l_2 \ l_3 \ \ (P([], l_2, l_3) \ \& \ \forall l \ (P(l, l_2, l_3) \implies \forall a \ P(a :: l, l_2, l_3)))$$

Proof of $P([], l_2, l_3)$:

$$\begin{aligned}
&\text{append}([], \text{append}(l_2, l_3)) \\
&= \text{append}(l_2, l_3) && \text{(definition of append)} \\
&= \text{append}(\text{append}([], l_2), l_3) && \text{(definition of append)}
\end{aligned}$$

Proof of $\forall l \ (P(l, l_2, l_3) \implies \forall a \ P(a :: l, l_2, l_3)))$:

$$\begin{aligned}
&\text{append}(a :: l, \text{append}(l_2, l_3)) \\
&= a :: \text{append}(l, \text{append}(l_2, l_3)) && \text{(definition of append)} \\
&= a :: \text{append}(\text{append}(l, l_2), l_3) && \text{(induction hypothesis)} \\
&= \text{append}(a :: \text{append}(l, l_2), l_3) && \text{(definition of append)} \\
&= \text{append}(\text{append}(a :: l, l_2), l_3) && \text{(definition of append)}
\end{aligned}$$

3.4.8 Example: Using Generalization

The example that follows shows that in certain cases, it may be necessary to prove a more general property than the one we want.

Consider the following two functions:

```
#let rec fact = fun
   0 → 1
 | n → n*fact(n−1);;

#let rec facti = fun
   (0,r) → r
 | (n,r) → facti(n−1,n*r);;
```

We want to establish the property $\forall n \ \text{fact}(n) = \text{facti}(n, 1)$. If we try to show that directly by induction on the integer n, we get this:

- $\text{fact}(0) = 1 = \text{facti}(0, 1)$

- $\text{fact}(n + 1) = (n + 1) * \text{fact}(n) = (n + 1) * \text{facti}(n, 1) = ?$

In fact, we must establish a more general property:

$$\forall n \ \forall r \ \ r * \mathsf{fact}(n) = \mathsf{facti}(n, r)$$

Proof:

- $r * \mathsf{fact}(0) = r * 1 = r = \mathsf{facti}(0, r)$

- $r * \mathsf{fact}(n+1) = (r * (n+1)) * \mathsf{fact}(n) = \mathsf{facti}(n, r * (n+1)) = \mathsf{facti}(n+1, r)$

3.4.9   Example: Using Lemmas

The next example shows that in certain cases, it may be necessary to use auxiliary lemmas.

Consider the function

```
#let rec rev =
   fun [ ] → [ ]
    |  (a::l) → append(rev l,[ a ]);;
```

We want to show $\forall l \ \mathsf{rev}(\mathsf{rev}(l)) = l$. The case of the empty list $\mathsf{rev}(\mathsf{rev}([\ ])=[\ ]$ is obvious. In contrast, a direct attempt to show

$$\forall l \ (\mathsf{rev}(\mathsf{rev}(l) = l \ \implies \ \forall a \ \mathsf{rev}(\mathsf{rev}(a :: l)) = a :: l)$$

gives us

$$\mathsf{rev}(\mathsf{rev}(a :: l)) \ = \ \mathsf{rev}(\mathsf{append}(l, [a])) \ = \ ?$$

Consequently, we have to articulate and prove a property connecting the two functions **rev** and **append**. We take $\forall l_1, l_2 \ Q(l_1, l_2)$ where

$$Q(l_1, l_2) \ \equiv \ \mathsf{rev}(\mathsf{append}(l_1, l_2)) = \mathsf{append}(\mathsf{rev}(l_2), \mathsf{rev}(l_1))$$

We will establish successively

$$\mathsf{rev}(\mathsf{append}([], l_2)) = \mathsf{append}(\mathsf{rev}(l_2), \mathsf{rev}([]))$$

and

$$(\mathsf{rev}(\mathsf{append}(l, l_2)) = \mathsf{append}(\mathsf{rev}(l_2), \mathsf{rev}(l)))$$
$$\implies \ \forall a \ (\mathsf{rev}(\mathsf{append}(a :: l, l_2)) = \mathsf{append}(\mathsf{rev}(l_2), \mathsf{rev}(a :: l)))$$

$$
\begin{aligned}
&\mathsf{rev}(\mathsf{append}([], l_2)) \\
&\quad = \mathsf{rev}(l_2) &&\text{(definition of append)} \\
&\quad = \mathsf{append}([], \mathsf{rev}(l_2)) &&\text{(definition of append)} \\
&\quad = \mathsf{append}(\mathsf{rev}([]), \mathsf{rev}(l_2)) &&\text{(definition of rev)}
\end{aligned}
$$

$$\begin{aligned}
\mathsf{rev}(\mathsf{append}(a :: l, l_2)) & \\
= \mathsf{rev}(a :: \mathsf{append}(l, l_2)) & \text{(definition of } \mathsf{append}) \\
= \mathsf{append}(\mathsf{rev}(\mathsf{append}(l, l_2)), [a]) & \text{(definition of } \mathsf{rev}) \\
= \mathsf{append}(\mathsf{append}(\mathsf{rev}(l_2), \mathsf{rev}(l))), [a]) & \text{(hypothesis about recursion)} \\
= \mathsf{append}(\mathsf{rev}(l_2), \mathsf{append}(\mathsf{rev}(l), [a])) & \text{(associativity of } \mathsf{append}) \\
= \mathsf{append}(\mathsf{rev}(l_2), \mathsf{rev}(a :: l)) & \text{(definition of } \mathsf{rev})
\end{aligned}$$

Once we have established the lemma, we can then establish $\forall l \ \mathsf{rev}(\mathsf{rev}(l)) = l$:

$$\begin{aligned}
\mathsf{rev}(\mathsf{rev}(a :: l)) & \\
= \mathsf{rev}(\mathsf{append}(\mathsf{rev}(l), [a])) & \text{(definition of } \mathsf{rev}) \\
= \mathsf{append}(\mathsf{rev}([a]), \mathsf{rev}(\mathsf{rev}(l))) & \text{(property Q)} \\
= \mathsf{append}(\mathsf{rev}([a]), l) & \text{(hypothesis about recursion)} \\
= \mathsf{append}(\mathsf{append}(\mathsf{rev}([]), [a]), l) & \text{(definition of } \mathsf{rev}) \\
= \mathsf{append}(\mathsf{append}([], [a]), l) & \text{(definition of } \mathsf{rev}) \\
= \mathsf{append}([a], l) & \text{(definition of } \mathsf{append}) \\
= a :: \mathsf{append}([], l) & \text{(definition of } \mathsf{append}) \\
= a :: l & \text{(definition of } \mathsf{append})
\end{aligned}$$

3.4.10 Example: Proof under Hypothesis or Proof by Assumption

Let's consider two iterative functions on lists, it_list and list_it, for which we will use the following definitions:

```
#let rec it_list f x = fun
    [ ] → x
  | (a::l) → it_list f (f x a) l;;

#let rec list_it f l x =
  match l with [ ] → x
             | (a::l) → f a (list_it f l x);;
```

These functions have been Curryfied, and they each have a parameter that is a function, but as we have seen before, that will not change the way we go about the proof.

We will show that if the function f passed as a parameter is associative and has a neutral element e, then we have this:

$$\forall l \ \mathsf{it\_list} \ f \ e \ l = \mathsf{list\_it} \ f \ l \ e$$

We have

$$\begin{aligned}
\mathsf{it\_list} \ f \ e \ (a :: l) &= \mathsf{it\_list} \ f \ (f \ e \ a) \ l & \text{(definition of } \mathsf{it\_list}) \\
&= \mathsf{it\_list} \ f \ a \ l & \text{(neutral elt)}
\end{aligned}$$

and

$$\text{list\_it } f \ (a :: l) \ e \ = f \ a \ (\text{list\_it } f \ l \ e) \quad \text{(definition of list\_it)}$$

We can prove it by induction if we can establish by example the property

$$\forall x \ \forall l \ \ f \ x \ (\text{it\_list } f \ e \ l) = \text{it\_list } f \ x \ l$$

We have:

$$
\begin{aligned}
f \ x \ (\text{it\_list } f \ e \ []) \ &= f \ x \ e && \text{(def. it\_list)} \\
&= x && \text{(neutral elt.)} \\
&= \text{it\_list } f \ x \ [] && \text{(def. it\_list)}
\end{aligned}
$$

and

$$
\begin{aligned}
f \ x \ (\text{it\_list } f \ e \ (a :: l)) \\
&= f \ x \ (\text{it\_list } f \ (f \ e \ a) \ l) && \text{(definition of it\_list)} \\
&= f \ x \ (\text{it\_list } f \ a \ l) && \text{(neutral elt)} \\
&= f \ x \ (f \ a \ (\text{it\_list } f \ e \ l)) && \text{(induction hypothesis)} \\
&= f \ (f \ x \ a)(\text{it\_list } f \ e \ l) && \text{(associativity of f)} \\
&= \text{it\_list } f \ (f \ x \ a) \ l && \text{(induction hypothesis)} \\
&= \text{it\_list } f \ x \ (a :: l) && \text{(definition of it\_list)}
\end{aligned}
$$

Exercises

3.1 Consider the two functions

```
#let rec iter₁ n f =
  if n=0 then I else compose f (iter₁ (n−1) f);;

#let rec iter₂ n f x =
  if n=0 then x else f(iter₂ (n−1) f x);;
```

Show that the function exp defined by

```
#let rec exp a n =
  if n=0 then 1. else
  (if (n mod 2) = 0 then 1. else a) *. exp (a*a) (n/2);;
```

computes a^n.

3.2 Show that the function map defined on page 60 and the one defined by means of list_hom on page 61 are equivalent.

3.3 Show the correctness of the function quicksort defined on page 63.

3.5   Typing Expressions

When we defined computations in terms of rewrite rules, we made the implicit hypothesis that the expressions the rewrite rules worked on were typed. More precisely, we actually made two hypotheses:

- The expressions to evaluate are well typed.

- If an expression E is well typed and $E \Rightarrow E'$, then E' is also well typed.

These hypotheses have consequences. In particular, when an expression appearing in the course of a computation is an application of a basic operator, its arguments are valid types, and the application of this operator can be carried out. In sum, evaluation will not produce type errors.

We will not present a formal proof of this property here, but we will indicate how such a proof would be done. First, we have to define precisely how expressions are typed; that is done by means of a system of type rules.

Such a system uses a ternary relation

$$E \vdash e : t$$

which we read like this:

"The expression e is of type t in the type environment E."

A type environment is a function or a table associating types with the variables of a program. Here are the rules for that association:

$$\frac{E(x) = t}{E \vdash x : t} \quad (\text{Var})$$

$$\frac{E \vdash e_1 : t_1 \quad \ldots \quad E \vdash e_n : t_n}{E \vdash (e_1, \ldots, e_n) : (t_1 * \ldots * t_n)} \quad (\text{N-tuplet})$$

$$\frac{E \vdash e_1 : \textbf{bool} \quad E \vdash e_2 : t \quad E \vdash e_3 : t}{E \vdash \textbf{if } e_1 \textbf{ then } e_2 \textbf{ else } e_3 : t} \quad (\text{Cond})$$

$$\frac{(x:t_1)::E \vdash e : t_2}{E \vdash (\textbf{fun } x \to e) : t_1 \to t_2} \quad (\text{Fun})$$

$$\frac{E \vdash e_1 : t \to t' \qquad E \vdash e_2 : t}{E \vdash (e_1\ e_2) : t'} \text{ (App)}$$

We still have a problem with how to take **let** into account because this construction makes it possible to use the same variable with two different types (for example in **let** id=(**fun** x→x) **in** id id).

For now, we will deal with this phenomenon by replacing an expression such as **let** id=(**fun** x→x) **in** id id by (**fun** x→x)(**fun** x→x). That gives us adequate types for the two subexpressions (**fun** x→x). In Chapter 13, we will show you a more efficient way to deal with this issue.

$$\frac{E \vdash e_2[x \leftarrow e_1] : t}{E \vdash \textbf{let } x=e_1 \textbf{ in } e_2 : t} \text{ (Let)}$$

Also, we have to add rules for constants and basic operators, though they present no difficulties.

Here is how we demonstrate the type of the expression **let** id = **fun** x → x **in** id id.

$$\frac{\dfrac{[x{:}\alpha \to \alpha] \vdash x : \alpha \to \alpha}{[\ ] \vdash (\textbf{fun } x \to x) : (\alpha \to \alpha) \to (\alpha \to \alpha)} \qquad \dfrac{[x{:}\alpha\,] \vdash x : \alpha}{[\ ] \vdash (\textbf{fun } x \to x) : (\alpha \to \alpha)}}{\dfrac{[\ ] \vdash (\textbf{fun } x \to x)(\textbf{fun } x \to x) : \alpha \to \alpha}{[\ ] \vdash \textbf{let } id = \textbf{fun } x \to x \textbf{ in } id\ id : \alpha \to \alpha}}$$

This formal definition of types is the basis to establish the property

$$\text{if } (E \vdash e : t) \text{ and } (e \Rightarrow e'), \text{ then } (E \vdash e' : t).$$

3.6 Summary

A **computation** leading from an expression to its value is defined as a sequence of expressions where each one results from the preceding one by the application of a **rewrite rule**. An expression that cannot be rewritten further is said to be in **normal form**. Values are expressions in normal form.

The set of rewrite rules associated with programs form a **convergent** system, defined on page 74. In particular, this property implies that all finite computations associated with an expression terminate at the same normal form, which we consider the **value** of the expression. In that way, we define the **semantics** of the language we are using; that is, we have a formal way of associating a value (possibly undefined) with every expression in the language.

A **computation strategy** is a uniform and deterministic procedure to choose a rewrite rule to apply at each step from among all the possible rules. Strategies can be defined formally by means of **deduction rules**.

We say that a strategy is **complete** if it always leads to the value of an expression, whenever such a value exists. The strategy in CAML—known as evaluation **by value**—is not complete. Other strategies, such as **delayed evaluation**, are complete.

We can carry out proofs about the properties of programs by using rewrite rules such as formal equations and a general recursion principle on data structures. Such proofs establish partial correctness, so they must be accompanied by a proof of termination to estabish total correctness.

The formal definition of types lets us show that any computation starting from a well typed expression will produce only well typed expressions in turn. Static type synthesis thus guarantees the absence of type errors at execution.

3.7   To Learn More

The definition of a computation as a sequence of rewritten expressions and the idea of convergence were first used in the context of λ-calculus [5]. The idea of convergence also plays an important role in systems of automatic proof based on first order equational logic.

The kind of semantics we presented in this chapter can be qualified as **operational semantics**. It exploits mainly syntactic concepts. In particular, functions are handled in this context as texts within a mechanical application syntax, not as true functions in the mathematical sense.

In contrast, **denotational semantics** associates veritable mathematical objects with expressions in programs. The mathematician Dana Scott initiated this kind of semantics. He was the first to provide a model of expressions from λ-calculus based on the ideas of a **complete partially ordered set**, or **CPO**, and the continuous functions over such sets. The most accessible reference about denotational semantics is [15]. You might also consult [37] and [41].

A great deal of research has been devoted to proving the correctness of programs. As far as the correctness of functional programs, we should cite, among the most venerable, the system LCF from Milner [16, 30] and the system of Boyer and Moore [8].

Current research is oriented toward the development of systems based on constructive logic and the analogy between proofs and programs, both coded in a typed, higher order λ-calculus that allows the construction of only programs that terminate. An example of a system based on this approach is Coq [18].

About evaluation strategies, you can see two different approaches in existing languages. Languages in the ML family or languages such as SCHEME chose evaluation by value in a way that allows the use of non-functional constructions. Other languages chose delayed evaluation, also often called "lazy" evaluation. This is the case, for example, in the languages MIRANDA or HASKELL.

Chapter 4

Imperative Aspects

All those aspects of CAML that cannot be described in a purely functional view of the language are known as its **imperative** qualities

- either because they make sense only with respect to a particular evaluation strategy,

- or because they refer to the machine representation of data structures.

Among the imperative aspects of that first kind, there are exceptions and input-output.

Among the second kind of imperative aspects, we find **destructive** operations such as assignment. The effect of such operations can be explained completely only by reference to formal semantics or to a description of the implementation of data structures. (We will get to those ideas later in Chapter 12.) However, we can still give you a reasonable description here based on examples.

4.1   Exceptions

In Section 2.3.4, we touched on the problem of writing partial functions. To do that, we introduced the type

#type α option = None | Some **of** α;;

This solution can hardly take into account all the situations where we need partial functions. For example, division is a partial operation (since division by 0 (zero) is not defined), but it would not be practical to replace the types int and float by the types int option and float option in every numeric calculation because doing so assumes that all arithmetic operations foresee the case where one of their arguments is undefined. The chief effect of that assumption would be to make numeric calculations impractical simply because they would be too inefficient to perform!

Incidentally, when division by 0 occurs during a computation, there is no need to go on with it since it clearly does not lead to a result.

Rather, we will use instead the idea of **exceptions** to take into account any exceptional situations that arise during a calculation, including those that come from causes outside the calculation.

During evaluation, exceptions behave quite differently from other values.

4.1.1   Examples of Exceptions

Exceptions appear in CAML in many situations; for example, at division by 0 (zero)

```
#2+(1/0)* 3;;
Uncaught exception: Division_by_zero
```

or during an attempt to access the first element of an empty list

```
#hd [ ];;
Uncaught exception: Failure "hd"
```

When the system cannot recover from these exceptions (recovery will be explained shortly), they appear at the level of the interaction loop (also known as *toplevel*) as a message including the name of the exception (for example Division_by_zero or Failure) and possibly an associated value ("**hd**" in the second example).

4.1.2   Defining Exceptions

The set of exceptions defined at a given moment in the system make up a special type exn for which the constructors are the names of the exceptions. In particular, the type exn provided by CAML thus includes the constructors

```
type exn  =
     . . .
     | Division_by_zero
     | Failure of string
     | . . .
```

In contrast to ordinary types, the type exn can be extended. As a user, you can add constructors to it, so you might write this:

```
#exception Int_exception of int;;
Exception Int_exception defined.
```

which has the effect of adding a case to the definition of the type exn which then becomes this:

```
type exn =
    ...
    | Division_by_zero
    | Failure of string
    | Int_exception of int
    | ...
```

4.1.3 Creating an Exceptional Value

When we use them in an ordinary way, values of type exn behave in an ordinary way.

```
#Failure "oops";;
− : exn = Failure "oops"
```

They behave "exceptionally" only when we apply the function **raise** to them.

```
#raise (Failure "oops");;
Uncaught exception: Failure "oops"
```

Here, for example, is how to define a function hd with exactly the same behavior as the one provided by the system.

```
#let hd = fun
    [ ] → raise(Failure "hd")
  | (a::l) → a;;
hd : α list → α = ⟨fun⟩
```

When an exception has been triggered by means of the construction **raise** and the mechanism described in the next section has not been able to recover from it, then the exception appears at *toplevel*.

```
#hd [ ];;
Uncaught exception: Failure "hd"
```

4.1.4 Filtering Exceptional Values

As a user, you can recover from exceptions triggered by **raise**. To do so, you use the construction **try−with**. Its complete syntax looks like this:

try e **with** $p_1 \rightarrow e_1$
$\qquad$ | ...
$\qquad$ | $p_n \rightarrow e_n$

The value of such an expression is computed first by evaluating the expression e. If that evaluation proceeds normally to a value v, then the result of the entire expression is v. If the computation of e produces an exceptional value, then the set of patterns $p_1, \ldots, p_n$ (which should all be of type exn) is used to filter this exceptional value. If p_i is the first pattern to match this value, then the result of the entire expression is e_i. If no pattern matches the exceptional value, then the exception will be propagated outside the **try—with** expression.

For example, we can filter the exception Division_by_zero, produced by numeric errors, in the following way:

```
#try 1/0 with Division_by_zero → 0;;
− : int = 0
```

When the expression 1/0 is evaluated, the computation is interrupted, and the result is the exceptional value Division_by_zero. This value is then filtered by the pattern Division_by_zero, so the final result is 0.

4.1.5 Using Exceptions

Of course, exceptions serve in particular to foresee cases of failure in certain functions.

```
#let rec find p = fun
    [ ] → raise (Failure "find")
  | (a::l) → if p a then a else find p l;;
find : (α → bool) → α list → α = ⟨fun⟩

#find (fun x → x mod 2 = 0) [3; 1; 7; 8; 13; 14];;
− : int = 8

#find (fun x → x mod 2 = 0) [3; 1; 7; 13];;
Uncaught exception: Failure "find"
```

They can also be used in the sort of positive situations that we will see more of later.

Notice the predefined function failwith, that we could define by:

```
#let failwith msg =
    raise (Failure msg);;
failwith : string → α = ⟨fun⟩
```

Exercise

4.1 Look again at the type α tree defined on page 54. Write a function of type $((\alpha \to \alpha \to bool) \to \alpha$ tree $\to \alpha)$ to search a binary tree for an element with a given property. First write this function without exceptions; then rewrite it to raise an exception when the target element has been found. If you encapsulate the call to this function in the construction **try–with**, you can even return the target result.

4.2 Input and Output

Input and output operations make interaction possible, interaction either between a program and its user, or between a program and the operating system on the machine where it is executing so that it can save information in files, for example.

In modern operating systems, input and output are seen uniformly as reads or writes on **channels** connected either to the keyboard and screen of the machine, or to files. Here we are going to look particularly at the interaction channels std_in and std_out corresponding to the keyboard and screen.

When we get into input and output operations, we necessarily leave behind the world of pure evaluation and enter the world of action, introducing a temporal dimension into programming. Certain actions will necessarily be carried out before others. For that reason, we have to introduce the idea of a sequence into the language.

4.2.1 Sequence

In CAML, a sequence of instructions is separated by a semi-colon, as it is in most programming languages. The semantics of an expression $(e_1; e_2)$ is defined by the rule

$$\frac{\vdash e_1 \Rightarrow v_1 \qquad \vdash e_2 \Rightarrow v_2}{\vdash (e_1; e_2) \Rightarrow v_2} \text{ (Seq)}$$

That is, the value of $(e_1; e_2)$ is the value of e_2. From a purely functional point of view, that construction does not make much sense.

In contrast, things go differently if the language includes exceptions. In the presence of exceptions, this construction behaves differently, according to these two rules:

$$\frac{\vdash e_1 \Rightarrow (\text{exn } v_1 \text{ raised})}{\vdash (e_1; e_2) \Rightarrow (\text{exn } v_1 \text{ raised})} \text{ (Seqexn1)}$$

$$\frac{\vdash e_1 \Rightarrow v_1 \qquad \vdash e_2 \Rightarrow (\text{exn } v_2 \text{ raised})}{\vdash (e_1; e_2) \Rightarrow (\text{exn } v_2 \text{ raised})} \text{ (Seqexn2)}$$

The occurrence of an exception in e_1 is consequently significant in the evaluation of $(e_1; e_2)$. Moreover, this construction takes on its full meaning when the expressions e_1 and e_2 have an **effect**, as is the case for i/o functions.

4.2.2   The Type unit

When we consider i/o functions, we also face the problem of how to determine the type of functions that have no arguments or no return values. For example, the function read_int which reads an integer from standard input (the keyboard, say) has no argument. We could, of course, make up a function of type $\alpha \rightarrow$ int that takes anything as its argument, but it would not really be very natural to do so.

In this kind of situation, we use the CAML type unit, a type with one value denoted (). The function read_int will thus be of type unit $\rightarrow$ int.

The function print_int to print an integer on screen will be of type int $\rightarrow$ unit.

4.2.3   I/O Functions

The input and output functions of CAML work on channels of type in_channel (obviously the input channel) or out_channel (the output). The names of input and output functions are prefixed by input or output.

```
output_char : out_channel → char → unit
output_string : out_channel → string → unit
input_char : in_channel → char
input_line : in_channel → string
```

The i/o channels can be created, for example, when files are opened by these functions:

```
open_in : string → in_channel
open_out : string → out_channel
```

For example, to write the string "hello" in the file temp, we do this:

```
#let ch= open_out "temp" in
  output_string ch "hello"; close_out ch;;
```

Incidentally, there are specific functions to read or write standard i/o channels (the keyboard and screen), for example:

```
read_line : unit → string
read_int : unit → int
print_string : string → unit
print_int : int → unit
print_newline : unit → unit
```

4.2.4 Example: Print Function

Here is a print function for the type inttree defined on page 52:

```
#let rec print_inttree = fun
    (Leaf n) → print_int n
  | (Node(t₁,t₂))
    → print_string "("; print_inttree t₁; print_string ",";
        print_inttree t₂; print_string ")";;
print_inttree : inttree → unit = ⟨fun⟩
```

CAML lets you replace the standard print function for any type by a user-defined function. For example:

```
#new_printer "inttree" print_inttree;;
− : unit = ()

#Node(Leaf 3,Node(Leaf 4,Leaf 5));;
− : inttree = (3,(4,5))
```

4.2.5 Example: Interaction

Here is a little interactive program to compute grades on an examination. The system asks the user for the score on the written exam and the score on the oral exam; then it displays the final grade as computed by the function f passed as a parameter.

```
#let sentence f =
    print_string "Written score: ";
    let n₁ = float_of_string(read_line()) in
    print_string "Oralscore: ";
    let n₂ = float_of_string(read_line()) in
    f(n₁,n₂);;
sentence : (float * float → α) → α = ⟨fun⟩
```

Here is an example of how it is used:

```
#sentence (fun (x,y) →
                  let m = (x +. y) /. 2.0 in
                  print_string (if m >. 10.0 then "RECEIVED"
                                  else "ADJOURNED");
                  print_newline());;
Written score : 13
Oral score: 15
RECEIVED
- : unit = ()
```

When we use sequencing (;), we are sometimes surprised by the precedence rules that CAML invokes. For example, the expression (if t then e₁ else e₂;e₃) is analyzed as (if t then e₁ else e₂); e₃. If we want the expression e₃ not to be evaluated unless t is false, then we must write **if** t **then** e₁ **else** (e₂; e₃) or equivalently **if** t **then** e₁ **else begin** e₂; e₃ **end**.

Generally, the keywords **begin** and **end** can be used in CAML anywhere that parentheses can, but they are really meant for use in imperative programs.

Exercise
4.2 Write a function to solve a second degree equation; make it display messages indicating the number of solutions and their values.

4.3   Character Streams

In many applications, we want to analyze the character streams appearing in an input channel. To do so, we can retrieve this stream in the form of a CAML value of type char stream.

The type α stream can match patterns so it is very easy to program functions for analyzing a stream. This way of using pattern matching on streams is described in greater detail in Chapter 8.

4.3.1   Constructing Streams

At first glance, streams can be regarded as lists. In contrast to lists, however, the interaction loop in CAML does not print streams.

Like the empty list, there is an empty stream:

```
#[⟨ ⟩];;
- : α stream = ⟨abstract⟩
```

There are also streams that have elements. Here is a stream with three elements:

```
#[⟨ ''a'; ''b'; ''c' ⟩];;
− : char stream = ⟨abstract⟩
```

That last expression is similar to this list of three elements:

```
#[ 'a'; 'b'; 'c' ];;
− : char list = [ 'a'; 'b'; 'c' ]
```

You see, then, that syntactically elements of a stream are preceded by an apostrophe. These elements can not be constants, but they are generally the values of arbitrary expressions. For example:

```
#let n = 0 in
  [⟨ ' n+1; ' n+2; ' n+3 ⟩];;
− : int stream = ⟨abstract⟩
```

is the stream of integers consisting of the elements 1, 2, and 3.

Starting from existing streams, we can, of course, build new ones. For example:

```
#let s₁ = [⟨ ''a'; ''b'; ''c' ⟩] in
  [⟨ ''0'; s₁ ⟩];;
− : char stream = ⟨abstract⟩
```

represents the stream containing the element '0' as its first one, followed by the elements of s_1.

In the same way, we can construct the stream

```
#let s₁ = [⟨ ''a'; ''b'; ''c' ⟩] in
  let s₂ = [⟨ ''d'; ''e'; ''f' ⟩] in
  [⟨ s₁; ''0'; s₂ ⟩];;
− : char stream = ⟨abstract⟩
```

where the elements are from s_1, followed by the character '0', and then those from s_2.

Thus streams seem to be data structures that look like lists, but differ in these points:

- their value is not printed by the interaction loop;

- they are constructed by adding elements one by one (each added element is preceded by an apostrophe) or by concatenating substreams (which are in fact expressions, not preceded by an apostrophe).

Nevertheless, streams and lists are fundamentally different. Their primary difference is that the elements of streams are evaluated on demand; that is, they are subject to "lazy" evaluation. We use pattern matching, as you will see later, to make such a demand.

More precisely, when this list

```
#[1 ; (print_string "Hello\n"; 2); 3];;
Hello
- : int list = [1; 2; 3]
```

is evaluated, it provokes a side-effect printing the message `Hello`. In contrast, the evaluation of the corresponding stream

```
#[⟨ '1 ; '(print_string "Hello\n"; 2); '3 ⟩];;
- : int stream = ⟨abstract⟩
```

has no side-effects. The message `Hello` appears only when we consult the second element of the stream (or one of the later elements) and it never appears if the stream is not examined from its second element. Once again, we emphasize that we can examine the stream that way from its second element only if we try pattern matching, as you will see later.

Another example is the infinite stream of integers. We define it like this:

```
#let ints =
   let rec ints_from n = [⟨ 'n; ints_from (n+1) ⟩] in
   ints_from 0;;
ints : int stream = ⟨abstract⟩
```

The function `ints_from`, given an integer n, builds a stream of which the first element is n and the rest is the stream produced by the recursive call `ints_from` (n+1). If we were to try to evaluate all the elements of the stream we get that way, the evaluation would never terminate. The "laziness" in the way we construct streams protects this evaluation from that fate, and it lets us get a stream that is potentially infinite, yet we can examine its elements one by one, as long as we do not try to get the whole stream at once.

These characteristics of the way streams are constructed were designed to resemble input channels in CAML. An input channel, for example the channel `std_in` corresponding to the keyboard, can be regarded as an infinite stream of characters constructed on demand, that is, during reads, thus forcing the user to enter one or more characters. If we regard them as made up of an infinite number of characters, input channels are thus also "lazy." The following predefined function makes it possible to treat input channels as streams:

```
stream_of_channel : in_channel → char stream
```

Let's continue the analogy between streams and input channels (and their read functions). In that context, another important characteristic of streams is their imperative aspect. More precisely, if we see input channels as composed of a certain number of characters (a finite number in the case of a channel opened for a file, for example), when a character is read, it is removed from the channel, and another read will get the following character.

Likewise, when an element of a stream is accessed, it is *physically removed* from the corresponding stream. Reading streams is accomplished by pattern matching. Such pattern matching can be used only with the constructions **function** and **match—with**. The patterns here are patterns for streams; their syntax is similar to expressions for streams. Intuitively, a pattern for a stream tries to match an *initial segment* of the stream. For example, we could define a function read to return the first element of its argument, a stream, in this way:

#let read = **function** $[\langle\, 'x\, \rangle] \to x$;;
read : α *stream* $\to \alpha = \langle$**fun**$\rangle$

If we carry out many successive reads on the stream of integers that we defined earlier, we notice the imperative aspect of streams: every read produces a different element because earlier reads remove elements from the stream—the elements they read.

#read ints;;
$-$: *int* = 0

#read ints;;
$-$: *int* = 1

#read ints;;
$-$: *int* = 2

One pattern to match an initial segment of a stream is the empty pattern; it accepts any stream, empty or not.

#match $[\langle\, '1;\, '2;\, '3\, \rangle]$ **with** $[\langle\, \rangle] \to$ true;;
$-$: *bool* = *true*

In that case, the stream is not modified, though it is matched.

Granted, these examples are simple, and granted that the purpose of pattern matching for streams is to make it easy to program syntactic analyzers, the semantics of pattern matching for streams is relatively complicated. Here we have used simple examples to give you insight into the topic, but if you want to exploit its full power, then you should look at Section 8.5 where pattern matching for streams is presented in the context of syntactic analysis.

4.4   Modifiable Data Structures

CAML allows you to modify such data structures as vectors, records, references, circular lists, and doubly-linked lists. This section explores the implications of this facility.

4.4.1   Vectors

Vectors are data structures that simultaneously look like tuples and lists.

- Vectors are objects of type α vect. Like lists, they can contain only objects of the same type. They can be any length.

- The type α vect does not support an operation that resembles cons (::) for lists. Like tuples, vectors are constructed only once in a single operation, and they cannot be extended afterwards. The vector containing the values $e_1, \ldots, e_n$ is denoted as $[| e_1; \ldots; e_n |]$.

- We access elements of a vector by **rank** or index. The rank of elements in a vector of length n must lie between 0 (zero) and $(n-1)$, inclusive. Given a vector v and a rank p, we denote access to the element at that rank by v.(p). Accessing an element of a vector takes constant time, and little time at that, because elements of a vector are organized sequentially in memory; the address of each element can thus be computed simply by adding its rank to the address of the first element.

- The elements of a vector can be modified.

If we organize an array of elements into a vector of elements in increasing order, it is possible to test whether an element belongs to the array in time proportional to the logarithm of the size of the array. To do so, we simply conduct a binary search, like this:

```
#let mem_vect c e v =
   let rec find m n =
     if m > n then false else
     let p = (m+n)/2 in
     if v.(p) = e then true else
     if c (v.(p)) e then find (p+1) n
     else find m (p−1)
   in find 0 (vect_length v);;
 mem_vect : (α → α → bool) → α → α vect → bool = ⟨fun⟩
```

```
#mem_vect (prefix <) 7 [| 2; 3; 5; 6; 7; 10; 12; 15 |];;
- : bool = true
```

The elements of a vector can be modified by assignment. To replace the ith element of a vector v by the value of an expression e, we write

$$v.(i) \leftarrow e$$

```
#let v = [| 0;1;2;3 |];;
v : int vect = [| 0; 1; 2; 3 |]

#v.(1) ← 7;;
- : unit = ()

#v;;
- : int vect = [| 0; 7; 2; 3 |]
```

Of course, that operation breaks away completely from the programming style we have maintained up to now. In effect, we have always considered that after having executed a definition of the form **let** v=e, the variable v and the expression e are totally interchangeable, notably in proofs about the correctness of programs. That is no longer the case with assignment, as the previous example clearly shows. The implications of this change will be discussed in greater depth later in Section 4.5.

Since assignment is available to us now, obviously we can program in the same style as PASCAL or C. In that spirit, here is a function that exchanges the elements at ranks i and j in a vector v.

```
#let swap v i j=
   let x = v.(i) in
   begin
     v.(i) ← v.(j);
     v.(j)← x
   end;;
swap : α vect → int → int → unit = ⟨fun⟩
```

Here is a version of the quicksort algorithm to order the elements of a vector. It uses only swaps between elements. The function place partitions the region [i,j] in the vector v by using the element v.(i) as a pivot.

```
#let place c v i j =
   place_rec (i+1) j
   where rec place_rec i' j' =
     let rec move_right p =
```

```
      if c (v.(i)) (v.(p)) or p=j' then p else move_right (p+1)
    and move_left p =
      if c (v.(p)) (v.(i)) or p=i' then p else move_left (p−1) in
    let k = move_right i' and l = move_left j' in
    if k>l then (swap v i l; l) else
    if k=l then
      if c (v.(l)) (v.(i)) then (swap v i l; l) else i
    else (swap v k l; place_rec (k+1) (l−1));;
```
place : $(\alpha \to \alpha \to bool) \to \alpha\ vect \to int \to int \to int = \langle\mathbf{fun}\rangle$

```
#let quicksort c v =
  quick 0 (vect_length v−1)
  where rec quick i j=
    if i<j then
      let p = place c v i j in
      quick i (p−1);
      quick (p+1) j;;
```
quicksort : $(\alpha \to \alpha \to bool) \to \alpha\ vect \to unit = \langle\mathbf{fun}\rangle$

```
#let v=[| 18; 2; 13; 4; 6; 25; 1; 10; 12; 9; 15; 7; 3 |];;
```
v : *int vect* = $[|\,18; 2; 13; 4; 6; 25; 1; 10; 12; 9; 15; 7; 3\,|]$

```
#quicksort (prefix <) v;;
```
− : *unit* = ()

```
#v;;
```
− : *int vect* = $[|\,1; 2; 3; 4; 6; 7; 9; 10; 12; 13; 15; 18; 25\,|]$

```
#quicksort (prefix >) v;;
```
− : *unit* = ()

```
#v;;
```
− : *int vect* = $[|\,25; 18; 15; 13; 12; 10; 9; 7; 6; 4; 3; 2; 1\,|]$

4.4.2   Records with Modifiable Fields

Just as it is possible to modify the elements of a vector, it is also feasible to modify the fields of a record. In CAML, this is possible if the field has been declared as **mutable** in the declaration of the record.

For example, we can define a type planar_point where the fields xcoord and ycoord are modifiable.

```
#type planar_point = {mutable xcoord: float; mutable ycoord: float};;
```
Type planar_point defined.

The function translate moves a point by changing its components. The function does not create a new point; it modifies the existing one.

```
#let translate (dx,dy) pt =
    pt.xcoord ← pt.xcoord+.dx; pt.ycoord ← pt.ycoord+.dy; pt;;
translate : float * float → planar_point → planar_point = ⟨fun⟩
```

```
#let point= {xcoord=2.0; ycoord=2.0};;
point : planar_point = {xcoord=2; ycoord=2}
```

```
#translate (1.2,2.8) point;;
− : planar_point = {xcoord=3.2; ycoord=4.8}
```

```
#point;;
− : planar_point = {xcoord=3.2; ycoord=4.8}
```

This introduction of modifiable fields gives each record its own independent status. Although in functional programming, two equal values are essentially indistinguishable, in imperative programming, values acquire the status of individualized objects, each one having its own history. In applications that implement a model representing situations in the physical or social world, objects and individuals can thus be represented by a data structure that can evolve as they do.

Undeniably, imperative programming is attractive because it resembles our usual experience of a world shaped from real entities in evolution. In that way, it differs profoundly from the mathematical world where two isomorphic objects are considered interchangeable.

This new point of view about values poses the problem of defining equality. The only equality that we have used so far corresponds to the infix symbol =. It involves a structural equality that explores two values to compare in order to see whether they are effectively equal. For example, two pairs, (a_1,a_2) and (b_1,b_2), are equal if a_1 is equal to b_1 and a_2 is equal to b_2. Likewise, two points, {xcoord=x_1; ycoord=y_1} and {xcoord=x_2; ycoord=y_2}, are equal if x_1 is equal to x_2 and y_1 is equal to y_2.

If we change our point of view and now see each value constructed as an object having its own identity, then we must have a predicate that lets us test whether two values are identical and not only structurally equal. In CAML, this predicate corresponds to the infix symbol ==. Here are a few examples to show how it works.

```
#let pt₁= {xcoord=2.0; ycoord=2.0};;
pt₁ : planar_point = {xcoord=2; ycoord=2}
```

```
#let pt₂= {xcoord=2.0; ycoord=2.0};;
pt₂ : planar_point = {xcoord=2; ycoord=2}

#let pt₃=pt₁;;
pt₃ : planar_point = {xcoord=2; ycoord=2}

#pt₁=pt₂;;
− : bool = true

#pt₁=pt₃;;
− : bool = true

#pt₁==pt₂;;
− : bool = false

#pt₁==pt₃;;
− : bool = true
```

When two values are identical, like pt₁ and pt₃ in the preceding example, every modification of one occurs to the other. However, that is not the case if they are simply equal, like pt₁ and pt₂.

```
#pt₁.xcoord←1.0;;
− : unit = ()

#pt₃;;
− : planar_point = {xcoord=1; ycoord=2}

#pt₂;;
− : planar_point = {xcoord=2; ycoord=2}
```

Each application of a constructor or record construction in CAML creates a new object distinguished by == from all those existing before. In contrast, a link by **let** does not create a new object; it simply provides a new way to name an object that exists already.

In this context, we should note the construction **as** used in CAML patterns. It marks subpatterns that correspond to the parts of the argument that we want to re-use to the right of the arrow. For example, the expression (**fun** ((x,y),z) → (x,y)) can be replaced by (**fun** ((x,y) **as** t,z) → t).

Since we renamed the part (x,y) in the pattern **as** t, we do not have to build a new pair for the result. By using the construction **as**, we save a memory allocation.

Chapter 12 about compilation explains how values are created and linked at the machine level, so that you can understand the structure of values in CAML more deeply.

4.4.3 References

The idea of a **reference** represents in some ways the quintessence of modifiable objects. This idea corresponds to pointers in such languages as PASCAL or C.

We can create a reference to any object by using the constructor **ref** of type $\alpha \to \alpha$ ref.

```
#let c= ref 0;;
c : int ref = ref 0

#let s= ref "hello";;
s : string ref = ref "hello"

#let l= [ref 1; ref 2; ref 3];;
l : int ref list = [ref 1; ref 2; ref 3]
```

The referenced value (that is, the one being pointed to) is accessible with the operator "!".

```
#!c;;
− : int = 0

#!(hd l);;
− : int = 1
```

References can be modified by assignment, denoted by ":=".

```
#c:= !c+3;;
− : unit = ()

#c;;
− : int ref = ref 3

#hd(tl l):=7;;
− : unit = ()

#l;;
− : int ref list = [ref 1; ref 7; ref 3]
```

Among the many applications of the idea of referencing, we should cite the definition of functions with internal state and the construction of graph structures with their arcs and nodes.

In that first category, there is the function **gensym**, defined later. This function to generate symbols is of type unit $\to$ string, and it is defined so that it provides a new character string for each application. It gets that character string by suffixing an integer to the string "ident". This integer is stored by a reference linked to an internal variable of the function, one that is incremented by each call.

```
#let gensym =
   let count = ref (−1) in
   fun () → count := !count + 1;
              "ident" ^ (string_of_int !count);;
```
gensym : unit → string = ⟨**fun**⟩

```
#gensym ();;
```
− : *string =* "ident0"

```
#gensym ();;
```
− : *string =* "ident1"

```
#gensym ();;
```
− : *string =* "ident2"

4.4.4   Circular Lists

In circular lists, the last element contains a reference to the first. An element in such a list is defined as an object of type lnode.

```
#type α lnode = {info: α; mutable next: α lnode};;
```

The function mk_circular_list constructs a circular list from one element, like this:

```
#let mk_circular_list e=
   let rec x={info=e; next=x} in x;;
```
mk_circular_list : α → α lnode = ⟨**fun**⟩

In a circular list of only one element, the first is also the last. For lists of more than one element, by convention we let the point of access be the last element of the list. The functions first and last indicate the first and last elements of the list. They are written like this:

```
#let last ln= ln.info;;
```
last : α lnode → α = ⟨**fun**⟩

```
#let first ln = (ln.next).info;;
```
first : α lnode → α = ⟨**fun**⟩

This way of organizing things enables us to insert elements at the head or tail of the list.

```
#let insert_head e l=
    let x={info=e; next=l.next}
    in l.next←x;l;;
```
$insert\_head : \alpha \rightarrow \alpha \ lnode \rightarrow \alpha \ lnode = \langle \textbf{fun} \rangle$

```
#let insert_tail e l=
    let x={info=e; next=l.next}
    in l.next←x;x;;
```
$insert\_tail : \alpha \rightarrow \alpha \ lnode \rightarrow \alpha \ lnode = \langle \textbf{fun} \rangle$

The element at the head of a circular list can be eliminated by only one assignment operation, like this:

```
#let elim_head l=
    l.next←(l.next).next;l;;
```
$elim\_head : \alpha \ lnode \rightarrow \alpha \ lnode = \langle \textbf{fun} \rangle$

However, you have to be careful that this operation does not eliminate the head of a circular list of only one element. The circular list needs to contain at least two. (This problem is addressed later when we discuss the way queues are implemented.)

Figure 4.1 shows a graphic representation of the value of the expression

```
#let l = mk_circular_list 1
    in list_it insert_tail [5;4;3;2] l;;
- : int lnode
    = {info=5; next={info=1;
                    next={info=2;
                        next={info=3;
                            next={info=4;
                                next={info=5;
                                    next={info= ...;
                                        next= ...}}}}}}}}
```

The first element of the circular list is indicated by an arrow. Careful: remember that list_it handles elements of the list from right to left; that is, the elements are inserted at the tail in the order 2, 3, 4, 5.

We use such lists to implement a **queue** structure; that is, a storage structure that behaves as FIFO (first in, first out). Elements are inserted at the end of the list and retrieved from the head.

The type α queue, defined later, implements queues as a sum type with constructors. The constructor Emptyqueue corresponds to an empty queue, and the constructor Queue to a non-empty queue.

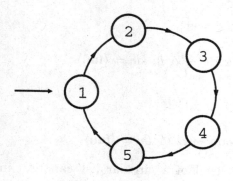

Figure 4.1. A circular list

#type α queue = Emptyqueue | Queue **of** α lnode;;

The function **enqueue** adds an element to the end of a queue. In the case where the initial queue is empty, this function creates a circular list from the element to insert. In cases where the initial queue is non-empty, the function insert_tail should be used.

```
#let enqueue x = fun
    Emptyqueue → Queue (mk_circular_list x)
  | (Queue ln) → Queue (insert_tail x ln);;
enqueue : α → α queue → α queue = ⟨fun⟩
```

The function **dequeue** removes the first element of the queue and returns a pair made from the new queue and the removed element. When the queue contains more than one element, we can use the function elim_head. When the queue contains a unique element, the new queue is simply empty. The problem is thus to detect whether a circular list contains only one element. To do so, we use the "physical" identity ==, defined on page 121, to test whether the first and last elements of the list are physically the same.

```
#let dequeue = fun
    Emptyqueue → failwith "dequeue: queue is empty"
  | (Queue ln) → if ln.next == ln then (Emptyqueue,ln.info)
                 else let x = first ln in
                      (Queue (elim_head ln),x);;
dequeue : α queue → α queue * α = ⟨fun⟩
```

To close this section, here is a function to make a list from elements found in a queue.

```
#let list_of_queue = fun
    Emptyqueue → [ ]
  | (Queue ln)
    → let ln₁ = ln.next in
       ln₁.info :: loq ln₁.next
      where rec loq ln =
        if ln == ln₁ then [ ]
        else ln.info :: loq ln.next;;
list_of_queue : α queue → α list = ⟨fun⟩
```

4.4.5 Doubly Linked Lists

The circular lists introduced in the previous section let us access the head and tail of a list; with them, we can also run through a list from head to tail; however, because of their orientation, we cannot run through such a list from tail to head. To overcome that limitation, now we will introduce doubly linked circular lists that can be traversed in both directions. We will use this type of list in Chapter 10 as one implementation of big numbers.

```
#type α dblnode = {info:α; mutable prev: α dblnode;
                   mutable next: α dblnode};;
```

Here is how we create a doubly linked list from one element:

```
#let mk_dbl_circular_list e =
    let rec x = {info=e; prev=x; next=x} in x;;
mk_dbl_circular_list : α → α dblnode = ⟨fun⟩
```

We will also define functions to insert a new element before or after a given element and to remove an element. We do not *a priori* privilege the place where the head of the list occurs, so it can be managed differently by various applications.

```
#let insert_before e l =
    let lprev = l.prev in
    let x = {info=e; prev=lprev; next=l} in
    lprev.next←x;
    l.prev←x;;
insert_before : α → α dblnode → unit = ⟨fun⟩
```

```
#let insert_after e l =
    let lnext = l.next in
    let x = {info=e; prev=l; next=lnext} in
    lnext.prev←x;
    l.next←x;;
insert_after : α → α dblnode → unit = ⟨fun⟩
```

The function we define here to remove an element assumes that there are at least two elements in the list. It removes the referenced element and returns the preceding one.

```
#let elim l =
   let lprev = l.prev
   and lnext = l.next
   in lprev.next←lnext;
       lnext.prev←lprev; lprev;;
elim : α dblnode → α dblnode = ⟨fun⟩
```

4.4.6 Comparing with Pascal, C, and Lisp

The various imperative constructions we introduced in this chapter let us program in CAML in a style close to that we would use in a more conventional language, like PASCAL or C. These constructions also let us destructively modify data, as we do in LISP or Scheme with such operations as rplaca, rplacd, or displace_obj. For those who enjoy those languages, no doubt it is interesting to discuss the differences between the approach in CAML and the others. In such a comparison, we distinguish the way variables are handled and the way data structures are managed.

With respect to variables, there is a fundamental difference between CAML on one side and PASCAL, C, and LISP on the other. The assignment operator in PASCAL (:=), the one in C (=), and the one in LISP (setq) can impinge on any variable and change its value. In CAML, that is not possible. The value of a variable is immutable, unchanging, and that fact can be easily verified. If we have defined a variable x, and we then define another variable y by let y = x, the test x == y always remains true. The only situation where we can write x := e in CAML is when the variable x is of a type of the form t ref. Therefore the link between x and its value is not modified, but rather the pointer located in the value is redirected. In conventional programming languages, any given occurrence of a variable will be interpreted differently depending on whether it appears to the left of an assignment sign or elsewhere. To the left of an assignment sign, an occurrence of a variable designates the variable itself[1] whereas in any other position, it designates its value and can be replaced by the value without altering the meaning of the text. For example, if the variable x has the value 3, the expression x := x+1 is equivalent to x := 3+1 but certainly not to 3 := 3+1 (which makes no sense).

In CAML, in contrast, a variable always represents its value, even to the left of an assignment sign. When this value is a reference, the reference is modified by the assignment.

---

[1]More precisely, its address

The dereference operator (!) makes the existence explicit of two levels of use of variables for which the value is a reference. We write x := !x+1 for the operation denoted by x := x+1 in a conventional language.

With respect to the dynamic construction of data structures, the languages CAML and LISP differ fundamentally from PASCAL and C. In CAML, simply writing a record or applying a constructor provokes the construction of a new object for which memory is implicitly allocated. Likewise in LISP, when we use the function cons or the operator quote. In contrast, in PASCAL, new objects can be constructed dynamically only by the function new, and in C by malloc. These objects are referenced by pointers which can be modified by assignment, as in CAML with references. As a consequence, even though objects are constructed in a way that appears very different, the management of pointers to dynamic data structures in PASCAL or C is very similar to that in CAML.

Finally, we note that the declaration of mutable fields in CAML records makes it possible to carry out operations similar to those of the functions rplaca and rplacd in LISP without introducing a supplementary level of reference.

In CAML and in LISP, the space occupied by objects that have become useless after pointer modifications is automatically recovered, although in PASCAL and in C, the user must explicitly declare that an object is no longer useful and then must exploit the functions dispose or free, with all the risks of error that they imply.

Chapter 12 about compilation briefly describes how memory is managed in an implementation of CAML.

Exercises

4.3 Modify the function gensym into a function of type string → unit → string so that the user can choose the character string to use.

4.4 Define a function reset_gensym:unit → unit to reset the counter used in gensym to 0 (zero).

4.5 Define a type to represent lists of priorities where the elements are pairs made up of some information and an integer representing the priority. The elements should be ordered by priority. Write the insertion function for such lists.

4.6 Write a sorting program like quicksort to work on doubly linked lists.

4.7 Define a type to represent nodes of graphs containing some information and the list of successors. By successors, we mean the set of nodes to which it is linked. Write functions to add or remove a node or an arc of the graph.

4.8 For those who know LISP, define a type to represent the data structures of LISP. In particular, define the operations rplaca and rplacd.

4.9 Show how references in CAML simulate passing parameters by reference in PASCAL.

4.5 Semantics of Destructive Operations

The semantics of the imperative aspects of CAML cannot be defined by using the idea of rewrites directly because that does not take into account modifications of data in memory.

However, it is possible to define semantics by translation in a formal system based on functions where the modifications in memory are managed explicitly.

To get an idea about this translation, consider the function **gensym**, defined on page 123, and assume for the moment that this function is the only one in the system with a definition that is not purely functional.

We will replace that function by a variant functional **sym** defined like this:

#let sym c = ("ident"^(string_of_int c), c+1);;

This function takes an integer as its argument and returns a pair consisting of the identifier that was built and the counter that has been incremented by one.

To use this new function **sym** in place of **gensym**, we change evaluation so that every CAML function takes a supplementary argument which is the value of a counter and returns a pair consisting of the veritable results and a new value for the counter which may have been modified. If the function under consideration does not call **sym**, the value of the counter will not be modified. For example, add_int simply becomes:

#let add_int c m n = (m+n, c);;

Composition of functions becomes:

#let compose c f g x =
    let (v_1,c_1) = g c x **in** f c_1 v_1;;

Thus the various functions "pass" the value of the counter, and that counter may be incremented by **sym** without any non-functional operations being necessary.

Now this way of going about things is not very realistic since it leads us to introduce a supplementary parameter in all functions every time we want to use a new mutable value. Instead of doing that, we could reorganize the set of mutable values into a single object known as **memory** of type loc → val where loc is the type of memory locations and val is the type of values used.

The function **update** functionally produces a modification in memory, like this:

#let update mem loc val =
    fun loc' → **if** loc' = loc **then** val **else** mem loc;;

Thus it suffices for each function to have a supplementary parameter corresponding to memory and to return a pair consisting of a result and a new piece of memory. In that way, we can simulate all operations that modify memory in a purely functional context.

This technique has traditionally been used in the denotational semantics of programming languages. We could then reason about non-functional programs by reasoning about their functional translation, and do so by using the methods you saw in Chapter 3 about semantics.

4.6 Summary

We have presented the main non-functional traits of CAML: sequences, exceptions, input and output, physical modification of objects. To understand them, you should place each of those traits in the context of CAML's strategy of evaluation by value. Moreover, the operations that physically modify objects depend on certain hypotheses about the representation of objects in memory.

With respect to the assignment operations that we find in more conventional languages such as C or PASCAL, such operations in CAML entail a few "guard rails" that control their use. In CAML, variables cannot be assigned, but only those values belonging to certain specific types. In that way, the fact that values not belonging to those types cannot be changed is preserved. Thus, for example, if a variable x is of an immutable type, we can be sure that every occurrence of that variable in a program represents the same value, even if x is passed as an argument to functions for which we do not know whether they make assignments or not.

4.7 To Learn More

We can give the semantics of the non-functional aspects of CAML or indeed more generally the semantics of more conventional languages only by making explicit the control mechanisms brought into play by exceptions and the memory-access mechanisms brought into play by assignment.

In the context of denotational semantics, the ideas of **continuation, environment function**, and **memory function** were introduced for that purpose. See [15] for an introduction to those ideas.

Part II

Applications

Here we begin the second part of this book; it is dedicated to writing various applications in CAML. Its chapters are largely independent of one another, so you can read them separately, choosing them according to your own interests or according to the needs of a course.

Chapter 5 covers symbolic computations over formal terms. In particular, it defines algorithms for pattern matching and unification used in many applications of symbolic computations, such as automatic proof, logic programming, or type synthesis.

Chapter 6 shows how to use balanced trees to represent large bodies of information. It uses the ideas of binary search trees and AVL trees as introduced in every course about algorithms.

Chapter 7 goes deeply into the methods of exploring graphs. It uses techniques of set representation introduced in Chapter 6 and presents applications from the domain of games such as the red donkey or solitaire.

Chapter 8 takes up the writing of lexical and syntactic analyzers. It uses the idea of a CAML stream.

Chapter 9 shows how to program drawing and designs. It first succinctly describes and then exploits the MLgraph library to draw trees and to tile planes and surfaces.

Chapter 10 deals with exact arithmetic, taking into account integers and rational numbers of arbitrary size. It does not attempt to describe a complete and efficient implementation of a library for large numbers, but rather, it tries to convince you that such a project is feasible.

Chapter 5

Formal Terms, Pattern Matching, Unification

In this chapter, we cover a general structure for terms with variables. We will present algorithms for pattern matching and unification—useful in many contexts where we handle expressions formally—such as type synthesis, evaluation, editing, formal computation, or even automatic proof. The chapter closes with an application of the unification algorithm to type synthesis.

5.1   Trees

The basic ideas we present in this section introduce the way we handle terms with variables in the next section.

We are interested in trees where the nodes have variable arity; that is, a node can have zero, one, or more children. The set of children of a node will be represented by a list. A leaf will simply be a node with an empty list of children. The type that we will use will thus have only one constructor.

#**type** α gentree = GenNode **of** $\alpha * \alpha$ gentree list;;

As usual, we assume there is a function to analyze syntax for the objects of this type.

The concrete syntax we use for trees is simple and parenthesized.

- "$a(t_1,\ldots,t_n)$" is the syntax of GenNode($a,[t_1;\ldots;t_n]$).

- "a" is syntactically equivalent to "a()".

#gentree_of_string;;
$-$: $(string \rightarrow \alpha) \rightarrow string \rightarrow \alpha$ gentree = $\langle$**fun**$\rangle$

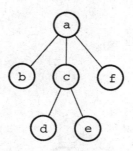

Figure 5.1. An *n*-ary tree

#gentree_of_string string_of_ident "a(b,c(d,e),f)";;
− : *string gentree* = *GenNode* ("a", [*GenNode* ("b", [ ]);
                                    GenNode ("c", [*GenNode* ("d", [ ]);
                                                   GenNode ("e", [ ])]);
                                    GenNode ("f", [ ])])

This tree is represented in Figure 5.1.

5.1.1   A Few Useful Functions

The **size** of a tree is the total number of nodes the tree contains. Size is defined by the following function.

#**let rec** gentree_size = **fun**
    (GenNode(x,l)) → 1 + sigma (map gentree_size l);;
gentree_size : α *gentree* → *int* = ⟨**fun**⟩

The **height** of a tree is the length of its longest branch. Height is defined by the following function.

#**let rec** gentree_height = **fun**
    (GenNode(x,l)) → 1 + (it_list max_int 0 (map gentree_height l));;
gentree_height : α *gentree* → *int* = ⟨**fun**⟩

It is often useful to compute the set of values appearing in a tree.

#**let rec** gentree_set = **fun**
    (GenNode(x,l)) → union [x] (it_list union [ ] (map gentree_set l));;
gentree_set : α *gentree* → α *list* = ⟨**fun**⟩

If we are interested only in the list of values (possibly redundant) appearing in a tree, then there are as many such lists possible as there are ways to traverse the tree visiting each node exactly once.

We say that a tree traversal is **breadth-first** if for every n, all the nodes of distance n from the root are visited before any of the nodes of distance $n + 1$. At every level, we can imagine visiting the nodes either from left to right or from right to left.

We say that a tree traversal is **depth-first** if for every node, all its children are visited before the next node is visited. A depth-first traversal is called **leftmost** if the children are visited from left to right; it is called **rightmost** if they are visited from right to left, of course. Moreover, during a depth-first traversal of a tree, the root can be visited either before or after its children, so we also distinguish **prefix** from **postfix** traversals.

For the tree in Figure 5.1, the various traversals correspond to the following orders for visiting the nodes.

breadth-first leftmost	a, b, c, f, d, e
breadth-first rightmost	a, f, c, b, e, d
depth-first prefix leftmost	a, b, c, d, e, f
depth-first prefix rightmost	a, f, c, e, d, b
depth-first postfix leftmost	b, d, e, c, f, a
depth-first postfix rightmost	f, e, d, c, b, a

Here, for example, is a function that gives the list of nodes in a depth-first, prefix, leftmost traversal.

```
#let rec flat_gentree = fun
  (GenNode (x,l)) → x :: list_it ((prefix @) o flat_gentree) l [ ];;
flat_gentree : α gentree → α list = ⟨fun⟩
```

5.1.2 Functionals for Trees

In Section 2.3.4, we presented a function, list_hom, to generalize all functions defined by recursion on the structure of a list. We call such a function a **homomorphism**. A similar approach prompts us to introduce this now:

```
#let rec gentree_hom f = fun
  (GenNode(x,l)) → f x (map (gentree_hom f) l);;
gentree_hom : (α → β list → β) → α gentree → β = ⟨fun⟩
```

All the functions we just defined can be redefined easily in terms of gentree_hom.

```
#let gentree_size = gentree_hom (fun x l → 1+sigma l);;
gentree_size : α gentree → int = ⟨fun⟩
```

```
#let gentree_height =
    gentree_hom (fun x l → 1 + it_list max_int 0 l);;
gentree_height : α gentree → int = ⟨fun⟩
```

```
#let gentree_set =
    gentree_hom (fun x l → union [x] (it_list union [ ] l));;
gentree_set : α gentree → α list = ⟨fun⟩
```

```
#let flat_gentree =
    gentree_hom (fun x l → x :: list_it (prefix @) l [ ]);;
flat_gentree : α gentree → α list = ⟨fun⟩
```

Incidentally, other functions, such as the application of a function f to all the nodes of a tree, or the mirror image of a tree, can also be defined from gentree_hom, like this:

```
#let rec map_gentree f =
    gentree_hom (fun x l → GenNode(f x, l));;
map_gentree : (α → β) → α gentree → β gentree = ⟨fun⟩
```

```
#let mirror_gentree =
    gentree_hom (fun x l → GenNode(x, rev l));;
mirror_gentree : α gentree → α gentree = ⟨fun⟩
```

However, it may be prohibitively inefficient to define a function by gentree_hom because the use of map forces gentree_hom to build an intermediate list before it applies f. It is possible to avoid that construction; for example, the function gentree_trav, defined later, avoids it. The only parameter f of gentree_hom is here decomposed into three parameters, h, g, and x. The parameters g and x compose the results of recursive applications on the children of a node by the function list_it. The result is then composed with information from the node by the function h.

```
#let rec gentree_trav h g x (GenNode (a,l))=
    h a (list_it (g o (gentree_trav h g x)) l x);;
gentree_trav : (α → β → γ) → (γ → β → β) → β → α gentree → γ
        = ⟨fun⟩
```

This definition gives a more efficient version of gentree_trav than does the following one from gentree_hom:

```
#let rec gentree_trav f g x =
    gentree_hom (fun a l → f a (list_it g l x));;
gentree_trav : (α → β → γ) → (γ → β → β) → β → α gentree → γ
        = ⟨fun⟩
```

All the functions we have just defined can be redefined with the help of gentree_trav, like this:

```
#let gentree_size =
    gentree_trav (fun x y → y+1) add_int 0;;
gentree_size : α gentree → int = ⟨fun⟩
```

```
#let gentree_height =
    gentree_trav (fun x y → y+1) max_int 0;;
gentree_height : α gentree → int = ⟨fun⟩
```

```
#let gentree_set =
    gentree_trav (fun x l → union [x] l) union [ ];;
gentree_set : α gentree → α list = ⟨fun⟩
```

```
#let flat_gentree =
    gentree_trav cons (prefix @) [ ];;
flat_gentree : α gentree → α list = ⟨fun⟩
```

```
#let map_gentree f =
    gentree_trav (fun x l → GenNode (f x,l)) cons [ ];;
map_gentree : (α → β) → α gentree → β gentree = ⟨fun⟩
```

The function mirror_gentree can also be defined this way, but its definition is awkward and expensive.

```
#let mirror_gentree =
    gentree_trav (fun x l → GenNode (x,l)) (fun x l → l@[x]) [ ];;
mirror_gentree : α gentree → α gentree = ⟨fun⟩
```

We can also traverse trees imperatively. The function do_gentree applies a function f to every value of a tree in a prefix leftmost traversal order.

```
#let rec do_gentree f (GenNode(x,l)) =
    f x; do_list (do_gentree f) l;;
do_gentree : (α → β) → α gentree → unit = ⟨fun⟩
```

5.1.3   Occurrences in a Tree

In certain circumstances, it is useful to be able to designate the various nodes of a tree precisely. To do so, we use the path from the root of the tree to each node. To define that path, it suffices to give the list of choices we make among the various children at each step to reach a given node. For that, we assume that when a node has n children, they are numbered from left to right, from 1 to n.

Here is how we thus designate a node:

- The root of a tree is designated by an empty list.

- If the node under consideration is located in the ith child of the root, the path to get there is (i :: path) where path is the path from the node under consideration in the ith child.

Paths denoted in that way are known as **occurrences**. They are represented in CAML as lists of integers. Formally, you can regard them as "words" (that is, strings of digits) over the alphabet **N** (natural numbers).

The function at, is declared as infix; it associates a subtree with an occurrence and a tree: the subtree located at the node pointed to by the occurrence, like this:

```
##infix "at";;
#let rec prefix at (GenNode (x,l) as t) = fun
    [ ] → t
  | (i::occ) → (nth l i) at occ;;
at : α gentree → int list → α gentree = ⟨fun⟩
```

In order to replace the subtree located at a given occurrence by a different tree, we use the function replace_occ.

```
.#let rec replace_occ (GenNode (x,l)) occ t₂ =
    match occ with
      [ ] → t₂
    | (i::occ) → let ti = nth l i in
                GenNode (x, replace_in_list l i (replace_occ ti occ t₂));;
replace_occ : α gentree → int list → α gentree → α gentree = ⟨fun⟩
```

5.1.4   Trees and Abstract Syntax

N-ary trees can represent any abstract syntax (or CAML type with constructors) in a unique type. In that way, they make it possible to write general functions to handle syntax.

Consider, for example, the following type:

#type ty = A | B **of** ty | C **of** ty * ty;;

If, for example, we make these constructors A, B, and C correspond to the strings "A", "B", and "C", then we can represent values of type ty by values of type string gentree, like this:

```
#let rec gentree_of_ty = fun
    A → GenNode("A",[ ])
  | (B(x)) → GenNode("B",[ gentree_of_ty x])
  | (C(x,y)) → GenNode("B",[ gentree_of_ty x;gentree_of_ty y ]);;
gentree_of_ty : ty → string gentree = ⟨fun⟩
```

You see clearly that this kind of translation can be generalized to the entire set of types with constructors. The reverse translation can also be programmed easily enough, but in doing so, we have to be careful of the fact that not all trees of type **string gentree** correspond to values of type ty. In effect, only the strings "A", "B", and "C" correspond to constructors, and these have an arity that must be respected.

Such information is conveyed by a **signature** in the form of an association list.

#type α signature == (α * int) list;;

The function arity gives the arity of a symbol in a given signature. It fails and raises the exception Sig_error when the symbol is unknown.

```
#exception Sig_error;;
Exception Sig_error defined.
```

```
#let arity sig x =
    try assoc x sig
    with _ → raise Sig_error;;
arity : (α * β) list → α → β = ⟨fun⟩
```

The following function verifies that a tree conforms to a given signature.

```
#let ok_sig sig t =
    try gentree_trav (fun x bl → for_all (fun b → b=true) bl
                              & arity sig x = list_length bl)
            cons [ ] t
    with Sig_error → false;;
ok_sig : (α * int) list → α gentree → bool = ⟨fun⟩
```

Verifying arity in this way is sufficient only in situations where we handle only one type of object. Such is generally not the case. For example, consider mutually recursive types, like these:

#type ty_1 = A | B **of** ty_1 * ty_2
  and ty_2 = C | D **of** ty_2 * ty_1;;

The idea of a signature must be extended to take types into account. Instead of associating an integer defining its arity with each constructor, we will associate a pair with it; that pair consists of the list of types of its arguments and the type of its result.

#type (α,β) signature == $(\alpha * (\beta \text{ list} * \beta))$ list;;

The following function tells us the type of a symbol in a given signature.

#let get_type sig x =
  try assoc x sig
  with _ $\rightarrow$ **raise** Sig_error;;
get_type : $(\alpha * \beta)$ *list* $\rightarrow$ α $\rightarrow$ β = $\langle$**fun**$\rangle$

In the case of the types ty_1 and ty_2, we will take:

#let sig_{12} = ["A",([ ],"ty1"); "B",(["ty1";"ty2"],"ty1");
                "C",([ ],"ty2"); "D",(["ty2";"ty1"],"ty2")];;
sig_{12}
    : *(string * (string list * string))* *list*
    = ["A", ([ ], "ty1"); "B", (["ty1"; "ty2"], "ty1"); "C", ([ ], "ty2");
        "D", (["ty2"; "ty1"], "ty2")]

The following function verifies whether a tree actually conforms to a given signature; the function tells its type in that case and fails in the opposite case.

#let typing sig t =
  gentree_trav (**fun** x ts $\rightarrow$ **let** (ts_1,t) = get_type sig x **in**
                        if ts=ts_1 **then** t **else** **raise** Sig_error)
      cons [ ] t;;
typing : $(\alpha * (\beta \text{ list} * \beta))$ *list* $\rightarrow$ α *gentree* $\rightarrow$ β = $\langle$**fun**$\rangle$

The function typing is a rudimentary type synthesizer—rudimentary in that it takes into account only "flat" types. The types it considers are constant types, represented in our example by character strings. Later, we will show you how to take into account more complicated types.

5.2 Terms with Variables

You have already seen that the type **gentree** lets us represent all kinds of expressions uniformly. However, those expressions included only operators and constants. Now any formal manipulation of expressions requires us to use the ideas of variables and substitution. It is possible to make certain kinds of substitutions with the help of the function **replace_occ**, defined in Section 5.1.3, but doing so assumes that the occurrence where the substitution has to be made must be designated absolutely (that is, by the path to get there from the root) a situation that is not at all convenient for most applications. It is much more natural to designate occurrences where substitutions should be made by variables, as we do in mathematics, so now we are going to introduce the idea of a variable explicitly.

5.2.1 Introducing Variables

The type (α,β) term, defined later, is similar to the type α gentree, but it adds the explicit idea of a variable represented by values of type β.

```
#type (α,β) term = Term of α * (α,β) term list
               | Var of β;;
```

In the rest of this section, we will use exclusively objects of type (string,string) term, so we will use a function to analyze syntax and a specialized print function, like these:

```
#term_of_string;;
```
$-$: $string \rightarrow (string, string)\ term = \langle\mathbf{fun}\rangle$

```
#print_term;;
```
$-$: $(string, string)\ term \rightarrow unit = \langle\mathbf{fun}\rangle$

We will syntactically distinguish variables from constants by representing constants as functions applied to an empty list of arguments.

```
#term_of_string "a(b(),c)";;
```
$-$: $(string, string)\ term = Term$ (“a”, [$Term$ (“b”, [ ]); Var “c”])

```
#new_printer "term" print_term ;;
```
$-$: $unit = ()$

```
#term_of_string "a(b(),c)";;
```
$-$: $(string, string)\ term = a(b(),c)$

To traverse the terms, we will use the function **term_trav**; in spirit, it is similar to **gentree_trav**, but it adds the idea of taking variables into account.

```
#let rec term_trav f g start v = fun
    (Term(oper,sons)) → f(oper, list_it (g o (term_trav f g start v)) sons start)
  | (Var n) → v n;;
```
$term\_trav : (\alpha * \beta \to \gamma) \to (\gamma \to \beta \to \beta)$
$$\to \beta \to (\delta \to \gamma) \to (\alpha, \delta)\ term \to \gamma = \langle\mathbf{fun}\rangle$$

The function vars computes the set of variables appearing in a term:

```
#let vars t = term_trav snd union [ ] (fun x → [x]) t;;
```
$vars : (\alpha, \beta)\ term \to \beta\ list = \langle\mathbf{fun}\rangle$

The function occurs tests whether a given variable occurs in a given term. It can be written like this:

```
#let occurs v t = mem v (vars t);;
```
$occurs : \alpha \to (\beta, \alpha)\ term \to bool = \langle\mathbf{fun}\rangle$

Like trees, terms should generally obey arity and type constraints. Functions defined in the previous section to verify arity and to compute type can be extended to terms with no difficulty. In the case of a simple verification of arity, variables are assimilated to constants. In the case of type synthesis, we must assume that variables themselves have types.

5.2.2 Substitutions

A **substitution** is an operation that replaces variables by terms. For example, the substitution that replaces the variable x by the term g(z), applied to the term f(x,y,x), will produce the term f(g(z),y,g(z)).

We will represent substitutions by association lists of type $(\beta * (\alpha,\beta)\ term)$ list. Any variables not appearing in this association list remain invariant during the substitution. Here is a function to print substitutions nicely:

```
#let print_subst subst =
    do_list (fun (x,t) → print_string x;
                         print_string "  -->  ";
                         print_term t;
                         print_newline())
        subst;;
```
$print\_subst : (string * (string, string)\ term)\ list \to unit = \langle\mathbf{fun}\rangle$

The function apply_subst applies a substitution to a term; that is, it replaces the occurrences of variables by their image in the substitution.

```
#let rec apply_subst subst =fun
   (Term (f,tl)) → Term(f,(map (apply_subst subst) tl))
 | (Var x as v) → try assoc x subst
                  with _ → v;;
apply_subst : (α * (β, α) term) list → (β, α) term → (β, α) term
            = ⟨fun⟩
```

```
#let subst= [ "x",term_of_string "g(z)" ]
  in apply_subst subst (term_of_string "f(x,y,x)");;
− : (string, string) term = f(g(z),y,g(z))
```

The composition of two substitutions, σ_1 and σ_2, can be computed simply from their representations as association lists. We get the image in the composition of a variable modified by σ_2 when we take the image by σ_1 of its image by σ_2. The image in the composition of a variable not modified by σ_2 is its image by σ_1. Thus we can get the representation by the association list of the composition. We do so in this way: first, we take the list corresponding to σ_2; in it, we modify the right members by σ_1; then we take the list corresponding to σ_1; from it, we remove the variables modified by σ_2; then we concatenate those results.

```
#let compsubst subst₁ subst₂ =
   (map (fun (v,t) → (v,apply_subst subst₁ t)) subst₂)
   @(let vs= map fst subst₂
      in filter (fun (x,t) → not(mem x vs)) subst₁);;
compsubst : (α * (β, α) term) list → (α * (β, α) term) list
                                  → (α * (β, α) term) list = ⟨fun⟩
```

```
#let subst₁= [ "x",term_of_string "g(x,y)" ]
  and subst₂= [ "y",term_of_string "h(x,z)" ] in
  print_subst (compsubst subst₁ subst₂);;
y → h(g(x,y),z)
x → g(x,y)
− : unit = ()
```

```
#let subst₁= [ "x",term_of_string "g(x,y)" ]
  and subst₂= [ "y",term_of_string "h(x,z)"; "x",term_of_string "k(x)" ] in
  print_subst (compsubst subst₁ subst₂);;
y → h(g(x,y),z)
x → k(g(x,y))
− : unit = ()
```

It is possible to simplify the definition of compsubst by not eliminating the variables modified by σ_2 from σ_1. Since association lists are traversed from left to right, only the leftmost definition will be taken into account, so we can write this:

```
#let compsubst subst₁ subst₂ =
    (map (fun (v,t) → (v,apply_subst subst₁ t)) subst₂) @subst₁;;
```
$$compsubst : (\alpha * (\beta, \alpha)\ term)\ list \rightarrow (\alpha * (\beta, \alpha)\ term)\ list$$
$$\rightarrow (\alpha * (\beta, \alpha)\ term)\ list = \langle \mathbf{fun} \rangle$$

5.2.3   Filtering and Pattern Matching

Filtering or pattern matching a term u by a term t is an operation where we search for a substitution that transforms t into u. If the term t is a simple variable x, then the substitution (x, u) clearly constitutes a unique solution. If the term t is of the form $f(t_1, ..., t_n)$, then for a solution to exist, these conditions are necessary:

- u must be of the form $f(u_1, ..., u_n)$.

- For every i, the pattern matching of u_i by t_i must be possible.

- The various substitutions corresponding to pattern matching u_i by t_i must be mutually compatible; that is, they must not produce different images of the same variable.

Otherwise, there is no solution.

The pattern matching function traverses the structure of the two terms verifying that these structures are compatible and breaking them down into pattern matching problems on simpler terms. When we encounter a pair in the form (x, u) where x is a variable, we add this pair to those already found by verifying that we have not already found a pair (x, u') where $u \neq u'$. This addition along with its verification is carried out by the function som_subst:

```
#exception Match_exc;;
Exception Match_exc defined.
```

```
#let som_subst s₁ s₂ =
    it_list (fun subst (x,t) → try let u = assoc x subst in
                                 if t=u then subst
                                 else raise Match_exc
                               with Not_found → (x,t)::subst)
       s₁ s₂;;
```
$$som\_subst : (\alpha * \beta)\ list \rightarrow (\alpha * \beta)\ list \rightarrow (\alpha * \beta)\ list = \langle \mathbf{fun} \rangle$$

The function matching produces this pattern matching:

```
#let matching (t₁,t₂) =
   matchrec [ ] (t₁,t₂)
   where rec matchrec subst =fun
     (Var v,t) → som_subst [v,t] subst
   | (t,Var v) → raise Match_exc
   | (Term(op₁,sons₁),Term(op₂,sons₂)) →
         if op₁ = op₂ then it_list matchrec subst (combine(sons₁,sons₂))
         else raise Match_exc;;
   matching : (α, β) term * (α, γ) term → (β * (α, γ) term) list = ⟨fun⟩
```

5.2.4   Unification

Given two terms, t and u, their **unification** involves a search to see whether there exists a substitution σ that unifies them, that is, a substitution such that $\sigma(t) = \sigma(u)$. The substitution σ is thus called the **unifier** of t and u.

If the term t is reduced to a variable x, then we have the solution (x, u) if the variable x does not appear in the term u. If the variable x appears in u, then there is no solution.

Likewise, if the term u is reduced to a variable x, we have the solution (x, t) as long as x does not appear in t.

In other cases, t and u are of the form $f(t_1, ..., t_m)$ and $g(u_1, ..., u_n)$. If the symbols f and g are different, then unification is not possible. If $f = g$, then we also have $m = n$, so our problem of unifying t and u is reduced to finding a substitution σ such that for all i, $\sigma(t_i) = \sigma(u_i)$.

As a consequence, in order to handle the problem of unifying two terms t and u, we must be able to handle the unification of a set of pairs of terms simultaneously.

To do so, we go about it this way. Given the set of pairs of terms to unify, $((t_1, u_1), ..., (t_n, u_n))$, we first unify t_1 and u_1. If this unification succeeds, and produces a unifier σ_1, then we will next try to unify the set

$$((\sigma_1(t_2), \sigma_1(u_2)), ..., (\sigma_1(t_n), \sigma_1(u_n)))$$

If that succeeds and produces a unifier σ, then the composition $\sigma \; o \; \sigma_1$ is sure to be a unifier for $((t_1, u_1), ..., (t_n, u_n))$.

The function unify implements this algorithm.

```
#exception Unify_exc;;
```
Exception Unify_exc defined.

```
#let rec unify =fun
   (Var v,t₂) → if Var v = t₂ then [ ] else
                   if occurs v t₂ then raise Unify_exc
                   else [v,t₂]
 | (t₁,Var v)→ if occurs v t₁ then raise Unify_exc
                   else [v,t₁]
 | (Term(op₁,sons₁),Term(op₂,sons₂)) →
       if op₁ = op₂ then
         (it_list subst_unif [ ] (combine(sons₁,sons₂))
          where subst_unif s (t₁,t₂) =
            compsubst (unify (apply_subst s t₁,apply_subst s t₂)) s)
       else raise Unify_exc;;
```

$$unify : (\alpha, \beta) \; term * (\alpha, \beta) \; term \to (\beta * (\alpha, \beta) \; term) \; list = \langle \textbf{fun} \rangle$$

Here is an example of it at work:

```
#let t₁= term_of_string "f(x,h(y))"
 and t₂= term_of_string "f(k(z),z)"
 in print_subst (unify(t₁,t₂));;
```
$x \to k(h(y))$
$z \to h(y)$
$- : unit = ()$

In contrast to the problem of pattern matching, the problem of unification does not generally have a unique solution. In fact, if σ is a unifier, then for every substitution ρ, the composition $\rho \; o \; \sigma$ is also a unifier. It is possible to show that the algorithm implemented by the function unify computes σ_0, a more general unifier than all others in the sense that we can get all the other unifiers by composing this particular unifier with a substitution; that is, all other unifiers are of the form $\rho \; o \; \sigma_0$. This unifier is known as the MGU, the **most general unifier.**

The unification algorithm is useful in many contexts of computer science. It makes it possible to synthesize types in CAML, for example.

5.3   Application: Type Synthesis

As we remarked in the previous section, the unification algorithm producing the most general unifier makes it possible for us to synthesize the most general type of an expression in CAML. Here is an application of that fact.

5.3.1 Constraints on Types

Here we will define a rudimentary type synthesizer. In particular, it will let us directly handle the constructions **let** and **let rec** only if we call expensive text substitutions like those discussed on page 152. A more efficient synthesizer for handling these constructions more naturally will be presented in Chapter 13 about types.

The synthesis method we present here starts from an expression for which we want to compute the type, then constructs a system of equations corresponding to the type constraints, and then resolves that system by unification.

The following constraints are generated that way:

- If c is an integer constant, then **type**(c) = int.

- If c is a Boolean constant, then **type**(c) = bool.

- If $e = (e_1, e_2)$, then **type**(e) = **type**(e_1)∗**type**(e_2).

- If $e = $ **if** e_1 **then** e_2 **else** e_3, then **type**(e_1) = bool, **type**(e) = **type**(e_2) and **type**(e) = **type**(e_3).

- If $e = ($**fun** $x \to e')$, then **type**(e) = **type**(x) $\to$ **type**(e').

- If $e = (e_1\ e_2)$, then **type**(e_1) = **type**(e_2) $\to$ **type** (e).

Moreover, all the occurrences of the same variable must have the same type.

This last constraint seems a contradiction of the fact that in CAML the variables having a polymorphic type can occur with different instances of that type. Remember, however, that such variables are defined in CAML by the constructions **let** and **let rec**, which we have decided not to treat directly here.

In Chapter 3, you saw that we could represent recursion by means of an operator Rec of type $((\alpha \to \alpha) \to \alpha)$. The constraints associated with an expression of the form Rec (**fun** $x \to e$) are thus:

- **type**(Rec (**fun** $x \to e$) = **type**(x) = **type**(e).

5.3.2 Generating Constraints

The abstract syntax of expressions will be defined by the following type:

```
#type ml_unop = Ml_fst | Ml_snd;;

#type ml_binop = Ml_add | Ml_sub | Ml_mult | Ml_eq | Ml_less;;
```

```
#type ml_exp =
      MI_int_const of int                              (* integer constant *)
    | MI_bool_const of bool                            (* Boolean constant *)
    | MI_pair of ml_exp * ml_exp                                  (* pair *)
    | MI_unop of ml_unop * ml_exp                      (* unary operation *)
    | MI_binop of ml_binop * ml_exp * ml_exp          (* binary operation *)
    | MI_var of string                                        (* variable *)
    | MI_if of ml_exp * ml_exp * ml_exp                    (* conditional *)
    | MI_fun of string * ml_exp                               (* function *)
    | MI_app of ml_exp * ml_exp                            (* application *)
    | MI_let of string * ml_exp * ml_exp                  (* declaration *)
    | MI_letrec of string * ml_exp * ml_exp    (* recursive declaration *)
;;
```

The abstract syntax of types will be the following:

```
#type ml_type =
      Int_type | Bool_type
    | Pair_type of ml_type * ml_type
    | Arrow_type of ml_type * ml_type
    | Var_type of string;;
```

Let's assume for the moment that we have functions to analyze and to print these types.

```
#new_printer "ml_type" print_ml_type;;
- : unit = ()
```

The function generate_type_constraints generates the list of type constraints that an expression must satisfy. The type terms are not expressed in the type ml_type but rather in the type term so that later the function unify can be used. The functions const, var, and arrow make it easier to construct these terms.

```
#let var n = Var ("v"^(string_of_int n));;
var : int → (α, string) term = ⟨fun⟩
```

```
#let const c = Term(c,[ ]);;
const : α → (α, β) term = ⟨fun⟩
```

```
#let pair(t₁,t₂) = Term("pair",[t₁;t₂]);;
pair : (string, α) term * (string, α) term → (string, α) term = ⟨fun⟩
```

```
#let arrow(t₁,t₂) = Term("arrow",[t₁;t₂]);;
arrow : (string, α) term * (string, α) term → (string, α) term = ⟨fun⟩
```

Subexpressions of the expression under consideration are numbered as they are traversed. We are sure that this numbering is unique because of the function new_int (similar to the function **gensym** on page 123). The function reset_new_int lets us re-initialize the counter before each type synthesis.

```
#let (new_int, reset_new_int) =
    let c = ref (−1) in
    (fun () → c:=!c+1 ; !c),
    (fun () → c:=−1);;
reset_new_int : unit → unit = ⟨fun⟩
new_int : unit → int = ⟨fun⟩
```

The types of basic operators are provided by the functions unop_type and binop_type. They furnish a pair or a triple of the types of arguments and the type of the result.

```
#let unop_type = fun
    Ml_fst → let a= var(new_int()) and b= var(new_int())
                in (pair(a,b),a)
  | Ml_snd → let a= var(new_int()) and b= var(new_int())
                in (pair(a,b),b);;
unop_type : ml_unop → (string, string) term ∗ (α, string) term = ⟨fun⟩
```

```
#let binop_type = fun
    Ml_add → (const "int", const "int",const "int")
  | Ml_sub → (const "int", const "int",const "int")
  | Ml_mult → (const "int", const "int",const "int")
  | Ml_eq → (const "int", const "int",const "bool")
  | Ml_less → (const "int", const "int",const "bool");;
binop_type : ml_binop → (string, α) term ∗ (string, β) term ∗
                        (string, γ) term = ⟨fun⟩
```

The function generate_type_constraints associates a type variable named v_i with each subexpression of number i; for each construction of the expression being treated, it also produces the set of associated constraints. The constraints produced that way are pairs of terms representing the equalities to satisfy. In order to ensure that all the occurrences of the same variable have the same type, we store the types that we associate with variables during their introduction by the construction **fun**. We store them in the **type environment**, a variable tenv.

```
#let generate_type_constraints e =
    reset_new_int();gen (new_int()) [ ] e
```

```
  where rec gen n tenv = fun
    (MI_int_const _) → [var n, const "int"]
  | (MI_bool_const _) → [var n, const "bool"]
  | (MI_unop (op, e)) →
      let (t₁,t₂) = unop_type op
      and nₑ = new_int() in
      (var n,t₂)::(var nₑ,t₁)::(gen nₑ tenv e)
  | (MI_binop (op,e₁,e₂)) →
      let (t₁,t₂,t₃) = binop_type op
      and n₁ = new_int() and n₂ = new_int() in
      (var n,t₃)::(var n₁,t₁)::(var n₂,t₂)
      :: (gen n₁ tenv e₁ @ gen n₂ tenv e₂)
  | (MI_pair(e₁,e₂)) →
      let n₁ = new_int() and n₂=new_int() in
      (var n,(pair(var n₁,var n₂)))::(gen n₁ tenv e₁@gen n₂ tenv e₂)
  | (MI_var x) → [var n,assoc x tenv]
  | (MI_if (e₁,e₂,e₃)) →
      let n₁ = new_int() and n₂ = new_int()
      and n₃ = new_int() in
      (var n₁,const "bool")::(var n,var n₂)::(var n,var n₃)
      ::((gen n₁ tenv e₁) @ (gen n₂ tenv e₂) @ (gen n₃ tenv e₃))
  | (MI_fun(x,e)) →
      let nₓ = new_int() and nₑ = new_int() in
      (var n, arrow(var nₓ,var nₑ))::
      (gen nₑ ((x,var nₓ)::tenv) e)
  | (MI_app (MI_var "Rec",MI_fun(f,e))) →
      let n_f = new_int() and nₑ = new_int() in
      (var n, var nₑ)::
      (gen nₑ ((f,var n)::tenv) e)
  | (MI_app (e₁,e₂)) →
      let n₁ = new_int() and n₂ = new_int() in
      (var n₁, arrow(var n₂,var n))::
      (gen n₁ tenv e₁ @ gen n₂ tenv e₂)
  | _ → failwith "Not implemented";;
generate_type_constraints
  : ml_exp → ((α, string) term * (string, string) term) list = ⟨fun⟩
```

In Chapter 3, we defined a function that let us make substitutions in programs. If we have that sort of function available now, we can handle the construction **let** by replacing every expression of the form **let** $x=e_1$ **in** e_2 by $e_2[x \leftarrow e_1]$. The effect of polymorphism that we get from **let** is simulated thus by our independently typing each occurrence of e_2. In the same way, we handle the construction   **let**

rec since **let rec** x = e_1 **in** e_2 can be replaced by **let** x = Rec (**fun** x → e).

5.3.3 Constraint Resolution

We need to define a function ml_type_of_term to convert between types **term** and
mltype.

```
#let rec ml_type_of_term = function
    Var s → Var_type s
  | Term("int",[ ]) → Int_type
  | Term("bool",[ ]) → Bool_type
  | Term("pair",[t₁;t₂]) →
        Pair_type(ml_type_of_term t₁,ml_type_of_term t₂)
  | Term("arrow",[t₁;t₂]) →
        Arrow_type(ml_type_of_term t₁,ml_type_of_term t₂);;
ml_type_of_term : (string, string) term → ml_type = ⟨fun⟩
```

We also need a function unify_list to unify lists of pairs of terms.

```
#let unify_list tl =
    it_list subst_unif [ ] tl
    where subst_unif s (t₁,t₂) =
    compsubst (unify (apply_subst s t₁,apply_subst s t₂)) s;;
unify_list : ((α, β) term * (α, β) term) list → (β * (α, β) term) list
        = ⟨fun⟩
```

The function for type synthesis generates the set of constraints, resolves those
constraints, and applies the substitution that it gets to the type variable v_0 corresponding to the type of the entire expression.

```
#let synthesize_type e =
    ml_type_of_term
        (apply_subst (unify_list (generate_type_constraints e))
        (var 0));;
synthesize_type : ml_exp → ml_type = ⟨fun⟩
```

Here are a few examples of how this works.

```
#synthesize_type (ml_exp_of_string "fun x -> x)");;
 − : ml_type = (v₁ → v₁)

#synthesize_type
    (ml_exp_of_string "fun f -> (fun x -> f (f x))");;
 − : ml_type = ((v₃ → v₃) → (v₃ → v₃))
```

```
#synthesize_type
  (ml_exp_of_string ("(fun f -> (fun x -> f (f x)))"
                    ^"(fun x -> x*x)"));;
```
$- : ml\_type = (int \rightarrow int)$

```
#synthesize_type
  (ml_exp_of_string "fun f -> (fun g -> (fun x -> f (g x)))");;
```
$- : ml\_type = ((v_8 \rightarrow v_6) \rightarrow ((v_5 \rightarrow v_8) \rightarrow (v_5 \rightarrow v_6)))$

```
#synthesize_type
  (ml_exp_of_string ("Rec (fun f -> (fun n -> if n=0 then 1 "^
                    "                        else n*f(n-1)))"));;
```
$- : ml\_type = (int \rightarrow int)$

Exercises

5.10 Extend type synthesis to a language that includes Cartesian products in their most general form.

5.11 Write a function to rename variables to make it easier to write the type you get.

5.12 Extend the syntax of the language to handle the constructions **let** and **let rec** by using the technique suggested on page 152.

5.4   Summary

We presented the types **gentree** and **term** for representing general n-ary trees and formal terms with variables.

The idea of **substitution** introduced an instantiation relation between terms in the sense that a term t' is an instance of a term t if there exists a substitution σ such that $\sigma(t) = t'$. When we say that t' is an instance of t, we mean that t' is a particular case of t or that t is more general than t'.

The problem of **pattern matching** involves testing whether one term is an instance of another. The problem of **unification** consists of testing whether two terms have a common instance. When it succeeds, the unification algorithm provides the most general substitution that produces an instance common to both terms.

Type synthesis is one application of the unification algorithm. The synthesized type is the most general one compatible with the type constraints under consideration.

5.5   To Learn More

Historically, the unification algorithm appeared in automatic proofs. In 1965, Robinson completely explicated it as the essential element of the **resolution rule**, but it had been suggested earlier by Herbrand in the thirties.

The resolution rule found an important application in computer science in 1973 when the language PROLOG [36] was introduced. PROLOG uses unification for what corresponds to procedure calls in more conventional languages. Other applications of unification can be found in various domains of artificial intelligence.

Milner, the creator of the language ML, deserves credit for using unification in type synthesis.

Chapter 6

Balanced Trees

This chapter defines a group of functions to manage large-scale data sets. These functions use trees as data structures because they are so well adapted to representing data sets that evolve dynamically, that is, data sets where the size can grow or shrink during computations.

The specific data structure we use is a binary tree. The algorithms we propose make it possible to keep these binary trees balanced, and this property ensures the efficiency of operations we want to carry out.

The main operations for managing a data set are these:

- **searching** for an element in the data set;

- **adding** an element to the data set;

- **removing** an element from the data set.

To search naively for an element in a data set, we can simply sweep sequentially through all the elements of the set, but that takes time proportional to the size of the data set. Its complexity is thus $O(n)$. This technique is the only one[1] we can use when we are managing data sets generically because we do not know any particular properties of the set.

In order to search more efficiently, we have to make hypotheses about the structure of the data set under consideration. For example, if we can assume that the data are ordered, then we can use a binary search as we did in Section 4.4.1 to represent sets by sorted arrays. The search time then is proportional to the logarithm of the size of the data set, that is, complexity is $O(\log(n))$.

However, inserting an element into a sorted array is a costly operation. If we do not want the insertion of an element to result in a new allocation of the array, then we are tempted from the beginning to allocate an array equal in size to the

---

[1]Short of hashing the internal representation of the elements.

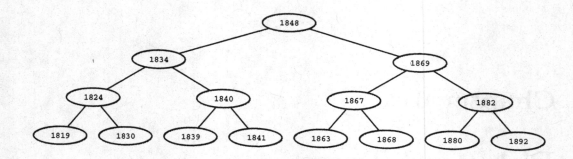

Figure 6.1. A few dates

maximal size of the data set that we have to manage—a temptation that leads to useless waste of memory. Moreover, in that case, adding an element assumes an offset of larger elements, which in turn leads to a time for insertion proportional to the size of the array.

In contrast, if we use trees as data structures, in the case of ordered data sets, we get logarithmic costs for all three operations: searching, adding, and removing. To achieve that, we use balanced binary search trees.

Consider, for example, a set of dates: 1819, 1824, 1830, 1834, 1839, 1840, 1841, 1848, 1863, 1867, 1868, 1869, 1880, 1882, 1892. We will represent this data set by a tree, as in Figure 6.1.

This tree has the following interesting property: at each node, the date there is later than those dates appearing in the subtree to the left of this node and earlier than those appearing in the right subtree. To search for a date in this tree, we do the following.

We first compare the date we are searching for with the date at the root of the tree.

- If they are equal, we have found it.

- If the date we are searching for is earlier than the date at the root, then we search the left subtree.

- Otherwise, we search the right subtree.

Our search for a date thus traverses only one branch of the tree; that is, at most four comparisons.

Trees organized in this way are known as binary search trees. Among the binary search trees, the one in Figure 6.1 is a special one because it is a complete binary search tree in which every branch has the same length. (In this context, complete means that every node that is not a leaf has exactly two children.) Generally, this will not be the case. However, the algorithms we present will guarantee that the trees they construct will be "sufficiently balanced" so that the length of their longest branch will be bounded by a logarithmic function of the total size of the tree. This condition will ensure logarithmic search times in the worst case.

The remarkable fact is that adding and removing elements can be managed as operations that also have a logarithmic complexity in the worst case, even though these operations must maintain the balance of the tree. To achieve that, we will use the well known technique of AVL trees, introduced by Adelson-Velskii and Landis. We will say more about these later in Section 6.5.2.

Management of data sets by balanced trees is useful in widely diverse applications. It is possible to use balanced trees to represent dictionaries where information is associated with "keys." A dictionary might be used, for example, to implement a symbol table or a function with a finite domain. Elements appearing at the nodes of the tree are thus pairs formed from a key and some information. For example, we can imagine a dictionary associating the dates of the tree in Figure 6.1 with the list of famous people born in that year.

Formally, the order used to organize the keys induces a pre-order among the pairs (key, information). In order to implement searching, adding, and removing in the most general way possible, and in particular, so that we can implement dictionaries, we will make sure that they can be organized by a pre-order and not necessarily by an order. (For an explanation of the difference, see Section 6.3 about order.)

6.1 Binary Trees

Our fundamental data structure in this chapter will be a binary tree. A **binary tree** can be empty, or it may be formed from a main node, known as the **root**, with its own data and two children, a right and left child, that are in turn binary trees themselves. Such trees are defined by the CAML type btree.

#type α btree = Empty | Bin **of** α btree $* \alpha * \alpha$ btree;;

It may also be useful to have functions to access various fields of the root of a tree. These functions will raise an exception when the tree is empty.

#exception Btree_exc **of** string;;

#let root = **fun**
    Empty $\rightarrow$ raise (Btree_exc "root: empty tree")
 | (Bin (_,a,_)) $\rightarrow$ a;;
root : α btree $\rightarrow \alpha$ = ⟨**fun**⟩

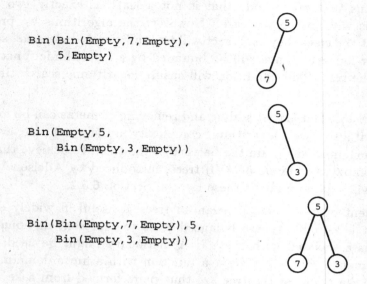

```
Bin(Bin(Empty,7,Empty),
       5,Empty)



Bin(Empty,5,
      Bin(Empty,3,Empty))




Bin(Bin(Empty,7,Empty),5,
      Bin(Empty,3,Empty))
```

Figure 6.2. A few binary trees

#let left_son = **fun**
   Empty → raise (Btree_exc "left_son: empty tree")
 | (Bin (t,_,_)) → t;;
left_son : α btree → α btree = ⟨**fun**⟩

#let right_son = **fun**
   Empty → raise (Btree_exc "right_son: empty tree")
 | (Bin (_,_,t)) → t;;
right_son : α btree → α btree = ⟨**fun**⟩

The type **btree** is not exactly a particular case of the type **gentree**, defined in Section 5.1. Actually, the type **btree** distinguishes whether a node having only one non-empty child has a left or right child.

Figure 6.2 illustrates that fact by showing graphically a few simple elements of type **int btree**.

The trees used in the rest of this chapter will be represented by instances of the type α **btree**. As a consequence, functionals we define in the following section to traverse trees will be applicable without change to particular trees introduced later.

In order to enter elements of type **btree** easily, we will need, as usual, a function to analyze syntax. We assume that we have defined such a function, **btree_of_string**.

```
#btree_of_string;;
```
$- : (string \rightarrow \alpha) \rightarrow string \rightarrow \alpha\ btree = \langle$**fun**$\rangle$

The concrete syntax used for binary trees is essentially the same as that we used in Section 5.1 for general trees, but the number of children of any node will now be exactly two.

Here is an example.

```
#btree_of_string int_of_string "2(3,4)";;
```
$- : int\ btree = Bin\ (Bin\ (Empty, 3, Empty), 2, Bin\ (Empty, 4, Empty))$

In that example, the analyzer int_of_string that we passed as an argument to btree_of_string recognizes an integer and returns that integer as a result in the form of a value of type int.

Likewise, we can assume the existence of a print function.

```
#print_btree;;
```
$- : (\alpha \rightarrow unit) \rightarrow \alpha\ btree \rightarrow unit = \langle$**fun**$\rangle$

We will use it very little, however, since we prefer to display trees in a graphic form, as in Figures 6.1 and 6.2.

6.2 Tree Traversals and Morphisms

For binary trees, we can define functionals similar to those we introduced in Section 5.1 for more general trees. However, their type is a little different to the degree that a constructor corresponding to the empty tree will lead us to handle that case specifically.

For example, the homomorphism of binary trees involves two parameters, f and v, corresponding to the two constructors, Bin and Empty.

Given a constant v of type β and a ternary operation f of type $(\beta * \alpha * \beta) \rightarrow \beta$, we can associate a value of type β with every tree of type α btree by recursion on the structure of the tree by taking

- val() = v

- val(a(t_1,t_2)) = f(val(t_1),a,val(t_2))

We call such an operation a **homomorphism**. The function btree_hom produces all possible homomorphisms.

```
#let rec btree_hom f v t =
    match t with
      (Bin (t₁,a,t₂)) → f(btree_hom f v t₁, a ,btree_hom f v t₂)
    | Empty → v;;
```
$btree\_hom : (\alpha * \beta * \alpha \rightarrow \alpha) \rightarrow \alpha \rightarrow \beta\ btree \rightarrow \alpha = \langle$**fun**$\rangle$

The height of a tree is the length of its longest branch. Its size is the total number of binary nodes. These two functions, btree_height and btree_size can be seen as homomorphisms to the integers.

#let btree_height t = btree_hom (**fun** $(x_1,\_,x_2) \rightarrow$ 1+ max_int x_1 x_2) 0 t;;
btree_height : α *btree* $\rightarrow$ *int* = $\langle$**fun**$\rangle$

#let btree_size t = btree_hom (**fun** $(x_1,\_,x_2) \rightarrow$ 1+x_1+x_2) 0 t;;
btree_size : α *btree* $\rightarrow$ *int* = $\langle$**fun**$\rangle$

The function map_btree applies a function f to each node of a binary tree and returns the resulting tree. This function is a homomorphism of binary trees.

#let map_btree f t =
    btree_hom (**fun** $(t_1,a,t_2) \rightarrow$ Bin$(t_1,$f a$,t_2)$)
      Empty t;;
map_btree : $(\alpha \rightarrow \beta) \rightarrow \alpha$ *btree* $\rightarrow \beta$ *btree* = $\langle$**fun**$\rangle$

The function mirror_btree returns the mirror image of a tree; that is, the tree we get by permuting the left and right children at every level. This function is a homomorphism of binary trees, too.

#let mirror_btree t = btree_hom
               (**fun** $(t_1,a,t_2) \rightarrow$ Bin(t_2,a,t_1))
               Empty t;;
mirror_btree : α *btree* $\rightarrow \alpha$ *btree* = $\langle$**fun**$\rangle$

In this chapter, the only binary trees we use will be search trees; that is, trees for which the infix traversals correspond to the order among the elements. Consequently, we will favor functions oriented toward the left and right infix traversals. The functions btree_it and it_btree produce infix traversals; their types are inspired by those of list_it and it_list.

#let rec btree_it f t x =
    match t **with**
      Empty $\rightarrow$ x
    | Bin $(t_1,a,t_2) \rightarrow$
        btree_it f t_1 (f a (btree_it f t_2 x));;
btree_it : $(\alpha \rightarrow \beta \rightarrow \beta) \rightarrow \alpha$ *btree* $\rightarrow \beta \rightarrow \beta$ = $\langle$**fun**$\rangle$

#let rec it_btree f x t =
    match t **with**
      Empty $\rightarrow$ x
    | (Bin $(t_1,a,t_2)) \rightarrow$
        it_btree f (f (it_btree f x t_1) a) t_2;;
it_btree : $(\alpha \rightarrow \beta \rightarrow \alpha) \rightarrow \alpha \rightarrow \beta$ *btree* $\rightarrow \alpha$ = $\langle$**fun**$\rangle$

The function flat_btree uses btree_it to produce the list of values present in a tree, and it does so in a left infix traversal.

```
#let flat_btree t = btree_it (fun x l → x :: l) t [ ];;
flat_btree : α btree → α list = ⟨fun⟩
```

Finally, we can also produce imperative traversals in binary trees. The function do_btree applies a function f to every value of a tree in a left infix traversal order.

```
#let do_btree (f:α → unit) =
   do_f where rec do_f = fun
        Empty → ()
      | (Bin (t₁,a,t₂)) →
             do_f t₁; f a; do_f t₂;;
do_btree : (α → unit) → α btree → unit = ⟨fun⟩
```

6.3 Order and Pre-Order Relations

Order relations are represented by functions with values of the type comparison.

```
#type comparison = Smaller | Equiv | Greater;;
```

This choice has the advantage of combining order and equality in the same function. It also lets us represent pre-orders.

To build such a function from an order-relation given as a function with a value of the type bool, we will use the auxiliary function mk_order.

```
#let mk_order ord x y =
    if ord x y then Smaller else
    if x=y then Equiv
    else Greater;;
mk_order : (α → α → bool) → α → α → comparison = ⟨fun⟩
```

Here is an example using the order of the integers.

```
#let int_comp = mk_order (prefix <);;
int_comp : int → int → comparison = ⟨fun⟩

#int_comp 2 3;;
− : comparison = Smaller

#int_comp 2 2;;
− : comparison = Equiv
```

A **pre-order** is a reflexive and transitive relation that is not necessarily antisymmetric. There is an equivalence relation $\equiv$ associated with every pre-order $\leq$. That equivalence relation is defined by

$$x \equiv y \longleftrightarrow x \leq y \text{ and } y \leq x$$

If $\equiv$ is the identity relation, then $\leq$ is an order relation.

The pair made up of a pre-order and its associated equivalence relation will also be represented by a function with a value of the type comparison. We could build it by using this:

```
#let mk_preorder(lt,eq) x y =
  if lt x y then Smaller else
  if eq x y then Equiv
  else Greater;;
mk_preorder : (α → β → bool) * (α → β → bool)
              → α → β → comparison = ⟨fun⟩
```

In certain computations using an order or pre-order, it is convenient to assume that there is a minimal and maximal element. We will use the type

```
#type α minmax = Min | Plain of α | Max;;
```

and extend an order relation by

```
#let extend_order ord x y =
  match (x,y) with
    ((Min,Min)|(Max,Max)) → Equiv
  | ((Min,_)|(_,Max)) → Smaller
  | ((Max,_)|(_,Min)) → Greater
  | (Plain x,Plain y) → ord x y;;
extend_order : (α → β → comparison)
                → α minmax → β minmax → comparison = ⟨fun⟩
```

6.4   Binary Search Trees

A **binary search tree** is a binary tree in which the values belong to an ordered data set; at each node, the value there is greater than all the values in the left child and less than all those in the right child. This property makes it possible to search for a value in a tree and yet explore only one of its branches. In effect, to know whether a value x is located in a tree $t=a(t_1,t_2)$, all we have to do is to begin by comparing x to a:

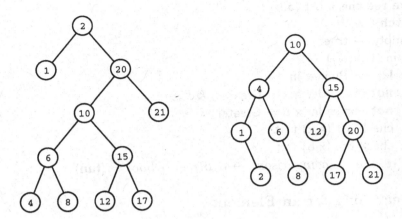

Figure 6.3. Two trees representing the same data set

- if x=a, then x is in t;

- if x<a, then x is in t if and only if x is in t_1;

- if x>a, then x is in t if and only if x is in t_2.

Binary search trees thus represent ordered data sets in such a way that the cost in the worst case of testing whether an element belongs to a tree is proportional to the length of the longest branch in that tree.

Many possible binary search trees correspond to any given ordered data set. For example, the two trees in Figure 6.3 represent the same set of integers: {1, 2, 4, 6, 8, 10, 12, 15, 17, 20, 21}.

Binary search trees are implemented as objects of type **btree**. This type does not distinguish between arbitrary binary trees and binary *search* trees. All functions that build, traverse, or modify binary search trees take an order relation as an argument, and they assume that the trees they work on are in fact binary search trees with respect to this relation.

When binary search trees implement various, more specialized data structures such as ordered sets or dictionaries, we would like to integrate the order relation in use with the corresponding types.

For example, the function to verify that a binary tree is in fact a binary search tree for a given relation could be written like this:

```
#let rec is_bst order =
    let ext_order = extend_order order in
    check_bst (Min,Max)
```

```
    where rec check_bst (a,b) t =
      match t with
        Empty → true
      | (Bin (t₁,x,t₂)) →
          let x= Plain x in
          not (ext_order a x = Greater) &
          not (ext_order x b = Greater) &
          check_bst (a,x) t₁ &
          check_bst (x,b) t₂;;
```

$is\_bst : (\alpha \rightarrow \alpha \rightarrow comparison) \rightarrow \alpha\ btree \rightarrow bool = \langle\mathbf{fun}\rangle$

6.4.1   Searching for an Element

The function search_bst traverses a binary search tree to find an element equivalent to e in the pre-order order. In a binary search tree, to find the element, we have to traverse only the branch of the tree in which the element is located. To get a response from this function, we apply the parameter answer to a subtree of the root, the subtree where the element we are looking for is actually found.

```
#exception Bst_search_exc of string;;

#let search_bst order answer e =
  search where rec search = fun
          Empty → raise (Bst_search_exc "search_bst")
        | (Bin(t₁,x,t₂) as t) →
            match order e x with
              Equiv → answer t
            | Smaller → search t₁
            | Greater → search t₂;;
```

$search\_bst : (\alpha \rightarrow \beta \rightarrow comparison)$
$\qquad \rightarrow (\beta\ btree \rightarrow \gamma) \rightarrow \alpha \rightarrow \beta\ btree \rightarrow \gamma = \langle\mathbf{fun}\rangle$

The function find_bst is a variation that returns the information (rather than the subtree of which the information is the root).

```
#let find_bst order = search_bst order root;;
```

$find\_bst : (\alpha \rightarrow \beta \rightarrow comparison) \rightarrow \alpha \rightarrow \beta\ btree \rightarrow \beta = \langle\mathbf{fun}\rangle$

We will also sometimes use the function belongs_to_bst, which returns a Boolean result.

```
#let belongs_to_bst order e t=
  try find_bst order e t; true
  with Bst_search_exc _ → false;;
```

$belongs\_to\_bst : (\alpha \rightarrow \beta \rightarrow comparison) \rightarrow \alpha \rightarrow \beta\ btree \rightarrow bool$
$\qquad = \langle\mathbf{fun}\rangle$

In the case where we are using a pre-order, it may be necessary to replace an element of a tree by an element equivalent in the sense of the pre-order. The function change_bst searches like find_bst, but it does not return the element it finds; rather, it returns a new tree in which the element has been modified by the function modify. It is the programmer's responsibility to ensure that this function preserves the equivalence associated with the pre-order. This operation entails copying the nodes (and only those nodes) found between the root of the tree and the modified element.

```
#let change_bst order modify e =
   change where rec change = fun
           Empty → raise (Bst_search_exc "change_bst")
         | (Bin(t₁,x,t₂) as t) →
               (match order e x with
                   Equiv → Bin(t₁,modify x,t₂)
                 | Smaller → Bin(change t₁,x,t₂)
                 | Greater → Bin(t₁,x,change t₂));;
change_bst : (α → β → comparison)
            → (β → β) → α → β btree → β btree = ⟨fun⟩
```

6.4.2   Adding an Element

There are two different ways to add an element e to a binary search tree: to the leaves or to the root. The simplest is adding to the leaves. We do that by searching the tree for an occurrence of an empty subtree that can be replaced by the element to add. To find such an occurrence, we only have to compare the element e to the root and then continue the search—in the left subtree when e is less than the root, and in the right subtree when e is greater than the root. When the element is equivalent to the root of the tree, what we must do depends on whether we want to keep the old root, replace it by the new one, or refuse the operation.

The function add_bottom_to_bst implements the algorithm that we have just briefly outlined. In the case where an element equivalent to the one we want to add is already present in the tree, we will use the parameter option to specify our choice between the old and new element.

- If we want to replace the old element by the new, we will use the function (**fun** x y → x) as the option.

- If we want to keep the old element, we will use (**fun** x y → y).

- In case we want to exclude this kind of conflict altogether, we could use, for example, the function (**fun** x y → raise (Bst_search_exc "clash")).

```
#let rec add_bottom_to_bst option order t e =
   add t where rec add = fun
        Empty → Bin(Empty,e,Empty)
      | (Bin(t₁,x,t₂) as t) →
           (match order e x with
               Equiv → Bin(t₁,option e x,t₂)
             | Smaller → Bin(add t₁,x,t₂)
             | Greater → Bin(t₁,x,add t₂));;
```

$add\_bottom\_to\_bst : (\alpha \rightarrow \alpha \rightarrow \alpha) \rightarrow (\alpha \rightarrow \alpha \rightarrow comparison)$
$$\rightarrow \alpha\ btree \rightarrow \alpha \rightarrow \alpha\ btree = \langle \textbf{fun} \rangle$$

The function add_list_bottom_to_bst adds a list of elements to a binary search tree.

```
#let add_list_bottom_to_bst option order =
   it_list (add_bottom_to_bst option order);;
```

$add\_list\_bottom\_to\_bst : (\alpha \rightarrow \alpha \rightarrow \alpha) \rightarrow (\alpha \rightarrow \alpha \rightarrow comparison)$
$$\rightarrow \alpha\ btree \rightarrow \alpha\ list \rightarrow \alpha\ btree$$
$$= \langle \textbf{fun} \rangle$$

The function mk_bst builds a binary search tree from a list of elements.

```
#let mk_bst option order = add_list_bottom_to_bst option order Empty;;
```

$mk\_bst : (\alpha \rightarrow \alpha \rightarrow \alpha) \rightarrow (\alpha \rightarrow \alpha \rightarrow comparison) \rightarrow \alpha\ list \rightarrow \alpha\ btree$
$$= \langle \textbf{fun} \rangle$$

Figure 6.4 shows you the trees that are built successively when we evaluate the expression mk_bst (**fun** x y → x) int_comp $[10; 15; 12; 4; 6; 21; 8; 1; 17; 2]$.

6.4.3   Adding an Element to the Root

It is also possible to add elements to the root of a binary search tree. This technique is useful when we want to produce an application where we often need to search for recently added elements. If such elements are close to the root, they will be found more rapidly.

For this purpose, given a tree t and an element e to add, we begin by "cutting" the original tree into two binary search trees, t_1 and t_2, where t_1 contains the elements less than e, and t_2 contains those greater than e. In the case where the original tree t does not contain an element equivalent to e, or in the case where we want to replace it by e, all we have to do is to build the tree Bin(t_1,e,t_2) to add the element. If we want instead to keep the old equivalent element, then the cutting procedure must also return the element plus the two subtrees. The next algorithm takes that possibility into account.

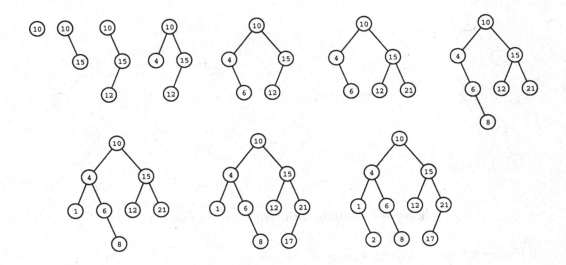

Figure 6.4. Adding at the leaves

To cut the Empty tree with respect to the element e, return the triple (Empty, e, Empty).

To cut the tree t=a(t_1,t_2) in two parts around the value e, we compare e and a.

- If e=a, return the triple (t_1,a,t_2).

- If e<a, cut the tree t_1 with respect to the element e. Doing so will provide a triple (t'_1,e',t'_2). Return the triple (t'_1,e',a(t'_2,t_2)).

- If e>a, do the symmetric operation.

The function cut_bst implements that algorithm.

```
#let rec cut_bst order e =
    cut where rec cut = fun
        Empty → (Empty,e,Empty)
      | (Bin(t₁,a,t₂)) →
            (match order e a with
                Smaller → let (t,e',t') = cut t₁ in
                          (t,e',Bin(t',a,t₂))
              | Equiv → (t₁,a,t₂)
              | Greater → let (t,e',t') = cut t₂ in
                          (Bin(t₁,a,t),e',t'));;
    cut_bst : (α → α → comparison)
            → α → α btree → α btree * α * α btree = ⟨fun⟩
```

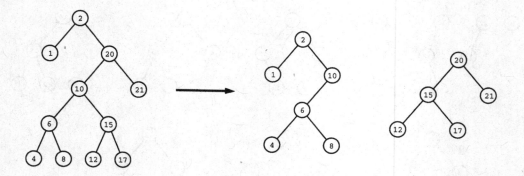

Figure 6.5. Cutting with respect to the value 11

Figure 6.5 shows you an example of cutting.

To add an element e to a binary search tree t, we cut t to get the triple (t_1,e',t_2), and then we build the tree $t=e(t_1,t_2)$ if we prefer the new element, or we build $t=e'(t_1,t_2)$ otherwise. Notice that when the tree t does not contain an element equivalent to e, the cut stops with a subtree, Empty, and thus $e'=e$.

The function add_root_to_bst implements that algorithm.

```
#let add_root_to_bst option order e t =
    let t₁,e',t₂ = cut_bst order e t in
    Bin(t₁,option e e',t₂);;
```
$$add\_root\_to\_bst : (\alpha \to \alpha \to \alpha) \to (\alpha \to \alpha \to comparison)$$
$$\to \alpha \to \alpha \; btree \to \alpha \; btree = \langle \mathbf{fun} \rangle$$

The function mk_bst₂ builds a binary search tree from a list of elements by successively adding to the root.

```
#let mk_bst₂ option order l = list_it (add_root_to_bst option order) l Empty;;
```
$$mk\_bst_2 : (\alpha \to \alpha \to \alpha) \to (\alpha \to \alpha \to comparison) \to \alpha \; list \to \alpha \; btree$$
$$= \langle \mathbf{fun} \rangle$$

Figure 6.6 shows you the successive trees built when we evaluate the expression mk_bst₂ (**fun** x y → x) int_comp $[10;15;12;4;6;21;8;1;17;2]$.

6.4.4   Removing an Element

When we remove an element located at the root of a binary search tree, if at least one of its two children is empty, then the removal of the root is immediate. It is sufficient then to replace the original tree by its non-empty child (if one exists) or by the empty tree otherwise.

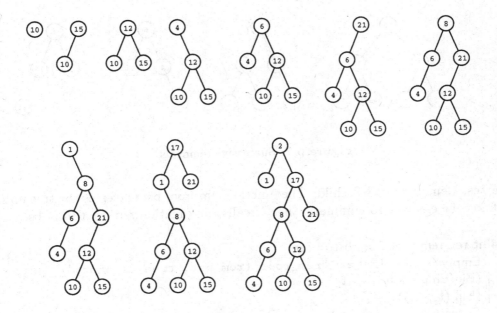

Figure 6.6. Adding at the root

In contrast, when the tree under consideration has two non-empty children, an element found at the root has to be replaced. There are, of course, two candidates for the role: either the greatest element in the left child or the least element in the right child.

Here, we will use the greatest element of the left child to replace the element that we remove. In other words, we choose the element located in the left child at the end of its rightmost branch. To get it, we will use the auxiliary function remove_biggest. When it is applied to a binary search tree, it returns a pair consisting of the greatest element and the original tree deprived of its greatest element.

#exception Bst_exc **of** string;;
Exception Bst_exc defined.

#let rec remove_biggest = **fun**
   (Bin(t_1,a,Empty)) → (a,t_1)
| (Bin(t_1,a,t_2)) →
    let (a',t') = remove_biggest t_2 **in** (a', Bin(t_1,a,t'))
| Empty → raise (Bst_exc "remove_biggest: tree is empty");;
remove_biggest : α *btree* → $\alpha * \alpha$ *btree* = ⟨**fun**⟩

The function rem_root_from_bst uses remove_biggest to replace the root by the

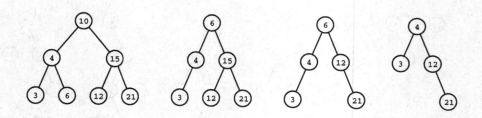

Figure 6.7. Successive removals

greatest element of its left child. The function rem_from_bst traverses the tree until
it finds the element to eliminate; then it calls the function rem_root_from_bst.

```
#let rec rem_root_from_bst = fun
    Empty → raise (Bst_exc "rem_root_from_bst: tree is empty")
  | (Bin(Empty,a,t₂)) → t₂
  | (Bin (t₁,_,t₂)) →
        let (a',t') = remove_biggest t₁ in
        Bin(t',a',t₂);;
rem_root_from_bst : α btree → α btree = ⟨fun⟩
```

```
#let rec rem_from_bst order e =
    rem where rec rem = fun
        Empty → raise (Bst_search_exc "rem_from_bst")
      | (Bin (t₁,a,t₂) as t) →
            (match order e a with
                Equiv → rem_root_from_bst t
              | Smaller → Bin(rem t₁,a, t₂)
              | Greater → Bin(t₁,a, rem t₂));;
rem_from_bst : (α → β → comparison) → α → β btree → β btree
            = ⟨fun⟩
```

The function rem_list_from_bst removes a list of elements from a binary tree.

```
#let rem_list_from_bst order =
    list_it (rem_from_bst order);;
rem_list_from_bst : (α → β → comparison)
                → α list → β btree → β btree = ⟨fun⟩
```

Figure 6.7 shows you the successive removal of the elements 10, 15, and 6
from a binary search tree.

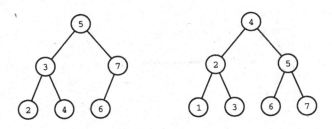

Figure 6.8. Adding the value 1

6.5   Balanced Trees

The cost of searching for an element in a binary search tree is proportional to the distance between the root of the tree and the element we are looking for. The maximal cost of a search is thus proportional to the length of the longest branch, and the average cost is proportional to the average distance of nodes from the root.

Thus among binary trees of size n, those that support best performance, both on average and in the worst case, are **completely balanced trees**; that is, those with height of $\lfloor \log_2(n) \rfloor$. To minimize the average search time, the ideal would thus be to use only completely balanced trees.

To do so, we must be able to keep this complete balance when we add or remove elements, and we must keep the balance at a reasonable cost. Alas, as you will see immediately from the following example, that is not possible. The left tree in the Figure 6.8 is a completely balanced binary search tree. If we add the value 1, the only completely balanced binary search tree possible will be the one on the right in the same figure. Notice that those two trees differ in every node; moreover, the relation of parent to child is totally different between the two trees. In short, building the tree on the right requires total reconstruction of the original tree.

We can reproduce this kind of example for trees of arbitrarily large size, so we conclude that the cost of re-organizing binary search trees after an addition is necessarily linear in the worst case if we try to keep the tree completely balanced.

To achieve logarithmic costs in the worst case for additions and removals, we have to loosen up our idea of "balanced." AVL trees, presented in Section 6.5.2, provide one solution to this problem. In that family of trees, we restore balance to a tree by means of local operations known as **rotations**.

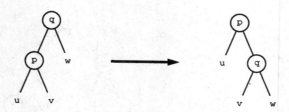

Figure 6.9. Right rotation

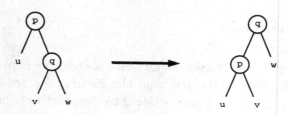

Figure 6.10. Left rotation

6.5.1 Rotations

Rotation is a way of re-organizing trees to preserve the structure of a binary search tree, but it allows us to modify the balance of the tree. There are two kinds of rotation: **right**, as you see in Figure 6.9, and **left**, as you see in Figure 6.10.

We program those operations like this:

```
#let rot_right = fun
   (Bin(Bin(u,p,v),q,w))
   → Bin(u,p,Bin(v,q,w))
```

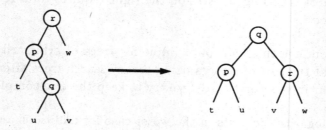

Figure 6.11. Left-right rotation

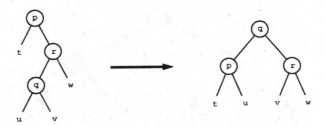

Figure 6.12. Right-left rotation

```
      | _ → raise (Btree_exc "rot_right");;
rot_right : α btree → α btree = ⟨fun⟩


#let rot_left =
   fun (Bin(u,p,Bin(v,q,w)))
        → Bin(Bin(u,p,v),q,w)
      | _ → raise (Btree_exc "rot_left");;
rot_left : α btree → α btree = ⟨fun⟩
```

We will also use combinations of these operations, known as **left-right rota-tion,** as you see in Figure 6.11, and **right-left rotation,** as you see in Figure 6.12. They are programmed like this:

```
#let rot_left_right = fun
   (Bin(Bin(t,p,Bin(u,q,v)),r,w))
      →
        Bin(Bin(t,p,u),q,Bin(v,r,w))
   | _ → raise (Btree_exc "rot_left_right");;
rot_left_right : α btree → α btree = ⟨fun⟩


#let rot_right_left = fun
   (Bin(t,r,Bin(Bin(u,q,v),p,w)))
      →
        Bin(Bin(t,r,u),q,Bin(v,p,w))
   | _ → raise (Btree_exc "rot_right_left");;
rot_right_left : α btree → α btree = ⟨fun⟩
```

It is easy to verify that these rotations preserve the structure of a binary search tree.

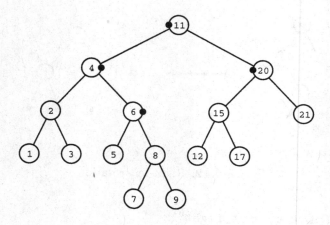

Figure 6.13. An AVL tree

6.5.2   AVL Trees

Let's define a function, δ, that associates a degree of "unbalance" with the root of every tree.

$$\delta(\mathrm{a}(t_1, t_2)) = \mathrm{height}(t_1) - \mathrm{height}(t_2)$$

A binary tree is said to be **H-balanced** if, for each of its subtrees, the function δ is at most one in absolute value. **AVL trees**[2] are H-balanced binary search trees.

Figure 6.13 shows you an AVL tree where the nodes leaning to the left are marked by a black spot on the left, and those leaning to the right are marked by a black spot on the right.

An H-balanced tree of size n has a height bounded by a logarithmic function of n. We can demonstrate this property quite simply. To do so, for every height h, we build the tree of height h that has a minimal number of summits.

- For height 1, we get a tree of size 1.

- To build a tree of height h, one of the children of the root must necessarily be of height $h - 1$; otherwise, if there were no such child, then the tree itself could not be of height h. Incidentally, the other child must necessarily be of height $h - 2$. If the height were strictly less than $h - 2$, then the constructed tree would not be H-balanced at its root; if it were of height $h - 1$, then the tree would not be of minimal size.

---

[2]These trees were introduced by Adelson-Velski and Landis.

If we denote the minimal size of an H-balanced tree of height h as $N(h)$, then we get a recursive definition of this function.

- $N(0) = 0$

- $N(1) = 1$

- $N(h) = N(h-1) + N(h-2) + 1$

By posing $N'(h) = N(h) + 1$, we get this equation:

$$N'(h) = N'(h-1) + N'(h-2)$$

No doubt you recognize that equation as our friend, the Fibonacci numbers. Since these numbers increase exponentially, the inverse function must grow logarithmically, and in fact, it is possible to show that the height of an H-balanced tree of size n is bounded by $1.44 \log_2(n+2)$.

To implement AVL trees, it would be most efficient to introduce a type with three constructors corresponding to the three cases $\delta = -1$, $\delta = 0$, and $\delta = +1$. However, this type would be different from the type btree, and that difference would prevent us from re-using the functions defined for btree. Consequently, we will implement AVL trees as binary trees with information of type balance at each node. The type balance has three values indicating whether the tree is balanced at that node ($\delta = 0$), whether it leans to the left ($\delta = 1$), or whether it leans to the right ($\delta = -1$).

#type balance = Left | Balanced | Right;;

The type used could be abbreviated like this:

#type α avltree == (α * balance) btree;;

As we did for binary search trees, we will use specific exceptions for AVL trees.

#exception Avl_exc **of** string;;
Exception Avl_exc defined.

#exception Avl_search_exc **of** string;;
Exception Avl_search_exc defined.

Many functions for AVL trees are directly inherited from binary search trees. However, the comparison function has to impinge on the useful information at every node and leave aside the details about balance.

For example, the function belongs_to_avl tests whether a value belongs to an AVL tree. It uses belongs_to_bst with a suitably modified comparison function.

```
#let belongs_to_avl order =
   belongs_to_bst (fun x y → order x (fst y));;
```
$belongs\_to\_avl : (\alpha \rightarrow \beta \rightarrow comparison) \rightarrow \alpha \rightarrow (\beta * \gamma)\ btree \rightarrow bool$
$\qquad = \langle \textbf{fun} \rangle$

Likewise, we can assume that these functions have been defined:

```
flat_avl : (α * balance) btree → α list
map_avl : (α → β) → (α * balance) btree → (β * balance) btree
do_avl : (α → unit) → (α * balance) btree → unit
```

Incidentally, when a function working on AVL trees raises an exception, we make sure that it involves an exception specific to AVL trees.

```
#let find_avl order e (t:(α*balance) btree) =
   try fst(find_bst (fun x y → order x (fst y)) e t)
   with Bst_search_exc _ → raise(Avl_search_exc "find_avl");;
```
$find\_avl : (\alpha \rightarrow \beta \rightarrow comparison) \rightarrow \alpha \rightarrow (\beta * balance)\ btree \rightarrow \beta$
$\qquad = \langle \textbf{fun} \rangle$

In contrast, all the functions that depend on information about balance have to be specially defined. For example, here is a function to test whether an AVL tree is correctly balanced:

```
#let h_balanced (t:(α*balance) btree) =
   let rec correct_balance= fun
     Empty → 0
   | (Bin(t₁,(x,b),t₂))
     → let n₁ = correct_balance t₁ and n₂ = correct_balance t₂ in
       if (b=Balanced & n₁=n₂ ) then n₁+1 else
       if (b=Left & n₁=n₂+1) then n₁+1 else
       if (b=Right & n₂=n₁+1) then n₂+1
       else raise (Avl_exc "not avl") in
   try correct_balance t; true
   with Avl_exc _ → false;;
```
$h\_balanced : (\alpha * balance)\ btree \rightarrow bool = \langle \textbf{fun} \rangle$

```
#let is_avl order (t:(α*balance) btree) =
   h_balanced t & is_bst (fun x y → order (fst x) (fst y)) t;;
```
$is\_avl : (\alpha \rightarrow \alpha \rightarrow comparison) \rightarrow (\alpha * balance)\ btree \rightarrow bool = \langle \textbf{fun} \rangle$

Here is a function to produce the mirror image of an AVL tree:

```
#let mirror_avl t =
  btree_hom
    (fun (t₁,(x,b),t₂)
        → Bin(t₂,(x,b'),t₁)
          where b' = match b with
            Left → Right
          | Balanced → Balanced
          | Right → Left)
    Empty t;;
mirror_avl : (α * balance) btree → (α * balance) btree = ⟨fun⟩
```

Adding elements to an AVL tree or removing elements from it can disturb its balance. For example, if we use the algorithm for adding leaves to a binary search tree in order to add the value 10 to the leaves of the AVL tree in Figure 6.13, we will produce a tree that is no longer AVL. The nodes 11, 4, and 6 would have δ equal to 2, -2, and -2 respectively. We also disturb the balance if we add 10 at the root. Consequently, the functions for adding elements that we have defined for binary trees can not be used here as they are.

Removing elements is also an operation likely to unbalance an AVL tree. If we remove the elements 12 and 17 from the tree in Figure 6.13, the root becomes unbalanced.

Consequently, the functions we defined for adding and removing in binary search trees cannot be used here as they are.

Fortunately, we can fix the disturbances introduced by these operations by using "rotation" functions.

6.5.3 Adding Elements to an AVL Tree

We will begin in the context of the algorithm we presented in Section 6.4.2 to add leaves to a tree. We will assume that we have an AVL tree $t=a(t_1,t_2)$ to which we want to add an element e. We start by comparing e to a.

If e=a, then we consider the option we chose and return either the tree t itself, or the tree $e(t_1,t_2)$.

If e<a, we add the element in the subtree t_1, which in turn gives rise to the tree t'_1. Now there are several cases to consider.

- If height(t'_1) = height(t_1)+1 and if $\delta(t)=0$ or $\delta(t)=-1$, then the result of our adding the element will still be $a(t'_1,t_2)$. However, we must correctly place the information about balance in the root of the resulting tree.

- If height(t'_1) = height(t_1)+1 and if $\delta(t)=1$, then the tree $t'=a(t'_1,t_2)$ is not an AVL tree because $\delta(t')=2$. We must rebalance it through rotations. To do so, we must consider the balance of the tree t'_1. We know that this tree

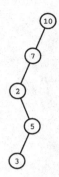

Figure 6.14. A tree built without rebalancing it

cannot be balanced. If it were, it would have the same height as t_1. Thus, there are only two possible cases:

- $\delta(t_1)=1$. t' can be rebalanced by a right rotation. The result of our adding the element will then be rot_right($a(t'_1,t_2)$) .

- $\delta(t_1)=-1$. t'=$a(t'_1,t_2)$ can be rebalanced by a left rotation of t'_1, followed by a right rotation of the entire tree. The result of our adding the element will then be rot_right($a(\text{rot\_left}(t'_1),t_2)$) .

- The other cases are symmetric to the preceding ones.

When a subtree must be rebalanced after the addition of an element, its height after rebalancing is the same as before the addition. It follows from this observation then that no subtree containing it will need to be rebalanced. An addition thus causes at most one rotation (whether simple or double).

An example will help you understand what is going on during these reorganizations of AVL trees after an addition. Figures 6.15 and 6.16 show the intervening rotations in an AVL tree built by successive additions of the elements 10, 7, 2, 5, and 3. If we had added these elements to a binary search tree with the algorithm from Section 6.4.2, the result would be the degenerate tree in Figure 6.14.

After we introduce elements 10, 7, and 2, we get the unbalanced tree on the left in Figure 6.15. It can be rebalanced by a right rotation.

When we successively add the elements 5 and 3, we get a new unbalanced tree, the one on the left in Figure 6.16. This one can be rebalanced by a double rotation: right-left.

With these ideas in mind, we can now write the function for adding elements. First, we will give you a new version of the rotation operations to take into

Figure 6.15. Rebalancing by right rotation

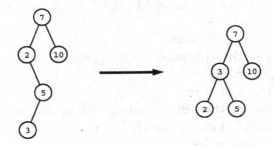

Figure 6.16. Rebalancing by right-left rotation

account any modifications of information about balance. Here is the definition of a right rotation. The others are redefined in a similar way.

```
#exception Avl_rotation_exc of string;;
```

```
#let rot_right = fun
    (Bin(Bin(u,(p,b),v),(q,_),w)) →
        (match b with
            Balanced → Bin(u,(p,Right),Bin(v,(q,Left),w))
          | Left → Bin(u,(p,Balanced),Bin(v,(q,Balanced),w))
          | Right → raise (Avl_rotation_exc "rot_right"))
    | _ → raise (Avl_rotation_exc "rot_right");;
rot_right : (α * balance) btree → (α * balance) btree = ⟨fun⟩
```

In order for us to decide whether a tree needs rebalancing, and also so that we can update balance information along the branch from the root to the insertion point (nodes not along that branch will not be bothered), the recursive procedure for adding an element must provide not only the resulting tree after an addition, but also information about whether the height of the tree has changed, and if so, in which child it changed. This information will be a value of type avl_add_info.

```
#type avl_add_info = No_inc | Incleft | Incright;;
```

Incleft is used when the height increases on the left, and Incright, on the right. If the original tree was empty, we can return either of those because the choice makes no difference in later computations. We use No_inc when the height has not changed.

```
#let rec add_to_avl option order t e =
    fst(add t)
    where rec add = fun
      Empty →
        Bin(Empty,(e,Balanced),Empty),Incleft
    | (Bin(t₁,(x,b),t₂) as t) →
        (match (order e x , b) with
          (Equiv,_) → Bin(t₁,(option e x,b),t₂),No_inc
        | (Smaller,Balanced) →
            let t,m = add t₁ in
            if m=No_inc then Bin(t,(x,Balanced),t₂),No_inc
            else Bin(t,(x,Left),t₂),Incleft
        | (Greater,Balanced) →
            let t,m = add t₂ in
            if m= No_inc then Bin(t₁,(x,Balanced),t),No_inc
            else Bin(t₁,(x,Right),t),Incright
        | (Greater,Left) →
            let t,m = add t₂ in
            if m=No_inc then Bin(t₁,(x,Left),t),No_inc
            else Bin(t₁,(x,Balanced),t),No_inc
        | (Smaller,Left) →
            let t,m = add t₁ in
            (match m with
              No_inc → Bin(t,(x,Left),t₂),No_inc
            | Incleft → rot_right (Bin(t,(x,Balanced),t₂)),No_inc
            | Incright → rot_left_right(Bin(t,(x,Balanced),t₂)),No_inc)
        | (Smaller,Right) →
            let t,m = add t₁ in
            if m= No_inc then Bin(t,(x,Right),t₂),No_inc
            else Bin(t,(x,Balanced),t₂),No_inc
        | (Greater,Right) →
            let t,m = add t₂ in
            (match m with
              No_inc → Bin(t₁,(x,Right),t),No_inc
            | Incleft → rot_right_left(Bin(t₁,(x,Balanced),t)),No_inc
            | Incright → rot_left(Bin(t₁,(x,Balanced),t)),No_inc));;
add_to_avl : (α → α → α) → (α → α → comparison)
```

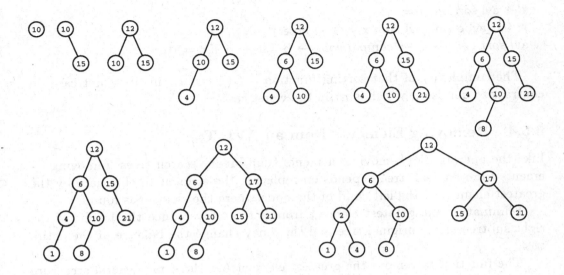

Figure 6.17. Successive addition in an AVL tree

$$\rightarrow (\alpha * balance)\ btree$$
$$\rightarrow \alpha \rightarrow (\alpha * balance)\ btree = \langle \mathbf{fun} \rangle$$

By iterating add_to_avl, we get the functions

#let add_list_to_avl option order = it_list (add_to_avl option order);;
$add\_list\_to\_avl : (\alpha \rightarrow \alpha \rightarrow \alpha) \rightarrow (\alpha \rightarrow \alpha \rightarrow comparison)$
$$\rightarrow (\alpha * balance)\ btree$$
$$\rightarrow \alpha\ list \rightarrow (\alpha * balance)\ btree = \langle \mathbf{fun} \rangle$$

#let mk_avl option order = add_list_to_avl option order Empty;;
$mk\_avl : (\alpha \rightarrow \alpha \rightarrow \alpha) \rightarrow (\alpha \rightarrow \alpha \rightarrow comparison)$
$$\rightarrow \alpha\ list \rightarrow (\alpha * balance)\ btree = \langle \mathbf{fun} \rangle$$

#let merge_avl option order =
  it_btree (**fun** t x → add_to_avl option order t (fst x));;
$merge\_avl : (\alpha \rightarrow \alpha \rightarrow \alpha) \rightarrow (\alpha \rightarrow \alpha \rightarrow comparison)$
$$\rightarrow (\alpha * balance)\ btree$$
$$\rightarrow (\alpha * \beta)\ btree \rightarrow (\alpha * balance)\ btree = \langle \mathbf{fun} \rangle$$

Figure 6.17 shows you the trees built successively by the evaluation of this:

mk_avl (**fun** x y → x) int_comp [10; 15; 12; 4; 6; 21; 8; 1; 17; 2]

We can get a sorting function from the function that builds AVL trees. To do so, we simply have to compose that one with a linearizing function, like this:

```
#let avl_sort order =
    flat_avl o (mk_avl (fun x y → x) order);;
```
$avl\_sort : (\alpha \rightarrow \alpha \rightarrow comparison) \rightarrow \alpha\ list \rightarrow \alpha\ list = \langle \textbf{fun} \rangle$

The complexity of that sorting function is $O(n \log(n))$ in the worst case, in contrast to quicksort, which is n^2 in the worst case.

6.5.4 Removing Elements from an AVL Tree

Like the operation of removing elements from binary search trees, removing elements from an AVL tree depends on replacing the element to eliminate by the greatest element of the left child of the node where the element is found.

Eliminating the greatest element from a tree may reduce the height of the right subtree of the original tree and thus may change the balance of the entire tree.

The function to remove the greatest element has the same general structure as the one in Section 6.4.4. It must also return supplementary information to indicate whether the height of the tree has decreased or not. For that, we use this type:

```
#type avl_rem_info = No_dec | Dec;;
```

For convenience, we have the following auxiliary functions:

```
#let balance = fun
    (Bin (_,(_,b),_)) → b
  | Empty → Balanced;;
```
$balance : (\alpha * balance)\ btree \rightarrow balance = \langle \textbf{fun} \rangle$

```
#let balance_right (t,x,t') =
    match balance t with
      (Left | Balanced) → rot_right (Bin(t,(x,Balanced),t'))
    | Right → rot_left_right (Bin(t,(x,Balanced),t'));;
```
$balance\_right : (\alpha * balance)\ btree * \alpha * (\alpha * balance)\ btree$
$\qquad\qquad \rightarrow (\alpha * balance)\ btree = \langle \textbf{fun} \rangle$

```
#let balance_left (t,x,t') =
    match balance t' with
      (Right | Balanced) → rot_left (Bin(t,(x,Balanced),t'))
    | Left → rot_right_left (Bin(t,(x,Balanced),t'));;
```
$balance\_left : (\alpha * balance)\ btree * \alpha * (\alpha * balance)\ btree$
$\qquad\qquad \rightarrow (\alpha * balance)\ btree = \langle \textbf{fun} \rangle$

Here is the function to remove the greatest element:

```
#let rec avl_remove_biggest = fun
    (Bin(t₁,(a,_),Empty)) → (a,t₁,Dec)
  | (Bin(t₁,(a,Balanced),t₂)) →
        let (a',t',b) = avl_remove_biggest t₂ in
        (match b with
            Dec → (a', Bin(t₁,(a,Left),t'),No_dec)
          | No_dec → (a', Bin(t₁,(a,Balanced),t'),No_dec))
  | (Bin(t₁,(a,Right),t₂)) →
        let (a',t',b) = avl_remove_biggest t₂ in
        (match b with
            Dec → (a', Bin(t₁,(a,Balanced),t'),Dec)
          | No_dec → (a', Bin(t₁,(a,Right),t'),No_dec))
  | (Bin(t₁,(a,Left),t₂)) →
        let (a',t',b) = avl_remove_biggest t₂ in
        (match b with
            Dec → (a', balance_right (t₁,a,t'),
                    match snd(root t₁) with
                    (Left|Right) → Dec
                  | Balanced → No_dec)
          | No_dec → (a', Bin(t₁,(a,Left),t'),No_dec))
  | Empty → raise (Avl_exc "avl_remove_biggest: empty avl");;
```

$avl\_remove\_biggest : (\alpha * balance)\ btree \rightarrow \alpha * (\alpha * balance)\ btree *$
$$avl\_rem\_info = \langle \textbf{fun} \rangle$$

The chief removal function repeats the same structure as the one in Section 6.4.4, too. It searches for the element to remove from the tree. When it finds that element, that is, when it finds a subtree of the form e(t₁,t₂) where e is the element to remove, it calls the function remove_biggest to which it passes t₁ as an argument. That function returns a triple made up of a new tree t'₁, the greatest element a from t₁, and information about the difference in height between t₁ and t'₁. That information is used later to balance the tree a(t'₁,t₂), if need be.

Moreover, rebalancing the tree a(t'₁,t₂) may produce a tree of lower height than e(t₁,t₂) (the one it replaces), and thus we must propagate that information to precipitate other rebalancings as we go back up toward the root.

Thus in contrast to what happened when we added an element, when we remove an element, we may have to carry out more than one rebalancing. There are no theoretic results about the average number of rotations needed by a removal. Experimental studies, though, have shown that on average, there is one rotation for five removals, whereas there is on average a rotation for every two additions.

Figure 6.18 shows the trees produced successively by our removing the elements 21, 17, 2, 4, 15, 12, 8, 10, and 6 from the AVL tree built in Figure 6.17.

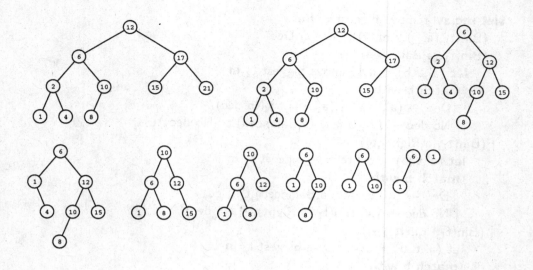

Figure 6.18. Successive removals from an AVL tree

Here, finally, is the function for removing elements.

```
#let rec remove_from_avl order t e =
  fst (remove t)
  where rec remove = fun
   Empty → raise (Avl_search_exc "remove_from_avl")
  | (Bin(t₁,(a,b),t₂)) →
      match order e a with
       Equiv →
          if t₁=Empty then t₂,Dec else
          if t₂=Empty then t₁,Dec else
          let (a',t',m) = avl_remove_biggest t₁ in
          (match m with
            No_dec → Bin(t',(a',b),t₂),No_dec
          | Dec → (match b with
                    Balanced → Bin(t',(a',Right),t₂),No_dec
                  | Left → Bin(t',(a',Balanced),t₂),Dec
                  | Right → balance_left(t',a',t₂),
                            if balance t₂ = Balanced
                            then No_dec else Dec))
      | Smaller →
          let t',m = remove t₁ in
          (match m with
            No_dec → Bin(t',(a,b),t₂),No_dec
```

```
            | Dec → (match b with
                        Balanced → Bin(t',(a,Right),t₂),No_dec
                      | Left → Bin(t',(a,Balanced),t₂),Dec
                      | Right → balance_left(t',a,t₂),
                                  if balance t₂ = Balanced
                                  then No_dec else Dec))
      | Greater →
          let t',m = remove t₂ in
          (match m with
            No_dec → Bin(t₁,(a,b),t'),No_dec
          | Dec → (match b with
                      Balanced → Bin(t₁,(a,Left),t'),No_dec
                    | Right → Bin(t₁,(a,Balanced),t'),Dec
                    | Left → balance_right(t₁,a,t'),
                                if balance t₁=Balanced
                                then No_dec else Dec));;
```

$$remove\_from\_avl : (\alpha \rightarrow \beta \rightarrow comparison)$$
$$\rightarrow (\beta * balance)\ btree \rightarrow \alpha \rightarrow (\beta * balance)\ btree$$
$$= \langle \textbf{fun} \rangle$$

6.6 Dictionaries

Here a **dictionary** is a structure to store information where the items of information are associated with keys from an ordered set. Dictionaries in the usual sense are the canonical example, but more generally, any function with a finite, ordered domain can be considered as a dictionary.

We will show you an implementation of dictionaries based on balanced AVL trees. With respect to performance, this implementation does not rival implementations based on hashing if the dictionary under consideration is of more or less fixed size or varies in size within foreseeable and reasonable limits. However, when the size of the dictionary cannot be foreseen or when it fluctuates greatly, implementation by balanced trees is a reasonable choice.

The type dictionary is a record with a field dict_rel indicating the order relation to use and another field dict_data containing the data to store. The information corresponds to the parameter α, and the key corresponds to the parameter β.

```
#type (α,β) dictionary =
      { dict_rel : β → β → comparison;
        dict_data: (α * β) avltree};;
```

Functions to search for, add, and remove elements directly exploit the corresponding functions for AVL trees. We have to modify only the comparison functions so that they access the keys. The search function is known as dict_assoc by analogy with the assoc function for lists.

```
#let dict_assoc e d =
    fst(fst(find_avl (fun x y → d.dict_rel x (snd y)) e d.dict_data));;
dict_assoc : α → (β * γ, α) dictionary → β = ⟨fun⟩
```

In a dictionary, adding an element usually entails replacing existing items.

```
#let dict_add_or_replace {dict_rel=c;dict_data=t} e =
    {dict_rel=c;
     dict_data=add_to_avl (fun x y → y) (fun x y → c (snd x) (snd y)) t e};;
dict_add_or_replace : (α, β) dictionary → α * β → (α, β) dictionary
                    = ⟨fun⟩
```

However, it is also possible to program other add functions if we choose a different option in the function add_to_avl.

The removal function looks like this:

```
#let dict_remove {dict_rel=c;dict_data=t} key =
    {dict_rel=c;
     dict_data=remove_from_avl (fun x y → c x (snd y)) t key };;
dict_remove : (α, β) dictionary → β → (α, β) dictionary = ⟨fun⟩
```

At times, we may also want to combine two dictionaries, like this:

```
#let dict_merge opt d₁ d₂ =
    if not(d₁.dict_rel==d₂.dict_rel) then
      failwith "dict_merge: dictionaries have different orders" else
    {dict_rel=d₁.dict_rel;
     dict_data= merge_avl opt (fun x y → d₁.dict_rel (snd x) (snd y))
                  d₁.dict_data d₂.dict_data};;
dict_merge : (α * β → α * β → α * β)
           → (α, β) dictionary
           → (α, β) dictionary → (α, β) dictionary = ⟨fun⟩
```

Exercises

6.1 To produce dictionaries for a natural language, we usually use a **trie** structure where we branch on each letter. (Fredkin says that the term trie comes from the word re*trie*val, and Sedgwick says that is it pronounced like try.) Take your inspiration from the type α gentree that you saw in Chapter 5 to define a type (α,β) trie to represent such dictionaries.

The type α corresponds to the letters, and the type β to the information associated with each word.

6.2 Write a function of type $(\alpha \rightarrow \alpha \rightarrow \mathsf{bool}) \rightarrow \alpha$ list $\rightarrow (\alpha,\beta)$ trie $\rightarrow \beta$ to retrieve the definition of a word in a dictionary. The first argument is the order to use to compare elements of type α (the letters), and the second argument is a word (a list of letters).

6.3 Write a function of type $(\alpha \rightarrow \alpha \rightarrow \mathsf{bool}) \rightarrow (\alpha$ list $* \beta)$ list $\rightarrow (\alpha,\beta)$ trie to build a dictionary from the order over the letters and a list of pairs (word, definition).

6.7   Ordered Sets

Balanced trees make it easy to implement ordered sets. The sets will be represented by records where the field **set_elements** contains the elements of the set organized as a balanced tree, and the field **set_order** indicates the order used in the tree.

```
#type α set =
      {set_elements: α avltree;
       set_order: α → α → comparison};;
```

The operation to build a set takes two arguments: an order relation and the list of elements in the set.

```
#let make_set c l =
    {set_elements=mk_avl (fun x y → x) c l;
     set_order=c};;
  make_set : (α → α → comparison) → α list → α set = ⟨fun⟩
```

Other operations no longer have to refer to the order among the elements since it is present in the internal representation of the set. They use operations that we have already defined for AVL trees.

Test for emptiness

```
#let set_isempty s =
    (s.set_elements=Empty);;
  set_isempty : α set → bool = ⟨fun⟩
```

Test for membership

```
#let set_member x s =
    belongs_to_avl s.set_order x s.set_elements;;
  set_member : α → α set → bool = ⟨fun⟩
```

Iterations over a set

The next two iteration functions let you program many uses of the elements in a set. Nevertheless, you must be careful of the fact that these iterators are sensitive to the representation of the set.

```
#let set_it f s =
    btree_it (fun x y → f (fst x) y) s.set_elements;;
set_it : (α → β → β) → α set → β → β = ⟨fun⟩

#let it_set f x s =
    it_btree (fun x y → f x (fst y)) x s.set_elements;;
it_set : (α → β → α) → α → β set → α = ⟨fun⟩

#let do_set f s = do_avl f s.set_elements;;
do_set : (α → unit) → α set → unit = ⟨fun⟩
```

Quantifications

```
#exception Set_exc of string;;

#let set_forall p s =
  try
    do_set (fun x → if not (p x)
                       then raise (Set_exc "")) s;
    true
  with Set_exc _ → false;;
set_forall : (α → bool) → α set → bool = ⟨fun⟩

#let set_exists p s =
  try do_set (fun x → if (p x)
                       then raise (Set_exc "")) s;
      false
  with Set_exc _ → true;;
set_exists : (α → bool) → α set → bool = ⟨fun⟩
```

Inclusion and equality

```
#let sub_set s₁ s₂ =
    set_forall (fun e → set_member e s₂) s₁;;
sub_set : α set → α set → bool = ⟨fun⟩

#let set_equiv s₁ s₂ =
    sub_set s₁ s₂ & sub_set s₂ s₁;;
set_equiv : α set → α set → bool = ⟨fun⟩
```

Ordered list of elements

```
#let list_of_set s =
    flat_avl s.set_elements;;
list_of_set : α set → α list = ⟨fun⟩
```

Choice of an arbitrary element

We will take the one at the root of the tree.

```
#let set_random_element s =
    fst (root s.set_elements);;
set_random_element : α set → α = ⟨fun⟩
```

Additions

```
#let add_to_set s x =
    {set_elements = add_to_avl (fun x y → x) s.set_order s.set_elements x;
     set_order=s.set_order};;
add_to_set : α set → α → α set = ⟨fun⟩
```

```
#let add_list_to_set s l=
    it_list add_to_set s l;;
add_list_to_set : α set → α list → α set = ⟨fun⟩
```

Removals

```
#let remove_from_set s x =
    try {set_elements= remove_from_avl s.set_order s.set_elements x;
         set_order=s.set_order}
    with _ → raise (Set_exc "remove_from_set");;
remove_from_set : α set → α → α set = ⟨fun⟩
```

```
#let remove_list_from_set s = it_list remove_from_set s;;
remove_list_from_set : α set → α list → α set = ⟨fun⟩
```

The operation remove_from_set fails when the element to remove does not belong to the set. It is also useful to have a function that does not fail in such a case. That function is particularly helpful for the operations of set difference and set intersection.

```
#let subtract_from_set s x =
    try remove_from_set s x
    with _ → s;;
subtract_from_set : α set → α → α set = ⟨fun⟩
```

Set operations

```
#let set_union s₁ s₂ =
  if not(s₁.set_order = s₂.set_order)
  then raise (Set_exc "set_union: different set orders")
  else it_set add_to_set s₁ s₂;;
```
set_union : α *set* $\rightarrow$ α *set* $\rightarrow$ α *set* = $\langle$**fun**$\rangle$

```
#let set_diff s₁ s₂ =
  if not(s₁.set_order = s₂.set_order)
  then raise (Set_exc "set_diff: different set orders")
  else it_set subtract_from_set s₁ s₂;;
```
set_diff : α *set* $\rightarrow$ α *set* $\rightarrow$ α *set* = $\langle$**fun**$\rangle$

```
#let set_intersection s₁ s₂ = set_diff s₁ (set_diff s₁ s₂);;
```
set_intersection : α *set* $\rightarrow$ α *set* $\rightarrow$ α *set* = $\langle$**fun**$\rangle$

6.8   Functional Queues

A queue is a structure to store information temporarily where the output order of elements is the same as their input. You have already seen (on page 125) an implementation that uses circular lists and destructive operations. In fact, a queue is a typical example of a data structure that is difficult to implement in a purely functional language. If we implement queues as lists, for example, we have to recopy the list completely every time we enter a new element.

The implementation we offer here is of limited interest to the degree that it takes logarithmic time for adds and removals whereas an implementation based on destructive operations takes constant time (and very little of it at that) for the same operations. Even so, this implementation shows that programming queues in a purely functional language is not totally impossible.

A queue is an AVL tree in which the elements are ordered by their entry date. The last element entered is considered the greatest, and it is placed at the end of the rightmost branch. The first element entered is considered the least and located at the end of the leftmost branch. Left rotation operations keep the AVL tree balanced.

```
#type queue_mod₁ = Inc | No_Inc;;
```
Type queue_mod₁ defined.

```
#let rec enqueue t e =
  fst (add t)
  where rec add = fun
    Empty → Bin(Empty,(e,Balanced),Empty),Inc
```

```
    | (Bin(t₁,(x,b),t₂))
       → let t,m = add t₂ in
         match (b,m) with
            Balanced,No_Inc → Bin(t₁,(x,Balanced),t),No_Inc
          | Balanced,_ → Bin(t₁,(x,Right),t),Inc
          | Left,No_Inc → Bin(t₁,(x,Left),t),No_Inc
          | Left,_ → Bin(t₁,(x,Balanced),t),No_Inc
          | Right,No_Inc → Bin(t₁,(x,Right),t),No_Inc
          | Right,Inc → rot_left(Bin(t₁,(x,Balanced),t)),No_Inc;;
```

enqueue : $(\alpha * balance)$ $btree \to \alpha \to (\alpha * balance)$ $btree = \langle$**fun**$\rangle$

```
#type queue_mod₂ = Dec | No_Dec;;
```
Type queue_mod₂ defined.

```
#let dequeue t =
   fst (sub t)
   where rec sub = fun
     Empty → failwith "dequeue: empty queue"
   | (Bin (Empty,(a,b),t₂)) → (a,t₂),Dec
   | (Bin (t₁,(a,b),t₂))
      → let (a',t'),m = sub t₁ in
        (match m with
           No_Dec → (a',Bin (t',(a,b),t₂)),No_Dec
         | Dec → (match b with
                    Balanced → (a',Bin (t',(a,Right),t₂)),No_Dec
                  | Left → (a',Bin (t',(a,Balanced),t₂)),Dec
                  | Right → (a',balance_left(t',a,t₂)),if balance t₂ = Balanced
                                                       then No_Dec else Dec));;
```

dequeue : $(\alpha * balance)$ $btree \to \alpha * (\alpha * balance)$ $btree = \langle$**fun**$\rangle$

By using a queue, we can program a breadth-first traversal of a tree.

```
#let breadth_it_btree orient f e t =
   trav e (enqueue Empty t)
   where rec trav x = fun
     Empty → x
   | q → let (t,q') = dequeue q in
         match t with
           Empty → trav x q'
         | Bin (t₁,a,t₂)
            → trav (f x a) (enqueue (enqueue q' t₁) t₂);;
```

breadth_it_btree : $\alpha \to (\beta \to \gamma \to \beta) \to \beta \to \gamma$ $btree \to \beta = \langle$**fun**$\rangle$

```
#let breadth_btree_it f t e =
  trav (enqueue Empty t)
  where rec trav = fun
    Empty → e
  | q → let (t,q') = dequeue q in
      match t with
        Empty → trav q'
      | Bin (t₁,a,t₂)
        → f a (trav (enqueue (enqueue q' t₁) t₂));;
```
$breadth\_btree\_it : (\alpha \to \beta \to \beta) \to \alpha\ btree \to \beta \to \beta = \langle \textbf{fun} \rangle$

```
#let breadth_flat_btree f t =
  breadth_btree_it (fun x l → f x::l) t [ ];;
```
$breadth\_flat\_btree : (\alpha \to \beta) \to \alpha\ btree \to \beta\ list = \langle \textbf{fun} \rangle$

6.9   Summary

We introduced the idea of a **binary search tree**, making it possible to search efficiently in ordered sets. Then we brought up the idea of an **AVL tree** with its associated algorithms to keep the **balance** in binary search trees in spite of our adding and removing elements. From there, we used AVL trees to define the types **set** and **dictionary** to manage sets and tables efficiently.

6.10   To Learn More

AVL trees are only one among many techniques possible to manage huge data sets of information. There are other important techniques, such as hashing. A great many books cover those other techniques, such as, for example, [35].

CAML provides libraries to manage dictionaries and tables (**set**, **map**) as well as to exploit hash tables (**hashtbl**).

Chapter 7

Graphs and Problem Solving

This chapter shows you how to define, implement, and use algorithms that explore graphs, and it does so from the perspective of problem solving.

A **graph** G is a structure defined by:

- a set of nodes S;

- a set of arcs; that is, a subset A of the Cartesian product $S \times S$.

This definition corresponds to the mathematical idea of a relation over a set S.

Graphs, in fact, constitute highly intuitive objects connected to ordinary experience. A subway map is a graph in which the nodes are subway stops; a road map is a graph in which the nodes are cities. Telecommunication networks (such as the telephone system or a computer network) provide other examples.

The intuitive character of a graph is reflected in the terminology we use about this subject. The existence of an arc between a node s_1 and a node s_2 can be interpreted by the fact that we can get from s_1 to s_2. A set of arcs that lets us get from one node to another is called a **path**. The **length** of a path is the number of arcs in it. A path is said to be **simple** if it does not pass the same node more than once. A node s_2 can be reached from a node s_1 if there is a path from s_1 to s_2. In that case, we say that s_2 is **reachable** from s_1. The **distance** between two nodes s_1 and s_2 is the length of the shortest path from s_1 to s_2. A **circuit** in a graph is a path from a node back to itself.

In the customary terminology of graphs, there is a distinction between oriented and non-oriented graphs. A **non-oriented** graph is one in which the arcs can be traversed in both directions. Any non-oriented graph can be represented by an oriented graph: all we have to do for every arc (s_1, s_2) is to add the opposing arc (s_2, s_1). Here, we will use the word "graph" to mean an "oriented graph."

In a graph defined by a set S of nodes and a set A of arcs, a **subgraph** is defined by a set $S' \subseteq S$ of nodes and a set $A' \subseteq A$ of arcs where the origin and destination both belong to S'. With every node s, we can associate the subgraph corresponding to the set of nodes that can be reached from s. The subgraphs of a graph are partially ordered by the relation of inclusion among the sets of nodes of that graph. A **partial subgraph** is defined by a set $S' \subseteq S$ of nodes and by the set $A' \subseteq A$ such that for every arc (s_1, s_2) of A', s_1 and s_2 belong to S'.

A graph is **strongly connected** if for every pair of nodes (s_1, s_2), there is a path from s_1 to s_2. A graph is **connected** if the non-oriented symmetric graph associated with it is strongly connected. A **connected component** of a graph is a maximal connected subgraph with respect to inclusion. Likewise, a **strongly connected component** of a graph is a maximal strongly connected subgraph with respect to inclusion.

Graphs may also be **valued**; that is, each arc may have an associated **cost**. The cost of a path is thus the sum of costs along the arcs that compose it. If all arcs have the same cost, then the cost of a path is obviously proportional to its length.

The structure of a graph can be generalized as a **hypergraph** where two nodes may be linked by more than one arc. Formally, a hypergraph is defined like this:

- a set S of nodes;

- a set A of arcs;

- a function $h : A \to S \times S$ that associates each arc with its origin and destination.

Hypergraphs are not directly useful in the applications presented in this chapter, but the algorithms we define here can easily be extended to hypergraphs.

We say that a graph is **finite** when its number of nodes and number of arcs are both finite. When a graph is finite, then it is possible to represent it by a data structure, such as a matrix or a list of lists of successors.

Representation of a graph as a matrix associates a finite graph with a square matrix M of size $n \times n$ where n is the number of nodes in the graph and where the element $M_{i,j}$ is the value 0 if the nodes i and j are not connected and the value 1 (or a value indicating cost) if they are connected by an arc. This representation is practical only for graphs, not for hypergraphs, of course.

Representation of a graph by a list of successive nodes associates each node with a list of its successors, possibly accompanied by the cost of the corresponding arc.

For the algorithms that we will develop here, we do not necessarily have to assume that the graphs are finite because we will not represent the graphs by data structures. We will simply assume that the set of nodes can be enumerated and that for every node s, the set of arcs originating at s is finite. With this hypothesis, a graph can be defined by a function that associates each node s with its list of successors, that is, the list of the destinations of the arcs that originate at s, possibly accompanied by supplementary information, such as cost. We call such a function a **transition** function.

The transition functions defined in this chapter all take an argument of type $\alpha \to \alpha$ list corresponding to a graph defined by that transition function.

For example, let's consider the graph where the nodes are natural numbers and where each integer is connected to the products when it is multiplied by 2, by 3, and by 5. The corresponding transition function is:

```
#let h= fun n → [2*n; 3*n; 5*n];;
h : int → int list = ⟨fun⟩
```

The kind of problem that interests us is the following: given the nodes s and s', is there a path from s to s'? or, given a node s, is there a path from s to some other node, satisfying a given property? We might also ask that the path we find should be minimal in length, or, if the graph is valued, that the cost be minimal.

In particular, we will apply the algorithms we define later to games like the red donkey, represented in Figure 7.1.

This game consists of a board and pieces. The board is made up of 5×4 squares where only 18 of the squares are occupied. The playing pieces are of various sizes. The point is to use the unoccupied squares to move the pieces. One of the traditional problems in this game is to start from the initial configuration in Figure 7.1 and then get to a configuration in which the largest piece reaches the bottom of the board, as in Figure 7.2.

In such a game, the search for a sequence of moves to get to a satisfying configuration makes us explore the graph of configurations that can be achieved from the initial configuration. A few nodes and arcs of that graph are represented in Figure 7.3.

In this game, the graph is finite, but it is not known at the beginning. However, it is possible to write a function to compute the set of configurations that can be reached from a given configuration. (We will solve the problem in Section 7.2.)

7.1   Algorithms to Explore Graphs

The problems that interest us take, as given, a graph and one of its nodes s, known as the origin, and they need a node s' having some given property as

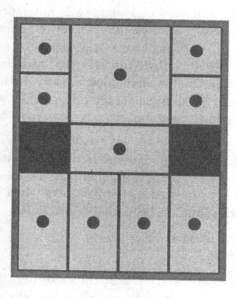

Figure 7.1. The game of the red donkey: initial configuration

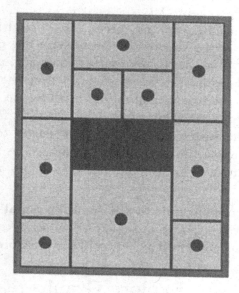

Figure 7.2. The game of the red donkey: final configuration

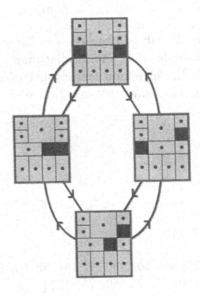

Figure 7.3. A small part of the graph of the red donkey

their result. When we search for such a node, we must explore the part of the graph that can be reached from s. The search principle is extremely simple: if s satisfies the property, then s is the result; otherwise, we explore the subgraphs corresponding to each of the successors of s. If the subgraph of the nodes that can be reached from s is a tree, that is, if for every node s' that can be reached from s, there is only one path from s to s', then the possible algorithms are just those classics for depth-first or breadth-first traversal of trees. In the opposite case, the difficulty is to detect when we reach a node whether it has already been visited before. If we can determine this point, then we reduce the exploration of the graph to a partial subgraph which is a tree.

We call such a subgraph a **covering tree**. In the case of a breadth-first traversal, the covering tree we build is of minimal depth.

We will begin by writing graph-traversal functions that do not test whether a node has already been visited. Later, we will add adequate tests to these functions.

7.1.1 Naive Breadth-First Search

We will use the function flat_map defined by

```
#let rec flat_map f = fun
    [ ] → [ ]
  | (a::l) → f a @ flat_map f l;;
```

$$flat\_map : (\alpha \rightarrow \beta\ list) \rightarrow \alpha\ list \rightarrow \beta\ list = \langle\mathbf{fun}\rangle$$

For every transition function h of type $\alpha \rightarrow \alpha$ list giving the list of its immediate successors for each node, the function flat_map h gives the list of all the immediate successors of all the elements for any list of nodes. In that way, we can easily get the list of successors at distance 2, 3, n. For example, we take the function h from page 197:

```
#h 1;;
- : int list = [2; 3; 5]
```

```
#flat_map h (h 1);;
- : int list = [4; 6; 10; 6; 9; 15; 10; 15; 25]
```

```
#flat_map h (flat_map h (h 1));;
- : int list
```
$$= [8;\ 12;\ 20;\ 12;\ 18;\ 30;\ 20;\ 30;\ 50;\ 12;\ 18;\ 30;\ 18;\ 27;\ 45;\ 30;$$
$$\quad 45;\ 75;\ 20;\ 30;\ 50;\ 30;\ 45;\ 75;\ 50;\ 75;\ 125]$$

Even when the function h provides a non-redundant list (normally the case), the lists of successors at distance n that we get from flat_map are generally quite redundant. A node will appear as many times as there are distinct paths of length n from the origin node to this node.

If we use the function union to produce the set-union of two lists, we can define the function union_map, which nicely replaces flat_map h.

```
#let rec union_map f = fun
    [] → []
  | (a::l) → union (f a) (union_map f l);;
union_map : (α → β list) → α list → β list = ⟨fun⟩
```

And thus we get non-redundant lists.

```
#h 1;;
- : int list = [2; 3; 5]
```

```
#union_map h (h 1);;
- : int list = [4; 6; 9; 10; 15; 25]
```

```
#union_map h (union_map h (h 1));;
- : int list = [8; 12; 18; 27; 20; 30; 45; 50; 75; 125]
```

Moreover, if we have an order among the nodes, we can even make the union more efficient. Indeed, in such a case, it is also possible to store the configurations that we encounter, and to do so efficiently, as we will do later.

We implement a depth-first algorithm by means of union_map to generate successively the nodes that can be reached by a path of length one, then those reached by a path of length two, and so forth.

The function naive_solve_breadth_first takes these arguments:

- ok of type $\alpha \to$ bool to indicate the property we are searching for;

- moves to define the graph in which we will search;

- start for the initial configuration.

It uses the function loop, defined on page 39, the function find, defined on page 110, and a function exists, predefined in CAML, to test whether an element satisfying a given property is in a list.

exists : $(\alpha \to$ bool$) \to \alpha$ list $\to$ bool

The nth recursive call of the function loop produces the list of nodes reached by a path of length n. If this list contains a node satisfying the predicate ok, then the corresponding node is returned. Otherwise, we call loop again to produce the list of nodes reached by a path of length $n + 1$.

```
#let naive_solve_breadth_first (ok,moves) start =
    find ok (loop (exists ok) (union_map moves) [start]);;
naive_solve_breadth_first : (α → bool) * (α → α list) → α → α
                        = ⟨fun⟩
```

This breadth-first function has the following properties:

- It always finds a solution if one exists. In other words, the search strategy is complete.

- It always finds a solution of minimal distance.

However, this one is not optimal among complete search strategies. In effect, the set of nodes reached by paths of length n may very well contain nodes which can be reached by paths of shorter length. In that way, the same node may well be visited more than once.

We can avoid that pitfall by storing the set of nodes that have already been visited and by saving only the nodes that have not yet been visited. To do so, we will use those functions that we introduced in Section 6.7 for handling sets.

7.1.2   Naive Depth-First Search

We have only limited interest in exploring a graph depth-first without storing the configurations we encounter if the graph is not a tree. In particular, such a procedure would loop if it encountered cycles. However, the structure of the search function we present here is interesting because simply by storing the configurations we encounter, we can make it into a reasonable search algorithm. We will do just that in Section 7.1.5.

   Here, we will simply use a list of nodes managed as a stack. If the top of the stack satisfies the predicate ok, then that node is returned as a result. Otherwise, we replace that node in the stack by the list of its successors.

```
#exception No_solution;;
Exception No_solution defined.


#let naive_solve_depth_first(ok,pos_moves) c =
    solve_rec [c]
    where rec solve_rec =
      fun [] → raise No_solution
       | (c::cl as cl') →
              if ok c then c
              else solve_rec (pos_moves c @ cl);;
naive_solve_depth_first : (α → bool) * (α → α list) → α → α
                      = ⟨fun⟩
```

7.1.3   Optimal Breadth-First Search

The function archive_map transforms a function of type $\alpha \to \alpha$ list into a function of type $(\alpha \ set * \alpha \ list) \to (\alpha \ set * \alpha \ list)$. It resembles the functions flat_map and union_map, but it stores the nodes it encounters; that is, only after producing the list of successors, it eliminates those that belong to the set of nodes already stored, and it adds only the nodes that do not yet belong to the set.

   The function archive_map uses the function select to extract a list of elements satisfying a property p from a list.

```
#let rec select p =fun
    [] → []
  | (a::l) → if p a then a::select p l
              else select p l;;
select : (α → bool) → α list → α list = ⟨fun⟩
```

```
#let archive_map f (s,l) =
    arch_map s [ ] l
    where rec arch_map s ll = fun
        [ ] → (s,ll)
      | (c::l) → let ll'= select (fun c → not (set_member c s)) (f c) in
                    arch_map (add_list_to_set s ll') (ll'@ll) l;;
```
archive_map : $(\alpha \rightarrow \beta\ list) \rightarrow \beta\ set * \alpha\ list \rightarrow \beta\ set * \beta\ list = \langle\textbf{fun}\rangle$

Notice that if the function f produces non-redundant lists, then in the same way, the function archive_map f will, too, because of the way it stores. In effect, for every configuration it treats, it adds the list of successors that are not already in its archive before it goes on to handle the following configuration.

Now we can define a new version of the function solve_breadth_first to store configurations it encounters.

```
#let solve_breadth_first (ok,moves,comp) start =
    (find ok o snd) (loop (exists ok o snd)
                    (archive_map moves)
                    (make_set comp [start],[start]));;
```
solve_breadth_first : $(\alpha \rightarrow bool) * (\alpha \rightarrow \alpha\ list) *$
$\qquad\qquad (\alpha \rightarrow \alpha \rightarrow comparison) \rightarrow \alpha \rightarrow \alpha = \langle\textbf{fun}\rangle$

Now this function is optimal. A node of the graph will cause its successors to be examined only if this node has not already been visited. The part of the search that expands into a tree, in fact, consists of a covering tree of minimal depth.

7.1.4   Variations and Improvements

Before we apply these search algorithms in specific situations (for example, in the games we will introduce in the following sections), we have to make them a little more flexible.

For one thing, a search algorithm is much more practical if it returns not just a node that satisfies a given property, but the *path* to reach that node. The elements we handle as we search should thus be put into pairs, for example, of a node and its access path or even into more complicated structures. In contrast, the storage mechanism only needs to archive the nodes themselves. For that reason, it will be useful to pass a function as a parameter to access the part that we want to store from the structures we are handling.

For another, the structure of the set that we have used for storage is not sufficiently general. For example, when the nodes of the graph are naturally partitioned, it could be more efficient for us to use arrays of sets, one array for each class in the partition. Doing so would lead us to use a storage mechanism that is not strictly the same as the one for managing sets.

Consequently, we will assume that incidentally we have defined a type α archive and its associated values.

> add_to_archive : α archive $\rightarrow$ α $\rightarrow$ α archive
> add_list_to_archive : α archive $\rightarrow$ α list $\rightarrow$ α archive
> make_archive : $(\alpha \rightarrow \alpha \rightarrow$ comparison$) \rightarrow \alpha$ list $\rightarrow \alpha$ archive
> archive_member : $\alpha \rightarrow \alpha$ archive $\rightarrow$ bool

The new function archive_map uses these new functions to manage archives; it also has a supplementary parameter arch_part to extract the part of a configuration that should be archived.

```
#let archive_map arch_part f (arch,l) =
   arch_map arch [ ] l
   where rec arch_map arch ll = fun
    [ ] → (arch,ll)
  | (c::cl) →
        let ll' = select
                    (fun c → not (archive_member (arch_part c) arch)) (f c) in
        arch_map (add_list_to_archive arch (map arch_part ll')) (ll'@ll) cl;;
```
$$archive\_map : (\alpha \rightarrow \beta) \rightarrow (\gamma \rightarrow \alpha\ list) \rightarrow \beta\ archive * \gamma\ list$$
$$\rightarrow \beta\ archive * \alpha\ list = \langle\mathbf{fun}\rangle$$

The new function solve_breadth_first also has a supplementary parameter arch_part.

```
#let solve_breadth_first (ok,pos_moves,comp) arch_part start =
   (find ok o snd)
     (loop
        (exists ok o snd)
        (archive_map arch_part pos_moves)
        (make_archive comp (map arch_part start), start));;
```
$$solve\_breadth\_first : (\alpha \rightarrow bool) * (\alpha \rightarrow \alpha\ list) *$$
$$(\beta \rightarrow \beta \rightarrow comparison) \rightarrow (\alpha \rightarrow \beta) \rightarrow \alpha\ list \rightarrow \alpha$$
$$= \langle\mathbf{fun}\rangle$$

7.1.5   Optimal Depth-First Search

To get a good algorithm for depth-first search, we need to add a way to store configurations encountered by the naive algorithm in Section 7.1.2. We will use the same functions to handle that archive as we did in the preceding section.

```
#let solve_depth_first(ok,pos_moves,comp) arch_part c =
    solve_rec (make_archive comp [ ]) [c]
    where rec solve_rec a = fun
       [ ] → raise No_solution
    | (c::cl) →
          if ok c then c else
          if archive_member (arch_part c) a then solve_rec a cl
          else solve_rec (add_to_archive a (arch_part c))
                (pos_moves c @ cl);;
```

$$solve\_depth\_first : (\alpha \to bool) * (\alpha \to \alpha\ list) *$$
$$(\beta \to \beta \to comparison) \to (\alpha \to \beta) \to \alpha \to \alpha$$
$$= \langle \mathbf{fun} \rangle$$

7.1.6 Exhaustive Search

We can modify our search functions to explore completely the subgraph corresponding to an initial configuration and get the whole set of nodes.

In the case of breadth-first search, we have to modify only the parameter of the function loop to redefine the halting condition. We will halt the search when the list of configurations we get is empty, and we will simply return the archive.

```
#let explore_breadth_first (pos_moves,comp) arch_map start =
    fst (loop
          (fun (s,l) → l = [ ])
          (archive_map arch_map pos_moves)
          (make_archive comp (map arch_map start),start));;
```

$$explore\_breadth\_first : (\alpha \to \alpha\ list) * (\beta \to \beta \to comparison)$$
$$\to (\alpha \to \beta) \to \alpha\ list \to \beta\ archive = \langle \mathbf{fun} \rangle$$

In the case of depth-first search, we have to eliminate the halting test that corresponds to a satisfactory configuration so that we halt only when the stack is empty.

```
#let explore_depth_first (pos_moves,comp) arch_part c =
    solve_rec (make_archive comp [ ]) [c]
    where rec solve_rec a = fun
       [ ] → a
    | (c::cl) →
          if archive_member (arch_part c) a then solve_rec a cl
          else solve_rec (add_to_archive a (arch_part c) )
                (pos_moves c @ cl);;
```

$$explore\_depth\_first : (\alpha \to \alpha\ list) * (\beta \to \beta \to comparison)$$
$$\to (\alpha \to \beta) \to \alpha \to \beta\ archive = \langle \mathbf{fun} \rangle$$

In both cases, we can still collect the solutions we encounter as we go. In breadth-first search, we get each solution in a minimum number of steps, so we know the distance of each solution from the origin.

7.1.7 Computing Connected Components

In non-oriented graphs, that is, in graphs where each arc has a reciprocal arc, the set of nodes that can be reached from a given node consists exactly of the (strongly) connected component from that original node. If we have a means to compute the set of nodes in the graph, it is possible to build the set of connected components from that. To do so, it suffices to take any node, to compute its connected component, to remove that from the set of nodes of the graph, and then to begin again.

The function findcc does that by hypothesizing that the type α archive is implemented by the type α set and that the configurations of the graph are archived without modification. This function returns a list of sets of configurations that are, in fact, the connected components of the graph.

```
#let rec findcc (pos_moves,comp) cset =
    if set_isempty cset then [ ]
    else let c= set_random_element cset in
        let CC = explore_breadth_first (pos_moves,comp) (fun x → x) [c]
        in CC :: findcc (pos_moves,comp) (set_diff cset CC);;
findcc : (α → α list) * (α → α → comparison) → α set → α set list
    = ⟨fun⟩
```

Exercises
7.1 Write a breadth-first search function for a graph that returns the total number of nodes that can be reached from a given configuration.
7.2 Write a breadth-first search function that finds not just one solution, but all solutions.
7.3 Write a function to return the length of the longest simple path in a graph, starting from a given node.
7.4 Write a function to find the greatest distance between a given node and a node that can be reached from that one.

7.2   The Red Donkey

The game of the red donkey belongs to a family of games known as brain teasers. We described it briefly on page 197. The game consists of moving the largest playing piece (the donkey) from one position to another, for example, from the top to the bottom of the board. Its graph is symmetric, that is, non-oriented, since any transition is also reversible. It is also relatively small: the total number of configurations for the 5×4 board is 65 880, so it is practical to compute all of them.

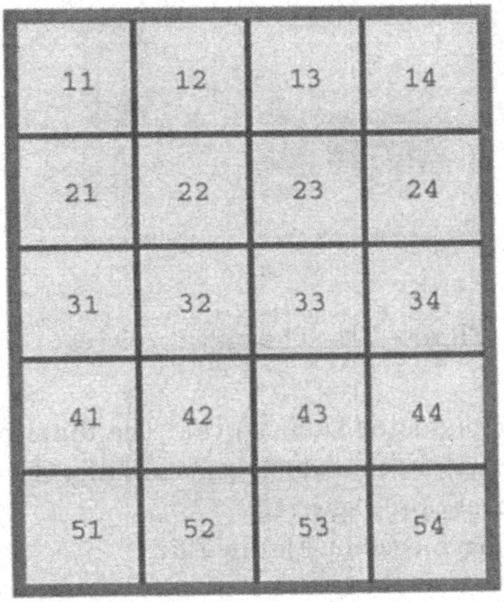

Figure 7.4. Numbered squares

The size of the connected component of the initial configuration represented in Figure 7.1 is 25 955 and the maximal distance between this configuration and the set of configurations that can be reached from it is 132. Nevertheless, there are much longer simple paths in this connected component.

The way we propose to implement configurations is fairly costly. To compute the entire graph on currently available hardware, we need a more compact representation—as we suggest in an exercise.

The positions on a 5×4 board will be represented as integers, as in Figure 7.4. We will use the following functions to move around the board.

```
#let up n = n−10 and left n = n−1
  and down n = n+10 and right n = n+1;;
up : int → int = ⟨fun⟩
left : int → int = ⟨fun⟩
down : int → int = ⟨fun⟩
right : int → int = ⟨fun⟩
```

The type piece will represent the playing pieces.

```
#type piece = Donkey | Square | Horiz | Vertic | None;;
```

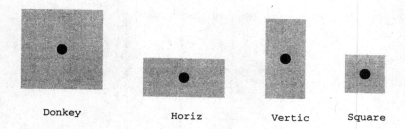

Donkey   Horiz   Vertic   Square

Figure 7.5. The playing pieces

We have added the constructor None so that the function get, from page 209, will be a total function. Later, that decision will simplify the way we write the functions moves₁ and moves₂ on page 210.

You can see the playing pieces in Figure 7.5.

We will use the type board to represent the configurations of the board.

```
#type board =
       {donkey: int;
        squares: int list;
        horiz: int;
        vertics: int list};;
```

The initial configuration in Figure 7.1 is defined by

```
#let start =
   {donkey= 12;
    squares= [11;14;21;24];
    horiz= 32;
    vertics= [41;42;43;44]};;
start : board = {donkey=12; squares=[11; 14; 21; 24]; horiz=32;
                 vertics=[41; 42; 43; 44]}
```

In the programs that follow, a configuration will, in fact, be represented most often by a value of type (int * int) * board where the pair of integers represent the two free squares. This information is redundant, but it will let us compute possible moves more quickly since possible moves depend first of all on the position of free squares. We will define the variable start like this:

```
#let start = ((31,34), start);;
start : (int * int) * board
      = (31, 34), {donkey=12; squares=[11; 14; 21; 24]; horiz=32;
                   vertics=[41; 42; 43; 44]}
```

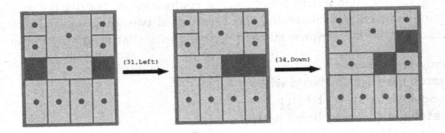

Figure 7.6. Moves

We want the pair of integers representing the two empty squares to be ordered, and likewise, for each field of a configuration containing a list of squares, we want those squares to be ordered, too. In that way, we can be sure that equality between configurations will be exactly equality between values of type (int*int)*board. Incidentally, we must define an order relation among configurations; we will call it donkey_comp, and we leave it as an exercise.

donkey_comp : board → board → comparison

The way pieces move is defined by a pair consisting of an integer and a direction. The integer indicates the square which is free before the move, which will be occupied afterwards, or in the case where two squares are used by the move, it indicates the higher and leftmost of the two.

#type direction = Left | Up | Right | Down;;

#type move == int * direction;;

Thus the list [(31,Left); (34,Down)] corresponds to the moves in Figure 7.6.

We will begin by writing a function to compute the set of possible moves from a given configuration. To do that, we have to use a function to indicate whether a given square is occupied or not by the upper left corner of a piece. If it is, the result is the name of the piece. Otherwise, the return result is None.

```
#let get cell board =
    if board.donkey=cell then Donkey else
    if board.horiz = cell then Horiz else
    if mem cell board.squares then Square else
    if mem cell board.vertics then Vertic
    else None;;
get : int → board → piece = ⟨fun⟩
```

Among the possible moves from a given configuration, we distinguish those that use only one empty square and those that need two squares simultaneously. Here is the function to compute all the possible moves that need only one square:

```
#let moves₁ b board =
  (match get (right b) board with
     (Square|Horiz) → [b,Left] | _ → [ ]) @
  (match get (down b) board with
     (Square|Vertic) → [(b,Up)] | _ → [ ]) @
  (match (get (left b) board, get (left(left b)) board) with
     ((Square,_)|(_,Horiz)) → [(b,Right)] | _ → [ ]) @
  (match (get (up b) board, get (up(up b)) board) with
     ((Square,_)|(_,Vertic)) → [(b,Down)] | _ → [ ]);;
moves₁ : int → board → (int * direction) list = ⟨fun⟩
```

For us to exploit two squares, they must be adjacent, either horizontally or vertically. The following functions test these properties by assuming that the two squares passed as arguments are ordered.

```
#let h_adjacent (n₁,n₂) = n₂=n₁+1;;
h_adjacent : int * int → bool = ⟨fun⟩
```

```
#let v_adjacent (n₁,n₂) = n₂=n₁+10;;
v_adjacent : int * int → bool = ⟨fun⟩
```

Here, then, is the function that computes all possible moves that need two squares:

```
#let moves₂ (b,b') board =
  if not(h_adjacent (b,b')) & not(v_adjacent (b,b')) then [ ] else
  if h_adjacent (b,b') then
    (match (get (up b) board, get (up(up b)) board) with
       ((_,Donkey)|(Horiz,_)) → [(b,Down)] | _ → [ ]) @
    (match get (down b) board with
       (Donkey|Horiz) → [(b,Up)] | _ → [ ])
  else
    (match (get (left b) board, get (left(left b)) board) with
       ((_,Donkey)|(Vertic,_)) → [(b,Right)] | _ → [ ]) @
    (match get (right b) board with
       (Donkey |Vertic) → [b,Left] | _ → [ ]);;
moves₂ : int * int → board → (int * direction) list = ⟨fun⟩
```

For the next step, we need to apply a move to a configuration. We leave this function as an exercise. We will assume that it is of type

```
#app_move;;
```
$- : (int * int) * board \rightarrow int * direction \rightarrow (int * int) * board = \langle\mathbf{fun}\rangle$

To apply a list of moves, we use the function app_moves:

```
#let app_moves c = it_list app_move c;;
```
$app\_moves : (int * int) * board \rightarrow (int * direction) \; list$
$$\rightarrow (int * int) * board = \langle\mathbf{fun}\rangle$$

We get the list of configurations that we can reach from a given configuration by applying all the possible moves in a given configuration, like this:

```
#let next_configs (((b₁,b₂),c) as c')=
    let moves = moves₁ b₁ c @ moves₁ b₂ c @ moves₂ (b₁,b₂) c in
    map (fun m → app_move c' m) moves;;
```
$next\_configs : (int * int) * board \rightarrow ((int * int) * board) \; list = \langle\mathbf{fun}\rangle$

When we are searching for a solution, we need to store the sequences of moves so that we can provide as results the ones that lead to a solution. For that, we will use a more complicated function that saves sequences of moves.

```
#let next_configs (ml,(((b₁,b₂),c) as c')) =
    let moves = moves₁ b₁ c @ moves₁ b₂ c @ moves₂ (b₁,b₂) c in
    map (fun m → (m::ml, app_move c' m)) moves;;
```
$next\_configs : (int * direction) \; list * ((int * int) * board)$
$$\rightarrow ((int * direction) \; list * ((int * int) * board)) \; list$$
$$= \langle\mathbf{fun}\rangle$$

Now we will use the function solve_breadth_first, defined on page 203, to define a search function for the optimal solution to the red donkey game. This function takes an initial configuration (start) and a search property for the final configuration (ok).

```
#let solve_red_donkey start ok =
    solve_breadth_first
      (ok, next_configs, donkey_comp)
      (snd o snd)
      [([ ], start)];;
```
$solve\_red\_donkey : (int * int) * board$
$$\rightarrow ((int * direction) \; list *$$
$$((int * int) * board) \rightarrow bool)$$
$$\rightarrow (int * direction) \; list * ((int * int) * board)$$
$$= \langle\mathbf{fun}\rangle$$

We will start from the initial configuration you saw in Figure 7.1, and we will search for a configuration where the donkey has dropped to the bottom of the board. We test for that situation like this:

```
#let ok_config c = (snd(snd c)).donkey / 10 = 4;;
ok_config : α * (β * board) → bool = ⟨fun⟩
```

Here is the solution we found, displaying only the list of moves.

```
#let ms=rev (fst(solve_red_donkey start ok_config));;
ms : (int * direction) list = [31, Left; 34, Down; 33, Left; 24, Down;
                               34, Down; 14, Right; 12, Right; 11, Up;
                               21, Up; 32, Left; 31, Left; 33, Left;
                               32, Left; 33, Down; 13, Right;
                               12, Right; 14, Right; 13, Right; 11, Up;
                               21, Up; 22, Right; 31, Up; 21, Up;
                               41, Left; 42, Down; 32, Down; 52, Down;
                               42, Down; 22, Left; 34, Up; 24, Up;
                               44, Right; 43, Right; 53, Down; ..., ...;
                               ... ]
```

You can reconstitute the final configuration by applying the sequence of moves ms to the initial configuration. You see that result in Figure 7.2.

```
#app_moves start ms;;
− : (int * int) * board
  = (32, 33), {donkey=42; squares=[22; 23; 51; 54]; horiz=12;
              vertics=[11; 14; 31; 34]}
```

The set of intermediate configurations appears in Figures 7.7 and 7.8.

If we start from the functions we have already defined, we can use other functions to explore the graph defined in the preceding section to compute the entire set of solutions of the problem under consideration or to solve other problems on the same board. For example, a more difficult problem to solve than the one we just showed starts from the configuration in Figure 7.9 and again moves the donkey (the largest playing piece) to the bottom of the board. In that case, the shortest possible solution requires 86 moves.

It is also possible to number the set of configurations in the graph and to count the set of connected components. The total number of configurations is 65 880. That includes two principal connected components that are images of each other because they are horizontally symmetric; each of them includes 25 955 configurations. The other configurations are distributed among a mere

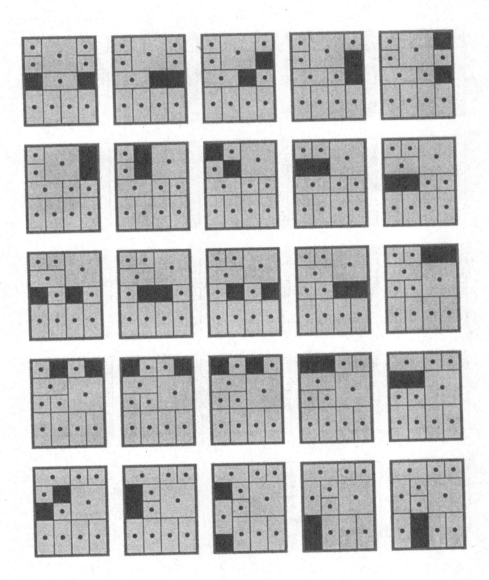

Figure 7.7. First 25 configurations

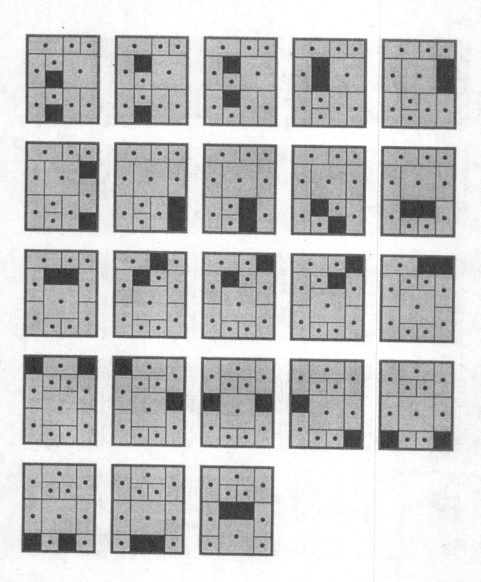

Figure 7.8. Last 23 configurations

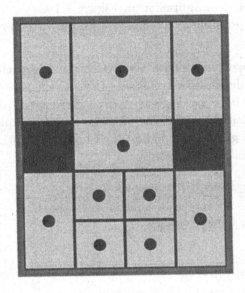

Figure 7.9. Another initial configuration

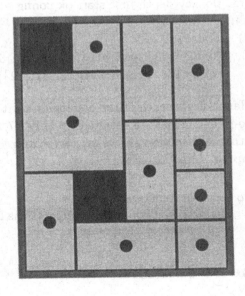

Figure 7.10. A connected component of size 2

896 other connected components; some of them have only two elements, like the
one corresponding to the configuration in Figure 7.10.

Of course, it is also possible to consider completely different games on a similar
board.

For the moment, we have not attempted to explore the graph of the red
donkey by means of a depth-first traversal. In fact, that would be a poor choice
because in this graph there are a great many different simple paths to get from
one configuration to another, and some of these paths are quite long. To explore
them depth-first would generally yield a much longer path than the optimal one,
as you can see in the following attempt.

```
#let solve_red_donkey_depth_first start ok=
   solve_depth_first
     (ok, next_configs, donkey_comp)
     (snd o snd)
     ([ ],start);;
solve_red_donkey_depth_first
   : (int * int) * board → ((int * direction) list *
                              ((int * int) * board) → bool)
              → (int * direction) list * ((int * int) * board)
   = ⟨fun⟩

#let (ml,c) = solve_red_donkey_depth_first start ok_config
 in (list_length ml, c);;
− : int * ((int * int) * board)
   = 1509, ((33, 34), {donkey=43; squares=[23; 24; 51; 52];
                       horiz=13; vertics=[11; 12; 31; 32]})
```

As you can see, a depth-first search found a solution that requires 1509 moves!
The same configuration can in fact be reached in only 77 moves by a breadth-
first search. Even so, the next section shows you an example in which depth-first
traversal is better adapted than breadth-first.

Exercises
7.5 Find a better way to code the configurations.
7.6 Write a program to generate the entire set of configurations for the red donkey.
7.7 From it, deduce the set of connected components.

7.3   The Game of Solitaire

Sometimes, solitaire is a card game, but the solitaire that we will play here is
a board game where there are cylindrical holes forming the nodes of a network
with pegs or marbles filling all but one of the holes. There are a great many

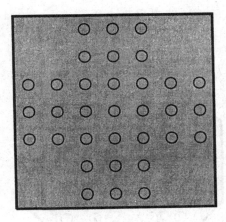

Figure 7.11. English solitaire

variations, but perhaps the two best known are English solitaire, in Figure 7.11, and French solitaire, in Figure 7.12.

The programs in this section are meant for English solitaire, but it is easy to adapt them to French solitaire or to other versions that you may know.

Starting from a configuration where there is at least one empty hole, the game is to take other pieces by jumping them to reach an empty hole. Any piece taken that way has to be removed from the board. Jumps can be horizontal or vertical.

The goal of the game is to reach a particular configuration, for example, one where there is only a single piece left on the board. Figure 7.13 shows you an initial configuration and a final configuration typical of English solitaire. The holes occupied by pieces are black in the figure.

The graph of solitaire is quite different from that of the red donkey. Here the moves are not reversible because a piece is removed from the board at every jump. We also know in advance the number of moves to arrive at a solution: it is the number of pieces in the final configuration subtracted from the number of pieces in the initial configuration.

However, the number of configurations is much, much greater ($2^{33} - 1$ for English solitaire). A problem like the one in Figure 7.13 has such a large graph that it is out of the question for us to explore all the possible moves breadth-first. A depth-first exploration is certainly a better choice, though it, too, may be prohibitively expensive. At the very least, it is clear that we must optimize our representation of configurations if we want to have a chance to find solutions.

We will represent a configuration as a 33-bit array indicating whether or not each hole is occupied. Unfortunately, such an array cannot be represented in one

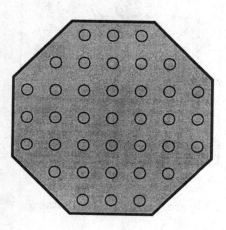

Figure 7.12. French solitaire

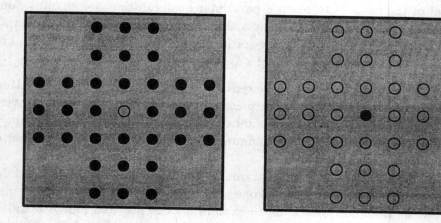

Figure 7.13. Initial and final configurations in English solitaire

byte of memory, since bytes are typically 32 bits. We thus have to use two, and in fact, we will use a pair of CAML integers of type int, providing us the necessary offset operations to access the bits representing the integers. How we use the bits in either of the two integers to represent configurations is fairly arbitrary. We have decided here to put three bits in the first integer and thirty in the second.

We define a function **compact** that starts from a list of length 33, containing integers of value 0 or 1 exclusively, and builds a compact representation. We also define uncompact for the opposite operation.

```
#let compact l = match l with
  n₀::n₁::n₂::l → (4*n₂+2*n₁+n₀, save 0 32 (rev l))
                     where rec save n i l =
                     if i<3 then n
                     else save ((n lsl 1) lor (hd l)) (i−1) (tl l)
 | _ → failwith "compact: list too short" ;;
compact : int list → int * int = ⟨fun⟩
```

```
#let uncompact (m,n) =
   (m mod 2)::((m lsr 1) mod 2)::((m lsr 2) mod 2)::unsave n 0
   where rec unsave n i =
   if i>29 then [ ] else (n mod 2):: unsave (n lsr 1) (i+1);;
uncompact : int * int → int list = ⟨fun⟩
```

Here is an example of what we mean:

```
#compact [
                     1; 1; 1;
                     1; 1; 1;
              1; 1; 1; 1; 1; 1; 1;
              1; 1; 1; 0; 1; 1; 1;
              1; 1; 1; 1; 1; 1; 1;
                     1; 1; 1;
                     1; 1; 1
              ];;
 − : int * int = 7, 1073733631
```

We also assume two functions, nth and set_nth, to work on the compact representation. We leave these two functions as an exercise for you to write.

```
#nth;;
 − : int → int * int → int = ⟨fun⟩
```

```
#set_nth;;
 − : int → bool → int * int → int * int = ⟨fun⟩
```

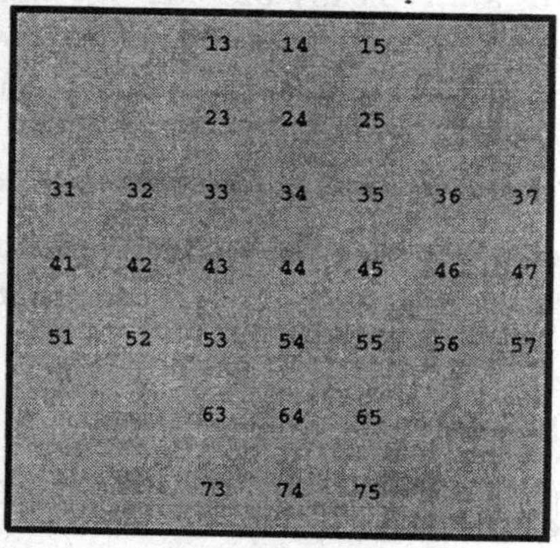

Figure 7.14. Positions are numbered for display

nth n rep accesses the nth bit of the representation rep, and set_nth n b rep replaces the nth bit of rep by b.

As we did in the game of the red donkey, again we will represent each position by an integer referring to its place in a square matrix. Figure 7.14 shows the way positions are numbered.

We will use this way of numbering positions to display solutions. Internally, we will work directly with the indices in the array of bits. You can see that internal representation in Figure 7.15.

Let's also assume we have the functions conv and iconv to convert between internal and external positions.

```
#conv 13;;
− : int = 0

#iconv 32;;
− : int = 75
```

The type direction will represent the orientation of moves on the board, and the function op_dir associates its opposite with a direction.

```
#type direction = Left | Up | Right | Down;;
```

```
#let op_dir=
    fun Left → Right | Right → Left | Up → Down | Down → Up;;
op_dir : direction → direction = ⟨fun⟩
```

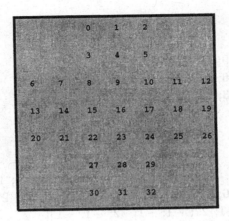

Figure 7.15. Positions internally numbered as well

Moves will be represented as they are in the game of the red donkey by a pair: the number of a position and a direction to move. The number refers to a position that will be empty before the move but occupied afterwards.

To speed up the computations about movements on the board, we will create look-up tables for the movement functions in various directions. To do so, we use integer vectors of length 33. For example, we tabulate the move to a position on the right by the vector *right*. For each position on the board, it gives the number of the position that is located to the right, if such a position exists, or -1 otherwise.

```
#let right = [|
                    1;   2;  -1;
                    4;   5;  -1;
              7;   8;   9;  10;  11;  12;  -1;
             14;  15;  16;  17;  18;  19;  -1;
             21;  22;  23;  24;  25;  26;  -1;
                   28;  29;  -1;
                   31;  32;  -1
        |];;
right : int vect = [| 1; 2; -1; 4; 5; -1; 7; 8; 9; 10; 11; 12; -1; 14; 15;
              16; 17; 18; 19; -1; 21; 22; 23; 24; 25; 26; -1;
              28; 29; -1; 31; 32; -1 |]
```

We assume that there are similar tables defined for the other directions. It will also be handy to have look-up tables for functions that move two positions in a given direction. For example:

```
#let right₂ = [|
                        2;  -1; -1;
                        5;  -1; -1;
              8;   9; 10; 11; 12; -1; -1;
             15; 16; 17; 18; 19; -1; -1;
             22; 23; 24; 25; 26; -1; -1;
                       29; -1; -1;
                       32; -1; -1
           |];;
```

$right_2$: *int vect* = [| 2; −1; −1; 5; −1; −1; 8; 9; 10; 11; 12; −1; −1; 15;
                    16; 17; 18; 19; −1; −1; 22; 23; 24; 25; 26; −1;
                    −1; 29; −1; −1; 32; −1; −1 |]

The function **table** maintains the correspondence between the look-up tables for directions and more move-functions.

```
#let table = fun
    Left 1 → left
  | Left 2 → left₂
  | Right 1 → right
  | Right 2 → right₂
  | Up 1 → up
  | Up 2 → up₂
  | Down 1 → down
  | Down 2 → down₂;;
```
table : *direction* → *int* → *int vect* = ⟨**fun**⟩

The configurations used by the search functions are of type **config**. The field **size** contains the number of pieces appearing on each board, so we do not have to recalculate that information. The field **moves** contains the sequence of moves needed to reach the configuration under consideration, starting from the initial configuration. The field **board** contains the representation of the board, coded as a pair of integers.

```
#type config = {size:int; moves: (int*direction) list;
                 board: int *int};;
```

The function **correct_move** is a utility function to compute possible moves. The argument i is a position on the board. The argument **dir** is a direction. The third argument is a configuration. If a movement in direction **dir** arriving in position i is possible, then the function returns a list containing a unique element, the configuration that it gets that way. Otherwise, it returns the empty list.

```
#let correct_move i dir {size=k; moves=ml;board=p} =
    let dir' = op_dir dir in
    let tab = table dir' 1 and tab₂ = table dir' 2 in
    let i₁ = tab.(i) and i₂ = tab₂.(i) in
    if nth i p = 0 & i₁ ≠ −1 & i₂ ≠ −1 &
        nth i₁ p = 1 & nth i₂ p = 1
    then [{size=pred k; moves=(i,dir)::ml;
            board=set_nth i true
                    (set_nth i₁ false (set_nth i₂ false p))}]
    else [ ];;
correct_move : int → direction → config → config list = ⟨fun⟩
```

Now here is the function that gives us the list of possible moves for a given configuration:

```
#let solit_moves config =
    pm 32 [ ]
    where rec pm n mvs =
        if n<0 then mvs
        else pm (n−1)
                (flat_map (fun d → correct_move n d config )
                    [Left;Right;Up;Down] @ mvs);;
solit_moves : config → config list = ⟨fun⟩
```

Before we apply a search procedure to that function, we must still define how to archive the configurations that we encounter as we search. A configuration is represented by a pair of integers, (n_1, n_2), where n_1 contains the first three bits of the representation. It is thus an integer between 0 and 7. With that idea in mind, we will use a vector of 8 sets, indexed by n_1. For each set, the order relation we use for storage in the archive will thus simply be the order among integers.

```
#type α archive = Arch of α set vect;;
```

```
#let add_to_archive (Arch arch) (n₁,n₂) =
    (arch.(n₁) ← add_to_set arch.(n₁) n₂);Arch arch;;
add_to_archive : α archive → int * α → α archive = ⟨fun⟩
```

```
#let add_list_to_archive= it_list add_to_archive;;
add_list_to_archive : α archive → (int * α) list → α archive = ⟨fun⟩
```

```
#let make_archive comp =
    add_list_to_archive (Arch (make_vect 8 (make_set comp [ ])));;
make_archive : (α → α → comparison) → (int * α) list → α archive
        = ⟨fun⟩
```

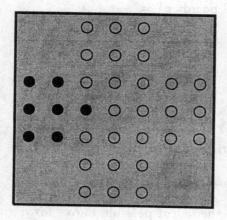 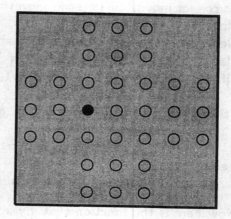

Figure 7.16. A sextuple game

#**let** archive_member (n_1,n_2) (Arch arch) = set_member n_2 (arch.(n_1)));;
*archive_member : int * $\alpha \to \alpha$ archive $\to$ bool* = ⟨**fun**⟩

Now we will define a depth-first search function for solitaire. It uses the general depth-first search function defined on page 204.

#**let** solve_depth_first_solit_game ok =
   solve_depth_first(ok,solit_moves,int_comp) (**fun** c $\to$ c.board);;
solve_depth_first_solit_game : (config $\to$ bool) $\to$ config $\to$ config
                    = ⟨**fun**⟩

Now we have the tools we need to tackle problems. First, we will consider problems where the goal is to reach a given configuration. Our halting test will thus be this:

#**let** ok_solit cgoal c = (c.board = cgoal);;
*ok_solit : int * int $\to$ config $\to$ bool* = ⟨**fun**⟩

To reach a final configuration c_2, starting from an initial configuration c_1, we simply have to evaluate this:

#solve_depth_first_solit_game (ok_solit c_2) ([ ],c_1);;

Here is a simple example first. Starting from the configuration on the left in Figure 7.16, we want to reach the configuration on the right.

These two configurations are defined by:

let b_1 = compact [

$$
\begin{array}{l}
0;\ 0;\ 0;\\
0;\ 0;\ 0;\\
1;\ 1;\ 0;\ 0;\ 0;\ 0;\ 0;\\
1;\ 1;\ 1;\ 0;\ 0;\ 0;\ 0;\\
1;\ 1;\ 0;\ 0;\ 0;\ 0;\ 0;\\
0;\ 0;\ 0;\\
0;\ 0;\ 0
\end{array}
$$

];;

$b_1 : int * int = 0,\ 400408$

let b_2 = compact [

$$
\begin{array}{l}
0;\ 0;\ 0;\\
0;\ 0;\ 0;\\
0;\ 0;\ 0;\ 0;\ 0;\ 0;\ 0;\\
0;\ 0;\ 1;\ 0;\ 0;\ 0;\ 0;\\
0;\ 0;\ 0;\ 0;\ 0;\ 0;\ 0;\\
0;\ 0;\ 0;\\
0;\ 0;\ 0
\end{array}
$$

];;

$b_2 : int * int = 0,\ 4096$

Let's assume that we have defined a function output_result to display the solution we found as well as the sequence of moves to get there.

Here is the statement of the problem and its result:

```
#output_result
    (solve_depth_first_solit_game
        (ok_solit b₂) {size=7; moves=[ ];board=b₁});;
Moves:
33 Right | 23 Up | 31 Up | 32 Up | 33 Right | 43 Down |

Final Configuration:
    0 0 0
    0 0 0
0 0 0 0 0 0 0
0 0 1 0 0 0 0
0 0 0 0 0 0 0
    0 0 0
    0 0 0
```

$-\ :\ unit\ =\ ()$

Now here is a larger example:

```
#let b₃ = compact [
                        1; 1; 1;
                        1; 1; 1;
                  1; 1; 0; 0; 1; 0; 0;
                  1; 1; 1; 1; 1; 1; 0;
                  1; 1; 0; 0; 1; 0; 0;
                        1; 1; 1;
                        0; 0; 0
                  ]
  and b₄ = compact [
                        0; 0; 0;
                        0; 0; 0;
                  0; 0; 0; 0; 0; 0; 0;
                  0; 0; 0; 1; 0; 0; 0;
                  0; 0; 0; 0; 0; 0; 0;
                        0; 0; 0;
                        0; 0; 0
                  ] in
  output_result
   (solve_depth_first_solit_game
     (ok_solit b₄) {size=21; moves=[ ];board=b₃});;
```

Moves:
33 Right | 31 Up | 32 Up | 34 Right | 33 Left | 34 Down | 32
Left | 33 Right | 35 Down | 25 Up | 53 Down | 33 Down | 43 Up
 | 53 Down | 63 Left | 43 Up | 45 Right | 35 Up | 45 Down | 4
4 Left |

Final Configuration:
```
    0 0 0
    0 0 0
0 0 0 0 0 0 0
0 0 0 1 0 0 0
0 0 0 0 0 0 0
    0 0 0
    0 0 0
```
$-$: *unit* = ()

Careful, though! Because of its complexity, the game of solitaire strongly resists a "brute force" approach for more complicated problems. To solve the problem in Figure 7.13 as we did, we needed considerable computing power. A

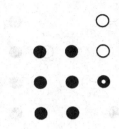

Figure 7.17. Block of 6

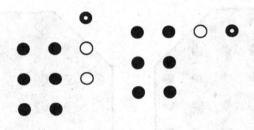

Figure 7.18. Other blocks of 6

configuration where there are only two pieces left on the board can be found in only a few minutes on a typical work station, but a solution with only one piece remaining requires several days of computation. To shorten the search time, we should exploit the symmetries of the board, but tests for symmetry themselves are quite complex.

By studying solitaire empirically it is possible to single out a few remarkable configurations. Our first example, in Figure 7.16, is notable. We observe here that position 43 never changes, and apart from the initial occupied positions, the only other positions used are 23 and 33. Thus we have successfully eliminated the six pieces in positions 31, 32, 41, 42, 51, and 52, using only the fact that positions 23 and 33 were empty and position 43 was occupied.

This observation is summarized pictorially in Figure 7.17 where the unmoving piece is black with a white center, the pieces that are removed are black, and the free positions are white.

You see other remarkable configurations in Figures 7.18 and 7.19.

If we exploit these blocks of moves, we can guide the search to arrive at a solution.

Of course, it would be even more satisfying to highlight global properties of the game to guide the search for solutions. Unfortunately, even though eminent

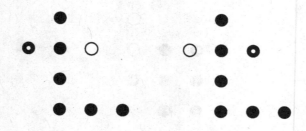

Figure 7.19. Blocks of 7

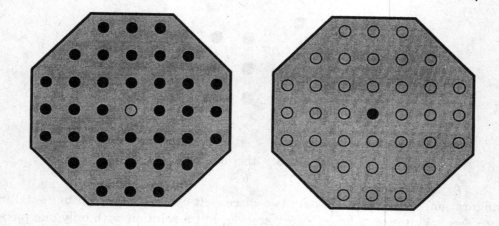

Figure 7.20. Initial and final configurations for French solitaire

mathematicians have been interested in this game, the only results they have obtained have been properties about the invariance of configurations linked by legal moves. These properties provide only negative results. If the values of the invariant are different for two configurations c_1 and c_2, then we know that it will be impossible to get from c_1 to c_2. However, even if the values of the invariant are the same for them, it may still be impossible to get from one to the other, and that fact does not offer any method to get there even if it is possible.

Even so, those negative properties at least let us eliminate right away any problems for which we know there is no solution. Their proofs can also be quite elegant. We will show you one such proof, due to Georges Gonthier, that the problem in Figure 7.20 has no solution. It is much the same problem as in Figure 7.13, but it appears on a French board.

The proof first partitions the positions into three classes, as you see in Figure 7.21.

Class 1 contains 12 positions; class 2, 13; and class 3, 12. In the initial

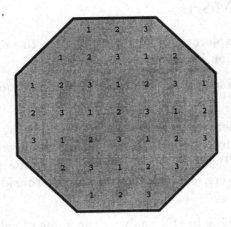

Figure 7.21. Partition the positions into 3 classes

configuration, each class contains 12 positions occupied by a piece. The important point here is not the number of occupied positions, but the *parity*, which is the same for the three classes initially. Notice that any move assigns three positions necessarily belonging to three different classes and modifies the parity of the number of positions occupied in each class. Starting from a configuration where the three parities are the same, we necessarily keep this property throughout all moves. It is thus impossible to reach a configuration where there is only one remaining piece on the board[1]. In particular, the problem in Figure 7.20 has no solution.

We can apply this technique of partitioning to all variations of solitaire. In doing so, we can show that no solution exists for a great many problems.

Exercises
7.8 Write the functions nth and set_nth on page 219.
7.9 Rewrite the function solit_moves on page 223 to include block moves as in Figures 7.16, 7.18, 7.19, and their symmetric images.

7.4 Summary

We introduced a group of functions to explore graphs defined by their transition functions. With these search functions, we tackled two games, the red donkey, where we exploited a breadth-first search, and solitaire, where we used depth-first.

---

[1]However, we can reach a configuration where there are two pieces on the board. These two pieces must belong to the same class, and they cannot reach each other.

7.5   To Learn More

The domain of graph exploration and its application to problem solving is vast; we have barely touched on it here.

Algorithms to traverse graphs are available in most books about algorithms, such as [35] and [7].

Graph traversal where the graphs are represented by transition functions rather than by data structures belongs to artificial intelligence. See [43] or [6] for more about that idea. Both those references take up the problem of strategies for games with two players, a topic that we did not consider here in our games for single players.

An article by P. Tougne in [40] analyzes the game of solitaire.

Chapter 8

Syntactic Analysis

Most programs, especially those that expect a character string as input, begin by recognizing such strings in order to determine whether or not one happens to represent valid input. Next—in fact, at the same time—such a program transforms the string into internal data that is easier to handle. The preceding chapters assumed the existence of such features and functions. This chapter indicates how to program them.

A command to an operating system (such as `ls` on UNIX, etc.) is a very simple example of a program that takes character strings as input and then decides to accept or reject them. A compiler is a more complicated program to take character strings as input; it accepts the concrete syntax of the program to compile. A compiler decides to accept or reject the program to compile; if it accepts, it transforms the program into more easily managed data, such as abstract syntax trees.

In each of these cases, we say that the command shell or the compiler accepts phrases belonging to a certain language; in the case of the command shell, we mean the options and arguments valid for a given command; for the compiler, the programming language to compile. In both cases, they reject any other phrases. In this chapter, we will call a **language** the set (possibly infinite) of acceptable character strings, and the chief problem that we take up is that of **recognizing** the phrases belonging to a given language.

In the case of a compiler, the recognition phase is followed by the transformation of input into data structures representing the program to compile. We have mentioned "phases," but in fact the phases of recognition and transformation are generally simultaneous, and we will speak of them together in this case as **syntactic analysis**.

In this chapter, we present a few methods of analysis particularly well adapted to CAML and to functional programming in general. We will first define two major classes of languages: those defined by regular expressions and those defined by context-free grammars. Initially, we will limit our efforts to recognizing phrases of these languages. Eventually, we will extend our recognition algorithms to analysis algorithms that transform their input into CAML data. Finally, we will study **predictive analysis**, a particular technique of analysis for which certain characteristics of CAML were specially designed.

8.1 Regular Expressions

Given an alphabet $\mathcal{A}$, a regular expression e over $\mathcal{A}$ is a concise way of representing a set $\mathcal{L}$, possibly infinite, of strings of elements of $\mathcal{A}$. For example, there exists a regular expression over the ASCII alphabet to represent the concrete form of a numeric constant.

We will define regular expressions by the set of strings that they represent:

- ϵ represents the set $\mathcal{L}_\epsilon = \{\epsilon\}$ containing only the empty string. The string itself is also denoted ϵ.

- an element c of $\mathcal{A}$ represents the singleton $\mathcal{L}_c = \{c\}$.

- $e_1 e_2$ represents the set $\mathcal{L}_{e_1} \cdot \mathcal{L}_{e_2}$ of all concatenations possible among the elements of $\mathcal{L}_{e_1}$ and $\mathcal{L}_{e_2}$. It is defined by

$$\mathcal{L}_{e_1} \cdot \mathcal{L}_{e_2} = \{s_1 s_2 \mid s_1 \in \mathcal{L}_{e_1}, \ s_2 \in \mathcal{L}_{e_2}\}$$

- $e_1 | e_2$ represents the set $\mathcal{L}_{e_1} \cup \mathcal{L}_{e_2}$.

- e^* represents the union

$$\bigcup_{i=0}^{\infty} \mathcal{L}_e^i \text{ where } \mathcal{L}_e^0 = \mathcal{L}_\epsilon \text{ and } \mathcal{L}_e^i = \mathcal{L}_e^{i-1} \cdot \mathcal{L}_e$$

In other words, e^* is equivalent to the infinite regular expression

$$\epsilon |e| ee |eee| \ldots$$

This iterator is called the **Kleene closure operator**.

In order to name regular expressions, we use the symbol "::=". For example, the regular expression *digit* representing digits is defined by

$$digit ::= \text{`0`}|\text{`1`}|\text{`2`}|\text{`3`}|\text{`4`}|\text{`5`}|\text{`6`}|\text{`7`}|\text{`8`}|\text{`9`}$$

A non-empty sequence of digits is defined by

$$digits ::= digit \ digit^*$$

An optional positive or negative sign is defined by

$$optsign ::= \; `-`|`+`|\epsilon$$

The optional decimal part of a number is made up of a decimal point followed by a sequence (possibly empty) of digits, like this:

$$optfrac ::= (`\;.\;` \; digit^*)|\epsilon$$

An exponent, which is also optional, consists of the letter **e**, possibly in upper case, possibly a sign, and one or more digits, like this:

$$optexp ::= ((`e`|`E`) \; optsign \; digits)|\epsilon$$

A number can now be defined as a sequence of digits, a decimal part, and an exponent, like this:

$$number ::= digits \; optfrac \; optexp$$

From now on, we will consider a regular expression $name_n$ as a sequence of such definitions.

$$name_1 ::= e_1; \; \ldots; \; name_n ::= e_n$$

Yet we must be careful that the resulting regular expression (the one we get by replacing names by their definition) remains finite. To guarantee that point, it suffices to impose the rule that no name $name_i$ with $i \geq k$ appears in e_k. In that way, we avoid recursive definitions.

Languages that can be represented by regular expressions are called, reasonably enough, **regular languages**. Typically, we use regular expressions to define the **tokens** of a language during lexical analysis, for example, as well as to search for patterns in a text, for example in the famous UNIX command, `grep`.

An example of a non-regular language is the language of nested parentheses: the alphabet $\mathcal{A}$ is reduced to $\{`(`,`)`\}$, and the phrases of the language are the well formed, nested parentheses like "((()))". That non-regular language can be defined by a context-free grammar, as you will see next.

8.2 Context-Free Grammar

The class of context-free languages includes those languages that can be defined by a context-free grammar. This class is larger than the class of regular languages.

Programming languages are habitually defined recursively, without the limitation that we introduced earlier. For example, arithmetic expressions (which we will call simply *expressions*) can be defined in the following way:

An expression is one of these:

- the addition of two expressions, that is, an expression followed by an addition sign, followed by another expression;

- the difference of two expression, that is, an expression followed by a subtraction sign, followed by another expression;

- the multiplication of two expressions;

- the division of one expression by another;

- an expression within parentheses;

- an identifier;

- a numeric constant.

Let's assume that the set of valid identifiers of the language is called *IDENT* and the set of numeric constants is *NUM*. The following succinct notation is known as BNF[1]:

$$
\begin{aligned}
expr \quad ::= \quad &expr + expr \\
| \quad &expr - expr \\
| \quad &expr * expr \\
| \quad &expr \,/\, expr \\
| \quad &(\ expr\ ) \\
| \quad &id \in IDENT \\
| \quad &n \in NUM
\end{aligned}
$$

To produce all the valid phrases of the language *expr*, it suffices to read each of those lines as a **production rule**; that is, it produces one of the following sets. In fact, if we adopt set notation, we can read the grammar as the definition of an infinite set that solves the following equation:

$$
\begin{aligned}
expr \quad = \quad &IDENT \\
\cup \quad &NUM \\
\cup \quad &\{\text{'('}e\text{')'} \mid e \in expr\} \\
\cup \quad &\{e_1\text{'/'}e_2 \mid (e_1, e_2) \in expr \times expr\} \\
\cup \quad &\{e_1\text{'*'}e_2 \mid (e_1, e_2) \in expr \times expr\} \\
\cup \quad &\{e_1\text{'-'}e_2 \mid (e_1, e_2) \in expr\} \\
\cup \quad &\{e_1\text{'+'}e_2 \mid (e_1, e_2) \in expr \times expr\}
\end{aligned}
$$

We read the symbol "|" as a set union, as we did for regular expressions.

We mentioned earlier that the language of nested parentheses could not be represented as a regular expression. However, we can represent it by a context-free grammar, like this:

---

[1]For *Backus-Naur Form*.

$$nested\_paren \quad ::= \quad `(` \ nested\_paren \ `)`$$
$$| \quad \epsilon$$

In the BNF notation of a context-free grammar, two kinds of symbols appear:

- Symbols such as '+', '(', or $n \in NUM$, are known as **terminal** symbols. They play the role of constants. They are symbols that are not defined by the grammar. They are analogous to tokens or lexemes in a natural language such as French or English: they are the basic elements that we can assume were identified during the **lexical analysis**, prior to the syntactic analysis.

- Symbols known as **non-terminals** represent the languages and sublanguages defined by a grammar. In our example, the only non-terminal is *expr*.

8.2.1 Types and Values

From the point of view of computer science, a grammar like this represents only the structure of the language being defined; it does not take into account the possible values that we might want to associate with each phrase of the language. Typically, we associate abstract syntax trees defined by a CAML type, like:

```
#type ast =
       Constant of float
     | Variable of string
     | Addition of ast * ast
     | Subtraction of ast * ast
     | Multiplication of ast * ast
     | Division of ast * ast;;
```

This type is similar to one we saw in Section 2.2.4 but differs somewhat: the constants are floating-point numbers, and we have two supplementary operations—multiplication and division.

The concrete syntax of arithmetic expressions will, of course, be character strings. Such a string will in turn be transformed into a sequence of tokens, which will be elements of the following type:

```
#type token =
       NUM of float | IDENT of string
     | LPAR | RPAR
     | PLUS | MINUS | STAR | SLASH;;
```

Each of the production rules of the grammar *expr* can thus be associated with an element of type ast. From now on, we will use a BNF notation enriched by a means to name intermediate values (e_1, e_2, s) and an action associated with each production rule. The grammar of arithmetic expressions thus can be written like this:

$$
\begin{array}{lcll}
expr & ::= & expr(e_1) \text{ PLUS } expr(e_2) & \rightarrow \quad \text{Addition}(e_1, e_2) \\
     & | & expr(e_1) \text{ MINUS } expr(e_2) & \rightarrow \quad \text{Subtraction}(e_1, e_2) \\
     & | & expr(e_1) \text{ STAR } expr(e_2) & \rightarrow \quad \text{Multiplication}(e_1, e_2) \\
     & | & expr(e_1) \text{ SLASH } expr(e_2) & \rightarrow \quad \text{Division}(e_1, e_2) \\
     & | & \text{LPAR } expr(e) \text{ RPAR} & \rightarrow \quad e \\
     & | & \text{IDENT}(s) & \rightarrow \quad \text{Variable}(s) \\
     & | & \text{NUM}(n) & \rightarrow \quad \text{Constant}(n)
\end{array}
$$

Now such a grammar can be associated with a type in the sense that its terminal elements are all of type token and its semantic actions all produce values of type ast. Intuitively, an analyzer of arithmetic expressions must have a type to associate ast with token list.

8.2.2 Ambiguities

A significant problem of the grammar in the previous section is that it is ambiguous. More precisely, two different trees can be associated with the sequence

NUM(1) MINUS NUM(2) MINUS NUM(3)

corresponding to the arithmetic expression $1 - 2 - 3$. It involves

Subtraction(Constant 1., Subtraction(Constant 2., Constant 3.))

and

Subtraction(Subtraction(Constant 1., Constant 2.), Constant 3.)

In the case of operators that are not semantically associative (like substraction), this choice is important. Yet nothing in the grammar tells us how to make the choice; the definition of the language is thus incomplete. Another source of ambiguity is the relative priority between addition and multiplication operators.

With respect to arithmetic operators, we will conform to tradition and decide that all the operators are "left-associative," that is, like (e_1 op e_2) op e_3. This choice shows up in the following new grammar that uses different non-terminals on each side of the operators.

Also we will define multiplication operators as higher priority than addition operators. For example, the expression e_1 + e_2 * e_3 will be recognized as

$$e_1 + (e_2 * e_3)$$

We can get a non-ambiguous grammar for these arithmetic expressions by introducing two auxiliary non-terminals: *term* to designate possible arguments of addition operators and *fact* to designate possible arguments of multiplication operators.

expr	::=	$expr(e_1)$ PLUS $term(e_2)$	$\rightarrow$	Addition(e_1, e_2)
	|	$expr(e_1)$ MINUS $term(e_2)$	$\rightarrow$	Subtraction(e_1, e_2)
	|	$term(e)$	$\rightarrow$	e
term	::=	$term(e_1)$ STAR $fact(e_2)$	$\rightarrow$	Multiplication(e_1, e_2)
	|	$term(e_1)$ SLASH $fact(e_2)$	$\rightarrow$	Division(e_1, e_2)
	|	$fact(e)$	$\rightarrow$	e
fact	::=	LPAR $expr(e)$ RPAR	$\rightarrow$	e
	|	IDENT(s)	$\rightarrow$	Var(s)
	|	NUM(n)	$\rightarrow$	Constant(n)

This grammar thus introduces a hierarchy among expressions, and it is easy enough to see that it eliminates the ambiguities that troubled us before.

In spite of a few differences in notation that we have introduced for grammars and regular expressions, we will use a common syntax for them; that is, we allow alternatives in the production rules of grammars, and we can use the * iterator there, too. Conversely, we will adopt the notation of grammars to associate values with regular expressions.

With this uniform notation, we will refer to grammars whether we are dealing with regular expressions or context-free grammars.

8.3   Recognizers

It may feel natural enough to read a grammar as the set of production rules to generate the language being defined. Even though this way of looking at a grammar lets us understand its meaning easily, this kind of reading gives us no idea of how to accept or reject a phrase on the basis of whether or not it belongs to the language.

Functional programming offers an interesting possibility here, in spite of a few limitations that we will look into later. The idea will be to read a grammar directly as a **recognizer**. For example, we could read the regular expression defining the concrete syntax of integer constants like this:

- to recognize *digit*, recognize '`0`', **or** recognize '`1`', **or** recognize ...;

- to recognize *digits*, recognize *digit*, **then** recognize **zero or more** *digit*;

- to recognize *optsign*, recognize '-', **or** '+' **or nothing**;

- etc.

This reading suggests that when we are given the basic recognition functions for characters, we can associate functions with the primary articulations, namely, **nothing, or, then,** and **zero or more.** We call these functions the **recognizer constructors.**

8.3.1   Recognizer Constructors

Recognizers work on lists; they consume part of a list and return either the rest of it or the value Fails, indicating that the attempt at recognition failed.

#type α remaining =
    Remains **of** α list
 | Fails;;

The type of a recognizer is an abbreviation:

#type α recognizer == α list $\rightarrow$ α remaining;;

Later we will use type constraints when necessary to force CAML to use this abbreviation.

    The recognizer associated with ϵ always succeeds and never consumes anything from its list-argument.

#let (empty : α recognizer) = **fun** toks $\rightarrow$ Remains toks;;
empty : α *recognizer* = $\langle$**fun**$\rangle$

#empty ['a'; 'b'];;
$-$: *char remaining* = *Remains* ['a'; 'b']

Given a predicate test, token produces the recognizer associated with the elements that make this predicate true:

#let (token : (α $\rightarrow$ bool) $\rightarrow$ α recognizer) = **fun**
  test (t :: ts) $\rightarrow$ **if** test t **then** Remains ts **else** Fails
 | _ _ $\rightarrow$ Fails;;
token : (α $\rightarrow$ *bool*) $\rightarrow$ α *recognizer* = $\langle$**fun**$\rangle$

#let char c = token (**prefix** = c);;
char : $\alpha \rightarrow \alpha$ *recognizer* = ⟨**fun**⟩

#char 'a' ['a'; 'b'];;
− : *char remaining* = *Remains* ['b']

#char 'a' ['b'];;
− : *char remaining* = *Fails*

We associate the recognizer p_1 **orelse** p_2 with the disjunction of the recognizers p_1 and p_2. That disjunction recognizer is defined by:

#let (orelse : α recognizer $\rightarrow \alpha$ recognizer $\rightarrow \alpha$ recognizer) =
    fun p_1 p_2 toks $\rightarrow$ **match** p_1 toks **with**
                Fails $\rightarrow$ p_2 toks
             | res $\rightarrow$ res;;
orelse : α *recognizer* $\rightarrow \alpha$ *recognizer* $\rightarrow \alpha$ *recognizer* = ⟨**fun**⟩

##infix "orelse";;

The recognizer p_1 **orelse** p_2 first tries p_1, and then p_2 if p_1 fails.

#((char 'a') orelse (char 'b')) ['b'];;
− : *char remaining* = *Remains* [ ]

Notice that **orelse** is not commutative, so we must be careful of the order of its arguments, especially when one of its arguments can recognize a substring recognizable by the other. As a general rule, the recognizer capable of recognizing the longest strings should be the first argument of **orelse**. The following example shows that **p orelse empty** behaves the way we expect, whereas **empty orelse p** always succeeds without consuming anything.

#((char 'a') orelse empty) ['a'];;
− : *char remaining* = *Remains* [ ]

#(empty orelse (char 'a')) ['a'];;
− : *char remaining* = *Remains* ['a']

Concatenation is represented by **andalso**. It tries to apply its arguments sequentially and fails when one of them fails.

#let (andalso : α recognizer $\rightarrow \alpha$ recognizer $\rightarrow \alpha$ recognizer) =
    fun p_1 p_2 toks $\rightarrow$
             match p_1 toks **with**
           Remains $toks_1$ $\rightarrow$ p_2 $toks_1$
           | _ $\rightarrow$ Fails;;
andalso : α *recognizer* $\rightarrow \alpha$ *recognizer* $\rightarrow \alpha$ *recognizer* = ⟨**fun**⟩

##infix "andalso";;

```
#((char 'a') andalso (char 'b')) ['a'; 'b'; 'c'];;
- : char remaining = Remains ['c']
```

Finally, the * iterator is translated by the recursive function zero_or_more:

```
#let rec zero_or_more p =
    (fun toks → ((p andalso (zero_or_more p))
                    orelse empty) toks : α recognizer);;
zero_or_more : α recognizer → α recognizer = ⟨fun⟩
```

Here we have been careful to make the choice empty the second argument of orelse so that it is called only as a last resort.

```
#zero_or_more (char 'a') ['a' ;'a' ;'a' ; 'b'];;
- : char remaining = Remains ['b']
```

```
#zero_or_more (char 'a') ['b'];;
- : char remaining = Remains ['b']
```

8.3.2 Limitations

We have to point out here the limitations of our recognizer constructors. They can **backtrack** but only in a limited way. Backtracking occurs with the constructor orelse, as you can see in the following example.

```
#let ab = (char 'a') andalso (char 'b')
 and ac = (char 'a') andalso (char 'c');;
ab : char recognizer = ⟨fun⟩
ac : char recognizer = ⟨fun⟩
```

```
#(ab orelse ac) ['a'; 'c'];;
- : char remaining = Remains []
```

The recognizer ab initially tests the first character by (char 'a'), then fails on the second one. Control is then handed to ac. It tests the first character again, then tests the second, and succeeds.

However, backtracking is limited, as the following example shows. Although $(a|\epsilon)a$ defines the same language as $aa|a$, you see that the associated recognizers are not equivalent.

```
#let opt_a = (char 'a') orelse empty;;
opt_a : char recognizer = ⟨fun⟩
```

```
#(opt_a andalso (char 'a')) ['a'];;
- : char remaining = Fails
```

```
#(((char 'a') andalso (char 'a'))
   orelse (char 'a')) ['a'];;
 − : char remaining = Remains [ ]
```

At first glance, you might think that it suffices to apply a rule about distribution over disjunction with respect to concatenation to a regular expression like $(a|\epsilon)a$.

$$(e_1 \mid e_2) \, e_3 \rightarrow e_1 e_3 \mid e_2 e_3$$

This rule transforms the expression $(a|\epsilon)a$ into $aa|a$, which in turn can easily be translated into the right recognizer. Unfortunately, the * operator complicates the problem a bit.

In effect, this operator behaves like a disjunction, so it tempts us to use the distributive rule we just defined in order to transform it into an iteration. Then we get the following rule:

$$e_1^* \, e_2 \rightarrow \epsilon e_2 \mid e_1 e_1^* e_2$$

that is,

$$e_1^* \, e_2 \rightarrow e_2 \mid e_1 e_1^* e_2$$

The pattern $e_1^* e_2$ occurs on the righthand side of the rule, so the transformation cannot be carried out completely.

Another limitation of our constructors involves the iteration of a recognizer that accepts the empty string (opt_a, for example). In such a case, we risk a loop like you see in the following example. In this example, we redefine opt_a so that it will not be called more than 100 times.

```
#let opt_a =
   let called = ref 0 in
   fun toks → if !called ≥ 100 then
                  (called := 0; failwith "Called 100 times! Aborting.")
              else incr called;
                  ((char 'a') orelse empty) toks
 in (zero_or_more opt_a) ['b'];;
Uncaught exception: Failure "Called 100 times! Aborting."
```

The recognizer (zero_or_more opt_a) tries to recognize an infinite sequence of ϵ and thus cannot decide whether the argument belongs to the language or not.

With respect to regular expressions, there is a way to avoid such problems with the help of a transformation of the regular expression under consideration. (See Section 8.6.) However, in the general case, writing recognizers or analyzers with these constructors demands a bit of prudence from the programmer! He or she must always write and transform the grammar into a simpler form that can be translated in a reliable way by means of the constructions in this chapter.

8.3.3   Recognizers for Regular Expressions

Now we are in a good position to produce the recognizer associated with *number*. An auxiliary predicate will help us test whether a character belongs to the union of closed intervals of characters.

```
#let rec char_range c = fun
    [ ] → false
 | ((c₁,c₂)::l) → (int_of_char c₁ ≤ int_of_char c &
                     int_of_char c ≤ int_of_char c₂)
                   or char_range c l;;
char_range : char → (char * char) list → bool = ⟨fun⟩
```

For example, we test whether a character is a digit like this:

```
#let is_digit c = char_range c [('0','9')];;
is_digit : char → bool = ⟨fun⟩
```

We test whether a character is a letter (either upper- or lower-case) like this:

```
#let is_letter c =
    char_range c [('a','z'); ('A','Z')];;
is_letter : char → bool = ⟨fun⟩
```

Just for review, here is the regular expression to define numbers:

$$
\begin{array}{lll}
digit   & ::= & \text{`0`}|\text{`1`}|\text{`2`}|\text{`3`}|\text{`4`}|\text{`5`}|\text{`6`}|\text{`7`}|\text{`8`}|\text{`9`}; \\
digits & ::= & digit\ digit^*; \\
optsign & ::= & \text{`-`}|\text{`+`}|\epsilon; \\
optfrac & ::= & (\text{`.`}\ digit^*)|\epsilon; \\
optexp & ::= & ((\text{`e`}|\text{`E`})\ optsign\ digits)|\epsilon; \\
number & ::= & digits\ optfrac\ optexp
\end{array}
$$

To construct the recognizer for numbers, we follow the same scheme:

```
#let digit = token is_digit;;
digit : char recognizer = ⟨fun⟩

#let digits = digit andalso (zero_or_more digit);;
digits : char recognizer = ⟨fun⟩

#let optsign =
    (token (fun ('-'|'+') → true | _ → false))
    orelse empty;;
optsign : char recognizer = ⟨fun⟩
```

The decimal part *optfrac* is recognized by this:

```
#let optfrac =
    (token (fun ' . ' → true | _ → false) andalso (zero_or_more digit))
    orelse empty;;
```
optfrac : *char recognizer* = ⟨**fun**⟩

We leave the recognizer optexp as an exercise for you to program. Finally, the recognizer for numbers itself is defined by:

```
#let number = digits andalso optfrac andalso optexp;;
```
number : *char recognizer* = ⟨**fun**⟩

In the definition of the language for numbers, we have been careful not to use iterations of regular expressions that accept the empty string; we have also avoided any need to backtrack. These precautions let us translate the regular expressions easily into recognizers.

In order to test our recognizers and analyzers more easily, we assume that we also have the following functions:

explode : string → char list
implode : char list → string

one to expand a string into a list of characters, and the other to change a list of characters into a string.

```
#number (explode ("123abc"));;
```
− : *char remaining* = *Remains* ['a'; 'b'; 'c']

```
#number (explode ("123.45e-67"));;
```
− : *char remaining* = *Remains* [ ]

```
#number (explode ("abc"));;
```
− : *char remaining* = *Fails*

8.3.4 Recognizers for Grammars

If we look again at the grammar for arithmetic expressions that we developed earlier, we see that we cannot directly translate it into a recognizer, as we did for regular expressions defining numbers. The reason is that, for example, the recognizer expr associated with *expr* would be defined like this:

let rec expr toks = (expr andalso plus andalso term) toks

implying that the first task of expr would be to call itself, leading thus to an infinite loop.

The problem is that because of the operators being left-associative, the grammar is left-recursive. The solution is to transform more of this grammar beforehand in order to eliminate recursion. However, we must keep in mind that, when we produce abstract syntax trees, we build them so that they correctly represent left-associativity.

We transform the grammar by noticing that *expr* always gives at least one *term*, followed zero or more times by an addition operator followed by *term*. We notice the same about *term*, a multiplication operator, and *fact*. If we use the * iterator from regular expressions, then we can rewrite the grammar, like this:

expr   ::=   *term* ((PLUS |MINUS) *term*)*

term   ::=   *fact* ((STAR |SLASH) *fact*)*

fact   ::=   LPAR *expr* RPAR
        | IDENT
        | NUM

This grammar is no longer left-recursive, and we take advantage of that fact to unite the two cases of operators into a single rule in *expr* and *term*.

Now it is possible to define the recognizer expr directly from that grammar.

```
#let recognize_expr =
    (*Recognizer for tokens *)
    let addop = token (fun (PLUS | MINUS) → true | _ → false)
    and mulop = token (fun (STAR | SLASH) → true | _ → false)
    and lpar = token (fun LPAR → true | _ → false)
    and rpar = token (fun RPAR → true | _ → false)
    and ident = token (fun (IDENT _) → true | _ → false)
    and num = token (fun (NUM _) → true | _ → false) in
    (*Main non-terminals *)
    let rec expr toks =
      (term andalso (zero_or_more (addop andalso term))) toks
    and term toks = (fact andalso (zero_or_more (mulop andalso fact))) toks
    and fact toks = ((lpar andalso expr andalso rpar)
                      orelse ident
                      orelse num) toks
    in expr;;
recognize_expr : token list → token remaining = ⟨fun⟩
```

Example:

```
#recognize_expr
    [NUM 2.0; PLUS; LPAR; NUM 3.0; MINUS; NUM 4.0; RPAR];;
- : token remaining = Remains [ ]
```

However, even if the input cannot be entirely recognized, the first and longest valid expression is still recognized:

```
#recognize_expr [NUM 2.0; PLUS; LPAR; RPAR];;
```
− : *token remaining = Remains [PLUS; LPAR; RPAR]*

8.3.5 Various Derived Forms

Before going on, we will now present a few derived forms that will be useful in building recognizers.

Especially useful for regular expressions, the recognizer any accepts all letters of the alphabet $\mathcal{A}$.

```
#let any x =
    token (fun _ → true) x;;
```
any : α list → α remaining = ⟨fun⟩

```
#any [ 'a' ];;
```
− : *char remaining = Remains [ ]*

The regular expression associated with any is customarily denoted by ".".

The recognizer associated with a production rule of the form $e|\epsilon$ will accept whatever the recognizer associated with e accepts or it will accept the empty string. We build these recognizers with the help of optional, defined by:

```
#let optional p =
    p orelse empty;;
```
optional : α recognizer → α recognizer = ⟨fun⟩

The expression $e|\epsilon$ is often denoted by $e?$.

In the same way that * signifies "zero or more," the $^+$ iterator designates "one or more." We use it often and represent it by this:

```
#let one_or_more p =
    p andalso (zero_or_more p);;
```
one_or_more : α recognizer → α recognizer = ⟨fun⟩

Considering a list of recognizers, we can construct its conjunction. The conjunction of an empty list is the recognizer empty.

```
#let and_list pl =
    list_it (prefix andalso) pl empty;;
```
and_list : α recognizer list → α recognizer = ⟨fun⟩

We get this conjunction from a list of analyzers of the same type and from the fact that for any analyzer p, p andalso empty recognizes the same language as p.

The disjunction of an arbitrary number of recognizers can be constructed only if that number is greater than or equal to one.

#let or_list p pl = it_list (**prefix** orelse) p pl;;
or_list : α recognizer → α recognizer list → α recognizer = ⟨**fun**⟩

Exercises
8.1 Write the function optexp from page 243.

8.4   Analysis = Recognition + Values

Now we will tackle the problem of constructing values during recognition. We call the complete process "analysis," and we qualify it as "lexical" or "syntactic" according to whether we consider regular expressions or context-free grammars.

We need two new types, similar to **remaining** and **recognizer** (which you have already seen). This time, they will have parameters according to the type of values returned.

#type (α, β) parsed =
      Returns **of** $\beta * (\alpha$ list)
   | AnalyzeFails;;

#type (α, β) parser == α list → (α,β) parsed;;

Basic analyzers, built by **token**, must no longer be constructed from a predicate, but rather from a function returning a value (when it succeeds). These values are contained in the following type:

#type α option =
      Some **of** α
   | None;;

Before we show you the constructors for analyzers, we will introduce a function, **accept**, to extract the return value of an analyzer:

#let accept = **fun**
   (Returns(v, [ ])) → v
  | (Returns(_, _::_)) → failwith "Couldn't consume all input"
  | AnalyzeFails → failwith "Failed";;
accept : (α, β) parsed → β = ⟨**fun**⟩

8.4.1   Constructors for Analyzers

We begin with the analyzer that recognizes the empty string:

#let (empty : $\alpha \rightarrow (\beta,\alpha)$ parser) = **fun** v toks $\rightarrow$ Returns (v, toks);;
empty : $\alpha \rightarrow (\beta, \alpha)$ parser = $\langle$**fun**$\rangle$

Its first argument v is the return value.

#empty 0.0 [ ];;
$-$: $(\alpha,$ float$)$ parsed = Returns $(0, [ ])$

The analyzers associated with tokens are built by means of functions returning a value of type option:

#let (token : $(\alpha \rightarrow \beta$ option$) \rightarrow (\alpha, \beta)$ parser) = **fun**
   test (t :: ts) $\rightarrow$ (**match** test t **with**
                 Some r $\rightarrow$ Returns (r, ts)
              | None $\rightarrow$ AnalyzeFails)
 | _ _ $\rightarrow$ AnalyzeFails;;
token : $(\alpha \rightarrow \beta$ option$) \rightarrow (\alpha, \beta)$ parser = $\langle$**fun**$\rangle$

#let char c =
   token (**fun** c' $\rightarrow$ **if** c = c' **then** Some c **else** None);;
char : $\alpha \rightarrow (\alpha, \alpha)$ parser = $\langle$**fun**$\rangle$

#let num =
   token (**fun** (NUM n) $\rightarrow$ Some (Constant n) | _ $\rightarrow$ None)
 and ident =
   token (**fun** (IDENT s) $\rightarrow$ Some (Variable s) | _ $\rightarrow$ None)
 and addop =
   token (**fun** PLUS $\rightarrow$ Some (**fun** e_1 e_2 $\rightarrow$ Addition(e_1,e_2))
          | MINUS $\rightarrow$ Some (**fun** e_1 e_2 $\rightarrow$ Subtraction(e_1,e_2))
          | _ $\rightarrow$ None)
 and mulop =
   token (**fun** STAR $\rightarrow$ Some (**fun** e_1 e_2 $\rightarrow$ Multiplication(e_1,e_2))
          | SLASH $\rightarrow$ Some (**fun** e_1 e_2 $\rightarrow$ Division(e_1,e_2))
          | _ $\rightarrow$ None);;
num : $($token, ast$)$ parser = $\langle$**fun**$\rangle$
ident : $($token, ast$)$ parser = $\langle$**fun**$\rangle$
addop : $($token, ast $\rightarrow$ ast $\rightarrow$ ast$)$ parser = $\langle$**fun**$\rangle$
mulop : $($token, ast $\rightarrow$ ast $\rightarrow$ ast$)$ parser = $\langle$**fun**$\rangle$

#num [NUM 3.0; LPAR];;
$-$: $($token, ast$)$ parsed = Returns $($Constant 3, [LPAR]$)$

The constructors for analyzers (notably **andalso**) produce values, so it will be handy to be able to change return values in order to re-organize them into data structures (for example, into lists) or more generally to apply a function to them. The function **gives** plays that role in the following:

```
#let (gives : (α, β) parser → (β → γ) → (α, γ) parser) =
    fun p f toks →
            match p toks with
               Returns(r₁, toks₁) → Returns(f r₁, toks₁)
             | AnalyzeFails → AnalyzeFails;;
gives : (α, β) parser → (β → γ) → (α, γ) parser = ⟨fun⟩

##infix "gives";;
```

```
#(num gives (fun (Constant n) → n | _ → 0.0)) [NUM 3.0; LPAR];;
− : (token, float) parsed = Returns (3, [LPAR])
```

The disjunction orelse differs little from its preceding version:

```
#let (orelse : (α, β) parser → (α, β) parser → (α, β) parser) =
    fun p₁ p₂ toks →
            match p₁ toks with
               AnalyzeFails → p₂ toks
             | res → res;;
orelse : (α, β) parser → (α, β) parser → (α, β) parser = ⟨fun⟩

##infix "orelse";;
```

```
#(num orelse (empty (Constant 0.0))) [NUM 3.0];;
− : (token, ast) parsed = Returns (Constant 3, [ ])
```

```
#(num orelse (empty (Constant 0.0))) [LPAR];;
− : (token, ast) parsed = Returns (Constant 0, [LPAR])
```

The conjunction of two analyzers builds the pair of values returned by each of them, like this:

```
#let (andalso : (α, β) parser → (α,γ) parser → (α, (β ∗ γ)) parser) =
    fun p₁ p₂ toks →
            (match p₁ toks with
               Returns(r₁, toks₁) → (match p₂ toks₁ with
                                       Returns(r₂, toks₂) →
                                             Returns((r₁, r₂), toks₂)
                                     | _ → AnalyzeFails)
             | _ → AnalyzeFails);;
andalso : (α, β) parser → (α, γ) parser → (α, β ∗ γ) parser = ⟨fun⟩

##infix "andalso";;
```

#((num andalso addop andalso num) gives (**fun** $((e_1, f), e_2) \rightarrow f\ e_1\ e_2$))
  [NUM 1.0; PLUS; NUM 2.0];;
$-$: (*token, ast*) *parsed* = *Returns* (*Addition* (*Constant* 1, *Constant* 2),
                                 [ ])

Now the iterator of regular expressions produces the list of results from calls of
its argument:

#**let rec** zero_or_more p =
  ((**fun** toks $\rightarrow$ (((p andalso (zero_or_more p)) gives (**fun** (x,xs) $\rightarrow$ x::xs))
                  orelse (empty [ ])) toks) : $(\alpha,\ \beta$ list) parser);;
zero_or_more : $(\alpha,\ \beta)$ *parser* $\rightarrow$ $(\alpha,\ \beta$ *list*) *parser* = ⟨**fun**⟩

#zero_or_more num [LPAR];;
$-$: (*token, ast list*) *parsed* = *Returns* ([ ], [*LPAR*])

#zero_or_more num [NUM 0.0; NUM 1.0; NUM 2.0];;
$-$: (*token, ast list*) *parsed*
  = *Returns* ([*Constant* 0; *Constant* 1; *Constant* 2], [ ])

Here we must note again that we have only a limited kind of backtracking, and
we also risk loops by iterating analyzers that accept the empty string. (See
Section 8.3.2 about limitations.)

8.4.2 A Lexical Analyzer

Now we have all the tools we need to build a lexical analyzer that returns lists of
tokens of type token. We will introduce analyzers for various lexical categories,
and then we will organize them into a single function for lexical analysis (lex).

Numeric constants

#**let** digit = token (**fun** c $\rightarrow$ **if** is_digit c **then** Some c **else** None);;
digit : (*char, char*) *parser* = ⟨**fun**⟩

#**let** digits = (digit andalso (zero_or_more digit)) gives (**fun** (c,cs) $\rightarrow$ c::cs);;
digits : (*char, char list*) *parser* = ⟨**fun**⟩

#**let** optsign =
  (token (**fun** ('$-$'|'+' **as** c) $\rightarrow$ Some [c] | _ $\rightarrow$ None))
  orelse (empty [ ]);;
optsign : (*char, char list*) *parser* = ⟨**fun**⟩

We leave you the exercise of programming the following analyzers:

optfrac : (char, char list) parser
optexp : (char, char list) parser

Each of those analyzers returns a list of characters, so number merely has to build the corresponding string and pass it to the predefined function float_of_string, which converts a string into a value of type float, like this:

```
#let number =
  (digits andalso optfrac andalso optexp)
  gives (fun ((csi, csf), cse) →
              NUM (float_of_string (implode (csi @ csf @ cse))));;
number : (char, token) parser = ⟨fun⟩

#number (explode "123.e-5 + 2");;
− : (char, token) parsed
  = Returns (NUM 0.00123, [' '; '+'; ' '; '2'])
```

Identifiers

```
#let letter =
  token (fun c → if is_letter c then Some c else None);;
letter : (char, char) parser = ⟨fun⟩

#let identifier =
  (letter andalso (zero_or_more letter))
  gives (fun (c,cs) → IDENT(implode (c::cs)));;
identifier : (char, token) parser = ⟨fun⟩

#identifier (explode "abcd + 2");;
− : (char, token) parsed
  = Returns (IDENT "abcd", [' '; '+'; ' '; '2'])
```

Operators and parentheses

```
#let operator = token (fun '+' → Some PLUS | '-' → Some MINUS
                         | '*' → Some STAR | '/' → Some SLASH
                         | _ → None);;
operator : (char, token) parser = ⟨fun⟩

#let paren =
  token (fun '(' → Some LPAR | ')' → Some RPAR | _ → None);;
paren : (char, token) parser = ⟨fun⟩
```

Blank space   Tokens may be separated by an arbitrary number of blank spaces, tabs, or ends of line. The analyzer **spaces** will ignore them.

```
#let space = token (fun (' '|'\t'|'\n') → Some () | _ → None);;
space : (char, unit) parser = ⟨fun⟩
```

```
#let rec spaces toks =
    (((space andalso spaces) gives (fun _ → ())) orelse
      empty ()) toks;;
spaces : char list → (char, unit) parsed = ⟨fun⟩
```

Now all that remains for us is to assemble these various elements to get a lexical analyzer. If we omit return values, the corresponding regular expression will be:

$$lex ::= spaces((identifier|number|operator|paren)spaces)^*$$

```
#let lex =
    spaces andalso (zero_or_more((identifier
                                    orelse number
                                    orelse operator
                                    orelse paren) andalso spaces
                                gives (fun (tok,_) → tok)))
    gives (fun (_,toks) → toks);;
lex : (char, token list) parser = ⟨fun⟩
```

```
#lex (explode " 1.e-2 - 3 * (4*5) / y + 6 ");;
− : (char, token list) parsed
    = Returns ([ NUM 0.01; MINUS; NUM 3;
                 STAR; LPAR; NUM 4; STAR;
                 NUM 5; RPAR; SLASH; IDENT "y"; PLUS; NUM 6], [ ])
```

8.4.3   Analyzer for Nested Parentheses

We can also directly translate the grammar of nested parentheses into the following analyzers:

```
#let open_paren = token (fun LPAR → Some () | _ → None)
  and close_paren = token (fun RPAR → Some () | _ → None);;
open_paren : (token, unit) parser = ⟨fun⟩
close_paren : (token, unit) parser = ⟨fun⟩
```

```
#let rec nested_paren toks =
    (((open_paren andalso nested_paren andalso close_paren)
      gives (fun _ → ()))
     orelse (empty ())) toks;;
nested_paren : token list → (token, unit) parsed = ⟨fun⟩
```

```
#nested_paren (accept (lex (explode "((((()))))")));;
− : (token, unit) parsed = Returns ((), [ ])
```

8.4.4   Derived Forms and Higher Order Analyzers

As we did for recognizers, we can also define derived forms of analyzer constructors. We will simply derive them, as they do not need any particular explanation. Our only comments are that any takes the value it must return as its argument, and optional receives as its argument whatever it must return in the case where its argument-analyzer recognizes nothing.

```
#let any v = token (fun _ → Some v);;
any : α → (β, α) parser = ⟨fun⟩
```

```
#let optional p v = p orelse (empty v);;
optional : (α, β) parser → β → (α, β) parser = ⟨fun⟩
```

```
#let one_or_more p = p andalso (zero_or_more p);;
one_or_more : (α, β) parser → (α, β * β list) parser = ⟨fun⟩
```

```
#let and_list pl =
    list_it (fun p₁ p₂ → (p₁ andalso p₂) gives (fun (x,xs) → x::xs))
       pl (empty [ ]);;
and_list : (α, β) parser list → (α, β list) parser = ⟨fun⟩
```

```
#let or_list p pl = it_list (prefix orelse) p pl;;
or_list : (α, β) parser → (α, β) parser list → (α, β) parser = ⟨fun⟩
```

We can also enrich our library of analyzers by a few useful features and functions here.

Analyzing Infix Operators

If we consider an analyzer of just any expressions, such as term, and another analyzer of infix operators, such as op, we can build an analyzer of expressions *expr* of the form:

$$expr \quad ::= \quad term\ op\ expr$$
$$| \quad term$$

We will assume that op produces functions with two arguments (for example, nodes of abstract syntax from two subtrees), and we will first define the function to produce the trees corresponding to right-associativity.

```
#let rec right_assoc term op =
    (fun toks →
              (((term andalso op andalso (right_assoc term op))
                 gives (fun ((t₁, f), t₂) → f t₁ t₂))
              orelse term) toks : (α,β) parser);;
    right_assoc : (α, β) parser → (α, β → β → β) parser → (α, β) parser
              = ⟨fun⟩
```

In the case of arithmetic expressions, an analyzer for operators will be of the form addop or mulop, defined on page 247:

```
addop : (token, ast → ast → ast) parser
mulop : (token, ast → ast → ast) parser
```

If we take numeric constants for *term*, we analyze addition or subtraction like this:

```
#right_assoc num addop
    [NUM 0.0; PLUS; NUM 1.0; PLUS; NUM 2.0];;
− : (token, ast) parsed
    = Returns (Addition
              (Constant 0, Addition (Constant 1, Constant 2)), [ ])
```

The function right_assoc has the drawback that it recognizes the same term twice. It is possible to "factor" it if we rewrite the corresponding production rule, like this:

$$expr ::= term \ (op \ expr \ | \ \epsilon)$$

```
#let rec right_assoc term op =
    (fun toks →
              ((term andalso (((op andalso (right_assoc term op))
                            gives (fun (f, t₂) → (fun t₁ → f t₁ t₂)))
                         orelse (empty (fun t → t))))
                 gives (fun (t₁, f) → f t₁)) toks : (α, β) parser);;
    right_assoc : (α, β) parser → (α, β → β → β) parser → (α, β) parser
              = ⟨fun⟩
```

To produce trees corresponding to left-associativity is a bit more complicated since the tree on the left must be built as soon as possible. More precisely, as soon as term has been called twice, the corresponding tree must be built, and the rest of the tree will be built on it.

For that, we must pass the value returned by the first call to term to the second call, and so forth. For that purpose, we introduce a new combinator:

```
#let (givento : (α,β) parser → (β → (α,γ) parser) → (α,γ) parser) =
    fun p₁ p₂ toks →
            match p₁ toks with
              Returns(r₁, toks₁) → p₂ r₁ toks₁
            | AnalyzeFails → AnalyzeFails;;
    givento : (α, β) parser → (β → (α, γ) parser) → (α, γ) parser
          = ⟨fun⟩
```

```
##infix "givento";;
```

The analyzer p_1 givento p_2 first calls p_1, which produces a value r_1. That value will then be sent to p_2, thus producing a new analyzer. The analyzer p_2 thus has a value as a parameter governing it. The analyzer for expressions with left-associative infix operators recognizes the following grammar:

$$expr ::= term \ (op \ term)^*$$

That analyzer can be defined by:

```
#let left_assoc term op =
    let rec sequence t₁ =
      (((op andalso term) gives (fun (f, t₂) → f t₁ t₂)) givento sequence)
      orelse (empty t₁) in
    term givento sequence;;
    left_assoc : (α, β) parser → (α, β → β → β) parser → (α, β) parser
          = ⟨fun⟩
```

```
#left_assoc num addop
    [NUM 0.0; PLUS; NUM 1.0; PLUS; NUM 2.0];;
  − : (token, ast) parsed
    = Returns (Addition (Addition (Constant 0, Constant 1), Constant 2)
                  , [ ])
```

Dynamically Constructing Analyzers

The constructor givento uses the fact that its second argument can be controlled by a value as a parameter. We used this value as a return value (an abstract syntax tree) in left_assoc, but we could also pass dynamically constructed analyzers and use them in other phases of recognition. We will use this possibility to construct an analyzer for a typical language that cannot be defined by a context-free grammar.

That language is defined like this:

$$\mathcal{L} = \{wcw \mid w \in (\mathsf{a}|\mathsf{b})^*\}$$

The problem of recognizing the words of $\mathcal{L}$ is thus to identify a prefix w, then a 'c', and then to recognize the *same* subword w in suffix position. The subword w must be a sequence (possibly empty) of characters 'a' or 'b'.

The solution[2] that we offer consists of building the analyzer to recognize the second occurrence of w during the recognition of its first occurrence.

```
#let a = token (fun 'a' → Some (char 'a') | _ → None)
 and b = token (fun 'b' → Some (char 'b') | _ → None);;
a : (char, (char, char) parser) parser = ⟨fun⟩
b : (char, (char, char) parser) parser = ⟨fun⟩

#let w_def = zero_or_more (a orelse b) gives and_list;;
w_def : (char, (char, char list) parser) parser = ⟨fun⟩
```

The analyzer w_def iterates the analyzer (a orelse b) and returns the sequential composition of the results. The ultimate analyzer w calls w_def, recognizes the character 'c', and then passes control to the analyzer built by w_def.

```
#let w =
    (w_def andalso (char 'c') gives (fun (f,_) → f))
    givento (fun x → x);;
w : (char, char list) parser = ⟨fun⟩

#w (explode "aaabbcaaabb");;
− : (char, char list) parsed = Returns (['a'; 'a'; 'a'; 'b'; 'b'], [ ])

#w (explode "c");;
− : (char, char list) parsed = Returns ([ ], [ ])

#w (explode "aaba");;
− : (char, char list) parsed = AnalyzeFails
```

8.4.5 An Analyzer for Arithmetic Expressions

We are now in a good position to complete our analyzer for arithmetic expressions by an easy assembly of various analyzers that we have already presented.

```
#let analyze_expr =
    let rec expr toks = (left_assoc term addop) toks
    and term toks = (left_assoc fact mulop) toks
    and fact toks =
```

---

[2]This example is from Daniel de Rauglaudre.

```
   (num
     orelse ident
     orelse ((open_paren andalso expr andalso close_paren)
              gives (fun ((_,e),_) → e))) toks
   in expr;;
 analyze_expr : token list → (token, ast) parsed = ⟨fun⟩

 #accept (analyze_expr (accept (lex (explode "1+2+3-4-x*6"))));;
 − : ast = Subtraction (Subtraction (Addition (Addition (Constant 1,
                                                         Constant 2),
                                              Constant 3), Constant 4)
                       , Multiplication (Variable "x", Constant 6))
```

Up to now, the analyses that we have done use the technique known as **recursive descent**—recursive because the analyzers are generally recursive and descent because the analysis or recognition *first* decides which non-terminal to recognize *before* traversing the rest of the tokens. There is also another major technique: **ascending analysis**. It consists of traversing the sequence of tokens and, on the basis of the tokens encountered, choosing to *reduce* this or that non-terminal. Ascending analysis generally uses look-up tables, and overall, it is more difficult to understand than our functional analyzers. YACC, the analyzer generator, uses an ascending technique; its version adapted to CAML is called CAML-YACC. As a general rule, ascending analyzers are not "written by hand", but rather, they are automatically produced from a grammar. These techniques require a very fine analysis of the grammar, so they do not support analyzers with parameters like the functional analyzers we presented in this chapter.

8.4.6   Predictive Analysis

Analysis by recursive descent (like we have been doing up to now) has a disadvantage: sometimes it requires more than one traversal of an initial segment of the list of tokens, and that requirement is a source of considerable inefficiency. We would like a guarantee that this list would be traversed only once at most, and thus that the first token alone would let us decide which analyzer to call. The implication of this choice is that two production rules that begin with the same token risk being incompatible, and consequently all production rules must have no common left factor. In general, that implies that the grammar must be factored before it is translated into an analyzer, but on the positive side, it will produce analyzers that are potentially more efficient.

To implement such predictive analyzers requires only a slight modification of the preceding analyzers. Up to now, values of type **parsed** distinguished between a successful and a failed analysis. In order to build predictive analyzers, we must further distinguish between two kinds of failure:

- A fatal failure occurs when a rule has been chosen but the analysis cannot lead to anything good. This failure is similar to the kind produced when pattern matching fails in CAML.

- A non-fatal failure occurs during the choice of a rule. This failure guides recognition.

Non-fatal failures are represented by the value AnalyzeFails. Fatal failures are produced when the exception AnalyzeError is raised. It is defined like this:

#exception AnalyzeError;;

Only the constructor andalso needs to be redefined in order to produce fatal errors from non-fatal errors in its second argument:

```
#let (andalso : (α,β) parser → (α,γ) parser → (α, (β * γ)) parser) =
    fun p₁ p₂ toks →
            (match p₁ toks with
                Returns(r₁, toks₁) →
                    (match p₂ toks₁ with
                        Returns(r₂, toks₂) → Returns((r₁, r₂), toks₂)
                      | _ → raise AnalyzeError)
              | _ → AnalyzeFails);;
    andalso : (α, β) parser → (α, γ) parser → (α, β * γ) parser = ⟨fun⟩
```

##infix "andalso";;

Since we redefined the other constructors for analyzers, let's verify that we no longer have any backtracking. The analyzer corresponding to (ab|a)b is written like this:

```
#((char 'a') andalso (char 'b') gives (fun _ → ())
    orelse ((char 'a') gives (fun _ → ()))
    andalso (char 'b') gives (fun _ → ())) ['a'; 'b'];;
Uncaught exception: AnalyzeError
```

Since disjunction distributes over concatenation, this regular expression is equivalent to abb|ab, where we must factor the prefix ab in order to translate it into predictive analyzers. The final expression is written as ab(b|ε). It translates into this:

```
#let optᵦ = (char 'b' gives (fun _ → ())) orelse (empty ()) in
    ((char 'a') andalso (char 'b') andalso optᵦ
      gives (fun _ → ())) ['a'; 'b'];;
  - : (char, unit) parsed = Returns ((), [ ])
```

The various examples that you have already seen (lexical and syntactic analyzers) can be programmed with no changes.

Exercises
8.2 Write the functions optfrac and optexp from page 249.

8.5   Streams and Pattern Matching

The analysis techniques that we have examined up to now obliged us to construct a list of tokens completely before we applied an analyzer. Moreover, in case of backtracking, we could not modify that list because we might need an arbitrary number of its elements before we could finish the analysis. In the case of a predictive analysis, since there was no backtracking, we could dispense with those constraints. What might be the ideal situation for us in these respects?

- We would like to build the list of tokens only on demand (that is, lazy style).

- We would like to empty the list as we go along, as the tokens are no longer useful to us.

CAML provides a data structure—streams—that fits those two criteria and serves as the argument to syntactic analyzers.

8.5.1   Streams

A stream is a data structure that takes specific syntax. You have already encountered streams as modifiable data structures in Chapter 4. Here we review their main characteristics.

Streams are constructed from the empty stream:

```
#[⟨ ⟩];;
− : α stream = ⟨abstract⟩
```

or from elements or from substreams:

```
#let s = [⟨ ''c'; ''d' ⟩];;
s : char stream = ⟨abstract⟩
```

```
#[⟨ ''a'; ''b'; s; ''e' ⟩];;
− : char stream = ⟨abstract⟩
```

The elements of a stream are preceded by an apostrophe. Substreams appear unquoted and are inserted into the stream that surrounds them.

A stream is a polymorphic data structure, and even though character streams and token streams are the most common, it is also possible to build streams of elements of arbitrary types.

Notice, too, that they are not printed completely: only the information ⟨**abstract**⟩ is provided. Only pattern-matching lets us examine the contents of a stream.

Streams are built in lazy style; that is, they are built only as we examine their elements. Several useful functions build streams from other data structures.

stream_of_string : string → char stream
stream_of_channel : in_channel → char stream
stream_from : (unit → α) → α stream

The function stream_of_string builds a stream associated with a character string, and the function stream_of_channel builds a stream associated with an input channel.

```
#stream_of_string "abc";;
− : char stream = ⟨abstract⟩
```

The function stream_from takes a function producing values of type α and returns the stream of values produced by successive calls. For example, an infinite list of 1 is built like this:

```
#stream_from (fun () → 1);;
− : int stream = ⟨abstract⟩
```

8.5.2 Stream Pattern Matching

The predefined function stream_next returns the first element of its stream argument. For example:

```
#let s = stream_of_string "abc";;
s : char stream = ⟨abstract⟩
```

```
#stream_next s;;
− : char = 'a'
```

```
#stream_next s;;
− : char = 'b'
```

```
#stream_next s;;
− : char = 'c'
```

Notice that an element is extracted *physically* from a stream. In fact, we can defined stream_next as a function defined by cases:

```
#let stream_next = function
    [⟨ 'x ⟩] → x;;
stream_next : α stream → α = ⟨fun⟩
```

The pattern matching of stream_next impinges only on the *initial segment* of the stream; it requires only a sole element in its stream argument. If we compare a stream to a list of tokens, stream_next accepts and recognizes any token. This function is thus comparable to our analyzer any. That pattern thus matches any stream of at least one element. That element is physically removed from the stream, just as any returned the rest of the list.

Again in comparison with analyzers, the function recognizing the empty string and leaving a stream unchanged is defined like this:

#let empty_stream v = **function**
  [⟨ ⟩] → v;;
empty_stream : $\alpha \rightarrow \beta$ *stream* $\rightarrow \alpha = \langle$**fun**$\rangle$

This function never fails, just as empty never does. In effect, the pattern [⟨ ⟩] must match an initial segment of the argument, and of course the empty stream is the initial segment of all streams.

The analyzer accepting the character 'a' and returning the same character is written like this:

#function [⟨ ''a' ⟩] → 'a';;
− : *char stream* $\rightarrow$ *char* $= \langle$**fun**$\rangle$

The equivalents of andalso and orelse are taken into account by the syntax of streams and functions defined by case. For example, the function accepting the character 'a' followed by 'b' can be defined like this:

#let ab = **function** [⟨ ''a'; ''b' ⟩] → ();;
ab : *char stream* $\rightarrow$ *unit* $= \langle$**fun**$\rangle$

Notice that the pattern matching here involves predictive analysis. Two kinds of failure, both represented by exceptions, can occur:

- The first is represented by the exception Parse_failure, involving the non-fatal failures that we coded in the previous section by the value AnalyzeFails.

- The second is represented by the exception Parse_error that we coded in the previous section by the value AnalyzeError.

For example:

#ab [⟨ ''a'; ''b' ⟩];;
− : *unit* = ()

#ab [⟨ ''c' ⟩];;
Uncaught exception: Parse_failure

#ab [⟨ ''a'; ''c' ⟩];;
Uncaught exception: Parse_error

The order of stream analyzers is also denoted by a semi-colon in a stream pattern. The following analyzer recognizes the sequence **abab**:

```
#function [⟨ ab _; ab x ⟩] → x;;
− : char stream → unit = ⟨fun⟩
```

If we adopt the terminology of grammar, in a stream pattern, an element is denoted as terminal when it is preceded by an apostrophe; a non-terminal is any other expression (in parentheses if it is not a simple identifier) followed by a pattern. In the previous example, the first occurrence of **ab** is such an expression (of type **char stream → unit**), and the pattern "_" indicates that we do not name the return value. In contrast, at the second occurrence of **ab**, we have named the return value x, and that value will become the final result.

Thus you see that a stream pattern simultaneously supports order like **andalso** and handles return values like **gives**. The role of **givento** is also taken into account, as the following example shows.

```
#let two_ints_added =
    let one_int_added_to n = function [⟨ 'm ⟩] → m+n in
    function [⟨ 'n; (one_int_added_to n) x ⟩] → x;;
two_ints_added : int stream → int = ⟨fun⟩

#two_ints_added [⟨'1; '2⟩];;
− : int = 3
```

An integer value acts as a parameter to the analyzer **one_int_added_to**, and the value n is passed to it in the definition of **two_ints_added**.

Like any function defined by case, an analyzer for streams can involve more than one case, with cases separated by vertical bars and playing the same role as **orelse**. We get from one case to the next in these situations:

- when the preceding case begins with a terminal that does not match the first element of the current stream (or if the current stream is empty);

- or when the first analyzer of the preceding case raises **Parse_failure**.

A stream pattern is not like other patterns: syntactically, it can follow only **function**, or else be used in the pattern-matching part of a **match** construction.

8.5.3 Lexical Analysis by Stream Pattern Matching

Let's look again at the lexical analyzer that you saw earlier. This time, we will program it by means of pattern matching with streams.

```
#let rec zero_or_more p = function
   [⟨ p x; (zero_or_more p) xs ⟩] → x::xs
 | [⟨ ⟩] → [ ];;
```
zero_or_more : $(\alpha\ stream \to \beta) \to \alpha\ stream \to \beta\ list$ = $\langle\textbf{fun}\rangle$

```
#let digit = function [⟨ '‘0‘..‘9‘ as d ⟩] → d;;
```
digit : *char stream* → *char* = $\langle\textbf{fun}\rangle$

```
#let digits = function [⟨ digit d; (zero_or_more digit) ds ⟩] → d::ds;;
```
digits : *char stream* → *char list* = $\langle\textbf{fun}\rangle$

```
#let optsign = function
   [⟨ '‘-‘|‘+‘ as c ⟩] → [c]
 | [⟨ ⟩] → [ ];;
```
optsign : *char stream* → *char list* = $\langle\textbf{fun}\rangle$

We leave you the exercise of programming the following analyzers:

optfrac : char stream → char list
optexp : char stream → char list

Here is an analyzer for numbers:

```
#let number = function
   [⟨ digits csi; optfrac csf; optexp cse ⟩]
   → NUM (float_of_string (implode (csi @ csf @ cse)));;
```
number : *char stream* → *token* = $\langle\textbf{fun}\rangle$

To define the letter analyzer, we use a pattern of the form "$c_1..c_2$" that accepts any character with an ASCII code situated between the codes for c_1 and c_2 (inclusive).

```
#let letter = function [⟨ ' (‘a‘..‘z‘ | ‘A‘..‘Z‘) as c ⟩] → c;;
```
letter : *char stream* → *char* = $\langle\textbf{fun}\rangle$

```
#let identifier = function
   [⟨ letter c; (zero_or_more letter) cs ⟩] → IDENT(implode(c::cs));;
```
identifier : *char stream* → *token* = $\langle\textbf{fun}\rangle$

```
#let operator = function
   [⟨ '‘+‘ ⟩] → PLUS | [⟨ '‘-‘ ⟩] → MINUS
 | [⟨ '‘*‘ ⟩] → STAR | [⟨ '‘/‘ ⟩] → SLASH;;
```
operator : *char stream* → *token* = $\langle\textbf{fun}\rangle$

We leave the parentheses analyzer as an exercise.

paren : char stream → token

```
#let rec spaces = function
    [⟨ ' ' | '\t' | '\n'; spaces _ ⟩] → ()
  | [⟨ ⟩] → ();;
spaces : char stream → unit = ⟨fun⟩
```

The following analyzer will be the token producer:

```
#let next_token = function
    [⟨ identifier tok ⟩] → tok
  | [⟨ number tok ⟩] → tok
  | [⟨ operator tok ⟩] → tok
  | [⟨ paren tok ⟩] → tok;;
next_token : char stream → token = ⟨fun⟩
```

It is used by the principal function lex:

```
#let lex s =
    stream_from (fun () → spaces s; next_token s);;
lex : char stream → token stream = ⟨fun⟩
```

```
#let rec list_of_stream = function
    [⟨ 'x ; list_of_stream xs ⟩] → x::xs
  | [⟨ ⟩] → [ ];;
list_of_stream : α stream → α list = ⟨fun⟩
```

```
#list_of_stream (lex (stream_of_string " 1 - 2 * (3*4) / y + 2 "));;
− : token list = [ NUM 1; MINUS; NUM 2; STAR; LPAR; NUM 3; STAR;
                   NUM 4; RPAR; SLASH; IDENT "y"; PLUS; NUM 2]
```

8.5.4 Higher Order Analyzers

In the same way that we programmed a general scheme of analyzers for infix operators in a purely functional context, we can also produce the same examples with stream pattern matching.

```
#let right_assoc term op =
    let rec sequence e₁ = function
        [⟨ op f; term e₂; (sequence e₂) e ⟩] → f e₁ e
      | [⟨ ⟩] → e₁ in
    function [⟨ term e₁; (sequence e₁) e ⟩] → e;;
right_assoc : (α stream → β) → (α stream → β → β → β)
                            → α stream → β = ⟨fun⟩
```

```
#let left_assoc term op =
    let rec sequence e₁ = function
```

```
        [⟨ op f; term e₂; (sequence (f e₁ e₂)) e ⟩] → e
      | [⟨ ⟩] → e₁ in
      function [⟨ term e₁; (sequence e₁) e ⟩] → e;;
  left_assoc : (α stream → β) → (α stream → β → β → β)
                                    → α stream → β = ⟨fun⟩
```

```
#let num = function
    [⟨ 'NUM n ⟩] → Constant n;;
num : token stream → ast = ⟨fun⟩
```

```
#let addop = function
      [⟨ 'PLUS ⟩] → (fun e₁ e₂ → Addition(e₁, e₂))
    | [⟨ 'MINUS ⟩] → (fun e₁ e₂ → Subtraction(e₁, e₂))
  and mulop = function
      [⟨ 'STAR ⟩] → (fun e₁ e₂ → Multiplication(e₁, e₂))
    | [⟨ 'SLASH ⟩] → (fun e₁ e₂ → Division(e₁, e₂));;
addop : token stream → ast → ast → ast = ⟨fun⟩
mulop : token stream → ast → ast → ast = ⟨fun⟩
```

```
#right_assoc num addop
    [⟨ 'NUM 1.0; 'PLUS; 'NUM 2.0; 'MINUS; 'NUM 3.0 ⟩];;
− : ast = Addition (Constant 1, Subtraction (Constant 2, Constant 3))
```

```
#left_assoc num addop
    [⟨ 'NUM 1.0; 'PLUS; 'NUM 2.0; 'MINUS; 'NUM 3.0 ⟩];;
− : ast = Subtraction (Addition (Constant 1, Constant 2), Constant 3)
```

We can also construct and dynamically call new analyzers. For this effect, we again take the example of the language wcw.

```
#let a = function [⟨ ''a' ⟩] → (function [⟨ ''a' ⟩] → 'a')
  and b = function [⟨ ''b' ⟩] → (function [⟨ ''b' ⟩] → 'b');;
a : char stream → char stream → char = ⟨fun⟩
b : char stream → char stream → char = ⟨fun⟩
```

```
#let rec and_list = function
      p :: ps → (function [⟨ p x; (and_list ps) xs ⟩] → x :: xs)
    | [ ] → (function [⟨ ⟩] → [ ]);;
and_list : (α stream → β) list → α stream → β list = ⟨fun⟩
```

```
#let c = function [⟨ ''c' ⟩] → ();;
c : char stream → unit = ⟨fun⟩
```

```
#let w_def = function
    [⟨ (zero_or_more (function [⟨ a p ⟩] → p
                            | [⟨ b p ⟩] → p)) ps ⟩] → and_list ps;;
```

w_def : *char stream* → *char stream* → *char list* = ⟨**fun**⟩

#let w = **function** [⟨ w_def p; ''c'; p r ⟩] → r;;
w : *char stream* → *char list* = ⟨**fun**⟩

#w (stream_of_string "aaabbcaaabb");;
− : *char list* = ['a'; 'a'; 'a'; 'b'; 'b']

#w (stream_of_string "c");;
− : *char list* = [ ]

8.5.5 Syntactic Analysis by Stream Pattern Matching

Let's look again at our language of arithmetic expressions. This time, we will write its analyzer with stream pattern matching.

```
#let rec expr toks = left_assoc term addop toks
  and term toks = left_assoc fact mulop toks
  and fact = function
    [⟨ 'NUM n ⟩] → Constant n
  | [⟨ 'IDENT s ⟩] → Variable s
  | [⟨ 'LPAR; expr e; 'RPAR ⟩] → e;;
expr : token stream → ast = ⟨fun⟩
term : token stream → ast = ⟨fun⟩
fact : token stream → ast = ⟨fun⟩
```

#expr(lex (stream_of_string "1+2+3-4-x*6"));;
− : *ast* = *Subtraction (Subtraction (Addition (Addition (Constant 1,*
                                        Constant 2),
                              Constant 3), Constant 4)
       , Multiplication (Variable "x", Constant 6))

Exercises
8.3 Write the parentheses analyzer paren from page 262.

8.6 Compiling Regular Expressions

In Section 8.3.3, you saw that even with limited backtracking, building a complete analyzer for an arbitrary regular expression was a more difficult task than it first appeared.

The problem that we encountered was that the recognizers could backtrack only if they were directly or indirectly called by the constructor **orelse**. In one of our examples, we showed that even if the regular expression **abb| ab** were equivalent to **ab|(b|ϵ)**, simply because of distribution, the associated recognizers

((char 'a') andalso (char 'b') andalso (char 'b'))
orelse ((char 'a') andalso (char 'b'))

and

(char 'a') andalso (char 'b') andalso ((char 'b') orelse empty)

were not equivalent.

You have also seen that direct or indirect iterative use of the analyzer **empty** could cause loops.

For all those reasons, we must have a compilation phase for regular expressions before we can interpret them straightforwardly.

8.6.1 Finite Automata

To compile a regular expression, we have the choice between two solutions; both depend on the transformation of the regular expression into a **finite automaton**. A finite automaton over an alphabet $\mathcal{A}$ consists of a finite set of **states** $\mathcal{S}$ and a set of **transitions** $\mathcal{T}$. The set $\mathcal{T}$ is the graph of a relation from $\mathcal{S} \times (\mathcal{A} \cup \{\epsilon\})$ to $\mathcal{S}$. A transition from $(s, \text{'a'})$ to s' will be denoted $s \overset{\text{'a'}}{\longmapsto} s'$, and we say that it is a transition on 'a', from s to s'.

Among the states of $\mathcal{S}$, one of them is known as the **initial state**; there must also exist a non-empty subset of **terminal states**. For example:

$$\mathcal{A} = \{\text{'a'}, \text{'b'}\}$$

$$\mathcal{S} = \{s_0, s_1, s_2, s_3\}$$

s_0 is the initial state
$\{s_3\}$ is the set of terminal states

$$\mathcal{T} = \{s_0 \overset{\text{'a'}}{\longmapsto} s_0, \; s_0 \overset{\text{'b'}}{\longmapsto} s_0, \; s_0 \overset{\text{'a'}}{\longmapsto} s_1, \; s_1 \overset{\text{'b'}}{\longmapsto} s_2, \; s_2 \overset{\text{'b'}}{\longmapsto} s_3\}$$

is a non-deterministic automaton represented graphically in Figure 8.1.

An automaton is said to be **deterministic** if there is no transition on ϵ and if for every state s and for all $c \in \mathcal{A}$, there exists at most one transition on c from s. In the case of a deterministic automaton, $\mathcal{T}$ is not merely a relation but rather a partial function from $\mathcal{S} \times \mathcal{A}$ to $\mathcal{S}$.

You can see clearly that we can directly interpret a deterministic finite automaton by means of our recognizers.

There is a simple algorithm to construct a non-deterministic automaton from a regular expression. It is known as Thompson's method. Unfortunately, such an automaton cannot be directly interpreted by our recognizers. We have to make

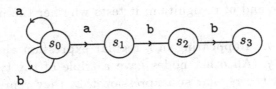

Figure 8.1. A non-deterministic automaton

such a non-deterministic automaton deterministic; that is, we have to build an equivalent deterministic automaton.

An alternative is to build a finite deterministic automaton directly from a regular expression. We have chosen this solution, and to do so, we use the algorithm presented in [2].

To produce this compilation, we must first have a representation of regular expressions as trees. In this representation, we need an explicit way to number various characters composing the regular expression. Once we compute the information that "this character may be followed by this or that character," compiling (strictly speaking) consists of starting in the initial state of the automaton and then recognizing or building the states that are accessible from the current state.

8.6.2 Abstract Syntax Trees for Regular Expressions

We begin by representing regular expressions as trees by using the type regexpr:

```
#type int_set == int set;;
```

```
#type regexpr =
      Epsilon
    | Symbol of char * int
    | Star of regexpr * pos
    | Or of regexpr * regexpr * pos
    | Seq of regexpr * regexpr * pos
    | Accept of int
  and pos =
      { Null : bool;
        First : int_set;
        Last : int_set
      };;
```

The constructors Epsilon, Symbol, Star, Or, and Seq correspond to ϵ, the characters of $\mathcal{A}$, the * iterator, disjunction, and concatenation. The constructor Accept corresponds to the end of recognition; it tests whether the input has been completely consumed.

The elements of $\mathcal{A}$ appearing in a regular expression along with Accept are numbered uniquely. All other nodes have a triple of the type pos to code the information about the regular subexpression that they represent. These triples have the following fields:

- Null: true if the regular subexpression recognizes the empty string; false otherwise;

- First: contains the set of symbols that can begin a string recognized by the regular subexpression;

- Last: contains the set of symbols that can terminate a string recognized by the regular subexpression.

The values of these records are computed during the construction of the abstract syntax tree of a regular expression. The type set that we use to represent sets of integers is defined in Section 6.7, page 189. Our empty set will be denoted like this:

empty_int_set : int_set

For example, the regular expression (a|b)*abb will be represented by the following expression:

```
Seq (Seq (Seq (Seq (Star (Or (Symbol ('a', 0),
                              Symbol ('b', 1), ...), ...),
                Symbol ('a', 2), ...),
            Symbol ('b', 3), ...),
        Symbol ('b', 4), ...),
    Accept 5, ...)
```

where "..." replaces the records of type pos.

The numbers are produced by an integer generator. We thus assume that the following functions are defined:

reset_labels : unit → unit
new_label : unit → int

8.6.3 Computing Null, First, and Last

For a given node, the value of its pos record depends only on the subexpressions of that node.

The value associated with Null is the simplest to compute. It is systematically true for an Epsilon node and for a Star node. It is systematically false for Symbol and Accept. For an Or node, it suffices for one of its two subexpressions to recognize the empty string. For a Seq node, both subexpressions must recognize the empty string. We define the function null_pos to extract the value of Null from a complicated expression and to return false when we present a symbol to it.

```
#let null_pos = function
    Epsilon → true
  | Symbol(_,i) → false
  | Or(_,_,p) → p.Null
  | Star(_,p) → p.Null
  | Seq(_,_,p) → p.Null
  | Accept i → false;;
null_pos : regexpr → bool = ⟨fun⟩
```

The set associated with a First field at a node contains the number associated with the symbols that can begin a string recognized by the regular expression represented by that node. It is defined by case according to the form of the node.

- Epsilon: the set is empty;

- Symbol or Accept number i: this set is $\{i\}$;

- Or (e_1, e_2, ...): this set is the union of sets associated with e_1 and e_2;

- Star(e): First is the set associated with e;

- Seq(e_1, e_2, ...): if e_1 recognizes the empty string, First is the union of sets associated with e_1 and e_2; otherwise, First is the set associated with e_1.

The set Last is computed according to similar rules that you can deduce from the following program.

We define the function to extract the value of First from its argument like this:

```
#let first_pos = function
    Epsilon → empty_int_set
  | Symbol(_,i) → make_set int_comp [i]
```

```
    | Or(_,_,p) → p.First
    | Star(_,p) → p.First
    | Seq(_,_,p) → p.First
    | Accept i → make_set int_comp [i];;
  first_pos : regexpr → int_set = ⟨fun⟩
```

The analogous function for Last is defined by:

```
#let last_pos = function
    Epsilon → empty_int_set
  | Symbol(_,i) → make_set int_comp [i]
  | Or(_,_,p) → p.Last
  | Star(_,p) → p.Last
  | Seq(_,_,p) → p.Last
  | Accept i → make_set int_comp [i];;
  last_pos : regexpr → int_set = ⟨fun⟩
```

The following functions effectively compute the values of Null, First, and Last. These functions build abstract syntax trees.

```
#let symbol p = Symbol (p, new_label())
 and star e =
   Star (e, {Null = true; First = first_pos e; Last = last_pos e})
 and mkor e₁ e₂ =
   Or(e₁, e₂, {Null = null_pos e₁ or null_pos e₂;
               First = set_union (first_pos e₁) (first_pos e₂);
               Last = set_union (last_pos e₁) (last_pos e₂)})
 and mkseq e₁ e₂ =
   let b₁ = null_pos e₁
   and b₂ = null_pos e₂ in
   Seq(e₁, e₂, {Null = b₁ & b₂;
                First = if b₁ then set_union (first_pos e₁) (first_pos e₂)
                        else first_pos e₁;
                Last = if b₂ then set_union (last_pos e₁) (last_pos e₂)
                       else last_pos e₂});;
 symbol : char → regexpr = ⟨fun⟩
 star : regexpr → regexpr = ⟨fun⟩
 mkor : regexpr → regexpr → regexpr = ⟨fun⟩
 mkseq : regexpr → regexpr → regexpr = ⟨fun⟩

#let accept e =
   let i = new_label() in
   mkseq e (Accept i);;
 accept : regexpr → regexpr = ⟨fun⟩
```

These functions are used by the syntactic analyzer for regular expressions. We are leaving its definition as an exercise, so we assume the definition of the following function.

parse_regexpr : string → regexpr * int

This function returns the pair composed of the regular expression and how many numbers have been allocated.

In order to display sets of integers concisely, from now on we will print them like this:

$[0, 1, 2, 3]$ for the set $\{0, 1, 2, 3\}$.

The regular expression (a|b)*abb will be represented by:

```
#parse_regexpr "(a|b)*abb";;
− : regexpr * int
  = Seq (Seq (Seq (Seq (Star ( ..., ...), ..., ...),
                Symbol ( ..., ...),
                {Null=false; First=[0, 1, 2];
                Last=[3]}), Symbol ('b', 4),
                {Null=false; First=[0, 1, 2]; Last=[4]}), Accept 5,
          {Null=false; First=[0, 1, 2]; Last=[5]}), 6
```

8.6.4 Computing follow

After the automaton has been constructed, the next step is to unite the information in First and Last in order to compute, for each of the (numbers of the) symbols in the regular expression, the (numbers of the) symbols that can follow. This information is stored in a vector; its length is equal to the number of symbols appearing in the regular expression.

The rules for computing follow involve only nodes about sequencing symbols, that is, the nodes Seq and Star.

In the case of Seq(e_1, e_2, p), each element of last_pos(e_1) can be followed by each of the elements of first_pos(e_2).

In the case of Star(e,p), each of the elements of last_pos(e) can be followed by each of the elements of first_pos(e).

While we are computing follow, we take advantage of it to store the association between numbers and characters of the regular expression. We put that information in a vector. We use the type option to do so, since the symbol Accept itself has a number, but it does not have an associated character.

```
#let compute_follow follow chars =
   let rec compute = function
```

```
        Seq(e₁,e₂,p) →
            compute e₁; compute e₂;
            let first₂ = first_pos e₂ in
            do_set (fun i → follow.(i) ← set_union first₂ (follow.(i))) (last_pos e₁)
    | Star(e,p) →
            compute e;
            do_set (fun i → follow.(i) ← set_union p.First (follow.(i))) p.Last
    | Or(e₁,e₂,p) → compute e₁; compute e₂
    | Epsilon → ()
    | Accept i → chars.(i) ← None
    | Symbol(c,i) → chars.(i) ← Some c
    in compute;;
compute_follow : int set vect → char option vect → regexpr → unit
            = ⟨fun⟩
```

This function is used like this:

```
#let regexpr_follow s =
    let (e,n) = parse_regexpr s in
    let follow = make_vect n empty_int_set in
    let chars = make_vect n None in
    compute_follow follow chars e;
    (e, follow, chars);;
regexpr_follow : string → regexpr * int_set vect * char option vect
            = ⟨fun⟩
```

In the regular expression (a|b)*abb, the characters are numbered like this:

$$(a|b)^*abb$$
$$0\ 1\quad 234$$

The computation by regexpr_follow produces this:

```
#regexpr_follow "(a|b)*abb";;
− : regexpr * int_set vect * char option vect
  = Seq (Seq (Seq (Seq (Star ( …, … ), …, … ), Symbol ( …, … ),
                {Null=false; First=[0, 1, 2]; Last=[3]}),
            Symbol ('b', 4), {Null=false; First=[0, 1, 2];
                            Last=[4]}), Accept 5,
        {Null=false; First=[0, 1, 2]; Last=[5]}),
    [| [0, 1, 2]; [0, 1, 2]; [3]; [4]; [5]; [ ] |],
    [| Some 'a'; Some 'b'; Some 'a'; Some 'b'; Some 'b'; None |]
```

The vector follow returned as a result is read like this:

- The first character of the regular expression (a, at number 0), can be followed by the characters numbered 0, 1, and 2; that is, the characters a, b, and a.

- The second (b) can be followed by the characters numbered 0, 1, and 2.

- The third (a) can be followed by the character numbered 3, that is, b.

- etc.

8.6.5 Representing Automata

Automata will be records with two fields. The field Pos will contain the set of elements of the regular expression that can be "active" in that state. More precisely, if Pos = [0, 1, 2] for a given state, it signifies that we are in a good position to recognize the symbols numbered 0, 1, or 2 in the regular expression.

Transitions are stored as lists of pairs consisting of a character and a state. A state can thus be a structure that loops over itself.

```
#type state = {
        Pos : int_set;
        mutable Tran : transitions
        }
and transitions == (char * state) list;;
```

8.6.6 Computing Automata

To compute the automaton, we maintain two lists: the list of marked and unmarked states. At the beginning of the algorithm, the only state we have will be unmarked, and its Pos field will contain first_pos(e), where e is the tree of the regular expression; its list of transitions will be empty.

For an unmarked state st, the algorithm does these things:

1. It calculates the set of numbers accessible from st, that is, a set of pairs (c,s), where c is a character and s is a set of integers. A number j is accessible from st by c if there exists i in st.Pos such that j belongs to follow.(i), and i numbers the character c. Notice that the pairs (c,s) in which s is empty are eliminated in that way.

2. For each of the pairs (c,s),

   - if there exists a state st' (whether marked or unmarked) such that s=st'.Pos, it adds (c,st') to the transitions of st;

- otherwise, it creates a new state st' without transitions, adds it to the transitions of st, and adds st' to the unmarked states.

3. It marks st.

It repeats this process as long as there are any remaining unmarked states. The result will be a vector of states obtained from the list of marked states. The terminal states are all those containing the number associated with **Accept**.

To implement this algorithm, we need some auxiliary functions. The first one, partition, takes the vector chars and the set s of numbers, and it returns a list of pairs (c,s') such that s' is the subset of s for which all the elements are associated with the same c. We simply assume that this function is defined, and we leave it to you as an exercise.

partition : char option vect → int set → (char option * int set) list

The second, accessible, effectively computes the list of sets accessible from a given state.

```
#let accessible s follow chars =
   let part = partition chars s.Pos in
   list_it (fun (Some c, l) rest →
                  (c, it_list set_union empty_int_set
                        (map (vect_item follow) (list_of_set l)))::rest
             | _ rest → rest)
      part [ ];;
accessible : state → int set vect → char option vect
                        → (char * int set) list = ⟨fun⟩
```

The function find_state takes a set s and two sets of states (marked and unmarked). It then searches for a state for which the set Pos is equal to s. It returns this state or it fails.

find_state : int set → state list → state list → state

Finally, we arrive at the function to compute the states.

```
#let rec compute_states marked unmarked follow chars =
   match unmarked with
     [ ] → vect_of_list marked
   | st::umsts →
         let access = accessible st follow chars in
         let marked₁ = st::marked in
         let unmarked₁ =
```

```
                list_it
             (fun (c, s) umsts →
                       if set_isempty s then
                           umsts                                    (* Suppress empty sets *)
                       else try st.Tran ← (c, find_state s marked₁ umsts)::st.Tran;
                              umsts
                          with Not_found →
                                    let state₁ = {Pos = s; Tran = [ ]} in
                                    st.Tran ← (c, state₁)::st.Tran;
                                    state₁::umsts)
             access umsts in
          compute_states marked₁ unmarked₁ follow chars;;
      compute_states : state list → state list → int set vect
                               → char option vect
                               → state vect = ⟨fun⟩
```

The following function computes the automaton. In doing so, it calls the function compute_states, then searches the vector for the index of the initial state, and puts the index in the first place in the vector. It got the index from the function vect_indexq, which knows how to search for the index of an element in a vector by testing for physical equality with the primitive ==. It uses that test because the usual test for equality (=) will not terminate on structures that loop. We take advantage of it to install the initial state in position 0 of the vector.

```
   #let dfa_of (e, follow, chars) =
      let init_state = {Pos = first_pos e; Tran = [ ]} in
      let dfa = compute_states [ ] [init_state] follow chars in
      (* Installing initial state at index 0 *)
      let idx_start = vect_indexq dfa init_state in
      dfa.(idx_start) ← dfa.(0);
      dfa.(0) ← init_state;
      dfa;;
   dfa_of : regexpr * int set vect * char option vect → state vect = ⟨fun⟩
```

Once again, we print automata in a special way, particularly the transitions. Various transitions from the same state are separated by **or**, and a transition on c to a state st is printed like this: c ↦ st.Pos.

```
   #dfa_of(regexpr_follow "(a|b)*abb");;
   − : state vect = [| {Pos=[0, 1, 2]; Tran=['b' ↦ [0, 1, 2] or
                                            'a' ↦ [0, 1, 2, 3]]};
                     {Pos=[0, 1, 2, 4]; Tran=['b' ↦ [0, 1, 2, 5] or
                                            'a' ↦ [0, 1, 2, 3]]};
                     {Pos=[0, 1, 2, 3]; Tran=['b' ↦ [0, 1, 2, 4] or
```

$$\text{`a`} \mapsto [0, 1, 2, 3]]\};$$

$$\{Pos=[0, 1, 2, 5];$$
$$Tran=[\text{`b`} \mapsto [0, 1, 2] \textbf{ or } \text{`a`} \mapsto [0, 1, 2, 3]]\} \,||$$

#dfa_of(regexpr_follow "abc");;
$- : state\ vect = [| \{Pos=[0]; Tran=[\text{`a`} \mapsto [1]]\};$
$\qquad\qquad\qquad \{Pos=[2]; Tran=[\text{`c`} \mapsto [3]]\};$
$\qquad\qquad\qquad \{Pos=[1]; Tran=[\text{`b`} \mapsto [2]]\}; \{Pos=[3]; Tran=[\,]\} \,||$

#dfa_of(regexpr_follow "");;
$- : state\ vect = [| \{Pos=[0]; Tran=[\,]\} \,||$

8.6.7   Interpreting a Deterministic Finite Automaton

In order to interpret an automaton, we could use any of the techniques for recognition or analysis that we covered in this chapter, but we will use the stream analyzers since they are the last we studied.

We will need the following analyzers and constructors of analyzers:

end_of_stream : α stream $\rightarrow$ unit

fails if the end of its argument stream is not reached.

```
#let parser_or p pl =
    it_list (fun p₁ p₂ → (function [⟨ p₁ x ⟩] → x | [⟨ p₂ y ⟩] → y))
        p pl;;
parser_or : (α stream → β) → (α stream → β) list → α stream → β
        = ⟨fun⟩
```

builds an alternative from a non-empty list of analyzers.

```
#let parser_of_char c =
    let pc = stream_check (prefix == c) in
    fun str → pc str; ();;
parser_of_char : α → α stream → unit = ⟨fun⟩
```

constructs the analyzer that exclusively recognizes the character c.

The predefined function stream_check takes a predicate and provides an analyzer that returns the first element of its argument stream, if that element satisfies that predicate.

stream_check : $(\alpha \rightarrow bool) \rightarrow \alpha$ stream $\rightarrow \alpha$

Now we can interpret an automaton by the following function:

```
#let rec interpret_dfa dfa accept =
   (* accept is the number associated with the token None *)
   (*building the vector of analyzers *)
   let fvect = make_vect (vect_length dfa) (fun _ → failwith "No value") in
   for i=0 to vect_length dfa − 1 do
     let trans = dfa.(i).Tran in
     let parsers =
       map (fun (c, st) →
                     let pc = parser_of_char c in
                     let j = vect_indexq dfa st in
                     function [⟨ pc _; (fvect.(j)) _ ⟩] → ()) trans in
     if set_member accept (dfa.(i).Pos) then
       fvect.(i) ← parser_or end_of_stream parsers
     else match parsers with
          [ ] → failwith "Impossible"
        | p::ps → fvect.(i) ← parser_or p ps
   done;
   fvect.(0);;
interpret_dfa : state vect → int → char stream → unit = ⟨fun⟩
```

All that is left for us to do is to assemble these various elements into a function regexpr that takes a regular expression in the form of a character string and returns a recognition function.

```
#let regexpr res =
   let ((e, follow, chars) as ast) = regexpr_follow res in
   let dfa = dfa_of ast in
   let p = interpret_dfa dfa (vect_length chars − 1) in
   fun s → p (stream_of_string s);;
regexpr : string → string → unit = ⟨fun⟩
```

```
#let e1 = regexpr "(a|b)*abb";;
e1 : string → unit = ⟨fun⟩
```

```
#e1 "abbaabb";;
− : unit = ()
```

```
#e1 "abb";;
− : unit = ()
```

```
#e1 "ab";;
Uncaught exception: Parse_error
```

```
#e1 "c";;
Uncaught exception: Parse_failure
```

Exercises

8.4 Write the analyzer for regular expressions parse_regexpr from page 271.

8.7   Summary

We presented how to write recursive-descent syntax-analyzers. First, we presented two ways to define a language: by regular expressions or by a context-free grammar.

Initially, we limited ourselves to the problem of recognition, that is, how to know whether or not a phrase belongs to a given language. In that context, we showed you a functional technique to build recognizers from basic functions.

Then we modified those recognizers so that they would be capable of producing values of arbitrary types during recognition.

CAML LIGHT includes a data structure dedicated to syntactic analysis: streams. It also has a special form of pattern matching to facilitate writing predictive analyzers. By predictive, we mean those analyzers that consult at most one token to make a decision. We used these facilities to compile regular expressions into deterministic finite automata and then to interpret the automata.

8.8   To Learn More

Burge's work [9] is a precursor to functional syntactic analysis. His ideas have been adapted within the framework of functional languages with delayed evaluation. In [1], for example, you will find an implementation of similar analyzers in such a context.

Streams, pattern matching, and various possible implementations in typed functional languages are defined in [26].

You should read this chapter as a description of one particular programming style and regard syntactic analysis as an example of a problem that this style solves. It is quite possible to develop similar solutions in rather different application domains. In effect, the type stream can be used for any stream of homogeneous information that must obey precise recognition rules.

More generally, this chapter illustrates a relatively consistent way of programming; we first build a basic toolbox, where the tools use a common protocol to communicate among themselves about the results of their effects. We then use various configurations of these tools to build solutions to a whole variety of problems. This technique is so general that it can certainly be applied to problems other than syntactic analysis.

The methods of syntactic analysis that we covered in this chapter are quite realistic. Even so, there are other, more conventional approaches that might prove more efficient. The following paragraphs give you a taste of those other approaches.

8.8.1 Comparing with Other Methods of Syntactic Analysis

As we mentioned before, there are two main families of techniques for syntactic analysis: ascendant and descendant analysis. We will not actually discuss more general techniques (such as Earley's algorithm [13]) because, though they are very powerful, they are not widely distributed.

Characteristically, descendant analysis recognizes a given non-terminal, whereas ascendant analysis collects the symbols it has read until a non-terminal can be recognized.

In this chapter, we insisted on descendant analysis and thereby profited from certain characteristics of functional languages generally and CAML in particular to build analyzers that we could parameterize. The chief difficulty that we encounter when we want to build a descendant analyzer is the transformation of the initial grammar that defines the language—transformation to get a grammar that can be systematically or even automatically translated into an analyzer. For example, the language of expressions that we looked at in Section 8.3.4 cannot be translated directly into an analyzer since it was left-recursive and ambiguous. We translated that grammar in a way that eliminated ambiguities and suppressed left-recursion. There is, however, a general technique for eliminating left-recursion; it works as long as no non-terminal of the grammar recognizes the empty word and if no non-terminal has a rule like this:

$$A \quad ::= \quad \ldots$$
$$\mid \quad A$$
$$\ldots$$

Frequently, ambiguities are resolved as we handled them (that is, rules about priority establish a hierarchy among operators), but in fact there is not an absolutely certain technique about this matter.

The goal of such transformations is to produce a grammar that belongs to the class LL(n)—one which it is relatively simple to translate into a descendant analyzer that consults at most the first n symbols of its input. To build a predictive analyzer (that is, one that consults at most one symbol), it suffices to build a grammar of the class LL(1).

Thus you see that automatically generating descendant analyzers from grammars actually presents a great many difficulties. Even so, you should not conclude that the descendant technique itself is the source of the difficulties! In fact, even though *generating* analyzers is hard, directly *programming* them leaves the programmer more freedom because he or she then has complete control over the activity, all the more so when the language the programmer uses is rich. If we consider functional languages, for example—dynamically building analyzers (just as we dynamically construct functional values), possibly storing them in data structures, perhaps passing them as arguments to other analyzers—they suggest solutions to problems where other more "classic" techniques fail.

We will only briefly mention the principal ascendant technique. It depends on generating analyzers driven by tables that contain actions to carry out for each possible symbol. (In short, they are symbol-table driven.) This is the technique used in YACC, the analyzer generator, which is the basis of the CAML-YACC generator which produces analyzers adapted to CAML. YACC also accepts a grammar as input and produces an analyzer that recognizes the language specified by that grammar on condition that the grammar belong to the class LALR(1). The grammars in this class are written in a natural way; in particular, they can be left-recursive. The analyzers produced this way are efficient, and this technique is well adapted if the language to recognize is fixed and the grammar for it readily available. Of course, with each rule of the grammar, you can associate an action to carry out during the rule reduction. The only difficulty is to foresee precisely when these actions will be carried out. In practice, the grammar has no operational connotations, so the behavior of the analyzer may sometimes be surprising. As a general rule, because of the declarative character of the grammar, controlling and debugging the generated analyzers may be quite a subtle problem. For that reason, such tools are best adapted to situations where the language to recognize is clearly defined.

8.8.2 Further References

It would take too long to catalogue all the various classes of grammar and to explicate in greater detail all the possible ways and means of producing analyzers here. Indeed, there are other analytic techniques even less widely known that we won't even mention. Instead, we will direct you to the standard references in the field. For example, [2] offers a reasonable and accessible approach to the problems of lexical and syntactic analysis, along with the most current solutions in the context of building compilers. And in [3], you will find a complete and detailed presentation of the theory of syntactic analysis.

Chapter 9

Geometry and Drawings

This chapter is devoted to functionally programming geometric drawings. We use types and graphic functions from the library MLgraph, and we briefly describe them before we use them.

The graphic approach of MLgraph is the same as PostScript, a language used particularly for programming laser printers. This approach is oriented toward programming drawings meant to illustrate documents, rather than toward the display of drawings on screen, though there is software to display PostScript drawings as well. Such software provides a reasonable approximation of the drawings, but the quality is limited by the actual screen resolution.

PostScript is an imperative language, indeed, a low-level imperative language, which was not meant to be used directly but rather to be generated by software to produce drawings or to type-set text. The approach we present here uses the graphic model of PostScript, but replaces that language by CAML. This enables us to provide much higher level construction functions for drawing.

The graphic model of PostScript freely uses an infinite Cartesian plane with no limit on the coordinates. The basic objects are initially sketched on this plane in absolute coordinates, but a user can then freely apply transformations to modify their size and position. Such transformations rapidly get out of the constraints about positioning and let us construct complicated drawings by functionally combining simpler ones.

At first glance, producing drawings by programming seems less pleasant than using software to draw interactively, especially if we want to produce a particular design rapidly. However, it has the advantage of producing uniformly families of designs with common characteristics. In particular, to display structured objects, such as trees or other data structures, a single program takes into account all the special cases, and in that way programming becomes much more efficient than interactive drawing. The drawings to illustrate this book were all programmed in CAML.

9.1 Meet MLgraph

Before we actually introduce this library, we should review a few basic concepts of geometry.

9.1.1 Geometric Plane

Figure 9.1 shows you a small part of the Cartesian plane where there are three particular points. Points are represented in CAML by values of type **point** defined like this:

```
#type point = {xc: float; yc: float};;
```

The variable **origin** designates the origin of the coordinate system.

```
#origin;;
```
$- : point = \{xc=0; \ yc=0\}$

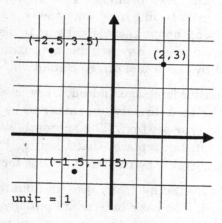

Figure 9.1. Points in the Cartesian plane

9.1.2 Geometric Elements

A basic geometric element can be one of these:

- an open polygon formed from a sequence of straight line segments; such an open polygon or polygonal line is defined by a list of points;

- an arc of a circle defined by its center, its radius, and two angles;

- a Béziers curve defined by its origin (a point of departure), two control points, and its endpoint (a point where it terminates). (Béziers curves resemble spline curves but differ mainly in that the two control points of Béziers curves do not lie on the curve.)

The corresponding CAML type is:

```
#type geom_element =
     Seg of point list
   | Arc of point * float * float * float
   | Curve of point * point * point * point;;
```

Given these points

$$A=(-3.,-3.) \quad B=(-3.,-1.) \quad C=(-1.,-1.)$$
$$D=(-1.,-3.) \quad E=(-3.,-4.) \quad F=(-2.,0.)$$
$$G=(0.,5.) \quad H=(1.,4.) \quad I=(3.,0.)$$

the expressions Seg [A; B; C; D; A], Curve(E, F, G, H), and Arc(I, 2., 30., 290.) correspond to the three elements drawn in bold in Figure 9.2.

A priori, a **transformation** is any function of type (point → point). However, the transformations most often used are linear ones that can be implemented efficiently. Conceptually, a linear transformation is a 3×3 matrix of the form:

$$\begin{pmatrix} m_{11} & m_{12} & m_{13} \\ m_{21} & m_{22} & m_{23} \\ 0 & 0 & 1 \end{pmatrix}$$

which works on vectors

$$\begin{pmatrix} x \\ y \\ 1 \end{pmatrix}$$

representing the coordinate point (x,y).

The type of linear transformations is:

```
#type transformation = {m11: float; m12: float; m13: float;
                        m21: float; m22: float; m23: float};;
```

The following function applies a transformation to a point:

```
##open "float";;

#let transform_point = fun
    {m11=a; m12=b; m13=c; m21=d; m22=e; m23=f} {xc=x; yc=y}
    → {xc = a*x+b*y+c ; yc = d*x+e*y+f};;
transform_point : transformation → point → point = ⟨fun⟩
```

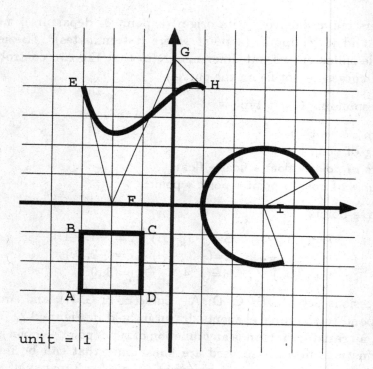

Figure 9.2. Geometric elements

The identity transformation is defined by:

#let id_trans = {m$_{11}$=1.; m$_{12}$=0.; m$_{13}$=0.; m$_{21}$=0.; m$_{22}$=1.; m$_{23}$=0.};;
id_trans : transformation = {m$_{11}$=1; m$_{12}$=0; m$_{13}$=0; m$_{21}$=0; m$_{22}$=1;
                                                  m$_{23}$=0}

The composition of a list of transformations is carried out from right to left.
It is defined by:

#let compose_transformations =
  let compose = **fun**
    {m$_{11}$=a$_{11}$; m$_{12}$=a$_{12}$; m$_{13}$=a$_{13}$; m$_{21}$=a$_{21}$; m$_{22}$=a$_{22}$; m$_{23}$=a$_{23}$}
    {m$_{11}$=b$_{11}$; m$_{12}$=b$_{12}$; m$_{13}$=b$_{13}$; m$_{21}$=b$_{21}$; m$_{22}$=b$_{22}$; m$_{23}$=b$_{23}$}
    → {m$_{11}$=a$_{11}$*b$_{11}$+a$_{12}$*b$_{21}$; m$_{12}$=a$_{11}$*b$_{12}$ + a$_{12}$*b$_{22}$;
      m$_{13}$=a$_{11}$*b$_{13}$+a$_{12}$*b$_{23}$+a$_{13}$;
      m$_{21}$=a$_{21}$*b$_{11}$+a$_{22}$*b$_{21}$; m$_{22}$=a$_{21}$*b$_{12}$+a$_{22}$*b$_{22}$;
      m$_{23}$ =a$_{21}$*b$_{13}$+a$_{22}$*b$_{23}$+a$_{23}$}
  in it_list compose id_trans;;
compose_transformations : transformation list → transformation
                              = ⟨**fun**⟩

```
##close "float";;
```

There are functions available to you so that you can construct an object of type **transformation** for the most common transformations, such as translation, rotation, symmetry around a point, symmetry around a line segment defined by two distinct points, and changes in scale.

> **translation** : float * float → transformation
> **rotation** : point → float → transformation
> **point_symmetry** : point → transformation
> **line_symmetry** : point * point → transformation
> **scaling** : float * float → transformation

Angles of MLgraph are represented by floating-point numbers; they are expressed in degrees.

Exercises
9.1 Write the functions sine and cosine to accept their arguments in degrees.
9.2 Write the functions translation, rotation, point_symmetry, and line_symmetry. (Their types were given before.)

9.1.3 Constructing Images

We will call a set of geometric elements a **sketch**. The type **sketch**, of course, is used to represent sketches. It is an abstract type; its implementation is hidden from the user. The function make_sketch builds a sketch from a list of geometric elements.

```
#make_sketch;;
- : geom_element list → sketch = ⟨fun⟩
```

In PostScript terminology, a sketch is called a "path."

Sketches constructed this way are connected in the sense that the straight line segments are added to link components. As a consequence, given four points A, B, C, D, the two expressions make_sketch [Seg[A; B; C; D]] and make_sketch [Seg[A; B]; Seg[C; D]] define equivalent sketches.

However, it is possible to define sketches with unconnected parts by this function:

```
#group_sketches;;
- : sketch list ↦ sketch = ⟨fun⟩
```

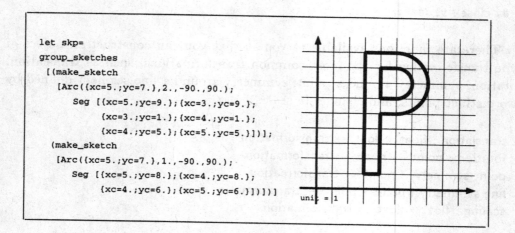

```
let skp=
group_sketches
 [(make_sketch
   [Arc({xc=5.;yc=7.},2.,-90.,90.);
     Seg [{xc=5.;yc=9.};{xc=3.;yc=9.};
          {xc=3.;yc=1.};{xc=4.;yc=1.};
          {xc=4.;yc=5.};{xc=5.;yc=5.}])]);
  (make_sketch
   [Arc({xc=5.;yc=7.},1.,-90.,90.);
     Seg [{xc=5.;yc=8.};{xc=4.;yc=8.};
          {xc=4.;yc=6.};{xc=5.;yc=6.}])]])]
```

unit = 1

Figure 9.3. A sketch of the letter P

Figure 9.3 shows the program that defines a sketch corresponding to the shape of the letter P as well as the graphic effect we get.

Sketches are pure geometric figures where the lines have no thickness. That is, they cannot be drawn as such. To produce a picture from a sketch, we have to give the lines a thickness, or we have to fill in the interior of the sketch.

To do so, we use information about "painting" which in turn uses the following types:

- for the extremeties of a line:

  #type linecap = Buttcap | Squarecap | Roundcap;;

- for the joint between two lines:

  #type linejoin = Beveljoin | Roundjoin | Miterjoin;;

- to define the characteristics of a line:

  #type linestyle = {linewidth:float;
                     linecap:linecap;
                     linejoin:linejoin;
                     dashpattern:int list};;

- for filling:

  #type fillstyle = Nzfill | Eofill;;

- for color:

```
#type color = Rgb of float * float * float
            | Hsb of float * float * float
            | Gra of float;;
```

We use the type picture to represent all the objects that can be seen. Like the type sketch, the type picture is abstract.

To create an object of this type from a sketch, we use other functions:

```
#make_draw_picture;;
```
— : *linestyle * color → sketch → picture* = ⟨**fun**⟩

```
#make_fill_picture;;
```
— : *fillstyle * color → sketch → picture* = ⟨**fun**⟩

- The function make_draw_picture produces a picture from a sketch by giving it a uniform line style and a color.

- The function make_fill_picture produces a picture from a sketch by closing its components and filling their interiors, as defined by fill style, with a certain color.

Figure 9.4 shows you two possible ways of using the same sketch from Figure 9.3.

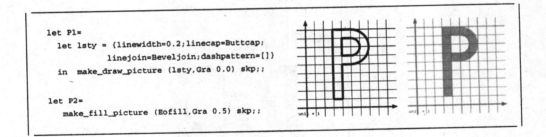

Figure 9.4. Two pictures from the same sketch

There are other kinds of pictures, in addition to those we get from sketches, for example, texts (that is, character strings written in a given font, of a certain size, and a particular color).

```
#type font_style =
        Courier | Helvetica | Symbol (*| ... *) ;;
```

```
#type font = { Style : font_style ; Size : float };;
```

```
#make_font;;
```
$-$: $font\_style \rightarrow float \rightarrow font = \langle \textbf{fun} \rangle$

```
#make_text_picture;;
```
$-$: $font \rightarrow color \rightarrow string \rightarrow picture = \langle \textbf{fun} \rangle$

Once a sketch or picture has been defined, it is possible to apply arbitrary linear transformations to it by these functions:

```
transform_sketch : transformation → sketch → sketch
transform_picture : transformation → picture → picture
```

Figure 9.5 shows you what we get when we apply the transformations $T_1=$ translation (2.,−9.), $T_2=$ scaling (0.5,0.5), and $T_3=$ rotation {xc=−2.; yc=−2.} 60.0 successively to a basic picture.

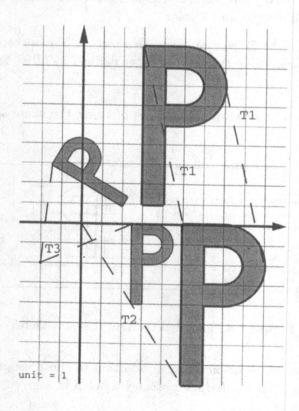

Figure 9.5. Transformations T1, T2, and T3

The function center_picture translates a picture so that its center coincides with a given point.

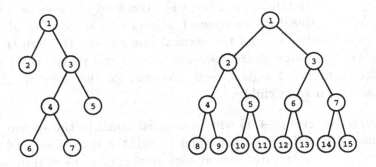

Figure 9.6. Two examples of binary trees

#center_picture;;
— : *picture → point → picture =* ⟨**fun**⟩

It is possible to group a list of pictures into a single one, each one keeping its own position. To do so, we use this function:

#group_pictures;;
— : *picture list → picture =* ⟨**fun**⟩

9.2 Drawing Trees

This section shows you how to draw binary trees, but the method used here is easily extended to more general trees.

9.2.1 Drawing Principles

The principal constraint to satisfy when we draw trees is to avoid superimposing the various subtrees. To do so, we must put the roots of siblings sufficiently far from one another so that they still lie side by side without overlaying each other. However, that is not the only constraint to satisfy. To limit clutter and for aesthetic reasons, too, a tree should fill the space allocated to it in a reasonably uniform way so that it does not contain useless blank spots. Figure 9.6 shows two trees, quite different in the way they are balanced, but which both satisfy the drawing rules we will apply. Those drawing rules are based on the following principles.

- The vertical distance between a node and its children is constant for all levels of a tree.

- At every level of a binary tree, there is a constant distance between sibling nodes. We call this distance **spread** at level n. The position of two sibling nodes is symmetric around the vertical line passing through their parent. In this way, the slope of arcs between a node and its left child will be the same for all nodes at a given level; likewise, for the slope of arcs between nodes and their right children.

- The spread at level $(n + 1)$ will be at most equal to the spread at level n. Incidentally, it will be at least equal to half the spread at level n because division by two of this distance at each level suffices to guarantee sufficient space between subtrees in any case.

- Two sibling subtrees will be drawn so that the distance between the rightmost node of the left subtree and the leftmost node of the right subtree will be at least equal to the spread between two siblings at that level, and this relation will hold for every level.

A binary tree will be drawn with these parameters: the vertical distance between a node and its children; the spread between the two children of the root; and a list of coefficients indicating for each level n the ratio between the spread at level $n+1$ and n. For now, we assume that these parameters have been computed to take into account the space occupied by each node. Later, you will see how to compute these quantities adequately.

Incidentally, we must also have a parameter to indicate the line style to trace the branches of the tree. All this information will be organized in the type tree_style.

```
#type tree_style =
     {vdist:float;
      hdist:float;
      coef_list:float list;
      tlsty:linestyle;
      tcolor: color};;
```

Trees to draw will be of type **picture btree**, and here is the drawing function:

```
#let draw_btree tsty t=
  let rec draw_r d cl ({xc=x; yc=y} as pt) = fun
    Empty → make_blank_picture (0.0,0.0)
  | (Bin(Empty,pict,Empty))
    → center_picture pict pt
  | (Bin(t_1,pict,t_2))
```

```
      → let d=d*.(hd cl) in
        let pt₁ = {xc=x−.d/.2.0;yc=y−.tsty.vdist}
        and pt₂ = {xc=x+.d/.2.0;yc=y−.tsty.vdist} in
        let line₁= make_draw_picture (tsty.tlsty,tsty.tcolor)
                     (make_sketch [Seg [pt;pt₁]])
        and line₂= make_draw_picture (tsty.tlsty,tsty.tcolor)
                     (make_sketch [Seg [pt;pt₂]]) in
      match (t₁,t₂) with
        (_,Empty)
        → group_pictures
             [line₁; center_picture pict pt; drawᵣ d (tl cl) pt₁ t₁]
      | (Empty,_)
        → group_pictures
             [line₂; center_picture pict pt; drawᵣ d (tl cl) pt₂ t₂]
      | _
        → group_pictures
             [line₁; line₂; center_picture pict pt;
                drawᵣ d (tl cl) pt₁ t₁; drawᵣ d (tl cl) pt₂ t₂]
   in drawᵣ tsty.hdist tsty.coef_list origin t;;
```

$draw\_btree : tree\_style \rightarrow picture\ btree \rightarrow picture = \langle \mathbf{fun} \rangle$

Notice that the order for drawing various elements is important. Branches must be drawn before nodes so that nodes hide the part of the branches inside the nodes.

To draw a tree, we must convert an object of type picture btree by associating a picture of each node with it. For that, we will use this function:

```
#map_btree;;
```
$- : (\alpha \rightarrow \beta) \rightarrow \alpha\ btree \rightarrow \beta\ btree = \langle \mathbf{fun} \rangle$

For the moment, we will use a function to associate an empty picture with each node so that the skeleton of the tree appears.

```
#fun x → make_blank_picture (0.0,0.0);;
```
$- : \alpha \rightarrow picture = \langle \mathbf{fun} \rangle$

Figure 9.7 represents the two pictures p₁ and p₂. Their computation is defined like this:

```
#let p₁ =
   let t₁= btree_of_string int_of_string "1(2,3(4(6,7),5))"
   and lsty={linewidth= 1.0;linecap=Buttcap;
```

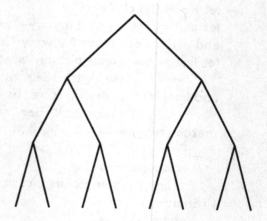

Figure 9.7. Two skeletons of binary trees

```
                linejoin=Beveljoin;dashpattern=[ ]}
    and cl₁=[1.0;1.0;1.0] in
    let tstyle₁= {vdist=50.0; hdist=50.0; coef_list=cl₁;
                tlsty=lsty; tcolor=black} in
    draw_btree
      tstyle₁ (map_btree (fun x → make_blank_picture (0.0,0.0)) t₁);;
p₁ : picture = ⟨abstract⟩

#let p₂ =
    let t₂= btree_of_string int_of_string
            "1(2(4(8,9),5(10,11)),3(6(12,13),7(14,15)))"
    and lsty={linewidth= 1.0;linecap=Buttcap;
                linejoin=Beveljoin;dashpattern=[ ]}
    and cl₂=[1.0;0.5;0.5] in
    let tstyle₂= {vdist=50.0; hdist=100.0; coef_list=cl₂;
                tlsty=lsty; tcolor=black} in
    draw_btree
      tstyle₂ (map_btree (fun x → make_blank_picture (0.0,0.0)) t₂);;
p₂ : picture = ⟨abstract⟩
```

To display the trees t_1 and t_2 completely, it suffices to associate a non-empty picture with the nodes. For that, we use this function:

```
#let draw_string_node r a =
    let s = center_picture
                (make_text_picture (make_font Helvetica r) black a)
```

               origin
    and f = make_fill_picture (Nzfill,white)
               (make_sketch [Arc(origin,r,0.0,360.0)])
    and c = make_draw_picture ({linewidth= r*.0.1;linecap=Buttcap;
                       linejoin=Miterjoin;dashpattern=[]},
               black)
          (make_sketch [Arc(origin, r, 0.0, 360.0)])
  in group_pictures [f;c;s];;
$draw\_string\_node : float \rightarrow string \rightarrow picture = \langle \mathbf{fun} \rangle$

#let draw_int_node r n = draw_string_node r (string_of_int n);;
$draw\_int\_node : float \rightarrow int \rightarrow picture = \langle \mathbf{fun} \rangle$

Figure 9.8 represents the two pictures p_1 and p_2. They are computed like this:

#let p_1 =
  let t_1= btree_of_string int_of_string "1(2,3(4(6,7),5))"
  and lsty= {linewidth= 1.0;linecap=Buttcap;
             linejoin=Beveljoin;dashpattern=[]}
  and cl_1= [1.0;1.0;1.0] **in**
  let $tstyle_1$= {vdist=50.0; hdist=50.0; coef_list=cl_1;
             tlsty=lsty; tcolor=black} **in**
  draw_btree $tstyle_1$ (map_btree (draw_int_node 10.0) t_1);;
$p_1 : picture = \langle \mathbf{abstract} \rangle$

#let p_2 =
  let t_2= btree_of_string int_of_string
         "1(2(4(8,9),5(10,11)),3(6(12,13),7(14,15)))"
  and lsty= {linewidth= 1.0;linecap=Buttcap;
             linejoin=Beveljoin;dashpattern=[]}
  and cl_2= [1.0;0.5;0.5] **in**
  let $tstyle_2$= {vdist=50.0; hdist=100.0; coef_list=cl_2;
             tlsty=lsty; tcolor=black} **in**
  draw_btree $tstyle_2$ (map_btree (draw_int_node 10.0) t_2);;
$p_2 : picture = \langle \mathbf{abstract} \rangle$

9.2.2   Computing the Reduction Coefficients

The following step automatically calculates the data needed to draw trees. The vertical distance between various levels and the minimal distance between sibling nodes depend on the size of the node drawing. Both are easy to get. In contrast,

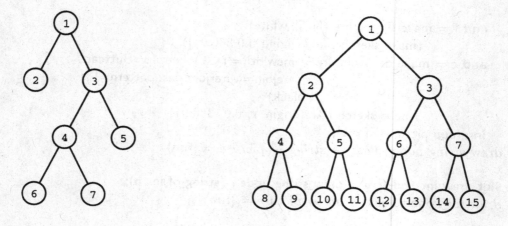

Figure 9.8. Two binary trees

the list of coefficients depends strongly on the general shape of a tree, so its computation is more difficult.

Here is a function to compute vertical and minimal horizontal distances. It takes a tree of type picture btree and a pair of coefficients as its arguments, and it returns a pair of floating-point numbers.

```
#let compute_height_width (hcoef,wcoef) t=
  let (h,w)= it_btree
            (fun (x,y) p → (max_float x (picture_height p),
                            max_float y (picture_width p)))
            (0.0, 0.0)
            t
  in (h*.hcoef, w*.wcoef);;
compute_height_width : float * float → picture btree → float * float
            = ⟨fun⟩
```

Now we will compute the list of coefficients to apply when we pass from one level of a tree to the next. We compute from bottom to top. We fix the minimal spread to apply to the deepest leaves (for example, the value 1) and then we work back up in the tree, computing the spread needed at each level. The ratio between the spreads at two levels, n and $n+1$, provides the coefficient at level n.

Let's assume we have a tree of the form $t=a(t_1,t_2)$, and that we know how to draw the trees t_1 and t_2 correctly. To know the spread between the roots of t_1 and t_2, we must know how much space these trees take; that is, more precisely, we have to know for each level the coordinates of the rightmost node of t_1 and the leftmost node of t_2 so that we leave sufficient space between these two nodes.

The function compute_coef_list recursively computes a pair (cl,trl) for all the subtrees of a binary tree.

- cl is the list of reduction coefficients to apply at each level. This information will be used eventually by the function draw_btree.

- trl is a list of triples (l,r,c), corresponding to each level of the tree where

  - l is the abscissa of the leftmost node at this level with respect to the root of the tree when we take the spread between the two children of the root as the unit of measure;
  - r is the abscissa of the rightmost node at this level with respect to the root of the tree when we take the spread between the two children of the root as the unit of measure;
  - c is the product of the reduction coefficients to apply between the root and this level. If the spread between the two children of the root is one, then the spread at this level is c.

For a binary tree $a(t_1,t_2)$, the function compute_coef_list begins by computing the information (cl_1,trl_1) and (cl_2,trl_2) corresponding to the two subtrees t_1 and t_2. Then the lists of coefficients cl_1 and cl_2 are combined so that at each level the most constraining coefficient is chosen (that is, the smallest). In that way, we get a list of coefficients cl which is valid for t_1 and t_2.

Compared to this new list of coefficients, the information in the triples trl_1 and trl_2 is no longer valid. Those triples are updated by the function recompute_triples so we get two new lists of triples trl'_1 and trl'_2.

Finally, we must take into account the supplementary constraint of juxtaposing the two subtrees t_1 and t_2 to build the tree $a(t_1,t_2)$. At each level, we consider the triples (l_1,r_1,c) and (l_2,r_2,c) from trl'_1 and trl'_2 corresponding to this level. (Notice that the reduction coefficient c is now the same in both triples.)

At a given level, in order for the rightmost node of the tree t_1 to be to the left of the leftmost node of the tree t_2 and at a distance at least equal to c, the algebraic distance between the roots of t_1 and t_2 must be at least equal to r_1-l_2+c. If this quantity is negative, it means that for the two subtrees t_1 and t_2 to overlap at that level, then the root of t_2 must be to the left of the root of t_1. That certainly is not true, so in this case, we take one as the coefficient; otherwise, we take $1/(r_1-l_2+c)$. Notice that if r_1-l_2+c is positive but less than one, the coefficient we get is greater than one. However, after we get coefficients for all levels, we take the minimum of this set and one; doing so guarantees that the final coefficient we choose is less than or equal to one.

Here are the functions for that computation:

```
#let rec minl = fun
    ([ ],l₂) → l₂
  | (l₁,[ ]) → l₁
  | (a₁::l₁,a₂::l₂) → min_float a₁ a₂ :: minl(l₁,l₂);;
minl : float list * float list → float list = ⟨fun⟩

#let recompute_triples cl =
    recomp (hd cl,tl cl)
    where rec recomp (n,cl) = fun
      [ ] → [ ]
    | ((l,r,c)::ll) → (l*.n/.c, r*.n/.c, n):: recomp (n*.(hd cl), tl cl) ll;;
recompute_triples : float list → (float * float * float) list
                              → (float * float * float) list = ⟨fun⟩

#let compute_head_coef (trl₁,trl₂) =
    it_list min_float 1.0 (comp_coef (trl₁,trl₂))
    where rec comp_coef = fun
      ([ ],_) → [ ]
    | (_,[ ]) → [ ]
    | ((_,r₁,c)::ll₁,(l₂,_,_)::ll₂)
      → let d=(r₁−.l₂+.c) in
          (if d≤.0.0 then 1.0 else (1.0/.d))
          :: comp_coef (ll₁,ll₂);;
compute_head_coef : (α * float * float) list * (float * β * γ) list
                              → float = ⟨fun⟩

#let combine_triples x (trl₁,trl₂) =
    (−.0.5, 0.5, 1.0) :: comb (trl₁,trl₂)
    where rec comb = fun
      ([ ],[ ]) → [ ]
    | ((l₁,r₁,c)::ll₁, [ ]) → (−.0.5+.x*.l₁, −.0.5+.x*.r₁, c*.x) :: comb(ll₁,[ ])
    | ([ ], (l₂,r₂,c)::ll₂) → (0.5+.x*.l₂, 0.5+.x*.r₂, c*.x) :: comb([ ],ll₂)
    | ((l₁,r₁,c)::ll₁, (l₂,r₂,_)::ll₂)
      → (−.0.5+.x*.l₁, 0.5+.x*.r₂, c*.x) :: comb(ll₁,ll₂);;
combine_triples : float → (float * float * float) list *
                              (float * float * float) list
                              → (float * float * float) list = ⟨fun⟩

#let compute_coef_list t =
    fst (comp t)
    where rec comp = fun
      Empty → [ ],[ ]
```

```
    | (Bin (Empty,_,Empty)) → [1.0],[ ]
    | (Bin (t₁,_,Empty))
      → let (cl,trl) = comp t₁ in
        (1.0::cl, (−.0.5,−.0.5,1.0)
                ::map (fun (l,r,c) → (−.0.5+.l, −.0.5+.r, c))
                  trl)
    | (Bin (Empty,_,t₂))
      → let (cl,trl) = comp t₂ in
        (1.0::cl, (0.5,0.5,1.0)
                ::map (fun (l,r,c) → (0.5+.l, 0.5+.r, c))
                  trl)
    | (Bin (t₁,_,t₂))
      → let (cl₁,trl₁) = comp t₁
        and (cl₂,trl₂) = comp t₂ in
        let cl = minl(cl₁,cl₂) in
        let trl1' = recompute_triples cl trl₁
        and trl2' = recompute_triples cl trl₂ in
        let x = compute_head_coef (trl1',trl2') in
        (1.0::x::tl cl, combine_triples x (trl1',trl2'));;
compute_coef_list : α btree → float list = ⟨fun⟩
```

Now we are in a good position to define a function to draw trees automatically. As arguments, it takes a function drn to draw nodes; a pair (vcoef,hcoef) to give two proportions: one between the maximal height of nodes and the height between levels of the tree, and the other between the maximal width of nodes and the minimal distance between nodes; a color; and a tree to draw. The width of the lines is arbitrarily fixed to one-fiftieth of the vertical distance between levels—empirically reasonable. We could, of course, make that another parameter.

```
#let make_btree_picture drn (vcoef,hcoef) color t =
    let tp = map_btree drn t
    and coef_list = compute_coef_list t in
    let (height,width) = compute_height_width (vcoef,hcoef) tp in
    let start_width = width /. (it_list mult_float 1.0 coef_list) in
    let tsty = {vdist=height; hdist=start_width;
                coef_list=coef_list;
                tlsty={linewidth= height/.50.0;
                       linecap=Buttcap;
                       linejoin=Beveljoin;dashpattern=[ ]};
                tcolor=color}
    in draw_btree tsty tp;;
make_btree_picture : (α → picture) → float * float
```

$$\rightarrow color \rightarrow \alpha \; btree \rightarrow picture$$
$$= \langle \textbf{fun} \rangle$$

The pictures in Figure 9.6 correspond to the following definitions:

```
#let p₁ =
    let t₁ = btree_of_string
                int_of_string
                "2(1,20(10(6(4(3,5),8(7,9)),15(12,17)),21))"
    in make_btree_picture (draw_int_node 10.0)
        (3.0,2.0) black t₁;;
p₁ : picture = ⟨abstract⟩

#let p₂ =
    let t₂ = btree_of_string
                int_of_string
                ("15(6(4(2(1,3),5),10(8(7,9),12(11,14(13,())))),"^
                "23(19(17(16,18),21(20,22)),25(24,26((),27))))")
    in make_btree_picture (draw_int_node 10.0)
        (3.0,2.0) black t₂;;
p₂ : picture = ⟨abstract⟩
```

Figure 9.9 shows how to draw two peculiar trees, defined like this:

```
#let t₃ = btree_of_string int_of_string "1(2((),3((),5)),4(2(6,()),()))";;

#let t₄ = btree_of_string int_of_string "1(2(3(4,()),()),2(3(4,()),()))";;
```

Exercise
9.3 Generalize the way we draw trees to handle trees of arbitrary arity.

9.3 Tiling

We use the term **tiling** to talk about paving a surface by repeating either a unique figure or a finite number of basic figures. Paving streets or sidewalks, tiling a kitchen or bathroom are typical examples of tiling in normal life. Many civilizations, particularly Arab civilizations, have used tiling to decorate monuments; in Arab culture a religious belief forbids the representation of human or animal images and has lead to the elaborate use of abstract geometric patterns. More recently, the Dutch engraver Maurits C. Escher has made tiling a plane one of the essential components of his works and has thus created many tilings based on animal figures.

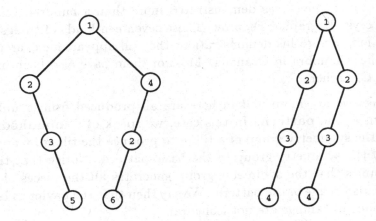

Figure 9.9. Two peculiar trees

Scientists have become interested in tiling through their study of regular mineral structures such as crystals. Crystallography in the nineteenth century initiated the theory of regular filling of space or planes. Since then, this theory has been greatly furthered by physicists and mathematicians, and it remains an active field of research.

The first principle for classifying the tilings of a plane is to define possible **symmetries**. When we say, "symmetry of a tiling," we mean the set of isometries under which it remains invariant. The set of isometries of the plane as well as the set of isometries that preserve a given tiling have the structure of a group (in the formal mathematical meaning of group). The tiling **symmetry groups** are organized into a few categories, like this:

- When the group contains no translations, it involves either a cyclic group of order n, generated by n rotations around the same center and angles of $2k\pi/n$, or a dihedral group of order $2n$, generated by n rotations and n symmetries along straight line segments that, among themselves, form angles of $2k\pi/n$.

- When the group contains translations all in the same direction, there are only seven possibilities. These seven groups are called frieze groups.

- When the group contains two translations in different directions, there are only seventeen possibilities. These seventeen groups are called crystallographic groups.

Tilings where the symmetry group contains two translations in different directions are also called periodic tilings. The fact that there are only seventeen groups of periodic tilings was demonstrated more than a hundred years ago by the Russian crystallographer Fedorov. These seventeen kinds of tilings had been widely used long before his demonstration; they all appear, for example, in the mosaics of the Alhambra in Granada. Most of them have also been used in the works of M. C. Escher.

The tilings we are interested in here are all produced from a unique basic figure, known as the **pattern**. In this case, we speak of a **monohedral** tiling. We will use the symmetry group of a tiling to produce the tiling by applying the isometries of the symmetry group to the basic pattern. Notice that this way of working assumes that the symmetry group generates all the pieces of the tiling from a particular image of the pattern. We say then that the paving is **isohedral**. Certain monohedral tilings are not isohedral.

We have already mentioned the **isometries** of a plane. They are the application of the set of points in the plane to itself which respect the dimensions of figures. That is, they simultaneously preserve distances and angles. In particular, an isometry transforms a triangle either into a triangle that can be superposed on the original (in that case, we speak of a direct isometry) or into a triangle that is the mirror image of the original (then we speak of an inverse isometry). Direct isometries are translations that leave no invariant points, rotations which leave a single point invariant, and the identity. Inverse isometries are the reflections with respect to a straight line segment called the axis of symmetry (they leave the points along that segment invariant) and glides (reflections followed by a translation in the same direction as the axis of symmetry) which do not leave any points invariant.

The inverse of an isometry is also an isometry of the same kind. In particular, symmetries with respect to a line segment are their own inverse.

The composition of two direct isometries or of two inverse isometries is also a direct isometry. The composition of a direct isometry and an inverse isometry is still an inverse isometry.

The fact that there are only seventeen possibilities for the symmetry groups of periodic tilings derives from the fact that the only rotations possible are of order 2, 3, 4, or 6. There are only five symmetry groups that include only direct isometries. Here are their traditional names in crystallography:

- **p1** generated by two independent translations;

- **p2** generated by three order-2 rotations;

- **p3** generated by two order-3 rotations;

- **p4** generated by one order-2 rotation and one order-4 rotation;

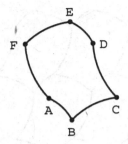

Figure 9.10. Pattern 1

- **p6** generated by one order-2 rotation and one order-3 rotation.

Our examples come from among those, though the programs we present are entirely independent of that choice. Indeed, if you are interested, you can use the programs to produce tilings of your choice.

9.3.1 The Method Used

We will give the basic pattern for a monohedral tiling in the form of an object of type picture or sometimes of type sketch if we want to produce colored tilings. The symmetries of a tiling will be given in the form of objects of type transformation.

The function make_tiling applies a set of transformations to a basic pattern and organizes the basic figure and its images into a unique value of type picture.

```
#let make_tiling p trans =
    group_pictures
      (map (fun t → transform_picture t p) trans);;
make_tiling : picture → transformation list → picture = ⟨fun⟩
```

The first kind of tiling that we will consider corresponds to a symmetry group generated by two independent translations (the group **p1**). Among the patterns that can serve as the basis for such a tiling, we find (besides the parallelograms) patterns like the one in Figure 9.10. It involves a surface where the outline includes six points A, B, C, D, E, F such that the segments AB and ED, BC and FE, CD and AF are images of each other by translation. Two such translations suffice to generate the symmetry group.

We assume that the six points A, B, C, D, E, F are values of the variables ptA_1, ptB_1, ptC_1, ptD_1, ptE_1, ptF_1, and we will use the function point_translation to associate the translation that gets from one to the other with any two points.

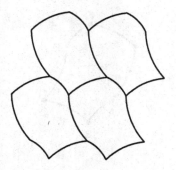

Figure 9.11. Tiling 1

#let point_translation = **fun**
   {xc=x_1; yc=y_1} {xc=x_2; yc=y_2} → translation (x_2−.x_1, y_2−.y_1);;
point_translation : *point* → *point* → *transformation* = ⟨**fun**⟩

The symmetry group could be generated by these two translations:

#let t_1 = point_translation ptA$_1$ ptC$_1$
   and t_2 = point_translation ptA$_1$ ptE$_1$;;
t_1 : *transformation* = {m_{11}=1; m_{12}=0; m_{13}=60; m_{21}=0; m_{22}=1; m_{23}=0}
t_2 : *transformation* = {m_{11}=1; m_{12}=0; m_{13}=20; m_{21}=0; m_{22}=1; m_{23}=70}

We will use a binary function to compose transformations from left to right.

#let comp_trans t_1 t_2 = compose_transformations [t_2;t_1];;
comp_trans : *transformation* → *transformation* → *transformation*
         = ⟨**fun**⟩

Figure 9.11 corresponds to the value of the expression:

#let tiling$_1$=
   make_tiling tile$_1$
      [id_trans; trans$_1$; trans$_2$; comp_trans trans$_1$ trans$_2$];;
tiling$_1$: *picture* = ⟨**abstract**⟩

The second kind of tiling that we will consider corresponds to a symmetry group generated by three central symmetries. (three rotations of π with three distinct points as the centers). For example, if we start from any quadrilateral, it is possible to tile a plane by using the symmetries that have as their center the midpoints of three of its sides; we get the symmetry with respect to the center of

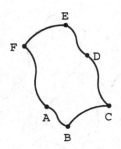

Figure 9.12. Pattern 2

the fourth side from those three others. We can get the same kind of tiling from a "brick" like the one in Figure 9.12.

It involves a surface where the outline includes six points A, B, C, D, E, F such that the segments AB, CD, DE, and FA have a center of symmetry, and the segments BC and FE are images of each other by translation.

The symmetry group can be generated by these three rotations:

```
#let middle pt₁ pt₂ =
    {xc=(pt₁.xc +. pt₂.xc) /. 2.0;
     yc=(pt₁.yc +. pt₂.yc) /. 2.0};;
middle : point → point → point = ⟨fun⟩
```

```
#let rot₁ = rotation (middle ptD₂ ptE₂) 180.0
  and rot₂ = rotation (middle ptA₂ ptF₂) 180.0
  and rot₃ = rotation (middle ptC₂ ptD₂) 180.0;;
```

$rot_1 : transformation = \{m_{11}=-1;\ m_{12}=-1.22460635382e{-}16;$
$\qquad\qquad\qquad\qquad m_{13}=660;\ m_{21}=1.22460635382e{-}16;$
$\qquad\qquad\qquad\qquad m_{22}=-1;\ m_{23}=730\}$

$rot_2 : transformation = \{m_{11}=-1;\ m_{12}=-1.22460635382e{-}16;$
$\qquad\qquad\qquad\qquad m_{13}=580;\ m_{21}=1.22460635382e{-}16;$
$\qquad\qquad\qquad\qquad m_{22}=-1;\ m_{23}=660\}$

$rot_3 : transformation = \{m_{11}=-1;\ m_{12}=-1.22460635382e{-}16;$
$\qquad\qquad\qquad\qquad m_{13}=700;\ m_{21}=1.22460635382e{-}16;$
$\qquad\qquad\qquad\qquad m_{22}=-1;\ m_{23}=650\}$

Figure 9.13 corresponds to the value of the expression:

```
#let tiling₂ =
    make_tiling tile₂ [id_trans;rot₁;rot₂;rot₃];;
tiling₂ : picture = ⟨abstract⟩
```

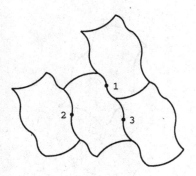

Figure 9.13. Tiling 2

9.3.2 Generating Transformations

To generate an arbitrarily large subset of a tiling of a plane, we must be able to generate automatically the elements of the group of transformations used. One approach is to use CAML objects of type **transformation** directly. Another approach, preferable for several reasons, is to manage the group of transformations formally. We will present that approach in Section 9.3.4.

In this section, we will use the CAML type **transformation** directly to represent the group generators. We will use **comp_trans** to compose transformations.

We have to test equality between transformations in a way that avoids redundant lists that lead to graphically correct but uselessly over-sized objects (over-sized because each instance of the pattern appears in many copies). However, equality between objects of type **transformation** depends on equality between floating-point numbers and thus cannot exactly reflect equality between products of generators. This equality can be taken into account perfectly only when we use a formal representation of symmetry groups, as we do in Section 9.3.4.

The function **power** is an auxiliary function to produce non-redundant lists of generators.

```
#let rec map_append f = fun
    [ ] → [ ]
  | (a::l) → (f a) @ map_append f l;;
map_append : (α → β list) → α list → β list = ⟨fun⟩

#let product f l₁ l₂ =
    map_append (fun x → (map (f x) l₂)) l₁;;
product : (α → β → γ) → α list → β list → γ list = ⟨fun⟩

#let power f x l =
    pwr [x]
```

where rec pwr ll = **fun**
   0 → ll
  | n → (set_of_list ll) @ pwr (product f l ll) (n−1);;
power : $(\alpha \to \beta \to \beta) \to \beta \to \alpha$ *list* $\to$ *int* $\to \beta$ *list* = ⟨**fun**⟩

The following function then simply generates the transformation group[1]:

#let generate_transformations_group =
   power comp_trans id_trans;;
generate_transformations_group
    : *transformation list* → *int* → *transformation list* = ⟨**fun**⟩

Figure 9.14 corresponds to the value of the expression:

#let $tiling_3$ =
   make_tiling $tile_2$ (generate_transformations_group
               [rot_1;rot_2;rot_3] 3);;
$tiling_3$: *picture* = ⟨**abstract**⟩

There we simply added the sequence of transformations to produce it to every copy of the basic pattern.

Obviously, you noticed that because the tilings we are considering are periodic, we can build them from the corresponding translations. To do so, we simply first construct the periodic pattern and then repeat it by translation. The following expression corresponds to the pattern in Figure 9.15.

#let $tiling_4$ =
  let tile = group_pictures
           [$tile_2$; transform_picture rot_3 $tile_2$]
  and tr_1 = comp_trans rot_3 rot_2
  and tr_2 = comp_trans rot_1 rot_3 **in**
  let tile' = make_tiling tile (generate_transformations_group [tr_1] 3)
  in make_tiling
      tile' (generate_transformations_group [tr_2] 3);;
$tiling_4$: *picture* = ⟨**abstract**⟩

9.3.3 Colored Tilings

We get colored tilings by associating permutations of a finite set of colors with the transformations of a symmetry group.

---

[1]We generate the entire group only if the list passed as an argument simultaneously contains the generators and their inverses, but in general it is not useful to produce tiling fragments.

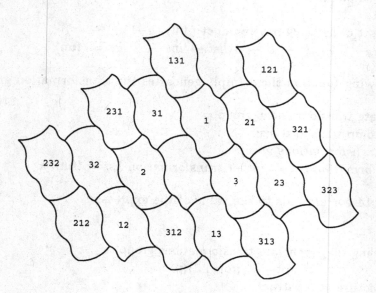

Figure 9.14. Tiling 3

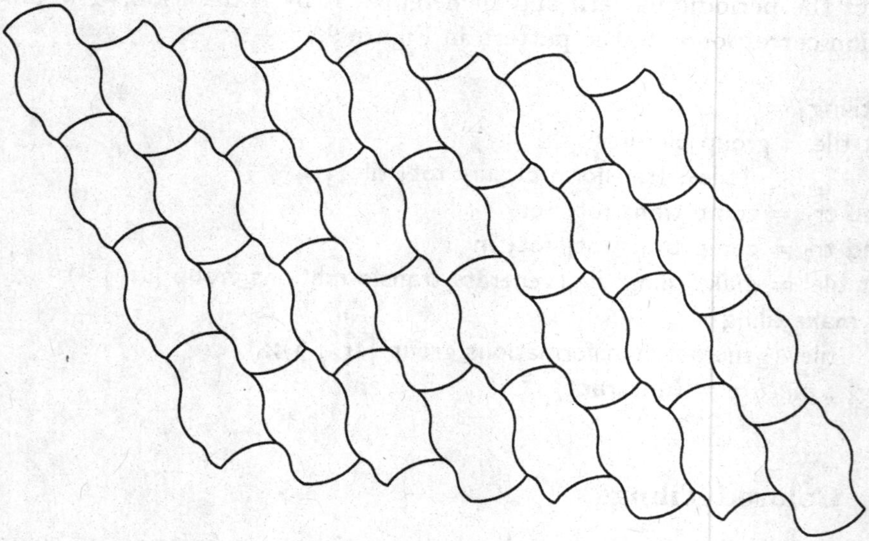

Figure 9.15. Tiling 4

These permutations could be represented, for example, by vectors of integers of size n where the values are a permutation of the set $\{0, 1, \ldots, n\}$. The following function composes permutations:

```
#let cpermut v v'=
    let n = vect_length v and n' = vect_length v' in
    if n ≠ n' then failwith "cpermut: non compatible args"
    else let w = make_vect n 0 in
        (try cp (n−1)
         with _ → failwith "cpermut: wrong arg")
        where rec cp=
        fun 0 → (w.(0)←v'.(v.(0)); w)
          | i → (w.(i)←v'.(v.(i)); cp(i−1));;
cpermut : int vect → int vect → int vect = ⟨fun⟩
```

The following function gives us the identity permutation of a set of k elements:

```
#let id_permut k =
    let w = make_vect k 0
    in ic (k−1)
        where rec ic = fun
            0 → (w.(0)←0; w)
          | i → (w.(i)←i; ic(i−1));;
id_permut : int → int vect = ⟨fun⟩
```

Colored transformations are represented by pairs consisting of a color transformation and a geometric transformation.
The following function generates a group of colored transformations:

```
#let pairing f g = fun
    (x,y) (x',y') → (f x x', g y y');;
pairing : (α → β → γ) → (δ → ε → φ) → α * δ → β * ε → γ * φ
        = ⟨fun⟩
```

```
#let generate_coltrans_group trl n =
    match trl with
      [] → []
    | _ → let k = vect_length (fst(hd trl)) in
            set_of_list
                (power (pairing cpermut comp_trans)
                    (id_permut k,id_trans) trl n);;
generate_coltrans_group : (int vect * transformation) list
                            → int → (int vect * transformation) list
                        = ⟨fun⟩
```

The basic patterns that transformations operate on will no longer be values of type picture, but rather values of type (int * linestyle * sketch), where the integer indicates a color.

The function make_tiling will now need a supplementary argument to handle the correspondence between colors and the integers appearing in the permutations.

```
#let make_colored_tiling (c,lsty,sk) col trans =
    group_pictures
      (map (fun (v,t) →
                    (transform_picture
                      t (group_pictures
                          [make_fill_picture (Nzfill,col v.(c)) sk;
                           make_closed_draw_picture (lsty,black) sk])))
          trans);;
```
*make_colored_tiling : int * linestyle * sketch*
$\rightarrow (\alpha \rightarrow color) \rightarrow (\alpha\ vect * transformation)\ list$
$\rightarrow picture = \langle$**fun**$\rangle$

We will go back to the example in Figure 9.14, associating permutations on three colors with the transformations there.

```
#let color_of_int =fun
    0 → Gra 0.2
  | 1 → Gra 0.4
  | 2 → Gra 0.7
  | _ → failwith "color_of_int: wrong int";;
```
color_of_int : int → color = $\langle$**fun**$\rangle$

```
#let ct₁ = [| 1; 0; 2 |] and ct₂ = [| 2; 1; 0 |];;
```
$ct_1 :$ *int vect* $= [|\ 1;\ 0;\ 2\ |]$
$ct_2 :$ *int vect* $= [|\ 2;\ 1;\ 0\ |]$

We get the tiling in Figure 9.16 in this way:

```
#let tiling₅ =
    let lsty = {linewidth= 2.0; linecap=Buttcap;
                linejoin=Beveljoin; dashpattern=[ ]}
    in make_colored_tiling (0, lsty, tile2sk) color_of_int
        (generate_coltrans_group
            [(ct₁,rot₁);(ct₁,rot₂);(ct₂,rot₃)] 4);;
```
$tiling_5 :$ *picture* $= \langle$**abstract**$\rangle$

Figure 9.16. Tiling 5

9.3.4 Handling Transformations Formally

The approach we have followed up to now—using the CAML type transformation to represent objects of a symmetry group—has a major drawback. With it, we cannot master the identity of transformations. Since this representation uses approximate numbers (namely, floating-point numbers), formally identical transformations are quite possibly considered distinct. More generally, this approach does not preserve the structure of elements in the group. For example, we cannot systematically reproduce tilings in which each tile contains information about how it was gotten. See Figure 9.14 for an example of what we mean.

To remedy this lamentable situation, we will use a formal representation of the transformations as a group. The composition of elements of the group will occur at a formal level, and the type transformation will be translated into objects once the computations have been carried out.

Notice that at this formal level, the identity is still problematic because the identity test of two elements given as a sequence of generators is not possible for every group. This test is known in group theory as solving the word problem. Fortunately, tiling groups pose a word problem that is decidable, and moreover, their elements have a canonical form that can be achieved through simplification. However, this canonical form that can be reached through simplification depends on the generators we choose. We will come back to this point later.

Elements of a transformation group will be represented by a list of generators.

The identity will be represented by the empty list.

The basic operation that we will use is composition of a generator by any element represented by a list.

A transformation group will be defined by a list of generators and a function. That function composes a generator with a list of generators representing an element of the group in order to get a new list of generators, like this:

```
#type α tgroup =
    {tgroup_gens:α list;
     tgroup_op: α → α list → α list};;
```

```
#let make_tgroup trl top =
  {tgroup_gens=trl;
   tgroup_op=top};;
```
$make\_tgroup : \alpha\ list \rightarrow (\alpha \rightarrow \alpha\ list \rightarrow \alpha\ list) \rightarrow \alpha\ tgroup = \langle\mathbf{fun}\rangle$

As we generate, we eliminate the elements that are not in canonical form. To do so, we make the composition function create an exception when the element being constructed is not in canonical form.

For example, the symmetry group **p1** in the example in Figure 9.11 has a particularly simple structure because it is generated by two translations, denoted A and B, that are commutative. Obviously, the canonical form involves first producing all the translations of the first type and then all the translations of the second type.

If we denote the inverse of A as a and the inverse of B as b, then the simplification rules to put the elements of a group into canonical form are the following:

$$
\begin{array}{rcl}
BA & \rightarrow & AB \\
Ba & \rightarrow & aB \\
bA & \rightarrow & Ab \\
ba & \rightarrow & ab
\end{array}
$$

```
#exception Group_gen_exc;;
```
Exception Group_gen_exc defined.

```
#type p1_gen = TA | TB | Ta | Tb;;
```

```
#let p1_op = fun
    TA → (fun [ ] → [TA]
            | (((TA|TB|Tb)::tl) as tl') → TA::tl'
            | (Ta::_) → raise Group_gen_exc)
  | TB → (fun [ ] → [TB]
            | ((TB::tl) as tl') → TB::tl'
```

```
                      |  ((TA|Ta|Tb)::_) → raise Group_gen_exc)
          |  Ta → (fun [ ] → [Ta]
                      |  (((Ta|TB|Tb)::tl) as tl') → Ta::tl'
                      |  (TA::_) → raise Group_gen_exc)
          |  Tb → (fun [ ] → [Tb]
                      |  ((Tb::tl) as tl') → Tb::tl'
                      |  ((TA|Ta|TB)::_) → raise Group_gen_exc);;
```

p1_op : p1_gen → p1_gen list → p1_gen list = ⟨**fun**⟩

```
#let p1_group =
    {tgroup_gens= [TA;TB;Ta;Tb];
     tgroup_op= p1_op};;
```

p1_group : p1_gen tgroup = {tgroup_gens=[TA; TB; Ta; Tb];
                            tgroup_op= ⟨fun⟩}

The generation functions must be modified slightly to take into account any possible exceptions. However, it is no longer necessary to eliminate redundancy in the lists produced, and this fact simplifies the function **power**.

```
#let rec map_try f = fun
    [ ] → [ ]
  | (a::l) → if (try f a; true with _ → false)
             then (f a) :: map_try f l
             else map_try f l;;
```

map_try : (α → β) → α list → β list = ⟨**fun**⟩

```
#let rec product f l₁ l₂ =
    match l₁ with
      [ ] → [ ]
    | (a::l) → map_try (f a) l₂ @ product f l l₂;;
```

product : (α → β → γ) → α list → β list → γ list = ⟨**fun**⟩

```
#let power f x l =
    pwr [x]
    where rec pwr ll = fun
      0 → ll
    | n → ll@ pwr (product f l ll) (n−1);;
```

power : (α → β → β) → β → α list → int → β list = ⟨**fun**⟩

The generation function takes only one argument: the group under consideration.

```
#let generate_transformations_group tgroup=
    power tgroup.tgroup_op [ ] tgroup.tgroup_gens;;
```

generate_transformations_group : α tgroup → int → α list list
                            = ⟨fun⟩

After we produce a list of the elements in the group, we translate these elements into geometric transformations. For examples that involve tiling a plane, like the ones we showed you earlier, these geometric transformations will be linear, represented by values of type transformation, but we reserve the right to produce non-linear transformations, which will simply be of type point $\rightarrow$ point.

For the group of the tiling you see in Figure 9.11, the function p1_transfo converts the list of generators into transformations.

```
#let p1_transfo =
  let transfo =
    let trans₁ = point_translation ptA₁ ptC₁
    and trans₂ = point_translation ptA₁ ptE₁
    in fun TA → trans₁
       |  TB → trans₂
       |  Ta → inverse_transformation trans₁
       |  Tb → inverse_transformation trans₂
    in it_list (fun t t' → comp_trans t (transfo t')) id_trans;;
p1_transfo : p1_gen list → transformation = ⟨fun⟩
```

Figure 9.17 is:

```
#let tiling₆ =
  make_tiling tile₁
    (map p1_transfo
       (generate_transformations_group p1_group 3));;
tiling₆ : picture = ⟨abstract⟩
```

The symmetry group **p2** corresponds to the tilings in Figures 9.14 and 9.15. When it is presented as three generators that are central symmetries, it does not have a canonical form that we can get through local simplifications.

In contrast, it is possible to get a canonical form when this group is presented as two translations and a central symmetry. If R_1, R_2, and R_3 are three central symmetries, we can generate the same group by keeping, say, R_2 and adding the translations $R_2 R_1$ and $R_2 R_3$.

If we denote the two translations as A and B, the rotation as C, and their inverses as a, b, and c, then we get the canonical form of the elements of the group through these simplifications:

$$
\begin{array}{rclrcl}
c & \rightarrow & C & CC & \rightarrow & 1 \\
Ca & \rightarrow & AC & Cb & \rightarrow & BC \\
CA & \rightarrow & aC & CB & \rightarrow & bC \\
BA & \rightarrow & AB & Ba & \rightarrow & aB \\
bA & \rightarrow & Ab & ba & \rightarrow & ab
\end{array}
$$

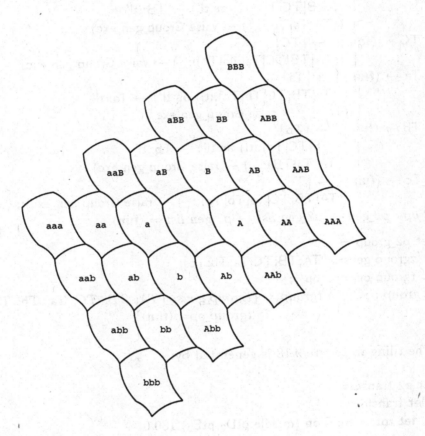

Figure 9.17. Tiling 6

```
#type p2_gen = TA | TB | TC | Ta | Tb | Tc;;


#let p2_op = fun
   TA → (fun [ ] → [TA]
           | (((TA|TB|TC|Tb|Tc)::tl) as tl') → TA::tl'
           | (Ta::_) → raise Group_gen_exc)
 | TB → (fun [ ] → [TB]
           | (((TB|TC|Tc)::tl) as tl') → TB::tl'
           | ((TA|Ta|Tb)::_) → raise Group_gen_exc)
 | TC → (fun [ ] → [TC]
           | ((TA|TB|TC|Ta|Tb|Tc)::_) → raise Group_gen_exc)
 | Ta → (fun [ ] → [Ta]
           | (((Ta|TB|TC|Tb|Tc)::tl) as tl') → Ta::tl'
           | (TA::_) → raise Group_gen_exc)
 | Tb → (fun [ ] → [Tb]
           | (((Tb|TC|Tc)::tl) as tl') → Tb::tl'
           | ((TA|Ta|TB)::_) → raise Group_gen_exc)
 | Tc → (fun [ ] → [TC]
           | ((TA|TB|TC|Ta|Tb|Tc)::_) → raise Group_gen_exc);;
```
*p2_op : p2_gen → p2_gen list → p2_gen list = ⟨**fun**⟩*

```
#let p2_group =
  {tgroup_gens= [TA;TB;TC;Ta;Tb;Tc];
   tgroup_op= p2_op};;
```
p2_group : p2_gen tgroup = {tgroup_gens=[TA; TB; TC; Ta; Tb; Tc];
                            *tgroup_op= ⟨**fun**⟩}*

The tiling in Figure 9.18 is generated by:

```
#let p2_transfo=
  let transfo =
    let rot₁= rotation (middle ptD₂ ptE₂) 180.0
    and rot₂= rotation (middle ptA₂ ptF₂) 180.0
    and rot₃= rotation (middle ptC₂ ptD₂) 180.0
    in fun TA → comp_trans rot₂ rot₁
        | TB → comp_trans rot₂ rot₃
        | TC → rot₂
        | Ta → inverse_transformation (comp_trans rot₂ rot₁)
        | Tb → inverse_transformation (comp_trans rot₂ rot₃)
        | Tc → rot₃
  in it_list (fun t t' → comp_trans t (transfo t')) id_trans;;
```
*p2_transfo : p2_gen list → transformation = ⟨**fun**⟩*

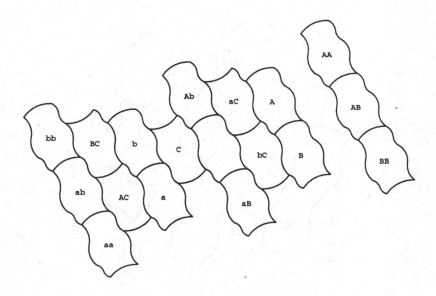

Figure 9.18. Tiling 7

```
#let tiling₇=
   make_tiling tile₂
      (map p2_transfo
         (generate_transformations_group p2_group 2));;
tiling₇ : picture = ⟨abstract⟩
```

From this example, you can see that representing a tiling as a group with our generation algorithm may result in unconnected partial tilings or simply in tilings that are badly distributed spatially. To remedy these problems, we have several possibilities.

We could reorganize the basic pattern with its image by the rotation C. We could then generate the tiling that we want by using only two translations, as in the preceding example. This solution is applicable to any tiling group that includes two translations. However, it is inconvenient since it does not exactly reflect the structure of the symmetry group. For example, it is quite impossible to produce an image like the one in Figure 9.18 (with its labels) this way. Likewise, producing colored tilings also generally becomes impossible this way.

Another solution is to take a set of generators that result in a good spatial distribution but to be careful to eliminate redundancy. This solution assumes that we compute the normal form for all the elements we build—a more costly task than purely and simply eliminating the elements that are not in normal form (as we have been doing up to now).

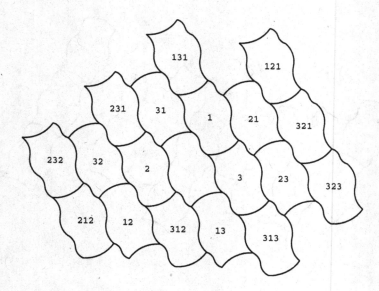

Figure 9.19. Tiling 8

We will not detail here the functions to compute normal forms and to eliminate redundant elements. Figure 9.19 shows you what we get for the tiling group **p2** when we use three rotations as generators. The three rotations are denoted 1, 2, and 3. This figure is identical to Figure 9.14.

To create a colored tiling, we simultaneously use a group of transformations and a group of permutations (of the colors). The type **ctgroup** organizes the necessary information, namely, the list of generators, the list of associated color permutations, and the composition operation.

```
#type α ctgroup =
      {ctgroup_tgens: α list;
       ctgroup_colgens: int vect list;
       ctgroup_top: α → α list → α list};;
Type ctgroup defined.

#let make_ctgroup trl ctrl top =
   if list_length trl ≠ list_length ctrl
     or list_length trl=0
       or (let n = vect_length (hd ctrl)
             in exists (fun v → vect_length v ≠ n) (tl ctrl))
   then failwith "make_ctgroup: wrong ctgroup"
   else {ctgroup_tgens=trl;
```

```
            ctgroup_colgens=ctrl;
            ctgroup_top=top};;
```
$make\_ctgroup : \alpha\ list \rightarrow int\ vect\ list \rightarrow (\alpha \rightarrow \alpha\ list \rightarrow \alpha\ list)$
$$\rightarrow \alpha\ ctgroup = \langle \mathbf{fun}\rangle$$

The generation function then becomes this:

```
#let generate_coltrans_group ctgroup =
   let k= vect_length (hd ctgroup.ctgroup_colgens)
   in
   power (pairing cpermut ctgroup.ctgroup_top)
      (id_permut k,[ ])
      (combine (ctgroup.ctgroup_colgens, ctgroup.ctgroup_tgens));;
```
$generate\_coltrans\_group : \alpha\ ctgroup \rightarrow int \rightarrow (int\ vect * \alpha\ list)\ list$
$$= \langle \mathbf{fun}\rangle$$

Now in this context, let's look again at the tiling in Figure 9.16. The color group is the group of permutations on a set of three elements.

```
#let p2_ctgroup =
   make_ctgroup [R₁;R₂;R₃] [ct₁;ct₁;ct₂] p2_op;;
```
$p2\_ctgroup : p2\_gen\ ctgroup$
$$= \{ctgroup\_tgens=[R_1;\ R_2;\ R_3];$$
$$ctgroup\_colgens=[[|\,1;\ 0;\ 2\,|];\ [|\,1;\ 0;\ 2\,|];\ [|\,2;\ 1;\ 0\,|]];$$
$$ctgroup\_top= \langle\mathbf{fun}\rangle\}$$

Here is how we write the elements of the colored group as effective transformations.

```
#let p2c_transfo=
   let transfo =
     fun R₁ → rotation (middle ptD₂ ptE₂) 180.0
      | R₂ → rotation (middle ptA₂ ptF₂) 180.0
      | R₃ → rotation (middle ptC₂ ptD₂) 180.0
   in fun (ct,tl) →
              (ct, it_list (fun t t' → comp_trans t (transfo t'))
                   id_trans tl);;
```
$p2c\_transfo : \alpha * p2\_gen\ list \rightarrow \alpha * transformation = \langle\mathbf{fun}\rangle$

We assume that the function simplify_p2c exists to eliminate redundancy from the list of transformations.

```
#simplify_p2c;;
```
$- : (\alpha * \beta\ list)\ list \rightarrow (\alpha * \beta\ list)\ list = \langle\mathbf{fun}\rangle$

Figure 9.20. Tiling 9

We get Figure 9.20 from the following definition:

```
#let tiling₉=
   let lsty = {linewidth= 2.0;linecap=Buttcap;
               linejoin=Beveljoin;dashpattern=[ ]}
   in make_colored_tiling (0,lsty,tile2sk) color_of_int
       (map p2c_transfo
           (simplify_p2c (generate_coltrans_group p2_ctgroup 4)));;
tiling₉ : picture = ⟨abstract⟩
```

9.4   Tiling a Hyperbolic Plane

By the same techniques, it is possible to produce drawings like the one in Figure 9.26 on page 334 which imitates an engraving known as **Circle Limit III**, by M. C. Escher. The first version of this drawing was programmed by Antoine Chambert-Loir.

This one involves not a tiling of an ordinary plane but of a hyperbolic plane. The main consequence for us is that the isometries in it are no longer linear transformations and thus can no longer be represented by the type **transformation**.

Hyperbolic geometry differs from Euclidean geometry in the fact that the Euclidean axiom

> Given a point A and a straight line d that does not pass through A, there exists at most one straight line d' passing through A and not intersecting d.

is replaced by the axiom

> Given a point A and a straight line d that does not pass through A, there exists at least one straight line d' passing through A and not intersecting d.

H. Poincaré developed a model of hyperbolic geometry where the points are points in the disk of radius one in the Euclidean plane, points on the circle of radius one being excluded. The "straight lines" are circle arcs perpendicular to the unit circle and diameters of this circle. In this model, through any point not on a straight line d, there are infinitely many straight lines that do not intersect d and exactly two straight lines "parallel" to d (those which "touch" d on the unit circle.

We represent the points of Poincaré's disk by complex numbers with modulus strictly less than 1 and therefore we need a complex arithmetic in CAML. Then, hyperbolic transformations will be defined as operations on complex numbers.

9.4.1 Complex Arithmetic

In this section, we will use the trigonometric functions sinus and cosinus working with angles expressed in degrees (rather than the usual CAML trig functions, that work with angles expressed in radians).

```
#type complex= {re_part:float; im_part:float};;
```

```
#let mk_cx r i= {re_part=r; im_part=i};;
mk_cx : float → float → complex = ⟨fun⟩
```

```
#let cx_1 = mk_cx 1.0 0.0
  and cx_0 = mk_cx 0.0 0.0;;
cx_1 : complex = {re_part=1; im_part=0}
cx_0 : complex = {re_part=0; im_part=0}
```

```
#let cx_of_pol rho theta= {re_part=rho*.cosinus theta;
                           im_part=rho*.sinus theta};;
cx_of_pol : float → float → complex = ⟨fun⟩
```

```
#let point_of_cx {re_part=r; im_part=i} = {xc=r; yc=i};;
point_of_cx : complex → point = ⟨fun⟩

#let cx_of_point {xc=r; yc=i} = {re_part=r; im_part=i};;
cx_of_point : point → complex = ⟨fun⟩
```

Here are the basic operations on complex numbers:

```
#let conjugate {re_part=r; im_part=i} = {re_part=r; im_part= −.i};;
conjugate : complex → complex = ⟨fun⟩

#let module {re_part=r; im_part=i}= sqrt(r*.r +. i*.i);;
module : complex → float = ⟨fun⟩

#let add_cx {re_part=r₁; im_part=i₁} {re_part=r₂; im_part=i₂}=
    {re_part=r₁+.r₂; im_part=i₁+.i₂};;
add_cx : complex → complex → complex = ⟨fun⟩

#let sub_cx {re_part=r₁; im_part=i₁} {re_part=r₂; im_part=i₂}=
    {re_part=r₁−.r₂; im_part=i₁−.i₂};;
sub_cx : complex → complex → complex = ⟨fun⟩

#let uminus_cx {re_part=r; im_part=i}= {re_part= −.r; im_part= −.i};;
uminus_cx : complex → complex = ⟨fun⟩

#let mult_cx {re_part=r₁; im_part=i₁} {re_part=r₂; im_part=i₂}=
    {re_part=r₁*.r₂−.i₁*.i₂; im_part=i₁*.r₂+.i₂*.r₁};;
mult_cx : complex → complex → complex = ⟨fun⟩

#let div_cx {re_part=r₁; im_part=i₁} {re_part=r₂; im_part=i₂}=
    let rho= r₂*.r₂ +. i₂*.i₂ in
    if rho=0.0 then failwith "cdiv: division by zero"
    else {re_part=(r₁*.r₂+.i₁*.i₂)/.rho;
          im_part=(i₁*.r₂−.r₁*.i₂)/.rho};;
div_cx : complex → complex → complex = ⟨fun⟩
```

9.4.2 Hyperbolic Isometries

In the Euclidean plane, any isometry can be obtained as compositions of reflections with respect to straight lines. Similarly, in Poincaré's model of hyperbolic geometry, the isometries are obtained as compositions of inversions.

The inversion with respect to a circle with center u and radius r is the transformation which associates with any complex z a complex z' defined by

$$z' - u = \frac{r^2}{\bar{z} - \bar{u}}$$

where $\bar{z}$ and $\bar{u}$ are the conjugates of z and u. This transformation can thus be presented as a negative homography, i.e. a function

$$z' = \frac{a\bar{z} + b}{c\bar{z} + d}$$

with $ad - bc \neq 0$.

Moreover, if the inversion circle is orthogonal to the unit circle, then $\bar{a}c = \bar{b}d$.

When two negative homographies are composed, the result is a positive homography, i.e. a function

$$z' = \frac{az + b}{cz + d}$$

with $ad - bc \neq 0$ and it is easy to check that if the two homographies satisfy $\bar{a}c = \bar{b}d$, then their compositions satisfy the same property.

In particular, the hyperbolic rotations that we will use for the Escher tiling can be obtained as the compositions of inversions with respect to two intersecting lines. They are positive homographies satisfying $\bar{a}c = \bar{b}d$ and any composition of such homographies still satisfy the same property.

This property enable us to present hyperbolic rotations in a more simple way using the form

$$h_{a,\mu} = \mu \frac{z + a}{1 + \bar{a}z}$$

For that purpose, it suffices to take $\mu = \frac{a}{d}$ and $a = \frac{b}{a}$. The positive hyperbolic isometries will thus be defined by giving two complex numbers a and μ.

```
#type hyp_isometry= {iso_m:complex; iso_a:complex};;
```

```
#let hyp_identity = {iso_m=cx_1; iso_a=cx_0};;
hyp_identity : hyp_isometry = {iso_m={re_part=1; im_part=0};
                               iso_a={re_part=0; im_part=0}}
```

The application of a hyperbolic isometry is defined by:

```
#let apply_hyp_iso {iso_m=mu; iso_a=a} z=
  mult_cx mu (div_cx (add_cx z a)
                     (add_cx cx_1 (mult_cx (conjugate a) z)));;
apply_hyp_iso : hyp_isometry → complex → complex = ⟨fun⟩
```

We get the composition of two isometries in left to right order by:

```
#let compose_hyp_iso {isoₘ=mu₁; isoₐ=a₁} {isoₘ=mu₂; isoₐ=a₂}=
   {isoₘ= div_cx (mult_cx mu₂ (add_cx mu₁ (mult_cx a₂ (conjugate a₁))))
           (add_cx cx_1 (mult_cx mu₁ (mult_cx (conjugate a₂) a₁)));
    isoₐ= div_cx (add_cx a₂ (mult_cx mu₁ a₁))
           (add_cx mu₁ (mult_cx a₂ (conjugate a₁)))};;
compose_hyp_iso : hyp_isometry → hyp_isometry → hyp_isometry = ⟨fun⟩
```

Hyperbolic rotations denoted $r_{a,\theta}$ of the center a and angle θ are defined as the conjugate of the Euclidean rotation of the center 0 and angle θ by the isometry $h_{a,1}$:

$$r_{a,\theta} = h_{a,1}^{-1} \circ r_{O,\theta} \circ h_{a,1}$$

```
#let hyp_rotation center angle=
   compose_hyp_iso
     {isoₘ=cx_1; isoₐ=uminus_cx center}
     (compose_hyp_iso
        {isoₘ=mk_cx (cosinus angle) (sinus angle);
         isoₐ=cx_0}
        {isoₘ=cx_1; isoₐ=center});;
hyp_rotation : complex → float → hyp_isometry = ⟨fun⟩
```

Hyperbolic isometries do not preserve Euclidean distance, but they do preserve angles, so you can still recognize figures in spite of these isometries. Triangles in hyperbolic geometry have a sum of angles strictly less than π, and reciprocally, for every triple of positive real numbers, a, b, and c, where $a + b + c < \pi$, there is a triangle with angles a, b, and c.

As a consequence, for the positive integers (that is, the natural numbers) n, p, and q such that $\frac{1}{n} + \frac{1}{p} + \frac{1}{q} < 1$, there exists a triangle with angles $\frac{\pi}{n}$, $\frac{\pi}{p}$, and $\frac{\pi}{q}$. Moreover, if we unite this triangle with one of its symmetries along one side, then we get a kind of hyperbolic "quadrilateral" to tile the plane in three rotations where the centers are the nodes of the triangle and the angles are $\frac{2\pi}{n}$, $\frac{2\pi}{p}$, and $\frac{2\pi}{q}$.

9.4.3   Escher's Fish

Escher chose a triangle with these nodes: a point A located on the x-axis, a point B which is the image of A in a 45 degree rotation around the origin, and a point C which is the origin of the coordinate system. The respective angles are 60, 60, and 45 degrees.

Point A is chosen so that there exists a hyperbolic line passing through A and B and making an angle of 120 degrees with the x-axis. Its x abscissa is defined by

$$x^2 = \frac{tan\frac{\pi}{6} - tan\frac{\pi}{8}}{tan\frac{\pi}{6} + tan\frac{\pi}{8}}$$

or

$$x^2 = \frac{sin\frac{\pi}{24}}{sin\frac{7\pi}{24}}$$

We add a point D, which is the image of A simultaneously in the rotation at an angle of 90 degrees around the center C and in the rotation at an angle of -120 degrees around the center B. In that way, we get the fundamental pattern for tiling. Instead of this quadrilateral itself, we can choose a slightly deformed figure so that this deformation will be compatible with rotations. For example, we could choose arbitrary lines for the sides AC and DB and get CD and BA by rotation around C and B.

Nevertheless, we have to be careful that the segments joining points are ordinary planar segments, not hyperbolic segments. If we want transformed figures that are not too deformed and in particular if we want the angles to be reasonably preserved, then we have to take sufficiently many points.

The basic pattern to produce Escher's tiling is the fish in Figure 9.21. The nodes of the triangle and the contour of the fish are defined like this:

```
#let ptA = cx_of_pol (sqrt(sinus 7.5 /. sinus 52.5)) 0.0;;
ptA : complex = {re_part=0.405616400802; im_part=0}

#let ptB = cx_of_pol (sqrt(sinus 7.5 /. sinus 52.5)) 45.0;;
ptB : complex = {re_part=0.286814107567;
                 im_part=0.286814107567}

#let ptC = cx_0;;
ptC : complex = {re_part=0; im_part=0}

#let rotA = hyp_rotation ptA 120.0;;
rotA : hyp_isometry = {iso_m={re_part=-0.707106781187;
                              im_part=0.707106781187};
                       iso_a={re_part=-0.594603557501;
                              im_part=-0.246292857752}}

#let rotB = hyp_rotation ptB 120.0;;
rotB : hyp_isometry = {iso_m={re_part=-0.707106781187;
                              im_part=0.707106781187};
                       iso_a={re_part=-0.246292857752;
                              im_part=-0.594603557501}}
```

```
#let rotC = hyp_rotation ptC 90.0;;
rotC : hyp_isometry = {iso_m={re_part=6.12303176911e-17;
                              im_part=1};
                       iso_a={re_part=0; im_part=0}}

#let ptD = apply_hyp_iso rotC ptA;;
ptD : complex = {re_part=2.48360210818e-17;
                 im_part=0.405616400802}


#let p_0 = ptA
  and p_1 = mk_cx (0.32) (-0.018)
  and p_2 = mk_cx (0.24) (0.0)
  and p_3 = mk_cx (0.2) (-0.1)
  and p_4 = mk_cx (0.09) (-0.14);;

#let p_5 = ptC
  and p_6 = apply_hyp_iso rotC p_4
  and p_7 = apply_hyp_iso rotC p_3
  and p_8 = apply_hyp_iso rotC p_2
  and p_9 = apply_hyp_iso rotC p_1
  and p_10 = apply_hyp_iso rotC p_0;;

#let p_11 = mk_cx (0.08) (0.355)
  and p_12 = mk_cx (0.155) (0.338)
  and p_13 = mk_cx (0.18) (0.25)
  and p_14 = mk_cx (0.25) (0.2);;

#let p_15 = ptB
  and p_16 = apply_hyp_iso rotB p_14
  and p_17 = apply_hyp_iso rotB p_13
  and p_18 = apply_hyp_iso rotB p_12
  and p_19 = apply_hyp_iso rotB p_11;;
```

This definition does not include the interior decorations.

9.4.4 The Isometry Group

For the hyperbolic tiling, the group of isometries that we used is (3,3,4) for which we happen to know a canonical representation. This representation uses three generators that we denote as TA, TB, and TC (they correspond to the three rotations around the centers A, B, and C) and their three inverses, denoted as Ta, Tb, and Tc.

```
#type escher_gen = TA | TB | TC | Ta | Tb | Tc ;;
```

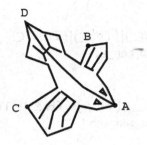

Figure 9.21. The basic fish pattern

Simplification rules let us put these elements into canonical form. If we leave out the obvious rules about inverses ($Aa = 1$ and $aA = 1$), and we compose from left to right, then those simplification rules are the following:

$$
\begin{array}{rclrcl}
cA & \rightarrow & Ba & bA & \rightarrow & Bc \\
cc & \rightarrow & CC & ca & \rightarrow & B \\
bc & \rightarrow & A & CB & \rightarrow & a \\
aa & \rightarrow & A & AA & \rightarrow & a \\
BB & \rightarrow & b & bb & \rightarrow & B \\
BA & \rightarrow & c & ab & \rightarrow & C \\
AC & \rightarrow & b & aB & \rightarrow & Cb \\
aC & \rightarrow & Ab & cB & \rightarrow & CCa \\
bCC & \rightarrow & Ac & CCC & \rightarrow & c
\end{array}
$$

The function escher_op constructs the elements of the group by eliminating the elements that can be simplified.

```
#let escher_op = fun
   TA → (fun [ ] → [TA]
             | ((TA::_)|(TC::_)|(Ta::_)) → raise Group_gen_exc
             | tl → TA::tl)
 | TB → (fun [ ] → [TB]
             | ((TB::_)|(TA::_)|(Tb::_)) → raise Group_gen_exc
             | tl → TB::tl)
 | TC → (fun [ ] → [TC]
             | ((TB::_)|(Tc::_)|(TC::TC::_)) → raise Group_gen_exc
             | tl → TC::tl)
 | Ta → (fun [ ] → [Ta]
             | ((Ta::_)|(Tb::_)|(TC::_)|(TB::_)|(TA::_))
                 → raise Group_gen_exc
```

```
                        |  tl → Ta::tl)
          | Tb → (fun [ ] → [Tb]
                    |  ((TA::_)|(Tc::_)|(Tb::_)|(TC::TC::_)|(TB::_))
                       → raise Group_gen_exc
                    |  tl → Tb::tl)
          | Tc → (fun [ ] → [Tc]
                    |  ((TA::_)|(Tc::_)|(Ta::_)|(TB::_)|(TC::_))
                       → raise Group_gen_exc
                    |  tl → Tc::tl);;
```

escher_op : escher_gen → escher_gen list → escher_gen list = ⟨**fun**⟩

We begin by producing an uncolored tiling in which we will display transformations.

```
#let escher_group =
   make_tgroup [TA;TB;TC;Ta;Tb;Tc] escher_op;;
```
escher_group
   : *escher_gen tgroup*
   = {*tgroup_gens*=[*TA*; *TB*; *TC*; *Ta*; *Tb*; *Tc*]; *tgroup_op*= ⟨**fun**⟩}

To convert the lists of generators into hyperbolic isometries, we use this function:

```
#let escher_transfo =
   let transfo = fun
     TA → hyp_rotation ptA 120.0
   | TB → hyp_rotation ptB 120.0
   | TC → hyp_rotation ptC 90.0
   | Ta → hyp_rotation ptA (−.120.0)
   | Tb → hyp_rotation ptB (−.120.0)
   | Tc → hyp_rotation ptC (−.90.0)
   in (fun (ct,tl) →
              (ct, it_list (fun t t' → compose_hyp_iso t (transfo t'))
                   hyp_identity tl));;
```
escher_transfo : α ∗ escher_gen list → α ∗ hyp_isometry = ⟨**fun**⟩

To display the transformations carried out, we will slightly modify this function so that it produces pairs of a tag and a transformation.

```
#let escher_tag_transfo =
   let transfo = fun
     TA → ("A", hyp_rotation ptA 120.0)
   | TB → ("B", hyp_rotation ptB 120.0)
```

```
  | TC → ("C", hyp_rotation ptC 90.0)
  | Ta → ("a", hyp_rotation ptA (−.120.0))
  | Tb → ("b", hyp_rotation ptB (−.120.0))
  | Tc → ("c", hyp_rotation ptC (−.90.0))
  in it_list (fun (s,t) c →
                    let (s',t') = transfo c
                    in (s^s', compose_hyp_iso t t'))
        ("", hyp_identity);;
escher_tag_transfo : escher_gen list → string * hyp_isometry = ⟨fun⟩
```

The basic patterns that we will use for the moment are formed from lists of points corresponding to the outline of the fish and the quadrilateral ABCD. Those lists are provided in the form of functions that take an isometry as argument and return a sketch (the list of points on the outline, transformed by this isometry).

```
#let body t = let tt z = point_of_cx (apply_hyp_iso t z)
             in make_sketch [Seg (map tt [P0;P1;P2;P3;P4;P5;P6;P7;P8;P9;
                                          P10;P11;P12;P13;P14;P15;P16;P17;
                                          P18;P19;P0])];;
body : hyp_isometry → sketch = ⟨fun⟩

#let quad t = let tt z = point_of_cx (apply_hyp_iso t z) in
             make_sketch [Seg (map tt [ptA;ptB;ptD;ptC;ptA])];;
quad : hyp_isometry → sketch = ⟨fun⟩


#let text size s =
  make_text_picture
    (make_font Helvetica size) black s;;
text : float → string → picture = ⟨fun⟩

#let make_pseudo_escher_tiling polygon n =
  let center = {re_part=0.2; im_part=0.15} in
  group_pictures
    (map (fun (tag, T) →
              let p = make_default_draw_picture (polygon T) in
              group_pictures
                [p; center_picture (text 0.05 tag)
                        (point_of_cx (apply_hyp_iso T center)) ])
      (map escher_tag_transfo
          (generate_transformations_group escher_group n)));;
make_pseudo_escher_tiling : (hyp_isometry → sketch) → int → picture
                          = ⟨fun⟩
```

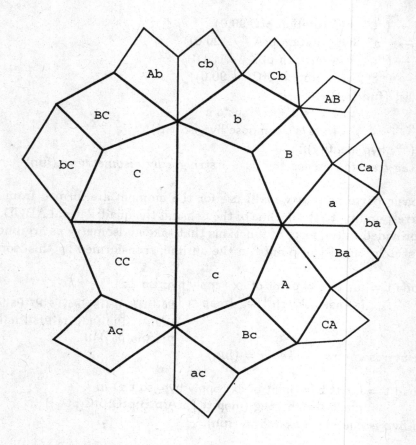

Figure 9.22. make_pseudo_escher_tiling quad 2

Figures 9.22 and 9.23 correspond to the following values:

#let pseudo_escher$_1$ =
   make_pseudo_escher_tiling quad 2;;
pseudo_escher$_1$: picture = ⟨**abstract**⟩

#let pseudo_escher$_2$ =
   make_pseudo_escher_tiling body 2;;
pseudo_escher$_2$: picture = ⟨**abstract**⟩

9.4.5 Escher's Circle Limit III

Now we will produce a colored image that comes close to Escher's engraving. To color it, we use four colors[2]. To get it, we use these permutations:

---
[2]Unfortunately, in print, you will see only four shades of gray.

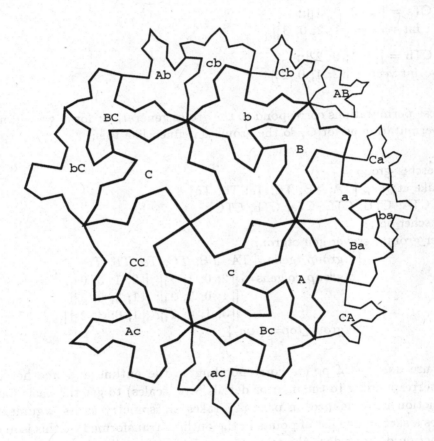

Figure 9.23. make_pseudo_escher_tiling body 2

```
#let CTA = [| 2; 0; 1; 3 |];;
CTA : int vect = [| 2; 0; 1; 3 |]

#let CTB = [| 2; 1; 3; 0 |];;
CTB : int vect = [| 2; 1; 3; 0 |]

#let CTC = [| 1; 0; 3; 2 |];;
CTC : int vect = [| 1; 0; 3; 2 |]

#let CTa = [| 1; 2; 0; 3 |];;
CTa : int vect = [| 1; 2; 0; 3 |]

#let CTb = [| 3; 1; 0; 2 |];;
CTb : int vect = [| 3; 1; 0; 2 |]
```

These permutations correspond to the group generators: for c, we will use the same permutation as for C, so the group is defined like this:

```
#let escher_group =
    make_ctgroup [TA; TB; TC; Ta; Tb; Tc]
      [CTA; CTB; CTC; CTa; CTb; CTC]
      escher_op;;
escher_group : escher_gen ctgroup
            = {ctgroup_tgens=[TA; TB; TC; Ta; Tb; Tc];
                ctgroup_colgens=[[| 2; 0; 1; 3 |]; [| 2; 1; 3; 0 |];
                                 [| 1; 0; 3; 2 |]; [| 1; 2; 0; 3 |];
                                 [| 3; 1; 0; 2 |]; [| 1; 0; 3; 2 |]];
                ctgroup_top= ⟨fun⟩}
```

We use one list of points corresponding to the outline and another list of points corresponding to the interior details (eye, scales) to get the basic pattern. The function **body** defined on page 327 takes an isometry as its argument and produces a sketch (the list of points in the outline, transformed by this isometry). The function **drawing** does the same for the interior details.

```
#body;;
 − : hyp_isometry → sketch = ⟨fun⟩

#drawing;;
 − : hyp_isometry → sketch = ⟨fun⟩
```

We get the drawing of an instance of the fish by filling in the outline with a given color and superposing the interior details on it.

```
#let color_of_int = fun
    0 → Gra 0.3 | 1 → Gra 0.5
  | 2 → Gra 0.7 | 3 → Gra 0.8
  | _ → failwith "wrong color";;
color_of_int : int → color = ⟨fun⟩
```

```
#let fish t col =
    let outline_sk = body t
    and decoration_sk = drawing t
  in group_pictures
        [ make_fill_picture
            (Nzfill, color_of_int col) outline_sk;
          make_default_draw_picture
            (group_sketches [outline_sk; decoration_sk]) ];;
fish : hyp_isometry → int → picture = ⟨fun⟩
```

To make the boundaries of the tiling more or less regular and to approximate a circle in shape, we eliminate instances where the center is located beyond a certain distance from the unit circle.

```
#let center= cx_of_point (sketch_center (body hyp_identity));;
center : complex = {re_part=0.202808200401;
                    im_part=0.132808200401}
```

```
#let simplify_escher d=
    select (fun (_,x)→ module (apply_hyp_iso x center) <. d);;
simplify_escher : float → (α * hyp_isometry) list
                        → (α * hyp_isometry) list = ⟨fun⟩
```

Here, finally, is the function to build the tiling. It takes two arguments: the maximal index of the elements of the group that we want to generate and the distance from the center that we use as a limit.

```
#let make_escher_tiling n d =
    group_pictures
      (map (fun (t₁,t₂) → (fish t₂ (t₁.(0))))
        (simplify_escher d
          (map escher_transfo
            (generate_coltrans_group escher_group n))));;
make_escher_tiling : int → float → picture = ⟨fun⟩
```

Figures 9.24, 9.25, and 9.26 provide a few examples. We have to go all the way to index 9 to get a drawing sufficiently regular because the generators we

Figure 9.24. make_escher_tiling 1 1.0

used do not provide an isotropic filling of the circle. However, at that index, the number of fish we generate is much greater than the number in the original engraving.

Exercises

9.4 Write two functions to construct tilings systematically like those in Figures 9.10 and 9.12.

9.5 Write a function to tile a plane with any arbitrary quadrilateral.

9.6 Produce a tiling like the one in Figure 9.27 where the symmetry group is **p4**.

9.5   Summary

We presented a few types and functions from the MLgraph library that make the graphic possibilities of the PostScript language available to you in CAML. We then exploited those functions to draw trees and to produce tilings.

The sections about tiling introduced a formal representation of symmetry groups. That representation let us generate tilings without redundancy. In particular, in that way we could reproduce a tiling of the hyperbolic plane due to M. C. Escher.

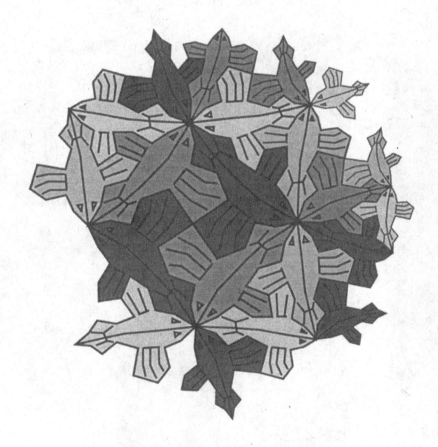

Figure 9.25. make_escher_tiling 2 1.0

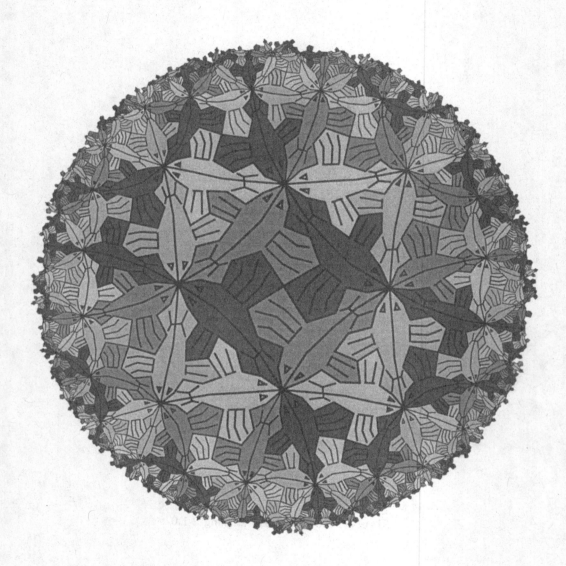

Figure 9.26. make_escher_tiling 9 0.95

Figure 9.27. A tiling for you to produce

9.6   To Learn More

9.6.1   About PostScript

As we mentioned before, the MLgraph library is modeled graphically on the language PostScript. That language was developed commercially by Adobe, Inc., from principles explained in an article by Warnock and Wyatt. The basic ideas underlying PostScript exploit a virtual coordinate system independent of any display device (particularly independent of printer- or screen-resolution, for example), and they freely exploit linear transformations in this coordinate system even for characters and bitmaps.

PostScript has become a standard for printing documents, whether artistic, scientific, or mainly textual. It is even used more and more to display graphic documents interactively on screen, ever since its adoption by NeXT as the only display tool in NeXTStep. References [39, 38] define the language and explain its use.

9.6.2   About Drawing Trees

How to represent the structure of trees graphically is a problem that has been studied widely and deeply in computer science because of the great number of objects in data processing that naturally lend themselves to representation as trees. The drawing algorithm that we explicated is not quite standard; we chose it for aesthetic reasons without much concern for its efficiency. When we display trees in the context of an interactive system (for example, in an editor), we may be obliged to recompute parts of the tree incrementally after a modification, an activity for which this algorithm is not really very well adapted. See [34] for other algorithms.

9.6.3   About Tilings

Coxeter's book [11] is an excellent introduction to the geometric principles under-lying tiling. Grünbaum and Shephard's book [17] summarizes just about every-thing that is currently known about tiling a plane, including non-periodic tilings recently explored by Wang, Robinson, and Penrose. Tiling groups are presented in [12], and simplifications to reach canonical forms are offered in [21].

Escher's engraving "Circle Limit III" has been analyzed from a mathematical perspective by Coxeter in [10].

Chapter 10

Exact Arithmetic

In this chapter, we show you how to represent exact numbers of arbitrary size. In certain applications, our ability to compute with such numbers is indispensible, especially so in computer algebra. Formal systems of symbolic computation, such as MAPLE [14], MATHEMATICA [44], or AXIOM [19], exploit an exact rational arithmetic. Moreover, programming languages oriented toward symbolic computation generally support exact computations. Such is particularly the case of CAML with the libraries bignum and ratio.

The sets of numbers that we will treat here are the natural numbers (also known as integers for counting), the signed integers (that is, both positive and negative), and the rational numbers. The natural numbers will be represented by the sequence of their digits in a given base. The sequence itself can be represented in various ways. We will represent natural numbers primarily by ordinary lists. This choice is not very efficient because it supports traversal in only one direction. If we decide to put least significant digits at the head of the list, then we can multiply and add fairly efficiently, but division will be inefficient because we must then turn the lists around.

Nevertheless, if we represent natural numbers as lists, then we can program the usual operations simply, and that model can serve later as the point of reference for getting into various other representations, such as representations by doubly linked circular lists or by arrays—representations used in "real" implementations. In principle, representation by arrays is simultaneously simple and efficient, but it implies that we ourselves must manage the allocation of arrays, a requirement that will blemish our algorithms somewhat, whereas, in contrast, allocation is implicit and invisible in the case of lists.

The representation of signed integers and of rational numbers uses the representation of natural numbers in a modular way like the abstract types defined in Section 2.2.8. If we ever replace our module of natural numbers by a more efficient one, then we directly improve the efficiency of these other modules as well.

10.1   Representing Integers by Lists

As we delve into our representation of natural numbers by lists, we need to consider a few practical issues.

10.1.1   Choosing a Base

When we choose a base to represent integers, we need one that supports ordinary integer arithmetic (type int) for operations on digits. Thus, in particular, the product of two integers that are less than the base must be an ordinary integer that can be computed without overflow. Moreover, for division, it is a good idea for any two-digit number to be an ordinary integer as well. Since the positive integers of CAML lie between -2^{30} and $2^{30} - 1$, we can take 2^{15} as our base. In fact, we prefer 10 000, which is less than that but it lets us display large numbers by concatenating the display of each digit. To change the base, anyway all we have to do is to redefine the constant nat_base.

```
#let nat_base = 10000;;
nat_base : int = 10000
```

In all programs that work on a representation with the least significant digits at the head, the lists of integers used will have a non-null significant digit (the one at the end of the list). This point implies in particular that [ ] will be the only representation accepted for the number 0, and more generally that every number will have a unique representation that we will call "canonic." All the functions that we will write will produce canonic lists.

The function nat_of_int produces a canonic list with the least significant digit at the head, starting from an ordinary positive integer.

```
#let rec nat_of_int n =
   if n=0 then [ ] else
   if n < nat_base then [n] else
   (n mod nat_base) :: nat_of_int (n/nat_base);;
nat_of_int : int → int list = ⟨fun⟩
```

```
#let zero_nat n= n=[ ];;
zero_nat : α list → bool = ⟨fun⟩
```

10.1.2   Operations with the Least Significant Digit at the Head

The following functions add, subtract, and multiply digits, all with carry. This subtraction assumes that $(n + c) \leq m$, so this property should be tested beforehand.

```
#let add_carry c (m,n) =
    let s = m+n+c in (s/nat_base, s mod nat_base);;
add_carry : int → int * int → int * int = ⟨fun⟩

#let sub_carry c (m,n) =
    let s = m−(n+c) in
    if s≥0 then (0,s) else (1,nat_base+s);;
sub_carry : int → int * int → int * int = ⟨fun⟩

#let mult_carry c (m,n) =
    let p = m*n + c in (p/nat_base, p mod nat_base);;
mult_carry : int → int * int → int * int = ⟨fun⟩
```

Now we will define addition and subtraction of a digit d and a number dl, as well as multiplication of a number dl by a digit d.

```
#let rec add_digit_nat d dl =
    if d = 0 then dl else
    match dl with
      [ ] → [d]
    | (a::dl') → let (c,n) = add_carry 0 (a,d)
                 in n :: add_digit_nat c dl';;
add_digit_nat : int → int list → int list = ⟨fun⟩

#let rec sub_digit_nat d dl =
    if d = 0 then dl else
    match dl with
      [ ] → failwith "sub_digit_nat:neg result"
    | [a] → let (c,n) = sub_carry 0 (a,d) in
                 if c = 0 then if n = 0 then [ ]
                               else [n]
                 else failwith "sub_digit_nat:neg result"
    | (a::dl') → let (c,n) = sub_carry 0 (a,d) in
                 if c = 0 then n::dl'
                 else n :: sub_digit_nat c dl';;
sub_digit_nat : int → int list → int list = ⟨fun⟩

#let mult_digit_nat d dl =
    let rec mult_rec c = fun
      [ ] → if c = 0 then [ ] else [c]
    | (a::dl') → let (c',n) = mult_carry c (a,d)
                 in n :: mult_rec c' dl'
    in if d = 0 then [ ] else mult_rec 0 dl;;
mult_digit_nat : int → int list → int list = ⟨fun⟩
```

These operations of addition, subtraction, and multiplication are the direct translation of the algorithms that we use "by hand" if we overlook the uncustomary representation of 0.

```
#let add_nat dl₁ dl₂ =
  let rec add_rec c = fun
    ([ ],[ ]) → if c = 0 then [ ] else [c]
  | ([ ],l) → add_digit_nat c l
  | (l,[ ]) → add_digit_nat c l
  | (a₁::dl₁,a₂::dl₂) → let (c',n) = add_carry c (a₁,a₂)
                          in n :: add_rec c' (dl₁,dl₂)
  in add_rec 0 (dl₁,dl₂);;
add_nat : int list → int list → int list = ⟨fun⟩
```

```
#let sub_nat dl₁ dl₂ =
  let rec sub_rec c = fun
    ([ ],[ ]) → if c = 0 then [ ]
                  else failwith "sub_nat:neg result"
  | ([ ],l) → failwith "sub_nat:neg result"
  | (l,[ ]) → sub_digit_nat c l
  | (a₁::dl₁,a₂::dl₂) → let (c',n) = sub_carry c (a₁,a₂) in
                          let r = sub_rec c' (dl₁,dl₂) in
                          if n = 0 & r = [ ] then [ ] else n::r
  in sub_rec 0 (dl₁,dl₂);;
sub_nat : int list → int list → int list = ⟨fun⟩
```

```
#let mult_nat dl₁ dl₂ =
  let rec mult_rec l' = fun
    [ ] → [ ]
  | [a] → mult_digit_nat a l'
  | (a::l) → add_nat (mult_digit_nat a l')
                (mult_rec (0::l') l) in
  if list_length dl₁ > list_length dl₂ then mult_rec dl₁ dl₂
  else mult_rec dl₂ dl₁;;
mult_nat : int list → int list → int list = ⟨fun⟩
```

Notice that the function mult_nat chooses to carry out recursion on its shortest argument.

10.1.3 Comparisons as Operations

Comparisons will be efficient only if we have rapid access throughout the length of the numbers. In the case where we must traverse the list of digits to know how long it is, then a comparison will require time linear in the length of the shortest number being compared.

Here is a function to compare two numbers represented with the least significant digit in the head of the list.

```
type comparison = Smaller | Equiv | Greater;;

#let comp_nat dl₁ dl₂ =
  comp_rec Equiv dl₁ dl₂
  where rec comp_rec comp dl₁ dl₂ =
    if dl₁ = [ ] then
      if dl₂ = [ ] then comp else Smaller else
    if dl₂ = [ ] then Greater else
    if hd dl₁ < hd dl₂ then comp_rec Smaller (tl dl₁) (tl dl₂) else
    if hd dl₁ = hd dl₂ then comp_rec comp (tl dl₁) (tl dl₂)
    else comp_rec Greater (tl dl₁) (tl dl₂);;
comp_nat : int list → int list → comparison = ⟨fun⟩
```

Starting from the function comp_nat, we can define more conventional comparison functions.

```
#let eq_nat l₁ l₂ = (comp_nat l₁ l₂ = Equiv);;
eq_nat : int list → int list → bool = ⟨fun⟩

#let lt_nat l₁ l₂ = (comp_nat l₁ l₂ = Smaller);;
lt_nat : int list → int list → bool = ⟨fun⟩

#let le_nat l₁ l₂ = match comp_nat l₁ l₂ with
    ((Smaller|Equiv)) → true
  | _ → false;;
le_nat : int list → int list → bool = ⟨fun⟩
```

In the case where the most significant digits are at the head, the comparison can be defined by this function:

```
#let rec icomp_nat l₁ l₂ =
    if l₁ = [ ] then
      if l₂ = [ ] then Equiv else Smaller else
    if l₂ = [ ] then Greater
    else let rec icomp_rec comp (l₁,l₂) =
          let (n₁,n₂) = list_length l₁,list_length l₂ in
          if n₁ < n₂ then Smaller else
          if n₁ = n₂ then comp else Greater in
          if hd l₁ < hd l₂ then icomp_rec Smaller (tl l₁,tl l₂) else
```

if hd l_1 = hd l_2 **then** icomp_nat (tl l_1) (tl l_2)
    else icomp_rec Greater (tl l_1,tl l_2);;
icomp_nat : int list → int list → comparison = ⟨**fun**⟩

The corresponding conventional comparison functions will then be these:

ieq_nat : int list → int list → bool
ilt_nat : int list → int list → bool
ile_nat : int list → int list → bool

Generally, for the moment we denote the functions that work on numbers with their significant digit at the head by identifiers that begin by the letter i. In Section 10.1.5, we will introduce nat, a type that lets us drop this distinction.

10.1.4   Division as an Operation

Division requires by far the most complicated algorithm. We begin by defining division in the particular case where the divisor consists of only one digit. If the dividend itself has only one digit or if it is null, then the result is immediate. Otherwise, we proceed recursively, using the first or the first two digits of the dividend at each step. When division of the first or the first two digits is exact (that is, when the remainder is zero), then we keep this zero for the head of the following dividend. In this way, we produce zeros naturally in the quotient.

However, this practice leads us to handle dividends that may not be "canonic" in the sense we defined on page 338. In particular, at the last step, when the dividend consists of only one digit, it may be [0] rather than [ ]. We take this possibility into account in the second case of the local function div_rec to get a normalized result.

In the following operations, the significant digit is at the head.

```
#let idiv_digit_nat dl d =
  if d = 0 then failwith "div_digit_nat: division by 0" else
  match d with
    1 → (dl,[ ])
  | _ → div_rec dl
        where rec div_rec = fun
          [ ] → [ ],[d]
        | [a] → let q = a/d
              and r = a mod d in
                ((if q=0 then [ ] else [q]), (if r=0 then [ ] else [r]))
        | (a₁::((a₂::dl) as dl'))
          → if a₁ < d
            then let m = a₁*nat_base + a₂ in
```

```
        let (q,r) = (m/d, m mod d) in
        let (q',r') = div_rec (r::dl) in
        (q::q', r')
      else let (q,r) = a₁/d,a₁ mod d in
        let (q',r') = div_rec (r::dl') in
        (q::q', r');;
idiv_digit_nat : int list → int → int list * int list = ⟨fun⟩
```

Given a divisor d of size $n > 1$, then the division of a number of size $n + p$ by d can be broken down into a series of divisions where the dividend is of size n or $n + 1$.

In order to write division, we will need an auxiliary function cut to cut the dividend dl into two lists, dl_1 and dl_2, where dl_1 is of size n; we also need an auxiliary function normalize to get rid of useless zeros in the intermediate dividends, since we use other operations that assume the numbers they handle have been normalized.

```
#let cut n (dl:int list) =
  let rec cut_rec (n,dl₁,dl₂) =
    if n = 0 then (dl₁,dl₂) else cut_rec(n−1,(hd dl₂)::dl₁,tl dl₂) in
  let (dl,dl') = cut_rec (n,[ ],dl) in
  (rev dl,dl');;
cut : int → int list → int list * int list = ⟨fun⟩
```

```
#let rec normalize = fun
  [ ] → [ ]
  | (0::dl) → normalize dl
  | dl → dl;;
normalize : int list → int list = ⟨fun⟩
```

We also assume that we have the operations of addition, subtraction, and multiplication which accept arguments with the significant digit at the head.

```
iadd_nat : int list → int list → int list
isub_nat : int list → int list → int list
imult_digit_nat : int → int list → int list
imult_nat : int list → int list → int list
```

Now we get to the complete algorithm for division. To limit the number of different cases we have to handle, we can always assume that the first digit of the divisor is greater than half the base. For that, it suffices to multiply the dividend and the divisor simultaneously by the integer quotient of the base divided by $d + 1$ if d is the first digit of the divisor and to divide the remainder at the end by the same digit. In this way, in the case of the division of an n-digit number by a smaller n-digit number, the quotient is always 1.

In the case of division of an $n + 1$-digit number by an n-digit number (where $n > 1$), the problem lies in "guessing" the first digit of the quotient. If we call the first three digits of the dividend u_0, u_1, u_2, and we call the first two digits of the divisor v_1, v_2, then the first quotient q to try is $(base - 1)$ if $u_0 = v_1$ and the integer quotient of $(u_0 * base + u_1)$ divided by v_1 otherwise. That quotient is then decreased by 1 repetitively until $v_2 \times q > (u_0 \times base + u_1 - q * v_1) \times base + u_2$. It is possible to prove that the probability for this quotient to be inexact is only $3/base$ and that if it is, then the spread from the true quotient is 1.

Here, then, is the function to compute the first likely digit of the quotient.

```
#let find_first_digit u₀ u₁ u₂ v₁ v₂ =
  let q₀ =
    if u₀ = v₁ then nat_base−1 else (u₀*nat_base+u₁)/v₁ in
  let rec find_q q =
    if v₂*q>(u₀*nat_base+u₁−q*v₁)*nat_base+u₂
    then find_q (q−1) else q in
  find_q q₀;;
find_first_digit : int → int → int → int → int → int = ⟨fun⟩
```

We will use the auxiliary function $first_2$ to extract the first two elements of a list, and $first_3$ to extract the first three elements.

```
first₂ : α list → α * α
first₃ : α list → α * α * α
```

Now we are getting to the division function at last. Its essential work is carried out by the auxiliary function div_rec, taking three arguments: quot, lg, and ld.

- quot is an accumulator. It contains the list of digits of the quotient. Since we compute these digits by going from the most to least significant digits, the successive digits of the quotient will be added to the end of the list.

- lg contains the successive dividends that serve in the computation of a digit of the quotient.

- ld contains the part of the original dividend that has not yet been used. At every step, we bring down a new digit from the dividend; that is, the first digit of ld is added to the right of lg.

```
#let rec idiv_nat dl₁ dl₂ =
    if ilt_nat dl₁ dl₂ then ([ ], dl₁) else
    let n₂ = list_length dl₂ in
    match n₂ with
        0 → failwith "Div_nat: divisor is 0"
      | 1 → idiv_digit_nat dl₁ (hd dl₂)
      | _ → let d = nat_base / (hd(dl₂)+1) in
            let dl₂ = imult_digit_nat d dl₂ in
            let (v₁,v₂) = first₂ dl₂ in
            (let (q,r) = div_rec [ ] [ ] (imult_digit_nat d dl₁)
             in (q, fst(idiv_digit_nat r d)))
            where rec div_rec quot lg ld =
                if ilt_nat lg dl₂ then
                    if ld = [ ] then (normalize quot,normalize lg) else
                    let lg' = normalize(lg@[ hd ld ]) in
                    if ilt_nat lg' dl₂ then div_rec (quot@[0]) lg' (tl ld)
                    else div_rec quot lg' (tl ld) else
                if list_length lg = n₂ then
                    let r₁ = isub_nat lg dl₂ in
                    div_rec (quot@[1]) r₁ ld
                else let (u₀,u₁,u₂) = first₃ lg in
                    let q₀ = find_first_digit u₀ u₁ u₂ v₁ v₂ in
                    let p = imult_digit_nat q₀ dl₂ in
                    let (q,p) =
                        if ilt_nat lg p then q₀−1,isub_nat p dl₂
                        else (q₀,p) in
                    let r₁ = isub_nat lg p in
                    div_rec (quot@[q]) r₁ ld;;
idiv_nat : int list → int list → int list * int list = ⟨fun⟩
```

In particular, the operation of division will be used to handle rational numbers. Rational numbers will be represented by fractions, so we will need division to simplify these fractions as well as to print rational numbers in decimal form.

The function compute_frac_part gives the sequence of the first n digits after the decimal point of a fraction $\frac{dvd}{dvs}$ where $dvd < dvs$ (or possibly fewer than n digits, if the division terminates before).

```
#let compute_frac_part dvd dvs n =
    cfp (normalize (dvd@[0])) n
    where rec cfp dvd =
        fun 0 → [ ]
          | n → let (q,r) = idiv_nat dvd dvs in
```

```
match r with
  [ ] → q
| _ → match q with
        [ ] → 0::cfp (normalize(r@[0])) (n−1)
      | [d] → d::cfp (normalize(r@[0])) (n−1)
      | _ → failwith "compute_frac_part: wrong arg";;
```
compute_frac_part : int list → int list → int → int list = ⟨fun⟩

The function pgcd computes the greatest common divisor of two integers. It uses Euclid's algorithm to do so.

```
#let rec pgcd dl₁ dl₂ =
  if dl₁ = dl₂ then dl₁ else
  if ilt_nat dl₁ dl₂ then pgcd dl₂ dl₁
  else let (q,r) = idiv_nat dl₁ dl₂ in
      if zero_nat r then dl₂ else pgcd dl₂ r ;;
```
pgcd : int list → int list → int list = ⟨fun⟩

10.1.5 A Type for Natural Numbers (Integers for Counting)

In what follows, we want to avoid preoccupation with the fact that the natural numbers we use are presented by either the most or least significant digit at the head. For relief, we are introducing nat, a type that foresees both cases.

```
#type nat = Left_nat of int list | Right_nat of int list;;
```
Type nat defined.

All operations must now be redefined to work with this type, so we will assume accordingly that all the functions such as add_nat, mult_nat, or div_nat, now work on the type nat.

```
div_nat : nat → nat → nat * nat
```

But we leave the definition of those new functions as an exercise.

10.1.6 Exponentiation

It will be useful to us to compute a^n only when n is an ordinary integer because otherwise the result we get would be much too large[1].

To compute a^n, we will use the following identities:

---

[1] Too large, that is, for the memory of a computer.

$$a^0 = 1$$
$$a^{2p} = (a^p)^2$$
$$a^{2p+1} = ((a^p)^2) \times a$$

They correspond to this program:

```
#let rec exp_nat a n =
    if n = 0 then nat_of_int 1 else
    let q = n/2
    and r = n mod 2 in
    let p = exp_nat a q in
    mult_nat (mult_nat p p) (if r = 0 then nat_of_int 1 else a) ;;
exp_nat : nat → int → nat = ⟨fun⟩
```

10.1.7 Computing Square Roots

To compute the integer square root of a natural number, we will use an iterative technique directly adapted from Newton's method to compute the approximate square root.

Newton's method, which you saw earlier on page 40, calculates a zero (that is, a root) of a function f by constructing a sequence where the recurrence relation is defined by:

$$x_{n+1} = x_n - \frac{f(x_n)}{f'(x_n)}$$

To compute the square root of a number a, it suffices to compute a zero of the function $x^2 - a$. The recurrence relation is thus:

$$x_{n+1} = x_n - \frac{x_n{}^2 - a}{2x_n} = \frac{1}{2}(x_n + \frac{a}{x_n})$$

It is possible to prove that we get the integer square root of a natural number a by this recurrence relation:

$$x_{n+1} = \left\lfloor \frac{(x_n + \frac{a}{x_n})}{2} \right\rfloor$$

If we start from a number greater than the square root, this recurrence relation defines a decreasing sequence that eventually becomes stable. When $x_{n+1} = x_n$, x_n is the root we are looking for.

We will begin the recursion by a number greater than the root but sufficiently close to it. This number is computed by the function guess_root.

```
#let guess_root n =
  let rec guess_rec n = fun
    [ ] → (0,n)
  | [x] → (1+int_of_float(sqrt(float_of_int x)),n)
  | [x₁;x₂] → (1 + int_of_float(sqrt(float_of_int (x₁ + nat_base*x₂))), n)
  | (_::_::l) → guess_rec (n+1) l in
  let (r,len) =
    guess_rec 0
      (match n with (Left_nat l) → l
                   | (Right_nat l) → (rev l)) in
  Right_nat (r:: gen_list 0 len);;
guess_root : nat → nat = ⟨fun⟩
```

The recursion itself and its halting test are defined by the function sqrt_nat.

```
#let sqrt_nat n =
  let x = guess_root n in
  let y = add_digit_nat 1 x in
  sqrt_rec x y
  where rec sqrt_rec x y =
    if le_nat y x then y else
      sqrt_rec (fst (div_digit_nat (add_nat x (fst (div_nat n x))) 2)) x;;
sqrt_nat : nat → nat = ⟨fun⟩
```

10.1.8 Reading and Printing Natural Numbers

As usual, we assume we have a function to enter large integers as data:

```
#nat_of_string "12345678";;
− : nat = Left_nat [5678; 1234]
```

To print natural numbers, we exploit the fact that the base is a power of 10 to produce a display digit by digit.

```
#let print_digit_nat n =
  let s = string_of_int n in
  match string_length s with
    1 → print_string ("000" ^ s)
  | 2 → print_string ("00" ^ s)
  | 3 → print_string ("0" ^ s)
  | 4 → print_string s
  | _ → failwith "print_digit_nat: wrong digit";;
print_digit_nat : int → unit = ⟨fun⟩
```

```
#let rec print_nat l =
   let rec print_rec = fun
     [ ] → ()
   | (a::l) → print_digit_nat a ; print_rec l in
   match
     (match l with (Left_nat l) → rev l | (Right_nat l) → l)
   with [ ] → print_int 0
       | [a] → print_int a
       | (a::l) → print_int a ; print_rec l;;
print_nat : nat → unit = ⟨fun⟩
```

CAML lets us associate a new print function with a type. To do so, we use the function new_printer.

```
#new_printer "nat" print_nat;;
- : unit = ()
```

Here is an example:

```
#let rec fact n =
   if n = 0 then nat_of_int 1
   else mult_nat (nat_of_int n) (fact (n−1));;
fact : int → nat = ⟨fun⟩

#fact 100;;
- : nat = 93326215443944152681699238856266700490715 9
          68264381621468592963895217599993229915608 9
          41463976156518286253697920827223758251185 2
          109168640000000000000000000000000
```

10.2 Other Representations of Natural Numbers

As we mentioned earlier, there are other possibilities to represent natural numbers.

10.2.1 Doubly Linked Circular Lists

If we use lists to implement large numbers, then we incur a cost due to the necessity of turning the lists around when, in the same computation, we use some operations that assume least significant digits at the head with others that assume most significant digits at the head. Moreover, when we use lists, we also entail the construction of many intermediate structures.

To get around these inconveniences, we can use doubly linked lists as data structures. They are introduced in Section 4.4.5. We will slightly modify the type dlnode to make the field info modifiable in this type of record. By means of this modification, we can use these lists as accumulators and thus avoid constructing too many intermediate structures.

```
#type α dlnode =
    { mutable info: α;
      mutable prev: α dlnode;
      mutable next: α dlnode
    };;
```

The number 0 will be represented by the circular list containing the integer 0 as its only element. Other numbers will be represented in such a way that the access node will be the least significant digit, and that a traversal of the list by the fields next corresponds to a traversal of the digits in increasing significance.

The test for equality to 0 will thus be defined simply by:

```
#let zero_nat n =
    n.info = 0 & n.next == n;;
zero_nat : int dlnode → bool = ⟨fun⟩
```

Here is the function to construct a natural number from a positive integer of type int, along with its inverse.

```
#let rec nat_of_int n =
    let n₀ = n mod nat_base and r=n/nat_base in
    let accu= mk_dbl_circular_list n₀ in
    nat_rec accu r
    where rec nat_rec dll p =
      if p = 0 then accu else
      begin
        insert_after (p mod nat_base) dll;
        nat_rec dll.next (p/nat_base)
      end;;
nat_of_int : int → int dlnode = ⟨fun⟩
```

```
#let int_of_nat n =
    int_rec n.prev n.prev.info
    where rec int_rec dll accu =
      if dll.prev==n.prev then accu else
      int_rec dll.prev (accu*nat_base+dll.prev.info);;
int_of_nat : int dlnode → int = ⟨fun⟩
```

We will also need a function to copy a circular doubly linked list.

```
#let copy n =
    let accu= mk_dbl_circular_list n.info in
    copy_rec accu n.next
    where rec copy_rec dl₁ dl₂=
      if dl₂ == n then accu else
      begin
        insert_after dl₂.info dl₁;
        copy_rec dl₁.next dl₂.next
      end;;
```
$copy : \alpha\ dlnode \rightarrow \alpha\ dlnode = \langle \textbf{fun} \rangle$

To add two natural numbers represented by circular lists, we copy the first one; then we destructively add the second one to it.

```
#let add_nat m n =
    if zero_nat m then n else
    if zero_nat n then m else
    let accu = copy m in
    add_rec 0 accu n
    where rec add_rec c dll dll'=
      let (c',n') = add_carry c (dll.info, dll'.info) in
      begin
        dll.info←n';
        if dll'.next==n then propagate_carry c' dll else
        if dll.next==accu
        then begin insert_after c' dll; add_rec 0 dll.next dll'.next end
        else add_rec c' dll.next dll'.next
      end
    and propagate_carry c dll =
      if c = 0 then accu else
      if dll.next == accu then begin insert_after c dll; accu end
      else let (c',n')= add_carry 0 (c,(dll.next).info) in
          begin
            (dll.next).info←n';
            if c'=0 then accu else propagate_carry c' dll.next
          end;;
```
$add\_nat : int\ dlnode \rightarrow int\ dlnode \rightarrow int\ dlnode = \langle \textbf{fun} \rangle$

To multiply two such numbers, we add the successive products of the first number multiplied by the digits of the second. To do so, we exploit an accumulator initialized to 0.

```
#let un_nat n =
```

```
      n.info = 1 & n.next == n;;
  un_nat : int dlnode → bool = ⟨fun⟩

#let mult_nat m n =
    if zero_nat m then m else
    if zero_nat n then n else
    if un_nat m then n else
    if un_nat n then m else
    let accu = nat_of_int 0 in
    mult_rec₁ accu n
    where rec mult_rec₁ dllaccu dlln =
      mult_rec₂ dllaccu m dlln.info;
      if dlln.next==n then accu else
      begin
        if dllaccu.next==accu then insert_after 0 dllaccu else ();
        mult_rec₁ dllaccu.next dlln.next
      end
    and mult_rec₂ dllaccu dllm d=
      let (c,n) = mult_carry dllaccu.info (dllm.info ,d) in
      begin
        dllaccu.info←n;
        if dllm.next==m then
          if dllaccu.next==accu & c≠0 then insert_after c dllaccu
          else () else
        begin
          (if dllaccu.next==accu then insert_after c dllaccu
            else (dllaccu.next).info ← (dllaccu.next).info + c);
          mult_rec₂ dllaccu.next dllm.next d
        end
      end;;
  mult_nat : int dlnode → int dlnode → int dlnode = ⟨fun⟩
```

For comparisons, we carry out a traversal of the numbers in the order of decreasing significance of their digits.

```
#let lt_nat m n =
    let rec lt_rec dll₁ dll₂ =
    dll₁.info < dll₂.info or
    dll₁.info = dll₂.info & not(dll₁.prev==m) &
    lt_rec dll₁.prev dll₂.prev in
    let lm=dll_length m and ln=dll_length n in
    lm < ln or lm = ln & lt_rec m n;;
  lt_nat : int dlnode → int dlnode → bool = ⟨fun⟩
```

10.2.2 Arrays

If we represent natural numbers by arrays, we get the most efficient representation in practice, but we also find it the most tricky to program because it means that we must manage the size of numbers and the boundaries of indices ourselves. In contrast, lists, whether simple or circular, avoid that kind of management problem. Even so, representation by arrays does not present any real difficulties for us.

Exercise
10.1 Write integer division assuming the representation of integers by doubly linked circular lists.

10.3 Signed Integers, Both Negative and Positive

To get signed integers (that is, both negative and positive integers), we can define these types, for example:

#type sign = Neg | Pos;;

#type big_int = {big_sign: sign; big_val: nat};;

Here is the function to coerce the types nat and big_int.

#let big_int_of_nat n = {big_sign=Pos; big_val=n};;
*big_int_of_nat : nat → big_int = ⟨**fun**⟩*

We will leave it to the reader to define most of the arithmetic functions for the type big_int from the ones that operate on the type nat.
Here is multiplication.

#let prod_sign= **fun**
    (Neg,Neg) → Pos
  | (Neg,Pos) → Neg
  | (Pos,Neg) → Neg
  | (Pos,Pos) → Pos;;
*prod_sign : sign * sign → sign = ⟨**fun**⟩*

#let mult_big n_1 n_2 =
    {big_sign = prod_sign (n_1.big_sign,n_2.big_sign);
      big_val = mult_nat n_1.big_val n_2.big_val};;
*mult_big : big_int → big_int → big_int = ⟨**fun**⟩*

Exercise
10.2 Define the other arithmetic functions and the comparison functions for the type big_int.

We assume that we have the function big_int_of_string in order to read large numbers. It builds a value of type big_int from a character string containing a sequence of digits, possibly preceded by a sign.

To print these numbers, we use the following functions.

```
#let print_big_int = fun
   {big_sign=s; big_val=l} →
      (match s with Neg → print_string "-" | Pos → ()) ; print_nat l;;
print_big_int : big_int → unit = ⟨fun⟩
```

```
#new_printer "big_int" print_big_int;;
− : unit = ()
```

```
#let n= big_int_of_string "-99999999999"
 in exp_big n 3;;
− : big_int = −999999999997000000000000299999999999
```

10.4   Rational Numbers

To define rational numbers, we use this type:

```
#type rat = {rat_sign: sign; rat_num: nat ; rat_den: nat};;
```

Rational numbers are represented in fractional form. It is easy to program the usual arithmetic operations on rational numbers: we do so with the help of operations on natural numbers. Here, for example, are multiplication and division.

```
#let mult_rat = fun
   {rat_sign=s₁; rat_num=n₁; rat_den=d₁}
   {rat_sign=s₂; rat_num=n₂; rat_den=d₂}
   → {rat_sign=prod_sign (s₁,s₂) ;
      rat_num=mult_nat n₁ n₂;
      rat_den=mult_nat d₁ d₂};;
mult_rat : rat → rat → rat = ⟨fun⟩
```

```
#let div_rat = fun
   r₁ {rat_sign=s₂ ;rat_num=n₂; rat_den=d₂}
   → mult_rat r₁ {rat_sign=s₂ ;rat_num=d₂; rat_den=n₂};;
div_rat : rat → rat → rat = ⟨fun⟩
```

Exercise
10.3 Write the functions to add, subtract, and compare numbers of the type rat.

Notice, for example, that the operation of division of rational numbers uses multiplication of natural numbers and does not reduce the fraction it gets that way. Thus rational numbers will generally be represented by unreduced fractions.

To put those fractions into canonic form (numerator and denominator relatively prime), we will use the function pgcd, defined on page 346, to compute the greatest common divisor of the numerator and denominator; then we divide both by it.

```
#let reduce {rat_sign=s; rat_num=num; rat_den=den}=
    let p = pgcd num den in
    {rat_sign=s; rat_num = fst (div_nat num p);
     rat_den= fst (div_nat den p)};;
reduce : rat → rat = ⟨fun⟩
```

We could decide to put rational numbers systematically into canonic form or to leave that choice to the end-users when they think it necessary. That latter solution is in practice often the best because the probability of two numbers picked at random being relatively prime is very great. Normalization into canonic form is a costly operation, but in view of that probability, on average it will not really be necessary. In contrast, in a specific application, users can actually know whether the numerator and denominator of a fraction have a greatest common denominator of sufficient size and thus whether it is worth the cost to simplify and reduce the size of the numbers they are handling.

Let's assume we have defined a syntactic analyzer and a print function for rational numbers. They both write a rational number in the form of a fraction, possibly preceded by a sign.

```
#reduce (rat_of_string "4446464/3256");;
− : rat = 50528/37
```

We might also prefer to print rational numbers in decimal form. To do so, we use the function compute_frac_part, defined on page 345. We define a global variable, default_frac_length, defining the length in digits of printed versions in the base nat_base. The practical length in digits of printing in decimal form will be four times as long.

```
#let default_frac_length= ref 3;;
default_frac_length : int ref = ref 3

#let set_frac_length n = default_frac_length:= n;;
set_frac_length : int → unit = ⟨fun⟩
```

```
#let print_frac_rat = fun
   {rat_sign=s; rat_num=num; rat_den=den}
  → (match s with Neg → print_string "-" | Pos → ());
    let q,r= div_nat num den in
    let frac_part= compute_frac_part r den !default_frac_length in
    begin
      print_nat q;
      print_string ".";
      print_nat (Right_nat frac_part)
    end;;
```
print_frac_rat : rat → unit = ⟨fun⟩

```
#new_printer "rat" print_frac_rat;;
```
− : unit = ()

```
#reduce (rat_of_string "4446464/3256");;
```
− : rat = 1365.621621621621

Printing like this is obviously costly.

Exercise
10.4 Write a function to convert rational numbers into floating-point numbers.

10.5   An Application: Computing π

This section looks at an example from Valérie Ménissier-Morain. She uses a formula from Dimitri and Gregory Chudnovsky to compute π.

$$\frac{1}{\pi} = \sum_{n=0}^{\infty} (-1)^n \frac{12(6n)!}{(n!)^3 (3n)!} \; \frac{13591409 + 545140134n}{(640320^3)^{n+\frac{1}{2}}}$$

We will use the following form since it lends itself more easily to computations:

$$\frac{1}{\pi} = \frac{1}{\sqrt{640320}} \sum_{n=0}^{\infty} (-1)^n \frac{12(3n+1)...(6n)}{(n!)^3} \; \frac{13591409 + 545140134n}{(640320^3)^n \times 640320}$$

We let

$$\frac{1}{\pi} = \sum_{n=0}^{\infty} \frac{A_n B_n}{D_n}$$

with

$$
\begin{aligned}
A_n &= (-1)^n 12(3n+1)...(6n) \\
B_n &= 13591409 + 545140134n \\
D_n &= (n!)^3 \times (640320^3)^n \times 640320
\end{aligned}
$$

and we assume that reductions to the same denominator have been carried out

$$\sum_{p=0}^{p=n} \frac{A_p B_p}{D_p} = \frac{N_n}{D_n}$$

leading to

$$\pi_n = \sqrt{640320}\frac{D_n}{N_n}$$

The recurrence relations are:

$$A_0 = 12, \qquad A_{n+1} = -\frac{(6n+1)(6n+2)(6n+3)(6n+4)(6n+5)(6n+6)}{(3n+1)(3n+2)(3n+3)}A_n$$

$$= -8(6n+1)(6n+3)(6n+5)A_n$$

$$\begin{aligned}
B_0 &= 13591409, & B_{n+1} &= 54514034 + B_n \\
N_0 &= 12 \times 13591409, & N_{n+1} &= (n+1)^3 640320^3 N_n + A_{n+1}B_{n+1} \\
D_0 &= 640320, & D_{n+1} &= (n+1)^3 640320^3 D_n
\end{aligned}$$

We still have to compute n^3 efficiently. $T_n = n^3$ is defined by:

$$T_0 = 1, \qquad T_{n+1} = (n+1)^3 = n^3 + 3n^2 + 3n + 1 = T_n + V_n$$

if we let $V_n = 3n^2 + 3n + 1$.

$$V_0 = 1, \qquad V_{n+1} = V_m + 6n + 6 = V_n + S_{n+1}$$

if we let $S_n = 6n$.
We can also use S_n to compute A_n, giving us:

$$A_{n+1} = -8(S_n + 1)(S_n + 3)(S_n + 5)$$

To compute $\frac{A_n B_n}{D_n}$ with d exact decimals, we must get as far as the index n satisfying:

$$\left|\frac{A_n B_n}{D_n}\right| < 10^{-d}$$

or

$$|A_n| \, B_n 10^d > D_n$$

that is,

$$\| A_n \| + \| B_n \| + d > \| D_n \|$$

if $\| x \|$ designates the number of decimal digits in a number x. We assume that the function size_nat tells us that number of digits.

```
#size_nat;;
- : nat → int = ⟨fun⟩
```

The halting test for the recurrence relation will be defined by:

```
#let test (x,y,z,t) = size_nat x + size_nat y + z > size_nat t;;
test : nat * nat * int * nat → bool = ⟨fun⟩
```

To compute the fraction to approximate π, we calculate the natural numbers D_n and N_n for a satisfactory index n, and then we multiply the fraction $\frac{D_n}{N_n}$ by $\sqrt{640320}$. We will get that quantity as the fraction

$$\frac{\sqrt{640320} \; 10^{2(d-2)}}{10^{d-2}}$$

guaranteeing d exact digits by using sqrt_nat, the function for integer square root.

The function sqrt$_{640320}$ carries out this computation:

```
#let sqrt₆₄₀₃₂₀ digits =
    let pow = exp_nat (nat_of_int 10) digits in
    {rat_sign=Pos;
     rat_num=sqrt_nat (mult_nat_list [nat_of_string "640320"; pow;pow]);
     rat_den= pow};;
sqrt₆₄₀₃₂₀ : int → rat = ⟨fun⟩
```

The function approx_pi calculates π with digits exact decimal digits.

```
#let approx_pi digits =
    let a₀ = nat_of_string "12"
    and b₀ = nat_of_string "13591409"
    and d₀ = nat_of_string "640320"
    and n₀ = mult_nat (nat_of_string "13591409")
              (nat_of_string "12")
```

```
    and s₀ = nat_of_string "0"
    and v₀ = nat_of_string "1"
    and t₀ = nat_of_string "0"
    and sqrt = sqrt₆₄₀₃₂₀ (digits−2)
    and pow₃ = exp_nat (nat_of_string "640320") 3
 in approx_rec a₀ b₀ t₀ d₀ n₀ s₀ v₀ true
    where rec approx_rec a b t d n s v pos=
      if test(a,b,digits,d)
      then let a =
              mult_nat_list [ nat_of_int 8;
                             add_digit_nat 1 s;
                             add_digit_nat 3 s;
                             add_digit_nat 5 s;
                             a ] in
           let b = add_nat (nat_of_string "545140134") b in
           let t = add_nat v t in
           let d = mult_nat_list [ t; pow₃; d ] in
           let n = (if pos then sub_nat else add_nat)
                   (mult_nat_list [ t; pow₃; n ])
                   (mult_nat_list [ a; b ]) in
           let s = add_digit_nat 6 s in
           let v = add_nat s v in
           approx_rec a b t d n s v (not pos)
      else mult_rat sqrt
           (div_rat (rat_of_nat d) (rat_of_nat n));;
approx_pi : int → rat = ⟨fun⟩
```

Here are the first 100 decimal digits of the number π:

```
#set_frac_length 25;;
− : unit = ()

#approx_pi 100;;
− : rat = 3.1415926535897932384626433832795028841971
          6939937510582097494459230781640628620899986
          280348253421170679
```

10.6   Summary

We offered a set of functions to compute exact arithmetic with no limit on the size. A module for computing natural numbers (the counting integers) represented as ordinary lists was completely defined. Then we outlined the way to build a similar module from more efficient representations.

From the module for natural numbers, we defined implementations for signed integers and for rational numbers. Arithmetic with rational numbers made it possible to define a function to compute the decimal representation of the number π to arbitrary precision.

10.7 To Learn More

The algorithms we used and in particular the algorithm for division of very large numbers were inspired by Knuth's book [20], though he uses arrays, not lists, as his preferred data structure.

Libraries defining arithmetic on very large numbers exist in many programming languages. In particular, the one for CAML is documented in [28]. We took our example for computing π from there. The basic layer of this library for natural numbers is written in C with certain crucial parts in assembly language.

You can imagine going beyond rational numbers to compute with real numbers represented, for example, as sequences of approximating rational numbers. That possibility, of course, no longer involves *exact* arithmetic, but rather arithmetic of arbitrary precision with the user defining how much precision is wanted for each number computed. Even though that kind of arithmetic has been studied and implemented, its effective use runs into many difficulties. In particular, there are difficulties due to the fact that the comparison of two numbers may take arbitrarily long when the comparison involves two numbers that are arbitrarily close. For more about that topic, see [27].

Part III

Implementation

This last part of the book describes techniques to implement a language like CAML. We do not pretend to give a complete description here of an implementation of CAML, but rather a demonstration that such an implementation is feasible. We treat a subset of CAML to show the major difficulties in compilation and type synthesis.

Chapter 11 defines a CAML evaluator in CAML. It highlights the main ideas that make it possible to produce a compiler: the idea of an environment is used to manage variables, and the idea of closure is used to represent functional values.

Chapter 12 tackles two topics simultaneously: compilation schema and techniques of memory management that come into play in the implementation of a functional language. With respect to memory management, only allocation is described precisely. Techniques for recovering memory (that is, garbage collection) are only briefly touched.

The set of machine instructions we use occurs at a relatively abstract level compared to all the instructions available in assembly language, but that set can nevertheless be translated into true machine instructions quite directly.

Chapter 13 describes a type synthesizer. We give you a preliminary version of it in a purely functional style; then we move on to a more efficient one, one that uses a destructive variety of the unification algorithm. This version is quite close to the actual type synthesizer in CAML.

Chapter 11

Evaluation

In Chapter 3, we presented a model for evaluation of expressions; it was based on the idea of rewrites. This model defined a semantics to which every implementation had to refer. However, an implementation that actually used textual rewrites would be highly inefficient. To achieve reasonable efficiency, we must replace textual rewrites by some other mechanism that simulates it. One possibility is to introduce the idea of an **environment**.

In this chapter, we present evaluation based on environments. We will write an evaluation function that takes an environment and a CAML expression as its arguments and returns the value of this expression as its result. The ideas for implementing this evaluation function will be refined in Chapter 12 to produce a compiler.

Section 11.1 describes evaluation of expressions with the help of environments. As in Chapter 3, it uses inference rules corresponding to each construction in the language to do so. These inference rules define evaluation by value, the evaluation strategy adopted by CAML. Section 11.2 then shows how to translate these rules into an evaluator written in CAML. Finally, Section 11.3 shows how to modify that evaluator to take into account delayed evaluation rather than evaluation by value.

11.1   Evaluation with the Help of Environments

An environment may be regarded as a look-up table in which certain variables are bound to values. For example, when we use CAML interactively to define, say, the variables $x_1, \ldots, x_n$, the values $v_1, \ldots, v_n$ associated with these variables are stored in an environment associated with the *toplevel*. That environment is a look-up table associating the value v_1 with the variable x_1, the value v_2 with x_2, and so forth.

It is possible to generalize the use of such tables during computations to store the values of variables of programs bound by the construction **fun** or by **let ... in** or by **let rec ... in**. When we have to evaluate an expression of the form (**fun** x → e) v, then rather than substitute v for x in e, we evaluate e in an environment where x is bound to v.

In this model, where we are computing with environments, functional values pose a special problem because they may contain free variables that have no meaning except in an environment. The value of a functional expression in an environment will thus be a pair: the expression and this environment. One such pair is known as a **closure**.

For example, consider the expression (**fun** x → **fun** y → x∗y) 3. In a computation that depends on substitution, its value is (**fun** y → 3∗y). In a computation based on an environment, its value will be the pair $<[x:3],($**fun** y → x∗y$)>$.

Formally, the evaluation of an expression in an environment will be defined by a ternary relation, denoted this way:

$$E \vdash e \Rightarrow v$$

It signifies

"The expression e has the value v in the environment E."

For each construction in the language, we then give a deduction rule. The following rules correspond to evaluation by value. (For more about this topic, see page 85.)

$$\frac{E(x)=v}{E \vdash x \Rightarrow v} \ (\text{Var})$$

The expression x, where x is a variable, has the value v in the environment E if v is precisely the value associated with x in that environment.

$$\frac{E \vdash e_1 \Rightarrow v_1 \quad .... \quad E \vdash e_n \Rightarrow v_n}{E \vdash (e_1,... e_n) \Rightarrow (v_1,... v_n)} \ (N\text{-tuple})$$

The expression $(e_1,... e_n)$ has the value $(v_1,... v_n)$ in the environment E if each expression e_i has the value v_i in that environment.

$$\frac{E \vdash e_1 \Rightarrow \textbf{true} \qquad E \vdash e_2 \Rightarrow v}{E \vdash \textbf{if } e_1 \textbf{ then } e_2 \textbf{ else } e_3 \Rightarrow v} \ (\text{Cond1})$$

The expression **if** e_1 **then** e_2 **else** e_3 has the value v in the environment E if, in this same environment, the expression e_1 has the value true and the expression e_2 has the value v.

$$\frac{E \vdash e_1 \Rightarrow \textbf{false} \qquad E \vdash e_3 \Rightarrow v}{E \vdash \textbf{if } e_1 \textbf{ then } e_2 \textbf{ else } e_3 \Rightarrow v} \quad \text{(Cond2)}$$

The expression **if** e_1 **then** e_2 **else** e_3 has the value v in the environment E if, in this same environment, the expression e_1 has the value **false** and the expression e_3 has the value v.

$$\frac{}{E \vdash (\textbf{fun } x \to e) \Rightarrow <E,(\textbf{fun } x \to e)>} \quad \text{(Fun1)}$$

The expression (**fun** $x \to e$) in the environment E has as its value the closure $<E,(\textbf{fun } x \to e)>$.

$$\frac{}{E \vdash (\textbf{fun } (x_1,\ldots,x_n) \to e) \Rightarrow <E,(\textbf{fun } (x_1,\ldots,x_n) \to e)>} \quad \text{(Fun2)}$$

The expression (**fun** $(x_1,\ldots,x_n) \to e$) in the environment E has for its value the closure $<E,(\textbf{fun } (x_1,\ldots,x_n) \to e)>$.

$$\frac{E \vdash e_1 \Rightarrow <E',(\textbf{fun } x \to e)> \qquad E \vdash e_2 \Rightarrow v_2 \qquad (x{:}v_2){::}E' \vdash e \Rightarrow v}{E \vdash (e_1\ e_2) \Rightarrow v} \quad \text{(App1)}$$

The expression $(e_1\ e_2)$ in the environment E has the value v if, in this same environment, the expression e_1 has for its value the closure $<E',(\textbf{fun } x \to e)>$ and the expression e_2 has the value v_2 and if in the environment E' of the closure augmented by the binding of v_2 to x, the expression e has the value v.

The notation that we use to augment an environment by a new binding assumes that the environment will be represented by an association list. In such lists, the same variable may appear more than once, but the effective binding is determined by the leftmost pair defining this variable, that is, the one closest to the head of the list or the one added most recently to the environment.

$$\frac{E \vdash e_1 \Rightarrow <E',(\textbf{fun } (x_1,\ldots,x_n) \to e)> \qquad E \vdash e_2 \Rightarrow (v_1,\ldots,v_n) \qquad (x_1{:}v_1){::}\ldots{::}(x_n{:}v_n){::}E' \vdash e \Rightarrow v}{E \vdash (e_1\ e_2) \Rightarrow v} \quad \text{(App2)}$$

The expression $(e_1\ e_2)$ in the environment E has the value v if, in the same environment, the expression e_1 has for its value a closure $<E',(\textbf{fun } (x_1,\ldots,x_n) \to e)>$ and the expression e_2 has a value $(v_1,\ldots,v_n)$ and if, in the environment E' of the closure augmented by the set of bindings between the values v_i and the variables x_i, the expression e has the value v.

$$\frac{E \vdash e_1 \Rightarrow v_1 \qquad (x{:}v_1){::}E \vdash e_2 \Rightarrow v}{E \vdash \textbf{let } x{=}e_1 \textbf{ in } e_2 \Rightarrow v} \quad \text{(Let)}$$

The expression **let** $x{=}e_1$ **in** e_2 has the value v in the environment E if, in the same environment, the expression e_1 has the value v_1 and if in the environment E augmented by the binding between v_1 and x, the expression e_2 has the value v.

To take recursion into account, we will adopt the following solution: a recursive function f defined by **let rec** f x = e will be represented by a closure $<E,(\textbf{fun } x \rightarrow e)>$ for which the environment E contains the infinite pair $f{:}<E,(\textbf{fun } x \rightarrow e)>$[1].

Given an environment E, a function name f, and a functional expression (**fun** $x \rightarrow e$) (where e may contain occurrences of f), we assume that we can construct an environment E' such that $E' = (f{:}<E',(\textbf{fun } x \rightarrow e)>){::}E$. The rule to take recursion into account is thus the following:

$$\frac{E' = (f{:}<E',(\textbf{fun } x \rightarrow e)>){::}E \vdash e_2 \Rightarrow v}{E \vdash \textbf{let rec } f\ x{=}e_1 \textbf{ in } e_2 \Rightarrow v} \quad \text{(Letrec)}$$

The expression **let rec** f $x{=}e_1$ **in** e_2 has the value v in the environment E if in the environment E' defined by $E' = (f{:}<E',(\textbf{fun } x \rightarrow e)>){::}E$ where the variable f thus has for its value the closure $<E',(\textbf{fun } x \rightarrow e)>$, the expression e_2 has the value v.

Notice that if you read these rules in reverse order (from bottom to top, as it were), they provide an effective means to evaluate any expression. We will exploit this observation to write a CAML evaluator in CAML.

11.2   Writing an Evaluator in Caml

A definition of CAML evaluation by an evaluation function written in CAML is in some respects a sleight of hand because it assumes that we already know how to evaluate the evaluation function. Nevertheless, this exercise is instructive because in doing it, we reduce the evaluation of all the expressions of the language to the evaluation of a very small number of simple functions. In particular, the evaluation function does not exploit higher order features, so to define the implementation of the language completely, it suffices to show how the evaluation function itself can be evaluated or compiled into machine langauage.

We begin by introducing a type ml_exp to define the abstract syntax of a kernel of CAML and another type val to define values that may result from a

---

[1]*A priori*, this kind of object is infinite, but it is possible to give it a finite representation as a data structure that loops.

computation. In closures, environments are represented by association lists of type (string * val) list.

The kernel of CAML to which we restrict ourselves for the moment contains no notion of *n*-tuples, but only pairs. As a parameter, every function has a unique variable—not an *n*-tuple of variables. Functions to access pairs (fst and snd) are predefined as are binary arithmetic operations (+, −, and *) as well as comparisons (= and <).

The predefined operations correspond in abstract syntax to the types ml_unop and ml_binop.

#type ml_unop = MI_fst | MI_snd;;

#type ml_binop = MI_add | MI_sub | MI_mult | MI_eq | MI_less;;

```
#type ml_exp =
      MI_int_const of int                         (* integer constant *)
    | MI_bool_const of bool                       (* Boolean constant *)
    | MI_pair of ml_exp * ml_exp                              (* pair *)
    | MI_unop of ml_unop * ml_exp                  (* unary operation *)
    | MI_binop of ml_binop * ml_exp * ml_exp      (* binary operation *)
    | MI_var of string                                   (* variable *)
    | MI_if of ml_exp * ml_exp * ml_exp               (* conditional *)
    | MI_fun of string * ml_exp                          (* function *)
    | MI_app of ml_exp * ml_exp                       (* application *)
    | MI_let of string * ml_exp * ml_exp             (* declaration *)
    | MI_letrec of string * ml_exp * ml_exp  (* recursive declaration *)
;;
```

The values of expressions are represented by the type val. They are integer constants, Booleans, pairs, and closures.

```
#type val =
      Int_Const of int
    | Bool_Const of bool
    | Pair of val * val
    | Clo of (string * val) list * ml_exp;;
```

We assume as usual that we have a function to analyze syntax corresponding to this type:

```
#ml_exp_of_string;;
— : string → ml_exp = ⟨fun⟩
```

```
#ml_exp_of_string "let x=1 in x+2";;
— : ml_exp = Ml_let ("x", Ml_int_const 1,
               Ml_binop (Ml_add, Ml_var "x", Ml_int_const 2))
```

The function ml_eval computes the value of an expression in an environment. To do so, it uses an auxiliary function ml_eval_binop to associate a function of type val → val → val with the basic operations.

```
#let ml_eval_binop = fun
    Ml_add (Int_Const m) (Int_Const n) → Int_Const (add_int m n)
  | Ml_sub (Int_Const m) (Int_Const n) → Int_Const (sub_int m n)
  | Ml_mult (Int_Const m) (Int_Const n) → Int_Const (mult_int m n)
  | Ml_eq(Int_Const m) (Int_Const n) → Bool_Const (eq_int m n)
  | Ml_less (Int_Const m) (Int_Const n) → Bool_Const (lt_int m n)
  | _ _ _ → failwith "ml_eval_binop: wrong types";;
ml_eval_binop : ml_binop → val → val → val = ⟨fun⟩
```

```
#let rec ml_eval env = fun
    (Ml_int_const n) → Int_Const n
  | (Ml_bool_const b) → Bool_Const b
  | (Ml_pair (e₁,e₂)) → Pair(ml_eval env e₁, ml_eval env e₂)
  | (Ml_unop (op,e)) → (match (op, ml_eval env e) with
                       (Ml_fst, Pair(v₁,v₂)) → v₁
                     |( Ml_snd, Pair(v₁,v₂)) → v₂
                     | _ → failwith "ml_eval: wrong types")
  | (Ml_binop (op, e₁, e₂)) → let v₂ = ml_eval env e₂
                       and v₁ = ml_eval env e₁
                       in ml_eval_binop op v₁ v₂
  | (Ml_var x) → (try assoc x env
                   with Not_found → failwith "unbound variable")
  | (Ml_if (c,e₁,e₂)) → (match ml_eval env c with
                       (Bool_Const true) → ml_eval env e₁
                     | (Bool_Const false) → ml_eval env e₂
                     | _ → failwith "ml_eval: wrong types")
  | (Ml_fun (x,e) as f) → Clo(env,f)
  | (Ml_app (e₁,e₂)) → (match (ml_eval env e₁, ml_eval env e₂) with
                       (Clo(env',Ml_fun (x,e)),v)
                       → ml_eval ((x,v)::env') e
                     | _ → failwith "ml_eval: wrong types")
  | (Ml_let (x,e₁,e₂)) → let v = ml_eval env e₁
                       in ml_eval ((x,v)::env) e₂
  | (Ml_letrec (f,e₁,e₂))
    → (match e₁ with
        Ml_fun _ → let rec env' = (f,Clo(env',e₁))::env
                   in ml_eval env' e₂
      | _ → failwith "illegal recursive definition");;
ml_eval : (string * val) list → ml_exp → val = ⟨fun⟩
```

Notice that recursive definitions exploit a recursive definition of an environment. This kind of recursive definition (impinging on objects, not on functions) is not handled by the evaluator that we just wrote. However, these recursive definitions of values will be well handled in the compiler you will see in Chapter 12.

Here are two examples of evaluation.

```
#ml_eval [ ]
   (ml_exp_of_string
      ("let double = fun f -> fun x -> f(f x) in " ^
       "let sq = fun x -> x*x in " ^
       "(double sq) 5"));;
```
— : val = Int_Const 625

```
#ml_eval [ ]
   (ml_exp_of_string
      ("let rec fact=" ^
       "  fun n -> if n=0 then 1 else n*(fact(n-1)) in " ^
       "fact 10"));;
```
— : val = Int_Const 3628800

Exercise
11.1 Complete the type ml_exp and the function ml_eval so that they handle tuples and functions with an n-tuple of parameters.

11.3   Evaluation by Necessity = Lazy Evaluation = Delayed Evaluation

Now we will modify our evaluator to take evaluation by necessity into account. To do so, it suffices to *delay* the evaluation of certain subexpressions until their value is *needed* to complete the computation[2].

We will use the following principle. In an evaluator built on the idea of environments, the evaluation of an expression depends on the evaluation environment that contains, in particular, the values of free variables in the expression. To defer the evaluation of an expression, we must consequently save that environment.

By associating an expression with its evaluation environment, we keep all the information necessary to evaluate the expression, and we can thus carry out the evaluation later.

As a consequence, to deal with an expression for which we want to delay evaluation, it suffices to construct a pair containing this expression and its environment. We call this procedure "freezing" an evaluation, and the structure we get that way is known as a **thunk** or a **promise**.

---

[2]In what follows, we use the terms "evaluation by necessity," "delayed evaluation," and "lazy evaluation" interchangeably.

When we need to know the effective value of a thunk, we must "thaw" it; that is, we have to carry out the evaluation that was delayed. To do so, it suffices to recall the evaluation function and pass it the environment and the expression.

Which evaluations should be delayed?

- the argument of an application;

- the components of a given data structure.

When should they be thawed? We must thaw them simply when we attempt to access them. An attempt to access a component in a data structure or even an argument of a function (that is, to access the value of a variable in the current environment) will be interpreted as the need to get the corresponding value.

The principle behind the evaluation function that we gave you earlier is the following: when it is called for an expression, that means that its value is needed. When its argument is an application $(e_1 \ e_2)$, we begin then by evaluating e_1 since it is needed. When this evaluation produces a closure, we evaluate the body of this closure with an environment enriched by the thunk of the expression e_2. During the evaluation of the body of the closure, the value of e_2 may (or may not) become necessary. Then and only then will we thaw e_2.

This evaluation function will thus never return a frozen value. Of course, it can return a value that has frozen components (data structures, for example).

Delayed evaluation is not really useful unless we use data structures; once we begin using them, we have the possibility of using infinite data structures. With that in mind, we will enrich our language so that we can compute with lists.

First, we introduce the type ml_constructor corresponding to constructors. For now, we will be content with constructors of lists, but the evaluation function we will show you later will accept any constructors.

```
#type ml_constructor = Nil | Cons;;
```

Next, we enrich the type ml_exp to accomodate functions defined by pattern matching (that is, the constructor Ml_func) and applications of constructors (that is, the constructor Ml_capp). We also enrich the type val to accommodate applications of constructors to values (that is, the constructor Constr) and especially the fact that certain expressions can be frozen. For that, we define the constructor Fre, similar to Clo; it stores an expression for which evaluation has been delayed along with the evaluation environment.

```
#type ml_exp =
        Ml_int_const of int                    (* integer constant *)
      | Ml_bool_const of bool                  (* Boolean constant *)
```

```
        | Ml_pair of ml_exp * ml_exp                          (* pair *)
        | Ml_unop of ml_unop * ml_exp                   (* unary operation *)
        | Ml_binop of ml_binop * ml_exp * ml_exp         (* base operation *)
        | Ml_var of string                                   (* variable *)
        | Ml_constr₀ of ml_constructor             (* nullary constructor *)
        | Ml_if of ml_exp * ml_exp * ml_exp                (* conditional *)
        | Ml_fun of string * ml_exp                          (* function *)
        | Ml_func of (ml_constructor * string list * ml_exp) list
                                             (* pattern matching function *)
        | Ml_app of ml_exp * ml_exp                       (* application *)
        | Ml_capp of ml_constructor * ml_exp list   (* constructor appl. *)
        | Ml_let of string * ml_exp * ml_exp             (* declaration *)
        | Ml_letrec of string * ml_exp * ml_exp    (* recursive declaration *)
;;

#type val =
        Int_Const of int
        | Bool_Const of bool
        | Pair of val * val
        | Clo of (string * val) list * ml_exp                (* closure *)
        | Fre of (string * val) list * ml_exp                  (* thunk *)
        | Constr₀ of ml_constructor
        | Constrₙ of ml_constructor * val list         (* data structures *)
;;
```

The patterns used in this syntax will be limited to the form $C(x_1,\dots,x_n)$ where n is the arity of the constructor C and the x_i are variables.

Here are a few examples of syntax:

```
#exp_of_string "Cons(x,1)";;
```
$-: ml\_exp = Ml\_capp\ (Cons, [\,Ml\_var\ "x";\ Ml\_var\ "1"\,])$

```
#exp_of_string "fun Nil -> Nil | (Cons(x,1)) -> x";;
```
$-: ml\_exp = Ml\_func\ [\,Nil, [\ ], Ml\_constr_0\ Nil;$
$$Cons, [\,"x";\ "1"\,], Ml\_var\ "x"\,]$$

The auxiliary function **select**, of course, will select the right case in a pattern to match. The auxiliary function **combine** will enrich the environment with all the bindings created by a case of pattern matching.

```
#let rec select p = fun
    (a::l) → if p a then a else select p l
    | _ → failwith "select";;
```
$select : (\alpha \rightarrow bool) \rightarrow \alpha\ list \rightarrow \alpha = \langle \mathbf{fun} \rangle$

```
#let rec combine = fun
   ([ ],[ ]) → [ ]
 | (a::l,a'::l') → (a,a')::combine(l,l')
 | _ → failwith "combine";;
combine : α list * β list → (α * β) list = ⟨fun⟩
```

The new evaluation function is accompanied by the function **unfreeze** to thaw frozen values.

```
#let rec ml_eval env = fun
   (Ml_int_const n) → Int_Const n
 | (Ml_bool_const b) → Bool_Const b
 | (Ml_pair (e₁,e₂)) → Pair(Fre(env,e₁), Fre(env,e₂))
 | (Ml_unop (op,e)) →(match (op, ml_eval env e) with
                        (Ml_fst, Pair(v₁,v₂)) → unfreeze v₁
                      | (Ml_snd, Pair(v₁,v₂)) → unfreeze v₂
                      | _ → failwith "ml_eval: wrong types")
 | (Ml_binop (op, e₁, e₂)) → let v₁ = ml_eval env e₁
                            and v₂ = ml_eval env e₂ in
                            (ml_eval_binop op) v₁ v₂
 | (Ml_var x) → unfreeze(assoc x env)
 | (Ml_constr₀ c) → Constr₀ c
 | (Ml_if (c,e₁,e₂)) → (match ml_eval env c with
                        (Bool_Const true) → ml_eval env e₁
                      | (Bool_Const false) → ml_eval env e₂
                      | _ → failwith "ml_eval: wrong types")
 | (Ml_fun _ as f) → Clo(env,f)
 | (Ml_func _ as f) → Clo(env,f)
 | (Ml_app (e₁,e₂))
   → (match ml_eval env e₁ with
       (Clo(env',Ml_fun (x,e)))
       → ml_eval ((x,Fre(env,e₂))::env') e
     | (Clo(env',Ml_func case_list))
       → let (c,vl) = match ml_eval env e₂ with
           (Constrₙ(c,vl)) → c,vl
         | (Constr₀ c) → c,[ ]
         | _ → failwith "ml_eval: wrong types" in
       let (c',sl,e) =
         select (fun (c',sl,e) → (c'=c)) case_list
         in ml_eval (combine(sl,vl)@env') e
     | _ → failwith "ml_eval: wrong types")
 | (Ml_capp (c,el)) → Constrₙ(c, map (fun e → Fre(env,e)) el)
```

```
    | (MI_let (x,e₁,e₂)) → ml_eval ((x,Fre(env,e₁))::env) e₂
    | (MI_letrec (f,e₁,e₂)) → let rec env' = (f,Fre(env',e₁))::env in
                              ml_eval env' e₂
  and unfreeze = fun
    (Fre(env',e)) → ml_eval env' e
    | v → v;;
  ml_eval : (string * val) list → ml_exp → val = ⟨fun⟩
  unfreeze : val → val = ⟨fun⟩
```

Here are a few examples to illustrate what we have been doing. The first example is a simple factorial computation. The following three examples illustrate the fact that the evaluator that we just defined lets us avoid useless calculations. In particular, the last example would not terminate in call by value.

```
#ml_eval [ ]
   (exp_of_string
      ("let rec fact = " ^
       " fun n -> if n=0 then 1 else n*(fact(n-1)) in " ^
       "fact 10"));;
 - : val = Int_Const 3628800

#ml_eval [ ]
   (exp_of_string
      ("let rec fact = " ^
       " fun n -> if n=0 then 1 else n*(fact(n-1)) in " ^
       "(fun x -> 1) (fact 100000)"));;
 - : val = Int_Const 1

#ml_eval [ ]
   (exp_of_string
      ("let rec fact = " ^
       " fun n -> if n=0 then 1 else n*(fact(n-1)) in " ^
       "(fst(1,fact 100000))"));;
 - : val = Int_Const 1

#ml_eval [ ]
   (exp_of_string
      ("let rec boucle =" ^
       " fun n -> boucle (n+1) in " ^
       "(fun x -> 1) (boucle 1)"));;
 - : val = Int_Const 1
```

Our new evaluator also handles infinite lists. The following example builds an infinite ordered list without repetition of multiples of 3 and 7. To display the beginning of this list, we define an auxiliary function in CAML, nfirst, that forms a list in the CAML sense from the first n elements of a list in the **val** sense. It does so by thawing the elements to display.

```
#let rec nfirst = fun
   0 → (fun _ → [ ])
 | n → (fun (Constrₙ (Cons,[x;l]))
               → (unfreeze x)::nfirst (n−1) (unfreeze l)
               | _ → failwith "nfirst: wrong data");;
nfirst : int → val → val list = ⟨fun⟩
```

```
#nfirst 20
  (ml_eval [ ]
    (exp_of_string
      ("let hd = fun (Cons(x,l)) -> x in " ^
      "let tl = fun (Cons(x,l)) -> l in " ^
      "let rec makelist=" ^
      "      fun f -> fun x -> " ^
      "                  Cons(x,makelist f (f x)) in " ^
      "let rec merge = " ^
      "      fun l -> fun ll ->" ^
      "           if (hd l) < (hd ll) then " ^
      "           Cons(hd l,merge(tl l) ll) else " ^
      "           if (hd l) = (hd ll) then " ^
      "           merge(tl l) ll " ^
      "           else Cons(hd ll,merge l (tl ll)) " ^
      "in merge (makelist (fun x -> x+3) 3)" ^
      "         (makelist (fun x -> x+7) 7)")));;
```
$-$: *val list* = [*Int_Const* 3; *Int_Const* 6; *Int_Const* 7; *Int_Const* 9;
                  Int_Const 12; *Int_Const* 14; *Int_Const* 15;
                  Int_Const 18; *Int_Const* 21; *Int_Const* 24;
                  Int_Const 27; *Int_Const* 28; *Int_Const* 30;
                  Int_Const 33; *Int_Const* 35; *Int_Const* 36;
                  Int_Const 39; *Int_Const* 42; *Int_Const* 45;
                  Int_Const 48]

To get a reasonably efficient implementation of delayed evaluation, we still need to modify our evaluator to avoid duplications of computations due to the fact that a variable may occur more than once. In effect, every time we access a variable in the environment, we provoke the thawing of a thunk, and multiple attempts to access the same thunk will provoke equally many evaluations.

What we have to do is make sure that every frozen value is systematically replaced by its value once calculated so that the value will be re-used (not recalculated) when it is needed again. In the evaluator we just showed you, a simple way to produce those changes is to represent environments and values by structures that can be physically modified. We leave one such way of doing that as an exercise.

When delayed evaluation is implemented in such a way as to avoid duplication of calculations, it is then called **lazy** evaluation.

11.4   Summary

We defined two evaluators of CAML, both written in CAML. These evaluators exploit the idea of **environments**. During a function call or during the evaluation of a **let**, the formal parameters of the function or the variables defined by the **let** are not replaced textually but the corresponding binding is stored in a look-up table known as the environment.

Functional values are presented in the form of **closures**, that is, pairs consisting of the text of a function and an environment.

A priori, this way of working is better adapted to evaluation by value, but it is possible to adapt it to delayed evaluation by "freezing" the stored values and "thawing" them when their value is needed. Delayed evaluation can be turned into lazy evaluation, where duplicate computations are avoided.

11.5   To Learn More

Landin, in 1965, introduced the idea of evaluating functional languages using the ideas of environments and closures. This technique is particularly useful to construct a compiler, as we do in the next chapter. At the end of that chapter, we will review the various implementation techniques for functional languages.

In comparison to a compiler, an evaluator like those we defined here suffers from inherent inefficiency. In effect, such evaluators continuously analyze the structure of the program they are evaluating in order to decide which actions to carry out, whereas in a compiler, such an analysis is carried out once and for all before execution. Even so, it is often instructive to write an evaluator; doing so helps you understand evaluation mechanisms that a compiler uses in a more obscure way.

Chapter 12

Compilation

In this chapter, we describe a technique to compile a functional language like CAML into machine code. This compilation technique is strongly connected to the evaluation technique developed in the preceding chapter. In particular, the idea of an environment again plays a central role here, and we keep the idea of closure to represent functional values. However, you will see that these two ideas correspond to slightly different objects in a compiler.

To keep the compiler at a sufficiently conceptual level of description, we have opted to use machine code made up of instructions specially adapted to our compilation scheme. These instructions produce operations more complicated than the "real" instructions of an assembly language. Even so, it is clear that these instructions can be expanded into a list of machine instructions producing the same effect. The compilation scheme we present thus leads directly to a real compiler.

To execute the code produced by our compiler, we use a stack to store the intermediate values needed in computations; we also store the addresses of subprograms there, a conventional and time-honored practice. What is special, though, about compiling functional languages are the instructions to allocate memory needed to build structured values, environments, and closures. To explain these instructions and their role in the compilation of functional languages, we must first explain how we use computer memory to represent complex objects. For that reason, this chapter begins with a section about the representation of data structures. We then go on to describe machine instructions and code generation in Section 12.3. We round things off by producing a compiler in CAML along with a code simulator in Section 12.4.

12.1 A Simplified Model of Computer Memory

A computer memory is essentially a large linear array of cells. These cells are numbered, starting from 0 (zero). Those numbers are known as **addresses**.

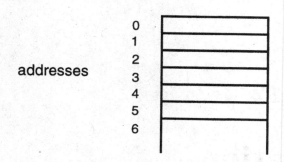

addresses

Figure 12.1. The structure of computer memory

Each cell contains information, generally in 32 bits. Such a model is represented in Figure 12.1.

The information contained in each memory cell can be decoded in various ways. We can read it as an integer, a floating-point number, a set of four characters, or even as an address or a machine instruction.

Generally, a user does not have direct access to the physical memory of a computer, but the user sees it through primitives that the system offers. In particular, the execution of a compiled program makes the computer create a process which has space in virtual memory available to it. At any given time, this virtual memory is divided among the main memory and the disks, yet everything works as though the executing program had direct access to physical memory.

The memory allocated to a process for computation is conceptually divided into zones. Here we are interested in three such zones: a **code zone** containing instructions, a **memory zone** containing (strictly speaking) data manipulated by the program (this zone is sometimes known as the heap), and a **stack zone** containing information about how the computation takes place. In addition, we assume that there are three special memory cells, known as **registers**. The code register (CR) contains an address in the code zone (the current instruction). The memory register (MR) contains an address in the memory zone (the first available cell). The stack register (SR) contains an address in the stack (the top of the stack). You see this kind of organization in Figure 12.2.

Instructions corresponding to elementary operations take their arguments from the stack and return their result to the stack as well.

12.2   Implementation of Data Structures

To avoid complicating our explanations, we will limit our descriptions to these kinds of data:

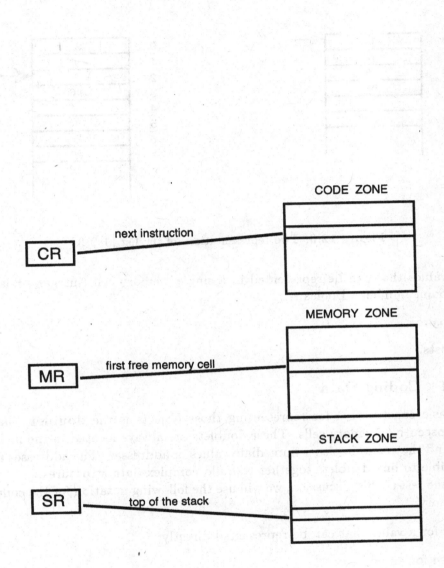

Figure 12.2. How a process is organized in memory

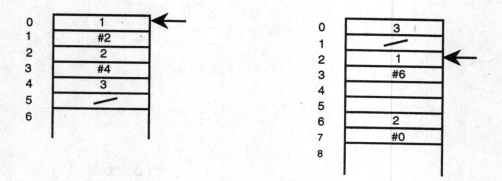

Figure 12.3. Two representations of the list $[1; 2; 3]$

- values that can be represented in a single memory cell (integers, floating-point numbers, Booleans);

- pairs;

- lists.

12.2.1 Coding Data

The basic construction for representing those objects is the **doublet**, that is, two consecutive memory cells. These doublets are always located in the memory zone, and they contain either immediate values or addresses. The addresses make it possible to link doublets together to build complex data structures.

In the rest of this discussion, we will use the following notation for the contents of memory:

- n for a value that can be represented directly;

- #n for an address;

- / a special value conventionally representing the empty list.

Figure 12.3 shows you two possible representations in memory for the list $[1; 2; 3]$ (which can also be written as 1::2::3::[ ]).

Notice that the order in which elements of the list appear in memory is independent of their order in the list. The way pointers (the addresses) are *linked together* defines the list.

When we want to see the memory representation of an object as an image independent of the way its memory cells are numbered, we will use a drawing like the one in Figure 12.4.

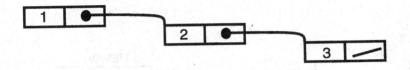

Figure 12.4. A more abstract representation

12.2.2   CONS as an Operation

When a CAML program contains an expression of the form (e_1,e_2) or $(e_1::e_2)$, the corresponding machine code must compute the values of the expressions e_1 and e_2 and then allocate a doublet where the first cell contains (the address of) the value of e_1 and the second cell contains (the address of) the value of e_2. We call this operation CONS. We assume that (the address of) the value of e_1 is found at the top of the stack (STACK[SR]) and that (the address of) the value of e_2 is right under it (STACK[SR−1]).

The effect of CONS as an operation can be defined by the following sequence of instructions:

```
MEM[MR] ← STACK[SR];
MEM[MR+1] ← STACK[SR−1];
STACK[SR−1] ← MR;
MR ← MR+2;
SR ← SR−1
```

(We assume that all the free doublets are located after the address MR; thus when the doublet of the address MR has been used, the new first free doublet is the address MR+2.)

Figure 12.5 shows you this operation in an example.

12.2.3   Sharing Data

When a structured value is referenced in a CAML expression, its address is used to designate this value in the compiled code of the expression. A value is thus always referenced by the contents of one sole word in memory.

When a complex value is used to build new values, only its address will be copied. For example, if the value v of the variable x is at the address #n, then the computation of the expression (x,x) does not entail a copy of the value v; rather, it occurs as the construction of a doublet where the two parts contain the address #n. In the representation of the value of (x,x), the value v is **shared** by the two elements of that pair, as you see in Figure 12.6.

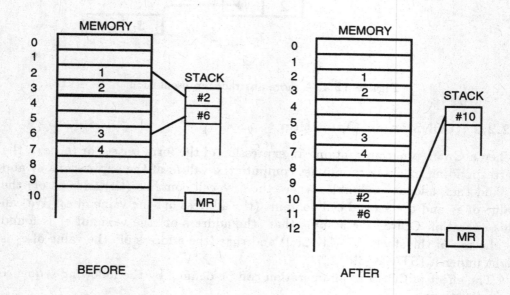

Figure 12.5. Operation CONS

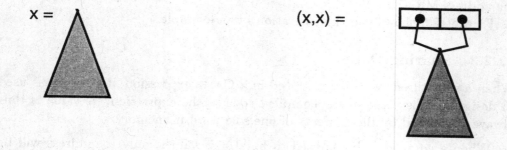

Figure 12.6. Sharing data

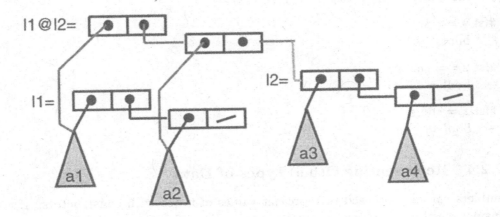

Figure 12.7. How append shares

Generally, then, the representation structure of values is not a tree but rather a graph (usually without cycles except for recursive values). Even when the expressions do not contain multiple occurrences of the same variable, evaluation may introduce sharing between a value being calculated and existing values. For example, the evaluation of the expression (l_1 @ l_2) concatenates two lists, l_1 and l_2; to do so, it constructs one structure which contains the addresses of elements of l_1 and the address of l_2.

Figure 12.7 shows you the result of this data sharing. Evaluation of the expression (l_1 @ l_2) allocates a number of doublets equal to the length of l_1, however complicated the elements in those lists.

At the level of CAML itself, you can detect sharing in the representation of values when you use the operator ==. In contrast to the operator = (which tests equality between *logical* values), == tests *physical* equality. That is, it checks whether the contents of memory cells containing its arguments are identical. The expression e_1==e_2 is true if the values of e_1 and e_2 are two equal immediate values or if they are two identical structured values (that is, located at the same address).

Here are a few examples to highlight what we mean:

#let x = (1,2);;
x : *int* * *int* = 1, 2

#let y = (x,x);;
y : (*int* * *int*) * (*int* * *int*) = (1, 2), (1, 2)

#let z = ((1,2),(1,2));;

$z : (int * int) * (int * int) = (1, 2), (1, 2)$

```
#fst y == snd y;;
```
$- : bool = true$

```
#fst z == snd z;;
```
$- : bool = false$

```
#fst z = snd z;;
```
$- : bool = true$

12.2.4   Representing Other Types of Data

Doublets can also be used to represent values of types with constructors. If we consider a value (C v) formed by the application of a constructor C to a value v, the first element of the doublet will contain an encoding of C and the second part will contain (the address of) the value v.

This representation can be optimized in various ways. For example, it is clear that if a type has only one constructor, then there is no need to represent it[1].

To represent n-tuples, records, and vectors, we cannot limit ourselves to individual doublets. We need to be able to allocate other sequences of memory cells, too.

Indeed, vectors and character strings need special structures in which the size of the object is indicated.

12.2.5   Recovering Allocated Memory

Frequently, a computation uses many intermediate values that are only temporarily useful. Once they have been used, they can be destroyed. However, it is not always possible for the programmer to determine exactly which values can be eliminated and which must be saved. This problem in general is undecidable.

The perspective adopted by functional languages is that the programmer should not have to worry about how long the data structures that he or she builds actually live. Clearly, however, for any given program, the size of usable memory is finite, and if memory is allocated without ever being recovered, a time will come when it will be used up entirely so that new values cannot be constructed. For that reason, we have to provide a means to recover memory occupied by useless structures. Such a means is known as a **garbage collector**, abbreviated **GC**.

There are many techniques of garbage collection in use. In general, they are variations on or combinations of two basic techniques:

---

[1]In practice, lots of other constructors can be eliminated if we exploit the representation of the values that the constructors impinge on.

- garbage collection by recovery of useless cells;

- garbage collection by copying useful cells.

In these two kinds of garbage collection, we determine the useful structures by following all the pointers that access values, either from the execution stack or from the symbol table where global variables are stored.

When the garbage collector recovers useless cells, any memory that has not yet been used is represented as a list of doublets. In this case, the means for allocating doublets is slightly different from the one we presented on page 382. The register MR points to the head of a list of available doublets and must point to the following doublet after a CONS. When this list is empty, the garbage collector must sweep through the memory zone twice. The first sweep finds and marks the useful doublets by following pointers. The second sweep takes the unmarked doublets to make a new list of available ones, and then normal computation starts again.

When the garbage collector copies useful cells, it divides memory into two zones to use them alternately. Memory that has not yet been used in the active zone is represented as a sequence of contiguous doublets allocated sequentially. When the active zone is full, the useful doublets are copied contiguously into the second zone. The second zone then becomes active, and its unoccupied part serves for allocations.

In theory, a garbage collector that copies useful cells is faster because it traverses only the useful cells whereas the other technique—of recovering useless cells—sweeps the entire memory zone. It has an additional advantage in that it compacts data and thus limits traffic between disks and main memory during a computation. However, it is inconvenient in that it does not use all of available memory since it has partitioned that available memory in two.

In practice, the efficiency of garbage collectors depends on highly complicated refinements that we will not go into here.

Exercises

12.1 Consider the type α gentree defined on page 135. The size of trees of type gentree is by definition the number of nodes, and it is computed by the function gentree_size on page 136. However, the actual size of the machine representation of such trees might be different from their theoretical size because some nodes might be shared. We call the "actual size" of such trees the number of physically distinct nodes that they contain, that is, the number of nodes distinguished by the predicate ==. Write a function to compute the actual size of a tree of type gentree.

12.2 When we handle very large trees, it is useful to reduce the size of their representation by sharing equal subtrees. Write a function of type α gentree $\rightarrow$ α gentree that starts with a tree t and then provides an equal tree represented by sharing all the equal subtrees. In other words, for every pair of subtrees (t',t") of the original tree t, we have t'=t" if and only if t'==t". This way of compacting trees is very useful, for example, when we exploit trees in spelling checkers. In fact, since verbs are conjugated as they are, there are a great many possibilities for sharing, so this kind of compacting usually reduces the number of nodes. In French, for example, it reduces them by more than 80%.

12.3   Producing Code

As compiled code, we will use a set of instructions that are not really machine instructions, but they are sufficiently simple to be easily translated into machine instructions. Some have arguments that are constants or addresses.

Since some instructions have arguments, we cannot assume that all the instructions fit into a single word in memory, nor that they all occupy the same number of words in memory. The way we increment the code register CR to get to the next instruction thus depends on the size of the instruction executed.

To simplify our presentation of various instructions, we will not make this modification of CR explicit for instructions that do not change the sequence of the program. However, we will, of course, make this modification explicit for any instructions, like CALL or RETURN, where the purpose is to change the sequence of the program.

Every instruction is defined by a set of transfers of the contents of memory cells. These transfers should happen in parallel, denoted by the sign " $\|$."

12.3.1   List of Instructions

Primitive operations

PLUS   STACK[SR$-$1] $\leftarrow$ (STACK[SR] $+$ STACK[SR$-$1]) $\|$ SR $\leftarrow$ SR$-$1
MULT   STACK[SR$-$1] $\leftarrow$ (STACK[SR] $*$ STACK[SR$-$1]) $\|$ SR $\leftarrow$ SR$-$1

The instruction PLUS replaces the two elements at the top of the stack by their sum. The instruction MULT replaces the two elements at the top of the stack by their product. We assume that all the binary arithmetic operations work the same way.

Stack operations

LOAD v   STACK[SR] $\leftarrow$ v
PUSH v   STACK[SR+1] $\leftarrow$ v $\|$ SR $\leftarrow$ SR+1
DUPL   STACK[SR+1] $\leftarrow$ STACK[SR] $\|$ SR $\leftarrow$ SR+1
SWAP   STACK[SR] $\leftarrow$ STACK[SR$-$1] $\|$ STACK[SR$-$1] $\leftarrow$ STACK[SR]
ROT$_3$ STACK[SR] $\leftarrow$ STACK[SR$-$1] $\|$ STACK[SR$-$1] $\leftarrow$ STACK[SR$-$2]
         $\|$ STACK[SR$-$2] $\leftarrow$ STACK[SR]
IROT$_3$ STACK[SR] $\leftarrow$ STACK[SR$-$2] $\|$ STACK[SR$-$1] $\leftarrow$ STACK[SR]
         $\|$ STACK[SR$-$2] $\leftarrow$ STACK[SR$-$1]

The instruction LOAD v replaces the top of the stack by v.

The instruction PUSH v pushes the value v onto the stack.

The instruction DUPL adds a copy of the top of the stack to the stack itself.

The instruction SWAP permutes the top of the stack with the element immediately below it in the stack.

The instruction ROT$_3$ circularly permutes the three elements above the stack.

The instruction IROT$_3$ inversely permutes the three elements above the stack.

Data structure instructions

FST	STACK[SR] ← MEM[STACK[SR]]
SND	STACK[SR] ← MEM[STACK[SR]+1]
SETFST	MEM[STACK[SR−1]] ← STACK[SR] ‖ SR ← SR−1
SETSND	MEM[STACK[SR−1]+1] ← STACK[SR] ‖ SR ← SR−1
CONS	MEM[MR] ← STACK[SR] ‖ MEM[MR+1] ← STACK[SR−1]
	‖ STACK[SR−1] ← MR ‖ MR ← MR+2 ‖ SR ← SR−1
SPLIT	STACK[SR+1] ← MEM[STACK[SR]]
	‖ STACK[SR] ← MEM[STACK[SR]+1]
	‖ SR ← SR+1

The instruction FST can be executed only if the top of the stack contains the address of a doublet. This address is then replaced by the first element of that doublet.

The instruction SND can be executed only if the top of the stack contains the address of a doublet. This address is then replaced by the second element of that doublet.

The instruction SETFST can be executed only if the element below the top of the stack contains the address of a doublet. The first element of that doublet is then replaced by the top of the stack, and the stack is popped.

The instruction SETSND can be executed only if the element below the top of the stack contains the address of a doublet. The second element of that doublet is then replaced by the top of stack, and the stack is popped.

The instruction CONS carries out the operation we described on page 382.

The instruction SPLIT does the opposite of CONS. It assumes that the top of the stack contains an address of a doublet, and it replaces the top of the stack by the two elements which are, of course, the first and second parts of that doublet.

Branching instructions

CALL	STACK[SR] ← STACK[SR−1] ‖ STACK[SR−1] ← CR+1
	‖ CR ← STACK[SR]
RETURN	CR ← STACK[SR−1] ‖ STACK[SR−1] ← STACK[SR]
	‖ SR ← SR−1
BRANCH a_1 a_2	STACK[SR] ← **if** STACK[SR] **then** a_1 **else** a_2

The instruction CALL modifies the value of the code register to execute a subprogram. It stores the return address to get back to the main program once the subprogram has been executed. We assume that at the time that CALL is executed, the top of the stack contains the address of the subprogram, and the element immediately below contains a value useful to the subprogram (its parameter). Before we hand over control to the subprogram, we put its parameter on top of the stack and we put the return address immediately below (that is, the value of the code register already conveniently incremented).

The instruction RETURN will be put at the end of subprograms to make it possible to get back to the calling program. We assume that at the end of execution of the subprogram the result of its computation will be found at the top of the stack, and the return address will be immediately below.

The instruction BRANCH a_1 a_2 assumes that the top of the stack is a Boolean. If it is true, it will be replaced by the address a_1; otherwise, it will be replaced by the address a_2.

12.3.2   Principle behind Compilation

The computation of an expression e containing the free variables $x_1, \ldots, x_n$ occurs in an environment $[v_1; \ldots; v_n]$, a list containing values of these free variables. Here it is not necessary to keep the names of variables because the information to access them is incorporated in the compiled code. We call $[x_1; \ldots; x_n]$ the **compilation environment** and $[v_1; \ldots; v_n]$ the **execution environment**.

The execution environment is represented in memory, and we assume that at the beginning of execution, the address of this environment is at the top of the stack. Compiled code is designed so that this property remains true for the evaluation of every subexpression. Moreover, this code will have the effect globally of replacing the environment at the top of the stack by the value of the computed expression without touching the rest of the stack.

As in the evaluation mechanism you saw earlier, functions are represented by closures, that is, pairs of an environment and some code. The difference lies in the way the environment and the code are represented. Now "code" is an address in the code zone, and the environment is a simple list of values.

We denote the code of the expression e compiled in the environment $[x_1; \ldots;$ $x_n]$ by $[\![\, e\,]\!]_{(x_1, \ldots, x_n)}$. For an expression e with no free variables, the compiled code will thus be denoted $[\![\, e\,]\!]_{[]}$.

Compiling a Constant

$$[\![\, c\,]\!]_E = \text{LOAD } c$$

The code of a constant c in an environment E will simply replace the environment E at the top of the stack by the value c.

Compiling a Variable

$$[\![\, x\,]\!]_{(x::E)} = \text{FST} \qquad\qquad [\![\, x\,]\!]_{(y::E)} = \text{SND}; [\![\, x\,]\!]_E$$

The code corresponding to a variable x_i in an environment $[x_1; \ldots; x_n]$ is $\text{SND}^{(i-1)}$; FST. It lets us access the value of the variable in the execution environment.

Compiling a Pair

$$[\![\, (e_1, e_2)\,]\!]_E = \text{DUPL}; [\![\, e_2\,]\!]_E; \text{SWAP}; [\![\, e_1\,]\!]_E; \text{CONS}$$

The code corresponding to an expression (e_1, e_2) in an environment E duplicates (the address of) the environment to use that environment twice: once to compute e_2, and again to compute e_1. After the execution of the code corresponding to e_2, the value v_2 of e_2 will be found at the top of the stack, above the second copy of (the address of) the environment E. The instruction SWAP then permutes v_2 and E so that the code corresponding to e_1 executes correctly. That produces a value v_1 which is then found at the top of the stack immediately above v_2. The only thing left to do then is to apply the instruction CONS to these two values to make a pair.

Compiling an Arithmetic Expression

$$[\![\, e_1 + e_2\,]\!]_E = \text{DUPL}; [\![\, e_2\,]\!]_E; \text{SWAP}; [\![\, e_1\,]\!]_E; \text{PLUS}$$

The code corresponding to an expression $(e_1 + e_2)$ in an environment E duplicates (the address of) the environment so that the environment can be used twice, once for the computation of e_2, and again for the computation of e_1. After the execution of the code corresponding to e_2, the value v_2 of e_2 is located at the top of the stack above the second copy of (the address of) the environment E. The instruction SWAP then permutes v_2 and E so that the code corresponding to e_1 executes correctly. That produces the value v_1, found at the top of the stack immediately above v_2. The only thing left to do is to apply the instruction PLUS to these two values.

Compiling a Function

$$[\![\ \mathbf{fun}\ \mathsf{x} \to \mathsf{e}\ ]\!]_E = \ \mathsf{PUSH}\ \mathsf{a};\ \mathsf{SWAP};\ \mathsf{CONS}$$
where **a** is the address of the code for the function, that is,
$$[\![\ \mathsf{e}\ ]\!]_{(x::E)};\ \mathsf{RETURN}$$

The code produced for the body of a function (**fun** x → e) in a formal environment E is the code for the expression e in the formal environment $(x :: E)$ that we get by adding the variable x to the environment E. At the end of execution of this code, the result of the evaluation of the function will be found at the top of the stack and the return address immediately below. The operation RETURN can thus be carried out. After the execution of RETURN, the result of the evaluation of the function will again be found at the top of the stack and can be used for the rest of the computation.

The code produced for the expression (**fun** x → e) itself consists of an instruction to PUSH the address of the code for the body of the function onto the top of the stack and then uses CONS to build a closure consisting of a code address and an environment.

Compiling an Application

$$[\![\ (\mathsf{e_1}\ \mathsf{e_2})\ ]\!]_E = \ \mathsf{DUPL};\ [\![\ \mathsf{e_2}\ ]\!]_E;\ \mathsf{SWAP};\ [\![\ \mathsf{e_1}\ ]\!]_E;\ \mathsf{SPLIT};$$
$$\mathsf{IROT_3};\ \mathsf{CONS};\ \mathsf{SWAP};\ \mathsf{CALL}$$

The code corresponding to an expression $\mathsf{e_1}\ \mathsf{e_2}$ in an environment E duplicates (the address of) the environment so that the environment can be used twice, once to compute $\mathsf{e_2}$, and again to compute $\mathsf{e_1}$. After the execution of the code corresponding to $\mathsf{e_2}$, the value v_2 of $\mathsf{e_2}$ will be at the top of the stack above the second copy (of the address of) the environment E. The instruction SWAP then permutes v_2 and E so that the code corresponding to $\mathsf{e_1}$ executes correctly. That produces a value, v_1, a closure, that is, a pair where the first part is the environment of the closure and the second part is the address of the code for the function. This pair is separated into its two components by SPLIT. Then the three elements at the top of the stack are re-ordered by the operation $\mathsf{IROT_3}$ so that the top of the stack contains v_2, the next element down contains the environment of the closure to apply, the next element below that contains the address of the code for that closure. The operation CONS constructs the correct environment to call this code. SWAP then permutes the address of the code and the environment so that CALL executes.

Compiling a Conditional Statement

$$[\![\ \mathbf{if}\ \mathsf{e_1}\ \mathbf{then}\ \mathsf{e_2}\ \mathbf{else}\ \mathsf{e_3}\ ]\!]_E = \mathsf{DUPL};\ [\![\ \mathsf{e_1}\ ]\!]_E;\ \mathsf{BRANCH}\ \mathsf{a_2}\ \mathsf{a_3};\ \mathsf{CALL}$$
where $\mathsf{a_2}$ is the address of the code $[\![\ \mathsf{e_2}\ ]\!]_E;\ \mathsf{RETURN}$

and a_3 is the address of the code $[\![\ e_3\ ]\!]_E$; RETURN

The code corresponding to the expression (**if** e_1 **then** e_2 **else** e_3) duplicates (the address of) the environment so that the environment can be used twice, once to compute e_1, and once again to compute e_2 or e_3, depending on the case. The execution of the code for e_1 produces a Boolean which is then used by BRANCH to push the address of the code for either e_2 or e_3 (depending on the case) onto the stack before carrying out the CALL.

Compiling a let

$$[\![\ \textbf{let}\ x{=}e_1\ \textbf{in}\ e_2\ ]\!]_E = \text{DUPL};\ [\![\ e_1\ ]\!]_E;\ \text{CONS};\ [\![\ e_2\ ]\!]_{(x::E)};$$

The code corresponding to an expression **let** $x{=}e_1$ **in** e_2 duplicates the environment, computes the value of e_1, and then uses CONS to add it to the second copy of the environment before it computes the value of e_2. Notice that e_2 is compiled in an environment to which x has been added.

Compiling a Functional let rec

$$[\![\ \textbf{let rec}\ f = e_1\ \textbf{in}\ e_2\ ]\!]_E = \ \ \text{PUSH nil};\ [\![\ e_1\ ]\!]_{(f::E)};\ \text{DUPL};\ \text{ROT}_3;\ \text{CONS};$$
$$\text{SETFST};\ \text{FST};\ [\![\ e_2\ ]\!]_{(f::E)};$$

The code corresponding to an expression **let rec** $f{=}e_1$ **in** e_2 is similar to that for **let**. The difference is twofold: e_1 is compiled in an environment containing f; the sequence of instructions DUPL; ROT$_3$; CONS; SETFST is used to build the closure and to replace its environment part (which is initially the empty environment) by the address of the total environment containing f. When we finally access the environment part of this closure by means of the instruction FST, we get the correct "loop" environment to execute the code for e_2.

Compiling a Non-Functional let rec

$$[\![\ \textbf{let rec}\ x = e_1\ \textbf{in}\ e_2\ ]\!]_E = \ \ \text{DUPL};\ \text{PUSH nil};\ \text{DUPL};\ \text{CONS};\ \text{DUPL};\ \text{ROT}_3;$$
$$\text{CONS};\ [\![\ e_1\ ]\!]_{(x::E)};\ \text{DUPL};\ \text{ROT}_3;\ \text{FST};\ \text{SETFST};$$
$$\text{SWAP};\ \text{SND};\ \text{SETSND};\ \text{CONS};\ [\![\ e_2\ ]\!]_{(x::E)};$$

The code corresponding to an expression **let rec** $x{=}e_1$ **in** e_2 makes the hypothesis that the value of the expression e_1 is represented by a doublet and that the expression is made up uniquely of constructions of doublets. It begins by duplicating (the address of) the environment; then it constructs a doublet (nil,nil) which is the temporary value of e_1. The sequence of instructions DUPL; ROT$_3$; CONS; $[\![\ e_1\ ]\!]_{(x::E)}$ produces the new value of e_1 at the top of the stack while still keeping immediately below it the address of the doublet (nil,nil) to represent its temporary value.

There is nothing left to do then but successively replace the first and second cell of this doublet (nil,nil) by the first and second cell of the doublet representing the value of e_1 to get an adequate "looped" structure. That is done by the sequence of instructions DUPL; ROT$_3$; FST; SETFST; SWAP; SND; SETSND. The looped value that we get that way is then added to the initial environment by CONS to produce the correct environment to evaluate e_2.

12.3.3   About the Compilation Scheme

We chose the compilation scheme presented here because it can be described simply. In particular, the fact that in our model the environment for computation is directly accessible in the form of a list of the values of variables which have been introduced so far makes the way that we construct closures very simple since we merely have to construct a pair from this environment and a code address. Incidentally, when we add an element to an environment, we merely allocate a doublet, so we easily induce shared subenvironments that way.

From the point of view of efficiency, however, this compilation scheme is subject to criticism. First of all, when we use lists, we impose linear access time although the use of arrays would support constant access time. Moreover, the environments for closures do not really need to contain the values of all the variables that exist at the time they are constructed; those environments actually need only the (free) variables that are used in the body of the function. The fact that the environments for closures contain too many values increases the access time, and more seriously prevents the garbage collector from recovering the space occupied by structures that belong to the environment of a closure but will not really be used. Finally, since we have to manage environments and build these closures, the evaluation of functional languages is penalized in comparison to more conventional languages where the stack is sufficient for all the values useful in computation. Since not all programs written in a functional language actually exploit all the power of functionality, it is very important when we target efficiency to know how to compile such programs efficiently. This aim assumes that we use the stack to its maximum potential and that we build environments and closures only when strictly necessary.

For all those reasons, the compilation scheme that we have presented must be considered above all as a demonstration of feasibility.

12.4   Implementation

We first sketch code simulation and then take up code production.

12.4.1 Code Simulation

Here we will limit ourselves to simulating the way a machine works at the "logical" level. The sequences of instructions will not be organized literally in memory in a code zone indexed by their addresses, but rather, we will handle them directly as objects of type list. The values and environments will not be organized literally in a memory zone but rather handled directly as CAML values. Even so, it is still clear that the execution function simulates the behavior of the machine defined in the preceding section.

```
#type instruction =
        STOP
      | LOAD of val
      | PUSH of val
      | DUPL | SWAP | ROT₃ | IROT₃
      | FST | SND | SETFST | SETSND
      | CONS | SPLIT
      | ADD | SUB | MULT | EQ
      | CALL | RETURN
      | BRANCH of val * val
  and val =
        Int_Const of int
      | Bool_Const of bool
      | Clo of val ref * instruction list        (* closure *)
      | Nil
      | Pair of val ref * val ref
      | Adr of instruction list;;
```

The type val represents the values occurring during the computation, the environments, and the sequences of instructions used here in place of addresses. Closures are represented by pairs. The elements of these pairs are references so we can physically modify them if necessary to handle recursion.

The function exec takes a list of instructions and a stack as arguments and executes the instructions one after the other. Normal execution begins with the Nil environment as the only value on the stack and ends with the instruction Stop. When that last instruction is executed, the stack should contain a unique value, the result of the computation.

```
#exception Exec_error;;
Exception Exec_error defined.

#let rec exec = fun
    ([STOP],[v]) → v
```

```
          | ((LOAD v)::code,v'::stack) → exec (code,v::stack)
          | ((PUSH v)::code,stack) → exec (code,v::stack)
          | (DUPL::code,v::stack) → exec (code,v::v::stack)
          | (SWAP::code,v::v'::stack) → exec(code,v'::v::stack)
          | (ROT₃::code,v₁::v₂::v₃::stack) → exec(code,v₂::v₃::v₁::stack)
          | (IROT₃::code,v₁::v₂::v₃::stack) → exec(code,v₃::v₁::v₂::stack)
          | (FST::code,(Pair(ref v₁,_))::stack)
            → exec(code,v₁::stack)
          | (SND::code,(Pair(_,ref v₂))::stack)
            → exec(code, v₂::stack)
          | (SETFST::code, v::(Pair(v₁,v₂) as p)::stack)
            → v₁:=v;exec (code,p::stack)
          | (SETSND::code, v::(Pair(v₁,v₂)as p)::stack)
            → v₂:=v;exec (code,p::stack)
          | (CONS::code, v₁:: v₂::stack)
            → exec(code,(Pair(ref v₁,ref v₂))::stack)
          | (SPLIT::code, (Pair(ref v₁,ref v₂))::stack)
            → exec(code, v₁::v₂::stack)
          | (ADD::code,(Int_Const v₁)::(Int_Const v₂)::stack)
            → exec(code, (Int_Const(v₁+v₂))::stack)
          | (SUB::code,(Int_Const v₁)::(Int_Const v₂)::stack)
            → exec(code,(Int_Const(v₁−v₂))::stack)
          | (MULT::code,(Int_Const v₁)::(Int_Const v₂)::stack)
            → exec(code, (Int_Const(v₁*v₂))::stack)
          | (EQ::code,(Int_Const v₁)::(Int_Const v₂)::stack)
            → exec(code, (Bool_Const(v₁=v₂))::stack)
          | (CALL::code,(Adr code')::v::stack)
            → exec(code', v::(Adr code)::stack)
          | (RETURN::code,v::(Adr code')::stack)
            → exec(code',v::stack)
          | (BRANCH(adr₁,adr₂)::code,(Bool_Const b)::stack)
            → if b then exec(code,adr₁::stack)
              else exec(code,adr₂::stack)
          | _ → raise Exec_error;;
        exec : instruction list * val list → val = ⟨fun⟩
```

12.4.2 Producing Code

The type of CAML programs is the same one we used in Section 11.2 about evaluation.

```
#type ml_unop = Ml_fst | Ml_snd;;
```

```
#type ml_binop = Ml_add | Ml_sub | Ml_mult | Ml_eq | Ml_less;;

#type ml_exp =
        Ml_int_const of int                      (* integer constant *)
      | Ml_bool_const of bool                     (* Boolean constant *)
      | Ml_pair of ml_exp * ml_exp                              (* pair *)
      | Ml_unop of ml_unop * ml_exp              (* unary operation *)
      | Ml_binop of ml_binop * ml_exp * ml_exp   (* binary operation *)
      | Ml_var of string                                   (* variable *)
      | Ml_if of ml_exp * ml_exp * ml_exp              (* conditional *)
      | Ml_fun of string * ml_exp                        (* function *)
      | Ml_app of ml_exp * ml_exp                     (* application *)
      | Ml_let of string * ml_exp * ml_exp           (* declaration *)
      | Ml_letrec of string * ml_exp * ml_exp  (* recursive declaration *)
;;
```

The compilation function compile uses three auxiliary functions, compile_unop, compile_binop, and compile_var, to translate basic operators and to compile access to the variables in an environment.

```
#let compile_unop = fun
      Ml_fst → FST
    | Ml_snd → SND;;
compile_unop : ml_unop → instruction = ⟨fun⟩

#let compile_binop = fun
      Ml_add → ADD
    | Ml_sub → SUB
    | Ml_mult → MULT
    | Ml_eq → EQ
    | _ → failwith "compile_binop: not implemented";;
compile_binop : ml_binop → instruction = ⟨fun⟩

#exception compile_error of string;;
Exception compile_error defined.

#let rec compile_var env v =
      match env
      with [ ] → raise(compile_error "unbound variable")
         | (x::env) → if x=v then [FST]
                          else SND::(compile_var env v);;
compile_var : α list → α → instruction list = ⟨fun⟩
```

Here is the compilation function that follows the description we gave in Section 12.3 exactly.

```
#let compile e =
   let rec comp env = fun
     (MI_int_const n) → [LOAD (Int_Const n)]
   | (MI_bool_const b) → [LOAD (Bool_Const b)]
   | (MI_pair(e₁,e₂)) → [DUPL]@(comp env e₂)@[SWAP]
                          @(comp env e₁)@[CONS]
   | (MI_unop(op,e)) → (comp env e)@[compile_unop op]
   | (MI_binop(op,e₁,e₂))
     → [DUPL]@(comp env e₂)@[SWAP]@(comp env e₁)@
        [compile_binop op]
   | (MI_var v) → compile_var env v
   | (MI_if(e₁,e₂,e₃))
     → [DUPL]@(comp env e₁)@
        [BRANCH(Adr(comp env e₂@[RETURN]),
                 Adr(comp env e₃@[RETURN])));
         CALL]
   | (MI_fun(x,e))
     → [PUSH(Adr(comp (x::env) e @[RETURN]));SWAP;CONS]
   | (MI_app(e₁,e₂))
     → [DUPL]@(comp env e₂)@[SWAP]@(comp env e₁)
        @[SPLIT;IROT₃;CONS;SWAP;CALL]
   | (MI_let(x,e₁,e₂))
     → [DUPL]@(comp env e₁)@[CONS]@(comp (x::env) e₂)
   | (MI_letrec(f,((MI_fun _) as e₁),e₂))
     → [PUSH Nil]@(comp (f::env) e₁)@[DUPL;ROT₃;CONS;SETFST;FST]
        @(comp (f::env) e₂)
   | (MI_letrec(f,e₁,e₂))
     → [DUPL;PUSH Nil;DUPL;CONS;DUPL;ROT₃;CONS]
        @(comp (f::env) e₁)
        @[DUPL;ROT₃;FST;SETFST;SWAP;SND;SETSND;CONS]
        @(comp (f::env) e₂)
   in (comp [] e)@[STOP];;
compile : ml_exp → instruction list = ⟨fun⟩
```

Now we can evaluate expressions by combining the functions compile and exec.

```
#let init_stack= [Nil];;
init_stack : val list = [Nil]
```

```
#let eval e = exec(compile e,init_stack);;
eval : ml_exp → val = ⟨fun⟩
```

12.5   Examples

Here are a few simple examples of our compiled code.

    #compile (ml_exp_of_string "2+3");;
    — : instruction list = [DUPL; LOAD (Int_Const 3); SWAP;
                            LOAD (Int_Const 2); ADD; STOP]

    #compile (ml_exp_of_string "fun x -> x*2");;
    — : instruction list = [PUSH (Adr [DUPL; LOAD (Int_Const 2);
                                    SWAP; FST; MULT; RETURN]);
                        SWAP; CONS; STOP]

    #compile (ml_exp_of_string "(fun x -> x*2) 3");;
    — : instruction list = [DUPL; LOAD (Int_Const 3); SWAP;
                        PUSH (Adr [DUPL; LOAD (Int_Const 2);
                                    SWAP; FST; MULT; RETURN]);
                        SWAP; CONS; SPLIT; IROT₃; CONS; SWAP;
                        CALL; STOP]

Now let's look again at the first two examples of Section 11.2 about evaluation.

    #let P₁=
      (ml_exp_of_string
        ("let double = fun f -> fun x -> f(f x) " ˆ
        "in let sq = fun x -> x*x " ˆ
        "   in (double sq) 5"));;

    #compile P₁;;
    — : instruction list
        = [DUPL; PUSH (Adr [PUSH (Adr [DUPL; DUPL; FST; SWAP; SND;
                                    FST; SPLIT; IROT₃; CONS;
                                    SWAP; CALL; SWAP; SND; FST;
                                    SPLIT; IROT₃; CONS; SWAP;
                                    CALL; RETURN]); SWAP; CONS;
                        RETURN]); SWAP; CONS; CONS; DUPL;
            PUSH (Adr [DUPL; FST; SWAP; FST; MULT; RETURN]); SWAP;
            CONS; CONS; DUPL; LOAD (Int_Const 5); SWAP; DUPL; FST;
            SWAP; SND; FST; SPLIT; IROT₃; CONS; SWAP; CALL; SPLIT;
            IROT₃; CONS; SWAP; CALL; STOP]

    #eval P₁;;
    — : val = Int_Const 625

```
#let P₂ =
  (ml_exp_of_string
    ("let rec fact=" ^
     " fun n -> if n=0 then 1 else n*(fact(n-1)) in " ^
     "fact 10"));;
```

#compile P₂;;
− : *instruction list*
= [*PUSH Nil; PUSH (Adr [DUPL; DUPL; LOAD (Int_Const 0);*
                          SWAP; FST; EQ;
                          BRANCH (Adr [LOAD (Int_Const 1);
                                        RETURN],
                                  Adr [DUPL; DUPL; DUPL;
                                        LOAD (Int_Const 1);
                                        SWAP; FST; SUB; SWAP;
                                        SND; FST; SPLIT; IROT₃;
                                        CONS; SWAP; CALL; SWAP;
                                        FST; MULT; RETURN]);
                          CALL; RETURN]); SWAP; CONS; DUPL;
   ROT₃; CONS; SETFST; FST; DUPL; LOAD (Int_Const 10); SWAP;
   FST; SPLIT; IROT₃; CONS; SWAP; CALL; STOP]

#eval P₂;;
− : *val = Int_Const* 3628800

Our last example shows you how a program that constructs a non-functional recursive value executes.

```
#let P₃ =
  (ml_exp_of_string
    "let rec p =  (1,(2,p)) in fst(snd(snd p))");;
```

#compile P₃;;
− : *instruction list* = [*DUPL; PUSH Nil; DUPL; CONS; DUPL; ROT₃;*
                         CONS; DUPL; DUPL; FST; SWAP;
                         LOAD (Int_Const 2); CONS; SWAP;
                         LOAD (Int_Const 1); CONS; DUPL; ROT₃;
                         FST; SETFST; SWAP; SND; SETSND; CONS;
                         FST; SND; SND; FST; STOP]

#eval P₃;;
− : *val = Int_Const* 1

Exercise
12.3 Modify the compiler to implement evaluation by necessity.

12.6   Summary

We presented the principles for representing the values of a functional language in memory, and we described a simple way to allocate doublets to support the implicit construction of data structures. We also highlighted **sharing** as induced by the way we constructed values.

Following that, we presented a set of low-level instructions to implement the functionalities of CAML. We also defined an algorithm to compile CAML in this instruction set. The algorithm works in three memory zones: code, heap, and stack. The execution model we used is one based on environments derived from the evaluators you saw in Chapter 11 about interpretation, but the idea of an environment here has been separated into a formal environment (used for compilation) and an execution environment.

We wrote the functions to compile and to simulate execution of the code in CAML.

12.7   To Learn More

There are few books describing techniques used to implement functional languages. Such descriptions usually appear in research articles that are hard to find or in articles that generally describe a theoretical model rather than implementation details.

Readers interested in the implementation technique used for CAML LIGHT should look at [23], even though it corresponds to a somewhat older version of this implementation.

A different compilation technique—based on the idea of continuation and implemented in the language Standard ML—is described in [4].

Finally, the techniques for implementing languages with lazy evaluation or delayed evaluation have been described more widely. In particular, you could look at [31] and [32].

Chapter 13

Type Synthesis

In the preceding chapters, we presented a few elements of type synthesis in CAML. Chapter 5 gave you a description that was almost complete, with the exception of how to manage polymorphism. In effect, Section 5.3.1 informally showed you constraints that must be respected for a program to be typable. Since CAML has a polymorphic type system, a value like e_1 introduced by **let** x = e_1 **in** e_2 may have different types, even types that are incompatible with one another, at every occurrence of x in e_2.

However, in Section 5.3.1, we suggested that the same effect could be achieved by typing the expression e_2 in which we substitute the expression e_1 for the free occurrences of x, that is, $e_2 [x \leftarrow e_1]$ in place of **let** x = e_1 **in** e_2. The major drawback of this technique is that we then have to synthesize the type of e_1 a great many times. To offset this inconvenience, the idea is to associate a type with e_1 so that we can decline the various occurrences of x differently, as we decline nouns or adjectives according to their context in certain natural languages.

More formally, in this chapter we will present CAML type synthesis, taking into account its polymorphism, and we will present an algorithm for realistic synthesis.

13.1 Type Rules

In CAML, type synthesis can be defined exactly as the evaluation relation, that is, by a ternary relation:

$$E \vdash e : t$$

We read that like this:

In the type environment E, the expression e is of the type t.

Just as an environment of values is a list of associations between variables and values, an environment of types will be a list of associations between variables and types.

13.1.1   Polymorphism by Substitution

Polymorphism complicates the relation for type synthesis. An expression such as (**fun** x → x) is of type int → int, but also of type bool → bool, as well as the polymorphic type $\alpha \rightarrow \alpha$. However, it is also possible to define it by deduction rules.

$$\frac{x{:}t \in E}{E \vdash x : t} \quad (\text{Var})$$

$$\frac{E \vdash e_1 : t1 \quad \ldots \quad E \vdash e_n : t_n}{E \vdash (e_1,\ldots,e_n) : (t_1 * \ldots * t_n)} \quad (N\text{-tuple})$$

$$\frac{E \vdash e_1 : \text{bool} \qquad E \vdash e_2 : t \qquad E \vdash e_3 : t}{E \vdash \textbf{if } e_1 \textbf{ then } e_2 \textbf{ else } e_3 : t} \quad (\text{Cond})$$

$$\frac{(x{:}t_1){::}E \vdash e : t_2}{E \vdash (\textbf{fun } x \rightarrow e) : t_1 \rightarrow t_2} \quad (\text{Fun})$$

$$\frac{E \vdash e_1 : t \rightarrow t' \qquad E \vdash e_2 : t}{E \vdash (e_1\ e_2) : t'} \quad (\text{App})$$

Now we have a problem taking the construction **let** into account because this construction lets us use the same variable with two different types (for example, in **let** id=(**fun** x→x) **in** id id). Back in Chapter 5, we suggested handling this phenomenon by replacing an expression such as **let** id = (**fun** x→x) **in** id id by (**fun** x→x)(**fun** x→x). That lets us adequately type the two subexpressions (**fun** x→x).

If we were to treat polymorphism that way, we would write the rule for typing the construction **let** like this:

$$\frac{E \vdash e_2[x \leftarrow e_1] : t}{E \vdash \textbf{let } x{=}e_1 \textbf{ in } e_2 : t} \quad (\text{Let})$$

However, in the case where x does not even appear in e_2, we would still have to require that e_1 could be typed, so we should write that rule like this:

$$\frac{E \vdash e_1 : t_1 \qquad E \vdash e_2[x \leftarrow e_1] : t}{E \vdash \textbf{let } x{=}e_1 \textbf{ in } e_2 : t} \quad (\text{Let})$$

To take recursion into account, we will use the constant Rec, introduced to define evaluation by rewrites, and the same kind of substitution as in the case of **let**.

$$\frac{E \;\vdash\; e_2[f \leftarrow \text{Rec } (\textbf{fun } f \rightarrow e_1)] : t}{E \;\vdash\; \textbf{let rec } f = e_1 \textbf{ in } e_2 : t} \quad \text{(Letrec)}$$

Here, too, in order to guarantee the correct typing of the entire program, we must guarantee that the expression e_1 can be typed, and this is not enforced by the rule above, because f does not necessarily occur in e_2.

This system will work only if we give rules elsewhere to synthesize the types of predefined constants in the language. We will allow the constant Rec to take any type of the form $((t_1 \rightarrow t_2) \rightarrow (t_1 \rightarrow t_2)) \rightarrow (t_1 \rightarrow t_2)$.

Unfortunately, it is not realistic to manage polymorphism by substitution of subprograms, so now we will bring up a new idea: a type scheme that can represent all the possible types of a given expression.

13.1.2 Parametric Polymorphism

A more realistic way to proceed is for us to introduce the idea of a **type scheme**. A type scheme corresponds to types for which we have specialized certain variables. We say such specialized variables are **generic**. A type scheme can be declined into a variety of different types (its instances) if we substitute the types of its generic variables.

A type scheme for which $\alpha_1, \ldots, \alpha_n$ are the generic variables will be denoted $\forall \alpha_1 \ldots \alpha_n.t$ where t is a type. We get an instance of this type scheme by substituting the types $t_1, \ldots, t_n$ for the variables $\alpha_1, \ldots, \alpha_n$ in t, so for the given types t_i, $t[\alpha_i \leftarrow t_i]_{i=1,n}$ is such an instance.

Thus with respect to (**fun** x → x) which has type t → t, for all t, we will say that this expression has the type scheme $\forall \alpha . \alpha \rightarrow \alpha$.

In the case where the set of generic variables of a type is empty, we will identify the two ideas of type and type scheme. A type is thus also a type scheme, one that we call **trivial**.

13.1.3 Generalizing Type Schemes

When we synthesize the type of a construction such as **let** x=e_1 **in** e_2, we will thus attribute a type t_1 to e_1; then we will compute the set of its generic variables, $\{\alpha_1, \ldots, \alpha_n\}$, and synthesize the type of e_2 in a type environment augmented by binding x to the type scheme $\forall \alpha_1 \ldots \alpha_n.t_1$.

Now we must determine which type variables can be generalized among all the variables that appear in a type.

In Section 5.3.1 about type constraints, type synthesis was presented as a search for solutions to a set of equations. From that perspective, type variables were seen as unknowns that take precise values when the system of equations is resolved (that is, when unification occurs). Among these unknowns, the ones that still do not have a value at the end of the resolution are the ones that can be generalized. In effect, since they do not have a precise value, they can thus represent an arbitrary type.

In terms of deduction rules, in the proofs, we want to change rules of the following form:

$$\frac{E \vdash e_2[x \leftarrow e_1] : t}{E \vdash \textbf{let } x{=}e_1 \textbf{ in } e_2 : t} \text{ (Let)}$$

into rules like this:

$$\frac{E \vdash e_1 : t_1 \quad (x : \forall \alpha_1 \ldots \alpha_n.t_1){::}E \vdash e_2 : t}{E \vdash \textbf{let } x{=}e_1 \textbf{ in } e_2 : t} \text{ (Let)}$$

and determine the set of α_i. Consequently, we must completely resolve the constraints that come from synthesizing the type of e_1, and then we must generalize the type variables that appear in t_1 and that cannot take a more precise value. As it turns out, those are the ones that do not depend on the context surrounding e_1, that is, the rest of the proof. The context is represented by the type environment E, so the variables that can be generalized are precisely those of t_1 that do not appear free in E. (Remember that E contains type schemes from now on.)

The set of variables that can be generalized will thus be $\textsf{vars}(t_1) \backslash \textsf{vars}(E)$.

13.1.4   Instantiation

Polymorphism allows the same identifier (introduced by **let**) to accept different types (instances) in various occurrences. The relation connecting each of these occurrences to the type scheme to which they belong is called the **instantiation relation**. It is denoted $\leq$. A type t' is an instance of the type scheme $\forall \alpha_1 \ldots \alpha_n.t$ if there exist types $t_1, \ldots, t_n$ such that $t' = t[\alpha_i \leftarrow t_i]_{i=1,n}$.

13.1.5   Type Rules with Parametric Polymorphism

Now we can articulate the new deduction rules about typing in our mini-language. These rules come from the system presented in Section 13.1.1 with the exception of the rules about identifiers and **let** constructions. Objects denoted by t, t_1, etc.

represent types here, not type schemes. In deductions about type, type schemes may appear only in the type environment.

The two new rules are:

$$\frac{x : \forall \alpha_1 \ldots \alpha_n.t \in E \quad t' \leq \forall \alpha_1 \ldots \alpha_n.t}{E \vdash x : t'} \text{ (Var)}$$

$$\frac{E \vdash e_1 : t_1 \quad \{\alpha_i\}_{i=1,n} = \text{vars}(t_1) \backslash \text{vars}(E) \quad (x : \forall \alpha_1 \ldots \alpha_n.t_1)::E \vdash e_2 : t_2}{E \vdash \textbf{let } x = e_1 \textbf{ in } e_2 : t_2} \text{ (Let)}$$

Notice that the type rule for **let** puts a type scheme into the type environment. (That type scheme may be trivial if no type variable can be generalized.) In comparison, the rule for **fun** does not put trivial type schemes (that is, just types) into the environment.

To simplify, we have omitted the rules about unary and binary operators.

Notice that one and only one type rule corresponds to each construction in the language. The program to synthesize the type of an expression will thus be a function defined by case according to the structure of its argument.

In contrast, the transformation of these deduction rules into an algorithm is not so simple as it was for the evaluation of programs. In the case of evaluation, an inference rule could always be read as a case in the definition of a function eval of an environment E and an expression e—a function that returns a value v. In each case of the rule, the value v expected in return could be computed by recursive calls (corresponding to premises of the rule) on expressions (either direct subexpressions of e or expressions we get from an intermediate value). During each of these calls, we compute an intermediate value which is saved to appear in the result or which is passed to the following recursive call. The last recursive call provides all or part of the final result.

In the case of type synthesis, the situation is far from simple. In effect, we are faced with two problems:

1. How shall we take into account the general equality constraints present in the application rule, where the type t must simultaneously be the type of e_2 and the argument part of the type of e_1?

2. When we type an abstraction, we must make a hypothesis (t_1) about the type of the formal parameter. How shall we make the right choice? In other words, how shall we propagate the resolution of the constraints we have already mentioned so that they reach the rest of the program?

The problem of propagating equality constraints seems particularly difficult. Those constraints are génerated in application sites, so we must propagate them backwards, for example, to the type of a parameter of a function. We see the same difficulties whichever philosophy we choose, whether polymorphism by substitution or parametric polymorphism.

Our solution, of course, is to exploit **unification**. (See Section 5.2.4 for an introduction to unification.) Equality constraints about types and the propagation of such constraints are both taken into account in two critical situations:

1. when we compute the substitutions to unify two types before they are equal;

2. when we return this substitution as part of the result in order to apply it to the type environment.

In effect, propagation of equality constraints is carried out through the type environment, since the type environment contains the partially known types that the equality constraint has just made somewhat more precise.

13.2   Writing a Program to Synthesize Types

Before we attack how to write a program to synthesize types, we must put into place the language, the type representation, the substitutions, as well as the toolkit for instantiation and generalization.

With respect to expressions of the language, the types, and the substitutions, we will recapture what we introduced in Section 5.3.1. The types of our language are coded by terms in which the variables are integers. For example, the following functions provide the source-types and goal-types of unary and binary operators:

```
#let unop_type = fun
    Ml_fst → let a = Var(new_int()) and b = Var(new_int())
               in (pair(a,b),a)
  | Ml_snd → let a = Var(new_int()) and b = Var(new_int())
               in (pair(a,b),b);;
```
$unop\_type : ml\_unop \rightarrow (string, int)\ term * (\alpha, int)\ term = \langle \textbf{fun} \rangle$

```
#let binop_type = fun
    Ml_add → (const "int", const "int",const "int")
  | Ml_sub → (const "int", const "int",const "int")
  | Ml_mult → (const "int", const "int",const "int")
  | Ml_eq → (const "int", const "int",const "bool")
  | Ml_less → (const "int", const "int",const "bool");;
```
$binop\_type : ml\_binop \rightarrow (string, \alpha)\ term * (string, \beta)\ term *$
$$(string, \gamma)\ term = \langle \textbf{fun} \rangle$$

We also have a new idea available: type schemes. We represent it by the following type:

#type α scheme = Forall **of** int list * α;;

For example,

#Forall([1], arrow(Var 1, Var 1));;
− : (*string, int*) *term scheme*
= *Forall* ([1], *Term* ("arrow", [*Var* 1; *Var* 1]))

represents the type scheme $\forall \alpha.\alpha \rightarrow \alpha$ associated with the function (**fun** x $\rightarrow$ x).

13.2.1 Generalizing a Type

As the (Let) rule expresses it, the generalization of a type is relative to the current type environment, so we need the following two functions:

subtract : α list $\rightarrow$ α list $\rightarrow$ α list
unique : α list $\rightarrow$ α list

The result of subtract l_1 l_2 is the list l_1 from which we have removed any possible elements of l_2. The function subtract is predefined.

The result of unique xs is the list xs from which we have removed duplicates. Each element of the resulting list xs' is thus unique in xs'. We leave you the definition of unique as an exercise.

The following function computes the non-quantified variables that appear in the type environment passed to it as an argument.

#let vars_of_tyenv env =
    flat_map (**fun** (_, Forall(gvars,t)) $\rightarrow$ subtract (vars t) gvars) env;;
vars_of_tyenv : (α * (β, int) *term scheme*) *list* $\rightarrow$ *int list* = $\langle$**fun**$\rangle$

The generalization function is simply defined like this:

#let generalize env t =
    let gvars =
        unique (subtract (vars t) (vars_of_tyenv env)) **in**
    Forall(gvars, t);;
generalize : (α * (β, int) *term scheme*) *list*
        $\rightarrow$ (γ, int) *term* $\rightarrow$ (γ, int) *term scheme* = $\langle$**fun**$\rangle$

13.2.2 Instantiation

Given a type scheme, the instantiation function returns a "minimal" instance of that scheme. That is, the function simply renames the generic variables of the scheme. It is up to unification to make the new type variables more precise once they are introduced this way.

```
#let instance = function
    Forall(gvars,t) →
        let renaming = map (fun n → (n, Var(new_int()))) gvars in
        apply_subst renaming t;;
```
instance : $(\alpha, int)\ term\ scheme \to (\alpha, int)\ term = \langle$**fun**$\rangle$

13.2.3 A Few Utilities

Now before we define the main function of the algorithm to synthesize types, we will define a few utility functions.

Substitutions.   First of all, since we have type schemes available in type environments (and thus we have quantified variables), we must be careful not to substitute them when a substitution is applied. The following function removes a variable from the definition domain of a substitution.

```
#let rec subst_but v = function
    [ ] → [ ]
  | (v₁,t₁)::subst →
        if v₁=v then subst_but v subst
        else (v₁,t₁)::(subst_but v subst);;
```
subst_but : $\alpha \to (\alpha * \beta)\ list \to (\alpha * \beta)\ list = \langle$**fun**$\rangle$

If we iterate this process over a list of variables, we remove a set of variables from the definition domain of a substitution, like this:

```
#let rec subst_minus subst vars =
    match vars with
      [ ] → subst
    | v::vs → subst_minus (subst_but v subst) vs;;
```
subst_minus : $(\alpha * \beta)\ list \to \alpha\ list \to (\alpha * \beta)\ list = \langle$**fun**$\rangle$

Now we can apply a substitution to a type environment.

```
#let subst_env subst env =
    map (fun (k, Forall(gvars,t)) →
                (k, Forall(gvars, apply_subst (subst_minus subst gvars) t))) env;;
```

$$subst\_env : (int * (\alpha, int)\ term)\ list$$
$$\rightarrow (\beta * (\alpha, int)\ term\ scheme)$$
$$list \rightarrow (\beta * (\alpha, int)\ term\ scheme)\ list = \langle\mathbf{fun}\rangle$$

Translating Terms into Types. In order to translate terms into types by means of functions from Section 5.2, we first need to change the variables of integer type into strings of characters. This is the role of the function make_string_vars.

```
#let rec term_map fop fleaf = function
    Term(oper, sons) → Term(fop oper, map (term_map fop fleaf) sons)
  | Var(n) → Var(fleaf n);;
```
$$term\_map : (\alpha \rightarrow \beta) \rightarrow (\gamma \rightarrow \delta) \rightarrow (\alpha, \gamma)\ term \rightarrow (\beta, \delta)\ term = \langle\mathbf{fun}\rangle$$

```
#let make_string_vars t =
    let var_of_int n =
      "v"^(string_of_int n) in
    term_map (fun x → x) var_of_int t;;
```
$$make\_string\_vars : (\alpha, int)\ term \rightarrow (\alpha, string)\ term = \langle\mathbf{fun}\rangle$$

13.2.4   Main Function

Here then is the main function to synthesize types. Before we show you its definition, let's consider a few issues to clarify its underlying principle.

The function type_expr accepts two arguments: a type environment E and an expression e; it returns a type t and a substitution σ. This substitution represents the effect of equality constraints on the type environment E; those equality constraints are encountered while e is being typed. We must thus interpret

$$(\sigma, t) = \text{type\_expr E e}$$

as

$$\sigma(E) \vdash e : t$$

As a consequence, managing substitutions in the algorithm that follows becomes really awkward for us. In particular, when the current expression includes several subexpressions (as conditional statements do), for each subexpression, we must:

- produce its type t and the resulting substitution σ;

- type the following subexpression in an environment modified by the substitution σ.

And that is not all: the substitutions produced by unification at the level of the current expression are added to this, and we must compose all this lovely stuff just to produce the resulting substitution!

Thus the typical (and interesting) cases of the function are these:

Constant: we return the corresponding type and produce the empty substitution.

Variable: we take an instance of the type scheme associated with it in the current environment.

Abstraction: we take a new type variable α, and we associate it with the formal parameter to synthesize the type t_2 in the body of the abstraction, and a substitution σ. The resulting type for the abstraction is thus $\sigma(\alpha) \to t_2$ because α was in the type environment of the body of the abstraction.

Let: we synthesize the type t_1 of the value declared locally. That gives us a substitution σ_1. We compute the type scheme ts_1 by generalizing t_1 with respect to the environment $\sigma_1(E)$. The body of the **let** is thus typed in the environment $\sigma_1(E)$ enriched by the binding between the identifier introduced by the **let** and the type scheme ts_1.

Application: we first type the two subexpressions of the application. To do so, we use the substitution computed for the first one to produce the type of the second. The type of the function part of the application must be a functional type $t'_1 \to t'_2$, and t'_1 must also be the type of the argument. If we name (σ_1, t_1) and (σ_2, t_2) as the results of typing the two subexpressions[1], then we must do the following:

- Unify $\sigma_2(t_1)$ with $t_2 \to \alpha$ (where α is a new type variable). Let's call their unifier μ.

- Return $(\mu \circ \sigma_2 \circ \sigma_1, \mu(\alpha))$ as the result.

Recursion: the idea is to associate a new type variable with the identifier defined recursively, then to type the body of the definition. With unification, that will produce a refinement of the type variable we introduced. Afterwards, we proceed as we did for **let**.

The remaining cases (even though they are generally longer than these) are simply variations on the application case.

---

[1]We assume that we began by typing the function part.

```
#let rec type_expr tenv expr =
  match expr with
    Ml_int_const n → ([ ], const "int")
  | Ml_bool_const b → ([ ], const "bool")
  | Ml_var s → ([ ], try instance (assoc s tenv)
                     with Not_found → failwith "Unbound variable")
  | Ml_fun(s, e) →
        let alpha = Var(new_int()) in
        let (su, t) = type_expr ((s,Forall([ ], alpha))::tenv) e in
        (su, arrow(apply_subst su alpha, t))
  | Ml_let(s,e₁,e₂) →
        let (su₁, t₁) = type_expr tenv e₁ in
        let ts₁ = generalize (subst_env su₁ tenv) t₁ in
        let (su₂, t₂) = type_expr ((s,ts₁)::(subst_env su₁ tenv)) e₂ in
        (compsubst su₂ su₁, t₂)
  | Ml_app(e₁,e₂) →
        let (su₁,t₁) = type_expr tenv e₁ in
        let (su₂,t₂) = type_expr (subst_env su₁ tenv) e₂ in
        let alpha = Var(new_int()) in
        let mu = unify (apply_subst su₂ t₁, arrow(t₂, alpha)) in
        (compsubst mu (compsubst su₂ su₁), apply_subst mu alpha)
  | Ml_unop(unop, e) →
        let (tᵢ, tₒ) = unop_type unop in
        let (su, t) = type_expr tenv e in
        let mu = unify (tᵢ, t) in
        (compsubst mu su, apply_subst mu tₒ)
  | Ml_pair(e₁, e₂) →
        let (su₁,t₁) = type_expr tenv e₁ in
        let (su₂,t₂) = type_expr (subst_env su₁ tenv) e₂ in
        (compsubst su₂ su₁, pair(apply_subst su₂ t₁, t₂))
  | Ml_binop(binop,e₁,e₂) →
        let (ta₁, ta₂, tᵣ) = binop_type binop in
        let (su₁, t₁) = type_expr tenv e₁ in
        let mu₁ = unify(t₁, ta₁) in
        let s₁ = compsubst mu₁ su₁ in
        let (su₂, t₂) = type_expr (subst_env s₁ tenv) e₂ in
        let s₂ = compsubst su₂ s₁ in
        let mu₂ = unify (t₂, apply_subst s₂ ta₂) in
        let s₃ = compsubst mu₂ s₂ in
        (s₃, apply_subst s₃ tᵣ)
  | Ml_if(e₁, e₂, e₃) →
        let (su₁, t₁) = type_expr tenv e₁ in
```

```
        let mu₁ = unify(t₁, const "bool") in
        let s₁ = compsubst mu₁ su₁ in
        let (su₂, t₂) = type_expr (subst_env s₁ tenv) e₂ in
        let s₂ = compsubst su₁ s₁ in
        let (su₃, t₃) = type_expr (subst_env s₂ tenv) e₃ in
        let s₃ = compsubst su₃ s₂ in
        let mu₃ = unify(t₃, apply_subst su₃ t₂) in
        (compsubst mu₃ s₃, apply_subst mu₃ t₃)
    | Ml_letrec(s,e₁,e₂) →
        let t₁ = Var (new_int()) in
        let ts₁ = Forall([ ], t₁) in
        let (su₁, t₁) = type_expr ((s,ts₁)::tenv) e₁ in
        let tsₛ = generalize (subst_env su₁ tenv) (apply_subst su₁ t₁) in
        let (su₂, t₂) = type_expr ((s,tsₛ)::(subst_env su₁ tenv)) e₂ in
        (compsubst su₂ su₁, t₂);;
```

type_expr : *(string * (string, int) term scheme) list*
              → *ml_exp* → *(int * (string, int) term) list ∗*
                          (string, int) term = ⟨**fun**⟩

13.2.5   Examples

The following function tests our algorithm in a few examples.

```
#let type_of e =
    reset_new_int();
    let (su, t) = type_expr [ ] e in
    ml_type_of_term (make_string_vars t);;
```
type_of : *ml_exp* → *ml_type* = ⟨**fun**⟩

In the examples that follow, the value returned by our type synthesizer is printed by this function:

print_ml_type : ml_type → unit

the default printer for values of type ml_type.

```
#type_of (ml_exp_of_string("let id = fun x -> x "^
                           "in (id 3, id true)"));;
```
− : *ml_type* = (*int ∗ bool*)

```
#type_of (ml_exp_of_string "fun x -> x");;
```
− : *ml_type* = (v_0 → v_0)

```
#type_of (ml_exp_of_string "(fun x -> x x)(fun x -> x)");;
Uncaught exception:  <local exception>
```

13.3   Synthesizing Types by Destructive Unification

No doubt you can see that the awkwardness of the function type_expr is due primarily to the substitutions that we must handle in order to propagate equality constraints we encounter during type synthesis. To remedy that, we will now present the same type-synthesizing algorithm, but this time, we will exploit destructive unification of specialized terms representing the types of the language.

In order to present the essence of this technique, we will limit ourselves to a sublanguage defined by the following type:

```
#type ml_exp =
        Ml_int_const of int                      (* integer constant *)
      | Ml_var of string                         (* variable *)
      | Ml_fun of string * ml_exp                (* function *)
      | Ml_app of ml_exp * ml_exp                (* application *)
      | Ml_let of string * ml_exp * ml_exp       (* declaration *)
;;
```

Thus we have only one type of constant available, and we have omitted the conditional statement, unary and binary operators, and recursive definitions. Extending the technique we are presenting here to a more nearly complete language is left as an exercise.

Types in our language will be represented by values of the following type:

```
#type ml_type =
        Unknown                          (* Val field of a type variable *)
      | Int_type
      | Var_type of vartype
      | Arrow_type of ml_type * ml_type
  and vartype = {Idx: int; mutable Val: ml_type};;
```

The idea of a type variable is now a little more complicated. Instead of conveying information of type string, a type variable will carry two kinds of information: first, a number in a non-modifiable field Idx, so that we can distinguish[2] two different variables; second, the modifiable field Val stores information about whether a type has been substituted for the variable.

Initially, the field Val in type variables is initialized as Unknown.

13.3.1   Destructive Unification

The unification principle is to make two terms identical, so up to now, we have unified two terms, t_1 and t_2, by computing a substitution σ such that $\sigma(t_1)$

---

[2]We can do without this information if we can test equality between the addresses of the representations of objects. The CAML primitive == lets us do that.

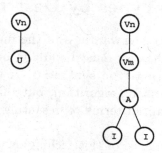

Figure 13.1. A variable before and after unification

$= \sigma(t_2)$. Incidentally, in the type algorithm of the previous section, we had to propagate the effect of these substitutions in the type environments and reproduce them in our results.

In the algorithm we present here, instead of computing these substitutions, we *physically* identify the terms to unify, and since the terms will then be shared in memory, we automatically propagate the effects of unification.

The type variables that we consider here are objects that can be physically modified. Indeed, they will be modified by unification, so we can no longer regard objects of type ml_type as trees, but we have to think of them as acyclic graphs. This kind of object is often referred to as a **directed acyclic graph**, abbreviated **DAG**.

For example, the variable

Var_type{Idx=n; Val=Unknown}

can be changed into

Var_type{Idx = n; Val = Arrow_type(Int_type, Int_type)}

or even into

Var_type{Idx = n;
        Val = Var_type{Idx = m; Val = Arrow_type(Int_type, Int_type)}}

where m ≠ n. These two objects are represented graphically in Figure 13.1, where the constructors Unknown, Int_type, and Arrow_type are denoted U, I, and A.

You see there several important points.

- Substitution of the variable n affects its structure, since that structure is physically modified by substitution. The two root nodes (denoted Vn) in Figure 13.1 are, in fact, the *same physical object*.

- Any other occurrence of the variable n is modified at the same stroke.

- An object Var_type{Idx=n; Val=t} represents an authentic type variable only if t is Unknown. In the opposite case, this object represents a non-variable type.

- In order to physically modify type variables, we create chains of indirection: the variable n represents the variable m that in turn represents the type int → int.

Shortening indirections. These chains of indirection are not in and of themselves a problem for us: we simply have to follow them to access the authentic value associated with a variable. Even so, we will shorten them when we encounter them. We do so by means of the function shorten, defined like this:

```
#let rec shorten t = match t with
    Var_type {Idx=_; Val=Unknown} → t
  | Var_type ({Idx=_; Val = Var_type {Idx=_; Val=Unknown} as tv}) → tv
  | Var_type ({Idx=_; Val = Var_type tv₁} as tv₂)
      → (tv₂.Val ← tv₁.Val); shorten t
  | Var_type {Idx=_; Val=t'} → t'
  | Unknown → failwith "shorten"
  | t' → t';;
shorten : ml_type → ml_type = ⟨fun⟩
```

This function returns the type represented by its argument, and if that type is constructed by Var_type, it shortens the indirections. So that we do not lose the advantage of sharing, when we must return an authentic variable, we keep one indirection (in the second case of pattern matching, we do not shorten the indirection) in order that any modification of this variable will be propagated to whatever it is the value of.

Testing occurrences. We test for an occurrence in the same way as we did in Section 5.2.4 about unification. However, the "type" Unknown (which, of course, is not really a type) should not be passed as an argument.

```
#let occurs {Idx=n;Val=_} =
    let rec occrec = function
      Var_type{Idx=m;Val=_} → (n=m)
    | Int_type → false
    | Arrow_type(t₁,t₂) → (occrec t₁) or (occrec t₂)
    | Unknown → failwith "occurs"              (* Should never happen *)
    in occrec;;
occurs : vartype → ml_type → bool = ⟨fun⟩
```

Unification. The unification function itself now merely traverses its two arguments, taking particular care in the case of variables. When the function unify
identifies its two arguments, it has already taken the trouble to shorten any possible indirections, and it returns no significant results.

```
#let rec unify (t₁,t₂) = match (shorten t₁, shorten t₂) with
    (Var_type({Idx=n; Val=Unknown} as tv₁),
     (Var_type {Idx=m; Val=Unknown} as t₂))          (* variables n and m *)
     → if n ≠ m then tv₁.Val ← t₂ else ()
  | (t₁, Var_type ({Idx=_;Val=Unknown} as tv))        (* type and variable *)
     → if not(occurs tv t₁) then tv.Val ← t₁
       else failwith "unify"
  | ((Var_type {Idx=_;Val=Unknown} as t₁), t₂)        (* variable and type *)
     → unify(t₂,t₁)
  | (Int_type, Int_type) → ()
  | (Arrow_type(t₁,t₂), Arrow_type(t'₁,t'₂))
     → unify(t₁,t'₁); unify(t₂,t'₂)
  | (_,_) → failwith "unify";;
unify : ml_type * ml_type → unit = ⟨fun⟩
```

13.3.2   Instantiation and Generalization

We will define the same utilities that we defined at the beginning of this chapter.
They let us instantiate type schemes and generalize types with respect to a given
type environment.

   The first of the following functions computes the (non-generic) type variables
that appear in a type; the second one computes those that appear in a type
environment.

```
#let vars_of_type tau =
  let rec vars vs = function
    Int_type → vs
  | Var_type {Idx=n; Val=Unknown}
     → if mem n vs then vs else n::vs
  | Var_type {Idx=_; Val= t} → vars vs t
  | Arrow_type(t₁,t₂) → vars (vars vs t₁) t₂
  | Unknown → failwith "vars_of_type"          (* Should never happen *)
  in vars [ ] tau;;
vars_of_type : ml_type → int list = ⟨fun⟩
```

```
#let vars_of_ty_env env =
  flat (map (fun(_, Forall(gvars,t)) → subtract (vars_of_type t) gvars) env);;
vars_of_ty_env : (α * ml_type scheme) list → int list = ⟨fun⟩
```

In order to generalize, essentially, we compute the variables that can be generalized from the type argument.

```
#let generalize tenv t =
    let genvars =
        unique (subtract (vars_of_type t)
                         (vars_of_ty_env tenv))
    in Forall(genvars, t);;
```
generalize : $(\alpha * ml\_type\ scheme)\ list \rightarrow ml\_type \rightarrow ml\_type\ scheme$
$\qquad = \langle \textbf{fun} \rangle$

To instantiate a type scheme, we associate a new type variable with each of the generic variables and substitute these new variables in the body of the type scheme. Thus we produce a copy of this type, complete with new variables which may possibly be modified eventually by unification.

```
#let instance = function
    Forall([ ], t) → t                                (* No generic variable *)
  | Forall(gvars,t) →
      let new_vars =
          (*Associate a new variable with each generic variable *)
          map (fun n → n, Var_type({Idx=new_int(); Val=Unknown})) gvars in
      let rec inst = function
          (*and replace generic variables in the type by these fresh ones *)
          (Var_type {Idx=n; Val=Unknown} as t) →
              (try assoc n new_vars
               with Not_found → t)
        | Var_type {Idx=_; Val= t} → inst t
        | Int_type → Int_type
        | Arrow_type(t₁,t₂) → Arrow_type(inst t₁, inst t₂)
        | Unknown → failwith "instance"              (* Should never happen *)
      in inst t;;
```
instance : $ml\_type\ scheme \rightarrow ml\_type = \langle \textbf{fun} \rangle$

13.3.3 The Algorithm for Synthesis

The algorithm is no more than a simple recursive traversal of the expression passed to it as an argument. It unifies types by imposing equality constraints between types.

```
#let rec type_expr tenv = function
    Ml_int_const _ → Int_type
  | Ml_var s →
```

```
            let ts =
               try assoc s tenv
               with Not_found → failwith "Unbound variable"
            in instance ts
         | Ml_let(s,e₁,e₂) →
            let t₁ = type_expr tenv e₁ in
            let ts = generalize tenv t₁
            in type_expr ((s,ts)::tenv) e₂
         | Ml_app(e₁,e₂) →
            let u = Var_type {Idx=new_int(); Val=Unknown}
            in unify(type_expr tenv e₁,Arrow_type(type_expr tenv e₂,u)); u
         | Ml_fun(x,e) →
            let alpha = Var_type {Idx=new_int(); Val=Unknown} in
            let ts = Forall([ ], alpha)
            in Arrow_type(alpha, type_expr ((x,ts)::tenv) e);;
```

$type\_expr : (string * ml\_type\ scheme)\ list \rightarrow ml\_exp \rightarrow ml\_type = \langle \mathbf{fun} \rangle$

Because we want to be concise, we will treat only a minimal language here. However, this algorithm can easily be extended to a richer language, such as the one we used at the beginning of this chapter.

The following function tests the algorithm in a few examples.

```
#let type_of e =
    reset_new_int ();
    type_expr [ ] e;;
```

$type\_of : ml\_exp \rightarrow ml\_type = \langle \mathbf{fun} \rangle$

We endowed the system with a tool for printing values of type ml_type, so we get:

```
#type_of (ml_exp_of_string("let id = fun x -> x "^
                           "in id id 2"));;
```

$- : ml\_type = int$

```
#type_of (ml_exp_of_string "fun f -> (fun x -> f x)");;
```

$- : ml\_type = ((v_1 \rightarrow v_2) \rightarrow (v_1 \rightarrow v_2))$

```
#type_of (ml_exp_of_string "(fun x -> x x)(fun x -> x)");;
Uncaught exception: Failure "unify"
```

13.4 Summary

We presented the rules for typing a representative kernel of CAML along with two algorithms for synthesizing types. The first uses unification over general terms which compute a substitution. This algorithm is close to the those appearing in the literature, and it is theoretically attractive because we can prove the following properties:

- Correctness: the results of the algorithm correspond to correct deductions from the inference system.

- Completeness: any deduction from the inference system can be found by applying a substitution to the result of the algorithm.

The second algorithm we presented is more realistic. It uses destructive unification, identifying terms physically in order to unify them.

13.5   To Learn More

The first presentation of the type system of the language ML is due to Milner [29]. You will find a recent presentation of it in [24], accompanied by proofs of its completeness and correctness.

Even though it is relatively realistic, our second algorithm is inefficient in two ways: instantiation and generalization.

Although types and type schemes are represented by graphs containing shared subterms, in the general case, the instantiation of a type scheme will disrupt this sharing during the substitution that it produces. A refinement of this function so that it preserves sharing would considerably improve its efficiency. For that, all the function has to do is store the nodes already encountered in the original type scheme, along with their instantiation; then the function should return what it stored when it again encounters one of these nodes.

Incidentally, computing the non-generic variables of the type environment is a costly operation because then the entire environment has to be traversed. To solve this problem, we should add the idea of levels to the type variables. The level increases during typing on the left of a **let** (that is, typing of e_1 in **let** $x=e_1$ **in** e_2) and goes back to its previous value during a typing on the right. During the unification of a type t with a variable tv, the unification algorithm should reduce the variables of t to that of tv when necessary. In [42], you can see levels managed in that way.

To generalize type t_1 from e_1 then comes down to a comparison of the levels of type variables appearing in t_1 to the current level: the variables at the current or higher level can be generalized because they are "local" to e_1, whereas those at a lower level are not.

There are still other possible improvements to make, especially with respect to the unification algorithm. The test for occurrences is also a relatively expensive operation because of its frequency. A possibility there is to delay these tests as long as possible. In [33], you will find a very efficient algorithm to synthesize types that delays tests for occurrences. The same source provides a formal system for a unification algorithm as the resolution of equations.

Quick Reference to the Syntax of Caml Light

In a relatively concise way, we present the syntax of CAML LIGHT. To keep it short, we have omitted certain points and perhaps introduced a little ambiguity, but our goal is to offer a quick reference guide. For a complete guide and definitive reference about the syntax of the language, see [22].

Conventions

In this guide, we use the following syntactic conventions:

keywords: enclosed in double quotation marks, like **"function"** or **"->"**;

terminals: entirely in upper-case (capital) letters, like INT, STRING;

non-terminals: begin with an upper-case letter, like Expr, Type, or SimplePattern.

Also, the constructions:

between brackets (like [**"rec"**]) are optional constructions;

between curly braces represent:

– if they are annotated by a + sign, a repetition of their contents at least once, like {SimplePattern}$^+$, which represents a non-empty sequence of SimplePattern;

– if they are annotated by an asterisk ∗, a repetition, possibly empty, of their contents, like { ";" Expr}∗, which represents a possibly empty sequence of ";" Expr.

You must be careful not to confuse the literal "{", which is a terminal, with {, which encloses an iteration like the ones we just described.

As far as possible, we put CAML comments to the right of productions.

Global Phrases

Global phrases are declarations of types, exceptions, and values, as well as directives.

Caml →   "#" IDENT STRING ";;"   *(* Directives *)*
         | **"type"** TyDecl   *(* Definitions of types/abbreviations *)*
            {**"and"** TyDecl}* ";;"
         | **"exception"** IDENT "=" IDENT ["of" Type]
            {**"and"** IDENT = ["of" Type]}* ";;"   *(* Declarations of exceptions *)*
         | **"let"** ["rec"] ValDecl {**"and"** ValDecl}* ";;"   *(* Declarations of values *)*
         | Expr ";;"   *(* Evaluation of expressions *)*

Expressions

Expressions of the langage

    We do not distinguish simple expressions (in parentheses, for example) from those that are not in the productions that follow. This choice, of course, introduces ambiguity and may be a source of error, so it is necessary in certain cases to add parentheses in your code to remove such ambiguity.

Constant →   STRING | CHAR | INT | FLOAT

Expr   →   IDENT   *(* Identifiers *)*
         | **"prefix"** INFIX
         | Constant   *(* Constants *)*
         | **"begin"** Expr **"end"**
         | "(" ")"
         | "(" Expr ")"   *(* Parenthesized expressions *)*
         | "[" "]"   *(* Lists *)*
         | "[" Expr {";" Expr}* "]"
         | "[|" "|]"   *(* Vectors *)*
         | "[|" Expr {";" Expr}* "|]"
         | "[(" ")]"   *(* Streams *)*
         | "[(" StrComp {";" StrComp}* ")]"
         | "(" Expr ":" Type ")"   *(* Type constraints *)*
         | "{" IDENT "=" Expr {";" IDENT "=" Expr}* "}"   *(* Records *)*
         | "!" Expr   *(* Dereference *)*
         | Expr "." IDENT   *(* Access to a record *)*
         | Expr "." "(" Expr ")"   *(* Access to a vector *)*
         | Expr {Expr}+   *(* Applications *)*
         | Expr {"," Expr}+   *(* N-Tuples *)*
         | **"−"** Expr   *(* Unary subtraction *)*
         | **"not"** Expr   *(* Logical negation *)*
         | Expr "." IDENT "<-" Expr   *(* Record assignments *)*
         | Expr "." "(" Expr ")" "<-" Expr   *(* Vector assignments *)*

    | Expr INFIX Expr   (* *Infix ops., including* ":", ":=",
                                arithmetic ops., logical ops., concatenation, etc. *)
    | **"if"** Expr **"then"** Expr **"else"** Expr   (* *Conditional* *)
    | **"while"** Expr **"do"** Expr **"done"**   (* *Loops* *)
    | **"for"** IDENT **"="** Expr **"to"** Expr **"do"** Expr **"done"**
    | **"for"** IDENT **"="** Expr **"downto"** Expr **"do"** Expr **"done"**
    | Expr **";"** Expr   (* *Sequences* *)
    | **"match"** Expr **"with"** Pattern **"->"** Expr   (* *Case analysis* *)
                 {**"|"** Pattern **"->"** Expr}*
    | **"match"** Expr **"with"** StrPattern **"->"** Expr   (* *Stream analysis* *)
                 {**"|"** StrPattern **"->"** Expr}*
    | **"try"** Expr **"with"** Pattern **"->"** Expr   (* *Exception handling* *)
                 {**"|"** Pattern **"->"** Expr}*
    | **"let"** [**"rec"**] ValDecl   (* *Local declarations* *)
       {**"and"** ValDecl}* **"in"** Expr
    | **"fun"** {SimplePattern}+ **"->"** Expr   (* *Functions* *)
       {**"|"** {SimplePattern}+ **"->"** Expr}*
    | **"function"** Pattern **"->"** Expr
           {**"|"** Pattern **"->"** Expr}*
    | **"function"** StrPattern **"->"** Expr   (* *Stream Analyzers* *)
           {**"|"** StrPattern **"->"** Expr}*

Components of expressions in streams

StrComp →   **"'"** Expr   (* *Terminals* *)
         | Expr   (* *Non-terminals* *)

Patterns

SimplePattern →   Constant
                   | **"_"**   (* *Catch-all* *)
                   | IDENT   (* *Identifiers and constant constructors* *)
                   | **"(" ")"**
                   | **"("** Pattern **")"**
                   | **"("** Pattern **":"** Type **")"**
                   | **"[" "]"**
                   | **"["** Pattern {**";"** Pattern}* **"]"**   (* *Lists* *)
                                          (* *Record patterns* *)
                   | **"{"** IDENT **"="** Pattern {**";"** IDENT **"="** Pattern}* **"}"**
                   | CHAR **".."** CHAR   (* *Intervals of characters* *)

Pattern   →   SimplePattern
                 | Pattern **"as"** IDENT   (* *Aliases* *)
                 | Pattern **"::"** Pattern   (* *Non-empty lists* *)
                 | Pattern {**","** Pattern}+   (* *N-Tuples* *)
                 | IDENT Pattern   (* *Constructors with non-null arity* *)
                 | Pattern **"|"** Pattern   (* *Disjunction of patterns (w/o variables)* *)

StrPattern   →   "'" Pattern   (* *Terminals* *)
               | Expr SimplePattern   (* *Non-terminals* *)

Expressions of types

Type →   TYVAR   (* *Type variables* *)
      | IDENT   (* *Non-parametric type* *)
      | Type IDENT   (* *Parametric type (one parameter)* *)
      | "(" Type {"," Type}* ")" IDENT   (* *Parametric type (one or more)* *)
      | "(" Type ")"
      | Type {"*" Type}+   (* *Cartesian product* *)
      | Type "->" Type   (* *Functional types* *)

Value bindings

ValDecl →   IDENT {SimplePattern}+ "=" Expr   (* *Functions* *)
        | Pattern "=" Expr   (* *Others* *)

Type bindings

TyDecl   →   [TyParams] IDENT "==" Type   (* *Type abbreviation* *)
          | [TyParams] IDENT "=" TyExpr   (* *Type declaration* *)

TyExpr   →   "{" IDENT ":" Type {";" IDENT ":" Type}* "}"   (* *Record types* *)
          | IDENT ["of" Type] {"|" IDENT ["of" Type]}*   (* *Sum types* *)

TyParams →   TYVAR | "(" TYVAR {"," TYVAR}* ")"

How to Get Caml, MLgraph, and the Examples

The software used in this book is available at no charge on the Internet, for example, with the help of a WWW browser or by **ftp**. For more information about how to use **ftp**, see the documentation at your installation.

Caml Light

The version of CAML we used here is available on the server **ftp.inria.fr** in the directory **/lang/caml-light**. There you will also find the UNIX version as well as versions for personal computers (PC and Macintosh). There is also English documentation there in various formats. The README file provides useful information about various files in that directory.

The WWW server **pauillac.inria.fr** contains lots of documents concerning CAML: answers to frequently asked questions (FAQ), documentation pointers to the CAML distribution, and gives access to various users' contributions. The URL of these CAML Web pages is:

> **http://pauillac.inria.fr/caml/**

MLgraph

The MLgraph library is available on the Web at the URL:

> **http://pauillac.inria.fr/mlgraph/**

Programs in this Book

The programs in this book are distributed by **ftp** from the server **ftp.inria.fr** in one of these directories:

- **/INRIA/Projects/cristal/Guy.Cousineau**
- **/INRIA/Projects/cristal/Michel.Mauny.**

References

[1] A. Aasa, *User-defined syntax*, Ph.D. thesis, Chalmers University of Technology, 1992.

[2] A. Aho, R. Sethi, and J. Ullman, *Compilers: Principles, techniques, and tools*, Addison-Wesley, 1990.

[3] A. Aho and J. Ullman, *Theory of parsing, translation and compiling. volume 1: Parsing*, Prentice Hall series in automatic computation, 1972.

[4] A.W. Appel, *Compiling with continuations*, Cambridge University Press, 1992.

[5] H.P. Barendregt, *The lambda-calculus: Its syntax and semantics*, North-Holland, 1987.

[6] A. Barr and E. Feigenbaum, *The handbook of artificial intelligence*, vol. 1, William Kaufmann, Inc., 1982.

[7] D. Beauquier, J. Berstel, and Ph. Chétienne, *éléments d'algorithmique*, Masson, 1992.

[8] R.S. Boyer and J.S. Moore, *A computational logic*, Academic Press, 1979.

[9] W.H. Burge, *Recursive programming techniques*, Addison-Wesley, 1975.

[10] H.S.M. Coxeter, *The non-euclidean symmetry of Escher's picture Circle Limit III*, Leonardo **12** (1979), Pergamon Press.

[11] ———, *Introduction to geometry*, North-Holland, 1981.

[12] H.S.M. Coxeter and W.O.J. Mauser, *Generators and relations for discrete groups*, Ergebnisse der Mathematik und ihrer Grenzgebiete **14** (1965).

[13] J. Earley, *An efficient context-free parsing algorithm*, Communications of the ACM **13** (1970), no. 2, 94–102.

[14] B. W. Char *et al.*, *Maple V: Langage reference manual*, Springer Verlag, 1991.

[15] M.J. Gordon, *The denotational description of programming languages*, Springer Verlag, 1977.

[16] M.J. Gordon, R. Milner, and C.P. Wadsworth, *Edinburgh LCF: a mechanized logic of computation*, Springer Verlag, 1979.

[17] B. Grünbaum and G.C. Shephard, *Tilings and patterns*, Wiley and Sons, 1987.

[18] G. Huet, G. Kahn, and C. Paulin-Mohring, *The Coq proof assistant: A tutorial*, Technical Report 204, INRIA-Rocquencourt, 1997.

[19] R.D. Jenks and R.S. Sutor, *Axiom: the scientific computation system*, Springer, 1992.

[20] D.E. Knuth, *The art of computer programming: Seminumerical algorithms*, vol. 2, Addison Wesley, 1969.

[21] Ph. Lechenadec, *Canonical forms in finitely presented algebras*, Pitman, 1986.

[22] X. Leroy, *The Caml Light system release 0.7: Documentation and user's guide*, URL http://pauillac.inria.fr/caml/man-caml/.

[23] ———, *The ZINC experiment: an economical implementation of the ML language*, Technical Report 117, INRIA, 1990.

[24] ———, *Polymorphic typing of an algorithmic language*, Research Report 1778, INRIA, 1992.

[25] X. Leroy and P. Weis, *Manuel de référence du langage Caml*, InterÉditions, 1993.

[26] M. Mauny and D. de Rauglaudre, *Parsers in ML*, Proceedings of the ACM International Conference on Lisp and Functional Programming (San Francisco, USA), 1992.

[27] V. Ménissier, *Arithmétique exacte*, Ph.D. thesis, Université Paris VII, December 1994.

[28] V. Ménissier and P. Weis, *An exact arithmetic package for ML*, Science of Computer Programming (1995).

[29] Robin Milner, *A theory of type polymorphism in programming*, JCSS **17** (1978), 348–375.

[30] L.C. Paulson, *Logic and computation: Interactive proof with Cambridge LCF*, Cambridge University Press, 1987.

[31] S.L. Peyton-Jones, *The implementation of functional programming languages*, Prentice-Hall International, 1987.

[32] R. Plasmeijer and M. van Ekelen, *Functional programming and parallel graph rewriting*, Addison-Wesley, 1993.

[33] D. Rémy, *Extending the ML type system with a sorted equational theory*, Research Report 1766, INRIA-Rocquencourt, 1992.

[34] E.M. Rheingold and J.S. Tilford, *Tidier drawing of trees*, IEEE Transactions in Software Engineering **SE-7** (1981).

[35] R. Sedgewick, *Algorithms*, Addison-Wesley, 1983.

[36] L. Sterling and E. Shapiro, *The art of Prolog*, MIT Press Series in Computer Science, 1979.

[37] J.E. Stoy, *Denotational semantics: the scott-strachey approach to programming languages theory*, MIT Press Series in Computer Science, 1979.

[38] Adobe Systems, *PostScript language: Reference manual*, Addison-Wesley, 1985.

[39] _____, *PostScript language: Tutorial and cookbook*, Addison-Wesley, 1985.

[40] P. Tougne, *Le solitaire*, La mathématique des jeux, Bibliothèque Pour la Science, 1993.

[41] J. van Leeuven, *Handbook of computer science*, vol. B, North-Holland, 1990.

[42] P. Weis and X. Leroy, *Le langage Caml*, InterÉditions, 1993.

[43] P.A. Winston, *Artificial intelligence*, Addison-Wesley, 1977.

[44] S. Wolfram, *Mathematica: a system for doing mathematics by computer*, Addison-Wesley, 1988.

Index

Index of Types and Functions